VICTORY

ALSO BY LINDA HIRSHMAN

Get to Work

Hard Bargains

A Woman's Guide to Law School

VICTORY

THE TRIUMPHANT GAY REVOLUTION

LINDA HIRSHMAN

HARPER
An Imprint of HarperCollins*Publishers*
www.harpercollins.com

Friendfactor, the gay rights organization for people with gay friends and family, says, "We sometimes use 'gay' when we mean LGBT (Lesbian, Gay, Bi, Trans) because not enough people know what LGBT means." "Gay" is the default term in this book as well, although I have tried to be faithful to historical patterns of nomenclature and to what institutions call themselves.

HarperCollins books may be purchased for educational, business, or sales promotional use. For information, please write: Special Markets Department, HarperCollins Publishers, 10 East 53rd Street, New York, NY 10022.

Grateful acknowledgment is made for permission to reproduce from the following:

FIRST EDITION

Designed by Michael Correy

Library of Congress Cataloging-in-Publication Data has been applied for.

ISBN 978-0-06-196550-0

12 13 14 15 16 OV/RRD 10 9 8 7 6 5 4 3 2 1

TOUCHED BY A FAIRY

As I turned to leave his San Francisco apartment after our interview, Arthur Evans (1943–2011), longtime gay activist, philosopher, and bongo-drumming Faerie, opened his arms and pulled me into a big hug. Still holding me, he explained the sudden onslaught of affection for a heterosexual woman he'd just met a few hours before. "You can do this, Linda," he said. "Tell them our story."

CONTENTS

Introduction: How an Army of Good Gays Won the West

At the height of the real estate boom in the 2000s, Robert M. "Robby" Browne, 2007 Corcoran Real Estate National Sales Person of the Year, put on his woman's bathing suit and silver heels and walked out onto the Club Exit stage. A thousand screaming, cheering, photo-snapping real estate brokers roared their approval. The openly gay Browne, six feet tall and nearly two hundred pounds, danced a sweetly amateurish version of the Village People's gay anthem, "YMCA," as ten half naked male Broadway dancers backed him up.

"Is there any question of who the star is?" Browne asks proudly, watching the video today. For most real estate brokers, a third year as Corcoran's top producer would have been stardom enough, but when Corcoran CEO Pam Liebman began planning the 2007 event, Browne thought he wouldn't bother to attend. He'd had enough top-earner, $100-million-club years. He was turning sixty, and he was thinking about his life as a whole. Finally he said he would show up, but only if he could accept the award in drag. Browne's beloved gay older brother, Roscoe Willett Browne, died of AIDS in 1985. He'd never forget the day when President George H. W. Bush said that dying of AIDS wasn't as important as losing your job. "George H. W. Bush did not acknowledge the sacrifice of my brother and our love. My brother. He's in his eighties and he still has his brothers and I don't have any brothers," says Browne. "And my brother was a Yalie and he was in Vietnam; Bush, how could he be more your person?" WE EXIST, says Browne, looking at the video of his awards ceremony. "This show says WE EXIST."

i

Exist? You can't pick up a paper without seeing evidence that gay people exist and are compelling American society to acknowledge them. The federal government protects them from homophobic violence and twenty-one states have laws against discrimination; 141 cities across the country constitute enclaves of equal treatment. A federal nondiscrimination bill gains more support in Congress with each passing year. Poll numbers show Americans overwhelmingly support protection for gays and lesbians against hate crimes and equality in health benefits, housing, and jobs. In July 2010, a federal judge struck down the federal law, the Defense of Marriage Act, that excluded gays from the federal benefits for which married people were eligible and that allowed the states to refuse to recognize the marriages if they pleased. In August, another federal judge invalidated the amendment to the California constitution, added by Proposition 8, that limited marriage to a man and a woman. September had hardly dawned when a third federal judge found the policy requiring gay soldiers to hide their sexual orientation, don't ask/don't tell, unconstitutional as well. The United States Congress repealed the law prohibiting out gays and lesbians from serving in the armed forces. Right after the Fourth of July in 2011, the federal courts in California ordered the United States military to stop screwing around getting ready and just cease enforcing it at once.

Gay playwright Edward Albee's play about the unbounded nature of love objects, *The Goat, or Who Is Sylvia?*, won the Tony Award for best play in 2002; the heroic biopic about San Francisco gay activist Harvey Milk, *Milk*, won two Oscars in 2009. So many people in show business have come out as gay that some gay media are now pooh-poohing their confessions as cheap shots meant to *bolster* their flagging careers.

Two of the most famous heterosexual lawyers in America, David Boies and Ted Olson, brought the suit against the California marriage ban in 2009. Win or lose, Boies and Olson's case has already achieved the crucial social goal of making same-sex marriage a legitimate claim. On the eve of the closing argument in the case in 2010, a *New York Times* editorial called same-sex marriage "A Basic Civil Right." In 2011 the poll numbers in favor of same-sex marriage crossed 50 percent. Regardless of intermittent setbacks, gay people like Robby Browne have succeeded in forcing society to acknowledge that they exist—as humans with a right to life and as American citizens with a claim to equality under the United States Constitution. Most of all, they have staked their claim to be treated, without lying or hiding, as moral persons, whose lives, loves, and ambitions have value and cannot be discounted.

The year 2009 saw the fortieth anniversary of the uprising in a New York gay bar called Stonewall. In 1969, "homosexuals," people who wanted to have sex with members of their own sex, were considered sinful by the church, their sexual practices were criminal in forty-nine states, the psychiatrists said they were crazy, and the State Department held that they were subversive. Forty-two years later, almost to the day, Andrew Cuomo, the governor of the state of New York, signed the law that enabled them to marry in New York. The Empire State Building was lit up in the rainbow colors of the symbolic gay flag.

ii

How did this tiny minority of despised and marginalized people do it?

They did it in America, what we philosophers call a "liberal (small *L*) state." America's roots go back to the beginning of modern Western political thought in the seventeenth century, when the philosopher Thomas Hobbes speculated that people create their governments; states are not handed down from God to Adam to the king. During the century and a half after Hobbes wrote, the English and their American colonists launched a variety of social movements—the English Revolution and the American Revolution among them—that pushed and pulled on the deal between people and government until they produced the basic outline of the modern western state, the liberal state. The liberal state makes three promises to its citizens. First, security: the state will protect its citizens from one another and not hurt them worse than the people it is protecting them from. Second, liberty: citizens have certain rights as human beings that even the state cannot interfere with. And finally, self-governance: for those aspects of life the state can control, citizens must decide for themselves on equal terms what they want the state to do. It's a good deal. No wonder so many people want in.

By the late twentieth century, Americans had already undertaken two great social movements for inclusion in the liberal state, the racial civil rights movement and the feminist movement. Since people aren't all that easy to organize, theorists have often speculated about how they did it. Their conclusions are that movements arise only when people come to see that their problems are political, not natural or personal, what theorists call "oppositional consciousness." This "aha!" moment in the civil rights movement dates back at least to W. E. B. Du Bois in 1903, when he observed that "the problem of the Twentieth Century is the problem of the color-line." In addition, movements need access to resources, as when the NAACP started getting hold of real money and the movement gained astute leaders, such as Martin Luther King Jr.

Students of the racial civil rights movement made the assumption that before people engage in new movements they do a rational cost-benefit analysis, weighing the benefits of political action against the cost. When people created social movements against all odds and acted against their own individual self-interest on behalf of the group, theorists had to rethink what really drives people to take action. As the racial civil rights movement gave way to other movements—the feminist, and, finally, the gay-liberation movement—

sociologists produced more theories to explain the new movements; indeed, the later thinking is often called "new social-movement" theory. In the newer thinking, theorists speculated that people draw their sense of who they are from the groups or social networks they are already in. From those starting places, they conceive a positive vision of themselves and then a desire to change the way the larger society perceives them all. New social movement theorists came to the realization that sometimes group identity is so strong that people act on behalf of the group whether it benefits them individually or not.

Classical or new, each of the movements before the gay movement was seeking citizenship in the liberal state. Women and racial minorities did not necessarily ask the dominant society to love them or approve of them. They sought to be secure against violence, to be tolerated as they exercised their human liberty, and to have equal access to political and economic life. Each movement got traction in these crucial areas. But both of them fell short of achieving all the elements of a full human life for most of the people they represented: they got little or no economic assistance or cultural validation, and, when the inevitable backlash came, they stalled or lost ground. It would take a newer new movement to make the next moves: it would take the gay revolution.

iii

The gay revolution achieved more because it faced different challenges. The path to liberal equality almost always involves mimicking as much as possible the behaviors and beliefs of the straight white men in power. The racial civil rights and feminist movements both made substantial detours into defending difference—black separatism and difference feminism. They failed to establish that their divergent cultures were as worthy as the dominant one and all they did was to split their movements. At the end of the day, both these modern movements got most of their traction from maximizing their similarity to dominant political and social hierarchies.

By definition, people involved in the gay revolution could not replicate the majority behavior. Their very political identity was behavior that distinguished them from the majority, including, but not limited to, their sex lives. The liberal state has a basic concept of a person entitled to be a citizen. When gay activists began their efforts, the churches considered them sinful, all but one state criminalized their sex acts, the doctors thought they were crazy, and politicians saw them as traitors to the nation. Sinners were kept away from sacred rites like marriage; criminals were imprisoned; crazy people were put in asylums; and people of doubtful loyalty were fired from their government jobs. Sinful, criminal, crazy, and subversive, the gays who made the gay revolution had the vastly harder task of convincing society to recognize they were even suitable candidates for citizenship despite their difference. Although liberalism pretends to be morally neutral, homosexual sexual behavior pressed that liberal commitment to the limit. In so doing, instead of bringing their marginal group into conformity with the mainstream norms, they challenged the accepted versions of sin, crime, sanity, and loyalty and changed America for everyone.

The movement succeeded, uniquely and in large part because, at the critical moments, its leaders made a moral claim. "Gay," as movement pioneer Franklin Kameny put it on the iconic button of the gay revolution in 1968, "Is Good." Even though it's different. No one told it better than activist Arthur Evans: "It was more than just being gay and having gay sex. We discovered who we were and we built authentic lives around who we were and we supported each other doing that and in the process came to very important questions about the meaning of life, ethics, the vision of the common good and we debated these issues and we lived them."

Morally ambitious and clearly identified as different, the gay movement came from further behind than either the civil rights or the feminist movements had done. It took on the liberal state and achieved formal equality, as did the other two movements. During the AIDS epidemic, it took on not just oppression, but neglect. And then it took on the traditional institutions of heterosexual morality—marriage and the military—and is rapidly conquering those arenas as well.

Fueled by its moral ambition, the gay movement is the model of a new era. It is ironic, yet fitting, that the only counterpart to the morally driven gay revolution is its contemporary and fiercest opponent, the morally driven religious right. Indeed, it is the moral certainty of the gay revolution that explains why, unlike the racial and feminist movements, it has been able to stand up to that powerful counterforce and, slowly but surely, prevail.

The theories all suggest that a whole lot of things have to go really right for people to act collectively against legitimate political authority. Lacking the religious and historical jet fuel of racial civil rights and the demographic advantage of feminism, the gay revolution started out from much the weakest position of any of the modern movements. Brilliantly led, endlessly resourceful, and stunningly creative, it came the furthest. When we ask how a cross-dressing homosexual activist got to be the poster boy of the most successful real estate brokerage firm in New York, we are also asking how people cooperate to get anything done, much less take on their whole society and wrench it onto a different path altogether. The gay Victory is not just a story, although that would be enough. It's an epic.

VICTORY

1

Gays and the Cities: Community First, Politics Later

When twenty-year-old "Jeb Alexander" chose his seat in Lafayette Square in Washington, DC, on a hot August night in 1920, he knew it was "the best bench in the park." In a matter of minutes, Randall Hare plucked him off that bench, and Jeb finally got laid. The shy, slender youngster with the widow's peak and the wide-set eyes started cruising the park every night, dreaming of an ideal love, but settling for sex when he found a man who met his finicky standards.

Jeb wasn't the first gay man to find sex in Lafayette Square. He wasn't even the first one to get it on that particular bench or get it at all. There had to be a first one. There's a lot of argument about who was the first person identified as "homosexual" at all. Everyone knows about the same-sex goings on at those old Greek chat-fests we call symposiums and scholars have found networks of "sodomites" in medieval Europe as well as early gay bars called "molly houses" in Reformation England. Letters and diaries reflect American women with warm "friendships" as their central emotional bond in the late nineteenth century. Of course it's one thing to have one drunken tryst with Socrates and another to *be* something you only do once in a while: "homosexual." For most of history, there could be no gay revolution because there was no category "gay." The word "homosexual" appears for the first time in Germany in 1869.

But identifiable gay history in America really got started after people began making stuff in factories rather than in the kitchens of their family farms. Immigrants and rural youths, male and female, gay and straight, flooded into American cities in the late nineteenth and early twentieth centuries.

Jeb Alexander, sitting on the bench in Lafayette Square, is the living embodiment of the birth of the American gay revolution. Gay men left the small towns, with their furtive bus stations and "bachelor" apartment rendezvous, and came to the anonymity of great cities like New York and San Francisco. Just like all newcomers, they wrote to friends back home about what they were finding in their new worlds. One homeboy followed the crumbs dropped by another, and, one link at a time, they created a chain of migration to American cities. Composer Gean (pronounced "Gene") Harwood, author, sixty years later, of *The Oldest Gay Couple in America*, found out where to go from an older gay friend in Albany, New York. Mississippi publisher George Henri Ford learned about gay New York from one of his writers. Jeb Alexander, whose diary would one day present an invaluable record of this much neglected world, made his way to Lafayette Park, one of the many urban neighborhoods where homosexuals gathered.

YMCA

The hall monitors were mostly looking the other way. As the great urbanization began, rural-based Protestant vice squads were focused on controlling the heterosexual behavior of males, especially of working-class males, and keeping the newly emancipated female factory workers safe. The vice squads—along with the anxious families back home—saw to it that urban boardinghouses and indeed whole neighborhoods were segregated by sex.

But in building single-sex residential hotels with shared bathrooms, the YMCA became "YMCA." The mere act of showering at the Sloane House YMCA in New York produced so many sexual encounters that gay diarist

Donald Vining once had to give up bathing in order to get some rest. Because boardinghouses had no kitchens, restaurants and cafeterias sprang up nearby.

Rooming houses, restaurants, the YMCA, and soon whole neighborhoods in growing cities like Los Angeles, Washington, New York, and San Francisco became centers of gay settlement. By the time gay people started keeping the diaries available to us, the young gay men pouring into the cities from farms and small towns already knew to go to Greenwich Village and DC's Lafayette Square.

The women were not so fortunate. In the late nineteenth century, when middle-class women started to attend women's colleges and hold jobs, the evidence of passionate female friendships multiplied in the historical record. Society pretty much left them alone. However, the Victorian concept of the sexless woman met up with reality and passionate same-sex relationships started looking more like social subversion than innocent friendship. Being private, female relationships were extremely vulnerable to social pressure to conform to a heterosexual norm. The combination of economic independence and social indifference that made a space for lesbian relationships in the late nineteenth century was more like a brief window into the future than the beginning of a social movement. Since women were never in command of the city streets the way men were, women would have to wait decades before they got a toehold in spaces like lesbian bars.

Jeb, on the other hand, was lucky to find a vacancy on a desirable bench at all. All over DC, New York, and Los Angeles, gay men were escaping the heat and crowding of their new urban homes and taking to the parks in search of sexual partners or just to meet their friends. Once out, they formed societies, gossiping and socializing as well as cruising. They even divided into subcultures based on looks and sexual tastes. In New York, conventional-looking men gathered in Brooklyn's Prospect Park, the sailors down in Battery Park, and gorgeous painted queens up in Bronx Park. And, of course, Central Park was central.

The city streets were filling up with gay society. Gay men gathered near their work; in New York the streets around Bloomingdale's windows and in the theater district blossomed into favorite gay gathering spots. Being on the street was a lot more dangerous than finding like-minded souls at the Y, so the men developed elaborate signaling mechanisms. They wore somewhat gaudy suits. At one point the clue was a red necktie. Gay men looked each other right in the eye and opened their eyes ever so slightly. They shared a secret language—including careful definitions of terms of self-description like "queer" and "swish"—advertising for "roommates" and "stopping by to see the apartment."

Jeb met a young man with a perfumed handkerchief at the DC library and went to a party at his apartment in the Riggs building. Apartments sprang up everywhere in America's growing cities between 1895 and 1920, and, as the apartments became available, gay tenants with a few extra bucks moved in and brought their friends. Sitting at the Riggs, listening to someone's recording of Enrico Caruso and lounging in a wicker chair, Jeb felt he had found his circle. A year later he left his family home and moved into a room at the local YMCA. The other gay men at the Y and in the Riggs gang introduced him around. They went to restaurants, galleries, and shows. Jeb took the civil-service exam and got a job as a publications clerk in the United States Department of Agriculture. With its rich clerical job pool, Washington was a very gay town.

Miraculously, Jeb's college crush J. J. Dasham showed up one day at the YMCA where Jeb was staying and went to work at the State Department. For the first, loving months of their relationship, they had breakfast every morning at the Allies Inn cafeteria. After Dash broke it off, their morning ritual was interrupted by visits from the many men Jeb thought had taken his place. Music-loving Randall, with the "beautiful eyes and sensuous lips" of Jeb's first sexual encounter; the tall, gangly German Hans Vermehren; the occasional cross-dresser Isador Pearson; the "effeminate" Junior Whorley all appeared, to Jeb's torment. Postcoital or postrelational, no one managing the Allies Inn cafeteria ever said a word to Jeb or Dash about their little gay breakfast club, including the effeminate and the cross-dressing. As the cities filled with restaurants, gay city dwellers figured out which ones, like the Allies Inn, were safe to patronize and pushed the envelope of how open they could be.

After 1920, Prohibition had transformed the urban restaurant scene, replacing the tony and respectable restaurants with a whole apparatus of social defiance—cheap cafeterias like the Childs chain, illegal clubs, and speakeasies. One Halloween, a bunch of Jeb's friends went to the DC Childs and put on "a reception there in one of the brightest spots on the Avenue, with the people inside Childs as spectators. Isador's face was flushed and hysterical. Junior put his arms around Dash and Isador, jumping up and down." Gay men colonized spaces like the Childs restaurants, turning their social life into a "show," sitting heavily made up at tables by the plate glass windows, camping it up, and loudly discussing their affairs.

The making of the gay male world, as historian George Chauncey calls the process in the subtitle of his book *Gay New York*, comes as close as Western culture has to answering the first question of Western political thought: what kind of society would people make if they suddenly "sprang up" with no preexisting ties or institutions? These men did not all come from the same European country or town, as other migrants did. They had no preexisting cuisines, anthems, or folk dances. And yet they did not fall into the brutish and short war of all against all that philosopher Thomas Hobbes imagined, but, rather, created places to work, live, and find—or seek—sex and love, a "collective," as Chauncey says, "social world."

A (Ball)room of Their Own

In 1903 the police raided a bathhouse in the basement of the Ariston Apartments at Fifty-fifth Street and Broadway in New York. Like the other fancy bathhouses around town, the Ariston had provided rooms obscure with steam and "cooling" rooms with cots for the men to use afterward. Caught having sex when the bath was raided, several men were sentenced to years or even decades in the penitentiary. As early as 1903, gay men had begun to create spaces they didn't have to share, gay speakeasies, gay bathhouses like the Ariston, and drag balls. The bars, baths, and balls were the locales that offered gay men the opportunities to transcend their private social circles of roommates, lovers, pals, and private apartments and create a web of community across race and class.

Like the Y, these semipublic institutions of gay culture were the unexpected consequence of institutions created by the dominant culture. Reformers and public officials tried to help tenement dwellers living without bathing facilities by opening public baths. Immediately, entrepreneurs began to open "Turkish" baths—private baths in hotels and apartments, with steam rooms, cafes, and other facilities, that emphasized pleasure over necessity. Some of them morphed into an extensive network of "gay" baths, which excluded people who were not gay and presumably kept the police away in the customary fashion of greasing palms. The grande dame of New York baths, the Everard, lasted as a gay institution from 1919 until it burned down in 1977.

Masked balls and masquerades mimicked the entertainments of some of the toniest groups in mainstream American society. In 1925, Jeb watched his pal Hans dressing up to go to the Bal Bohème, the annual gala of the snooty nongay Arts Club of Washington. Men routinely dressed up as women at the Bal Bohème, a contemporary newspaper reported, one guy in seven-inch heels and another in a red wig disguised as the Old Maid. Soon gay men were organizing their own, much livelier balls.

It was not a big leap. In New York, by a quirk of law, people were forbidden to appear masked on city streets unless they were going to a licensed masquerade ball (masked protesters had in the past engaged in genuinely disorderly conduct rather than the so-called disorderly conduct charge used against gays). Technically, there was no way to distinguish between something like an arts club asking to have a masquerade party and someone like the famed gay entertainer "Jackie" Mason organizing a drag ball in Greenwich Village. Men dressed up like women, the elaborately costumed "women" danced with the men, and before long Harlem's Hamilton Ball and comparable affairs in Chicago and New Orleans were attracting thousands of participants—and spectators, including the cream of heterosexual society. The toilet, one participant at a Chicago ball reported, was so crowded with men having sex that you could not even use it to pee. By the 1920s, there were enormous gay balls filled with participants in ostrich plumes, monkey fur, sequins, chiffon, silk, and satin at places like Madison Square Garden and the Astor Hotel.

The drag queens in their sequins and monkey fur are the ultimate in camp, that gay cultural behavior that adopts and mimicks female roles in exaggerated and humorous ways, which dates back at least to the twenties. Historian George Chauncey speculates that bitchy, humorous camp behavior helped gay men express anger at the loss of status that came from their being grouped with women, but also helped them to assert their superiority through humor and mockery.

However comforting camp culture was, some people were loath to close the closet door again so quickly after the ball. After the Harlem Balls of 1929 and 1931, two men—a telephone operator in a flame red dress and a ballet dancer in a velvet cape—were arrested for trying to eat in a restaurant. After spending time in the fantastic world of the drag ball, dressed to their wildest imaginings, dancing with each other, and having sex in the toilet, having to go under cover again turned out not to be so easy.

The Cold Comfort of the Closet

Jeb Alexander did not go to the balls. Instead, his diaries record a life of discreet aversion. He certainly didn't tell his family about his sexual orientation. When his brother Henry came to the Y to visit and remarked on what he'd like to do to the "'fairies' in the lobby," Jeb "wondered for a hellish moment if Henry knew that I was one of those he contemptuously speaks of as 'fairies' and if he was saying that for my benefit." Jeb spent many holidays eating two dinners, one with his parents and then a second one with his friends. (But, of course, they suspected. When he died forty-some years later in 1964, he left his diaries to his niece, Ina Russell. At the funeral, her parents and aunts came sidling up to her, one after another, to ask her point blank if Jeb was gay.)

Although no one actually ever confronted him directly, Jeb lived in terror of getting caught at work. When his homosexual companions Max and Junior showed up in drag at the theater where one of his coworkers happened also to be attending the play, he spent the evening in a pool of sweat. At the office Christmas party, secret Santas gave him cigarettes and a poem about "fags," along with a stuffed doll for his "lonely hours." When he wondered aloud why anyone would want to work at his office, his boss replied that it was the most "liberal" department in the government, except of course for that legendary refuge of the marginal, State, where, his boss noted, Jeb's "friend" Dash worked.

Jeb never contemplated revealing himself to his family or his coworkers. Most gays were closeted from the straight world and they supported one another in their efforts to conceal their sexual orientation from the hostile environment. Many closeted gay men saw nothing to reveal. They considered their forays into the gay neighborhoods to be random events that did not identify them as "homosexual," if they even knew there was such a category in the first place. According to Chauncey, the only moral discussion of coming out during the decades of gay community formation involved whether it was immoral for a gay man to conceal his homosexuality *from other gay men* whom he happened to meet.

It was indeed a dangerous world for men who had sex with men, no matter how hard they denied or tried to hide their same-sex attraction or activities. When Jeb was in college at Washington and Lee University, two classmates got the boot when the college found out they were "that sort." A few days later, one of them was found dead in the local river. Although the undercover cop in Lafayette Square was laughably obvious and known to all the regulars as the "Sneak," Jeb was terrified when the "hideous plain clothesman" interrupted

Jeb's regular lunch date with his father to tell Dad to "keep an eye on this fine young man." The Y suspected Dash and evicted him. One of the gang, Hans, had the bad fortune to be staying at the apartment of a gay friend one night in 1931 when the friend got caught shoplifting. When the police searched the apartment, they found Hans in bed with a visiting professor from Sweetbriar College and everyone got hauled off to jail. A day or two later, Hans saw his name in the local paper and decided to go back to Germany.

If Jeb did nothing to change his careful balance of private homosexual community and closeted work and family life, it wasn't for lack of insight. Jeb knew his same-sex desires were "congenital and entirely inescapable" and that he was still the "bashful good child" he once was, not someone who should be treated as a "criminal." "Filthy policemen!" Jeb wrote in his diary. "Why in hell can't the beasts leave us alone?" But, cocooned in the original regime of don't ask/don't tell, Jeb and Dash did not organize a rebellion. Protected by their willingness to limit their confrontation with straight society and by the temporary relaxation of moral vigilance during Prohibition, they and their friends drank bootleg liquor, moved from the Y to various lodgings, worked in their liberal government departments, and went to the theater or the movies.

The Closet Gets Even Smaller

But it was not to last. Prohibition had had the unexpected consequence of making behaviors like homosexuality, which had always been criminal under the sodomy laws, part of a whole culture of socially accepted criminality. Being gay got a sort of respectability by association. At the end of the Prohibition period, several New York speakeasies openly advertised drag entertainment to their mixed clientele, what contemporaries called the "pansy" craze.

One night in 1926, Jeb went to a local movie theater to see the German movie *Chained: The Story of the Third Sex*, an explicit depiction of an aging artist's infatuation with his beautiful young male model (played by the youthful Walter Slezak). Once *Chained* pushed the envelope, plays and other films followed. The irrepressible actress and self-promoter Mae West followed her heterosexual sex vehicle *Sex* with *The Drag*, set in a gay club and starring many of her gay friends. *The Drag* presented homosexuality as natural, positive, and pervasive among men not obviously gay. The newspapers went ballistic and began crusading against the featuring of gay entertainment in the nightclubs and onstage. While *The Drag* was in tryouts in New Jersey, the New York police raided *Sex* and arrested West. A prosecutor in New Jersey took after *The Drag.* The New York legislature passed a law allowing the theater licensing board to revoke a theater's license and close it down if the district attorney thought a production was obscene.

The campaign against homosexuality onstage was the end of the beginning of urban gay life in New York. Slowly, the whole lawless culture of Prohibition began to unravel. The same establishment forces that had created Prohibition in an effort to control the disorderly world of the male working-class saloon concluded that Prohibition merely spread disorder to the universe of law enforcement and, finally, it was repealed.

With the repeal of Prohibition, the line between respectable, law-abiding citizens and criminals was redrawn. Liquor could be sold, but regulation of liquor was delegated to the states, which established state licensing boards to control the bars. In place of the machinery of law enforcement came state regulation. New York, for example, established a requirement that places selling liquor must be orderly. The bars were dependent on their liquor licenses to survive and were completely vulnerable to the state authorities. The final nail was driven into public gay New York when the state liquor authority deemed the mere presence of homosexuals to constitute "disorder."

No longer could gay men—or lesbians for that matter—gather in pleasant illicit surroundings alongside nongay patrons. This was particularly hard on the lesbians, who would not meet on streets and beaches like the men. They had fought hard to establish and find bars in the major cities, and, later, in smaller places like Buffalo in the twenties. Now they had nowhere else to meet. "Arden" was initiated into lesbian life at Galante's, the gay, straight, and lesbian speakeasy in downtown Buffalo during Prohibition. As the lawless years declined, Galante's started getting raided. The cops even roughed up straight patrons who had just come for the spaghetti! Terrified, the lesbians stopped going and, after Prohibition ended, Galante's ended too. The mixed bars that remained had to monitor their gay patrons so as not to lose their licenses and livelihoods. At New York's famed Astor Bar, the saloon keeper even divided the actual bar into two segments, keeping the gay patrons to the most exquisite standards while the guys across the bar could throw their arms around each other in mannish camaraderie.

The crackdown weighed more on the public institutions of the gay community—the balls and the bars—than on the parallel private homosexual world of men like Jeb and fellow diarist Donald Vining. In 1932 Jeb reports that he was drunk enough to dance with other men at a mixed party thrown by a total stranger. In 1939, Vining, then an impoverished but aspiring drama graduate student at Yale, got picked up by a seductive fellow student with no more than hello and after, as he put it, years of talking and longing, finally had his first homosexual affair.

As the commercial institutions of gay life closed or went underground, Jeb's and Donald's lives of private homosexuality became the norm. Exclusively gay bars sprang up to fill the void but, lacking the cover of universal lawlessness, they were more like Nathan Detroit's permanent floating crap game than the open celebrations of the pansy craze. People in the payoff business opened them, they got raided, they closed. The broad and deep gay community that had taken hold through three or four preceding decades did not evaporate, of course. But instead of exuberantly displaying their camp culture in the plate glass windows of the Greenwich Village restaurants, gay New Yorkers had to be constantly on the alert just to know where to go for a drink.

There was, however, no organized resistance. There was no organization. People who wrote letters to the editors when crusading papers proposed to close the theaters for obscenity signed them with fake names. The only bar that fought back against the state liquor authority in New York was an apparently straight-owned place called Gloria's, which was trying to hang onto its gay business. It lost.

In these wilderness years, gay men and lesbians began to take vacations on Fire Island, a little barrier island on the south shore of Long Island. They used the power of their New York dollars during the Depression to buy property from the small, wary straight community that was there. When Willy Warren, a heavily closeted New York accountant, heard there was a place you could be gay without hiding all the time, he walked all the way from Fire Island's straight resort of Ocean Beach until he staggered into the bar at Duffy's Hotel in the gay colony of Cherry Grove. Warren and the rest of the rich Fire Island crowd thought they had found a place where they could buy an escape from actually having to engage in politics.

A Tale of Two Coasts

None of these concerns was on Mona Hood's mind when she launched her bar, Mona's, at the foot of Telegraph Hill when Prohibition ended in 1933. A classic San Francisco bohemian, the charming and popular Mona had been the center of social life in a group house of starving artists. An astute investor lent her the money to start a club. Mona's lesbian waitresses started singing as they waited, campy men were not far behind, and the bar, with its program of show songs, became a mainstay of San Francisco's always raffish tourist industry.

A lot of the story of the gay revolution is a "tale of two coasts"; this is one of the times that set them on a different course. California did not establish a state liquor authority, leaving the business of running the alcohol trade to a state agency interested only in taxation. The state board didn't care about disorder, it didn't let the cities or their police forces enforce the liquor rules, and, unlike New York, there was little or no Mafia presence.

Throughout the thirties, when New York gay men who wanted a drink were confined to a ghetto section in the Astor Bar or some rip-off Mafia joint, San Francisco's North Beach became a center of integration. Gay men, lesbian women, straight bohemians, and voyeuristic tourists all commingled in bars and clubs that offered the whole range of sexual companions and entertainments. The legendary North Beach club Finocchio's ("where boys will be girls") offered open drag performances, while, on the East Coast, the New York State Liquor Authority explicitly forbade drinking while gay.

In 1950, California authorities finally turned their attention to the Black Cat Bar, home to the drag version of *Carmen* performed in its entirety by waiter José Sarria. When the Board of Equalization suspended the bar's liquor license, the heterosexual owner, Sol Stoumen, sued and won. The California Supreme Court ruled that the authorities could not suspend the license merely because some of Stoumen's patrons were homosexuals who used his restaurant as a meeting place. Although California and San Francisco harassed the Black Cat and its patrons relentlessly for years, Stoumen didn't run out of money and give up until 1963.

The different regimes sent the West Coast and East Coast gay communities in very different directions. In New York, being forbidden to appear gay in any public place put a high premium on closeting, effective covert behavior, and sign reading. Gay New Yorkers' private relationships, like most private relationships, were generally conducted among people of the same race and class, exacerbating divisions which the open worlds of street and park and bar and ball had to some extent avoided. While gay New Yorkers gave parties at home or dressed up like straight men to have a drink at the pricey Rainbow Room or used the Metropolitan Opera as a site unlikely to be raided, poor gay men and the youngest gay runaways, often teens who lived on the street, were excluded from communal life.

San Francisco was never so stratified or closeted. With its history of disorderly conduct, from its origins as a mining camp to the raunchy port-city ambience from its shipping trade, San Francisco was always a harder sell for the forces of conformity. By the time the legions of sexual order came down on the institutions of the West Coast gay community, the early efforts at liberation were less than a decade away. For most of the movement's history, California gays, who faced less hostile conditions when they realized they were gay, were ahead of the curve. They recognized their common identity earlier, they claimed their difference sooner. When they made it to the threshold of the liberal state, they changed their strategy faster to move to normal politics of sameness and tolerance. Climbing higher, when their fellow Californians voted to forbid same-sex marriage in 2008, the fall was that much harder.

This Is the Army, Miss Jones

But first, New York, California, and the rest of the United States went to war. World War II changed the lives of everyone in America. Eighteen million American men were drafted. Women, not subject to the draft, signed up for the Women's Army Corps and Navy's WAVES. They were called in, classified, inducted or rejected, moved to cities they'd never dreamed of or seen, and sent to faraway places, sometimes to kill and sometimes to die. If they were not drafted, they changed jobs to work in the defense industries that had quickly started making what the government needed, again, often in places they'd never dreamed of living in.

Before the war, there was always an element of choice when gay Americans engaged with the nongay world. It may have been a hard choice, but gay people could decide the extent to which they wished to engage in a dialogue about their sexual orientation. They stayed in the closet or they revealed themselves. They stayed with Mom and Dad or moved to New York. They made a life in the gay community or they divided themselves in two—or three—or ten.

Conscription took that choice away from them. "Are you gay?" They might still lie, as most of them did. *But they had to answer the question.* They lost the option not to decide. In the course of making war, the US government subjected an entire generation of its citizens to a national examination of their physical and mental fitness. Gay and lesbian Americans, who had created an alternative world in the shadows—and, now and then, in the face—of the mainstream society, were tossed into the intake pipe, just like everyone else.

Fear of Freud

Self-described bottle blond and lisping nineteen-year-old Robert Fleischer was pretty sure of his physical fitness, but he was scared to death of the Army psychiatrist. He was sure the shrink was going to figure out he was gay and reject him, revealing his homosexuality to his family and all the world and depriving him of his much desired chance to fight.

Fleischer was correct to fear the doctors. The psychiatric profession, which had risen to power and some respectability in America during the years since World War I, had also become the proverbial friend that makes it unnecessary to find an enemy. The gay revolution would probably have happened sooner—although it would not have been as epochal—if the "science" of psychiatry had never happened. Before the cult of Freud developed, people's mental lives were considered mostly a matter of physical illness or religious belief. The only reason sex was treated as criminal in Western culture was that the American legal system, like its English progenitor, took much of its lead from the church, which forbade not only sodomy but also adultery and fornication. Had there been no psychiatric intervention, homosexual sex acts might sooner or later have gone the way of all criminal regulation of sexuality. Death of God, sexual revolution, right to privacy, game over.

But instead of that simple progression, the psychiatrists, starting with University of Vienna psychiatry professor Richard von Krafft-Ebing in 1886, began to analyze same-sex sexual attraction as a matter of mental health. Krafft-Ebing classified all sexual behaviors according to how they differed from the "norm" of heterosexual reproductive sex, which just happened to be the traditional Judeo-Christian standard. Following Krafft-Ebing, the ensuing "scientific" work adopted, without acknowledgment, the religious definition of sexual normality. The doctor then applied the concept of "degeneration" as it was used since the Middle Ages to mean the distance from God. Homosexuals found themselves categorized, along with masochists, fetishists, and the like, as "degenerate" invalids, people who fell away from the sexual ideal.

Krafft-Ebing also offered the smiley face of psychiatry: he was the first in a line of doctors who opposed throwing their sick patients in prison. Thereafter, many sex specialists, most notably the German homosexual activist Magnus Hirschfeld, argued for moderation of the criminal regime. The appeal of the medical model is understandable when the sheriff is after you, but the psychiatric establishment's offer of mental illness was a dangerous temptation. Over time, the treatments the psychiatrists prescribed for their sick patients went from Krafft-Ebing's innocuous-sounding prescription of hypnosis to treatments like electric shock.

Despite this inauspicious beginning, homosexuals kept going back to their purported ally, medical science. In 1935 New York lesbian activist Jan "Gay," née Greenburg, recruited the famed feminist and birth-control advocate Dr. Robert Dickinson to produce a scientific analysis of homosexual case studies. Gay had already amassed a wealth of information about lesbians from her own circles and from Hirschfeld's work in Germany before the Nazis closed him down in 1933. Dickinson raised a pile of money, added a committee of psychiatrists, and set about constructing a profile of "sex variants."

But the committee assigned Jan Gay to be the research assistant for one of their own, Robert Henry, who, unbeknownst to Gay, brought to the study his preexisting belief that homosexuality was an inversion. By the time the study, *Sexual Variants*, was published, Gay's perspective was nowhere to be found. Henry's version turned out to be a paean to the social importance of the heterosexual family along with ambitious prescriptions for parents and doctors to work together to ensure the rearing of children to become heterosexual adults. The subjects who had volunteered to participate in the study, including early self-consciously political lesbians and gay male prostitutes recruited by Gay, were furious.

The unraveling of Gay's relationship with the psychiatrists involved in the study perfectly symbolized the problem of homosexuality and psychiatry. The psychiatrists looked like possible allies to her and to many early activists. They consistently and honorably denounced the jailing of their patients. But the decriminalization of sexual behavior in the sexual revolution would eventually have ended the criminal punishment of homosexuals anyway. The tradeoff for the docs' support against the cops in the dark days was the medicalization of homosexuality. And the medicalization of homosexuality categorized same-sex attraction as a disease for which the sexual revolution was no cure.

The Disease Model in Action

Five years after the publication of *Sex Variants*, two powerful and well-connected psychiatrists, Drs. Henry Sullivan and Winfred Overholser, suggested themselves and their colleagues to the War Department as ideal gatekeepers for the United States armed forces. Sullivan—who was himself gay—and Overholser did not start out intending to screen recruits like Robert Fleischer for the degenerate homosexual variance. They were interested in protecting the armed services from mental weaklings, who might suffer from shell shock and the like.

As their suggestions made their way through the Selective Service Administration, other, less sympathetic members of their profession kept adding homosexuality to the list of disqualifying mental conditions. And so, as closeted Robert Fleischer tried to join the army in 1943, a doctor asked him if he liked girls. Being a sociable guy, he later recounted, he said he did like girls. Two years later, Bronze Star winner Fleischer found himself laying mines under heavy machine gun fire, on the far side of the Main River in Germany.

That was the last thing young Yale graduate Donald Vining wanted. Vining considered himself a conscientious objector, but the army was putting conscientious objectors into a camp without pay and Vining needed to support his single mother. When Vining's induction psychiatrist asked him about women, Vining told the doctor that he didn't know because he didn't associate with them much. Bingo. Although the psychiatrist tried to protect Vining with a coded diagnosis, the army brass kept leaning on him until he wrote Vining up as a "homosexual." Vining, like most "homosexuals," had been living part in and part out, exploiting society's marginal spaces to make a life. When he went back home to Pennsylvania after failing the draft, his closet door was flung open. Vining himself didn't care, but he worried about his mom, who was widely known in town.

Vining did the obvious thing and moved to New York. He felt sort of bad about it, but the war, by taking away so many competitors for jobs, made his life easy. He worked on his playwriting and held down a day job as a cashier at B. Altman's department store, and picked up servicemen in movie theaters in New York and, on trips to California, at Pershing Square in Los Angeles.

Vining's lovers were young military men, who, scholars speculate, being far from their families and hometowns and facing possible injury or death, experienced homosexual sex and community for the first time in the great disruption of the war. They came from military camps, some as large as small cities, where every imaginable kind of person, including many other homosexual men and lesbian women, were living together. When they got passes to go to town, they would take to the roads, thumbing for rides. In no time, the roads from bases to towns turned into cruising routes. Coming home from one of his jobs at the stage-door canteen, the ever resourceful Vining even identified a particular commuter he hoped would pick him up until somebody better came along.

The *San Francisco Chronicle* issued an appeal for people to pick up hitchhiking soldiers from the bases nearby. But when they arrived in town, they got a mixed reception, as MPs suddenly started patrolling in parts of San Francisco that had never known serious antivice crusades. The army's police stood outside two gay bars, the Silver Dollar and the Pirate's Cove, declaring them off limits to the service members whose patronage was crucial to their profits. Of course it wasn't all bad: when published in the local papers, the Armed Forces Disciplinary Control Board lists of off-limits places soon became a field guide to the whereabouts of San Francisco gay bars. The gay action was so hot at the San Francisco Pepsi-Cola Serviceman's Canteen that civilians poached military uniforms in order to get inside.

Combat veteran Fleischer and openly homosexual army reject Vining both enjoyed better fates than Marty Klausner, who was caught in the closet door. Although Klausner got through induction, he immediately started asking for trouble by doing things like pounding out "The Man I Love" on the service-club piano in order to attract potential mates. In the early days of the war, when every man was needed, people like Klausner could get away with it. Airman Woodie Wilson and an MP chum, "Kate," even started a newsletter, *Myrtle Beach Bitch*, in the orderly room at the base at Myrtle Beach, South Carolina, so that gay air corpsmen all over the country could keep up with their widespread buddies. Veterans recount dozens of stories of their commanding officers managing not to see the men who were otherwise of value to their units having sex under tarps and in deserted barracks in the desperate early years of the war.

Even as many officers were looking the other way, however, courts martial for sodomy were still choking the army courts system. By the time Klausner got caught, the army had replaced the legalistic court-martial system with a psychiatric program that applied a medical model of degrees of "perversion" to its homosexual servicemen and women. Some soldiers, "guilty" of only an infraction or two, were sent back to their units. Nonetheless, as with the medicalization of homosexuality in civilian life, the result was that many people who would never have been convicted under any criminal system with rudimentary due process standards were discharged as "undesirable." The discharged soldiers didn't even have to have committed the criminal act of sodomy to get the boot, because in this therapeutic system, it was the doctors' diagnosis of them as homosexuals that led to their discharges.

The system, which doctors like Klausner's "nice" and understanding psychiatrist devised, sent him from the army with the closest thing Americans had to the pink triangle the Nazis pinned on gay Germans—a "blue" discharge as mentally unfit for service. After the war, the Veterans Administration ruled that blue dischargees were not eligible for the G.I. Bill, with its generous benefits for education and housing. Worse, as Klausner found out when he went home to Pittsburgh, his blue badge kept him from getting a humble job as a hotel clerk or even getting unemployment compensation when he had exhausted his job opportunities. Bitterly, he asked a friend, "Why they don't just round us all up and kill us I don't know."

(Klausner was, happily, overstating the case, but, despite his sojourn in a psychiatric ward, he was certainly not delusional about gay vulnerability. On October 25, 1942, gay diarist Jeb Alexander noticed a folder lying on the dining room table of his old love and State Department employee J. J. Dasham. It was a list of men incarcerated in Nazi Germany, including their gay friend Hans, who had returned to Germany against Jeb's advice in 1931. "Are Hans and these others incarcerated for the same reason?" Jeb asked. "Dash said briefly, 'Pretty obvious.'" A footnote to the published diary notes simply "Hans' fate is not known.")

For a brief period after the war, a serious number of blue dischargees resisted the system, appealing their rejections and even gathering in small numbers in Washington to plead their cases to the military Discharge Review Board. In a sign of things to come, the homosexuals were aided by the nascent racial civil rights movement, since a disproportionate number of blue dischargees, homosexual or not, were black. Equally prophetic, however, was the army's response to pressure from institutions like the NAACP and the CIO. In 1947, after a period of administrative leniency, the government formally upgraded virtually all the blue discharges to general status and included the newly elevated dischargees in the program of veterans' benefits. Everyone, that is, except the homosexuals. They were explicitly excluded.

Even the Military Did Not Make Militants

Whether inducted into the armed services and serving in combat, as Robert Fleischer did, or servicing the soldiers and sailors in quite a different context as Donald Vining happily did, or trying, unsuccessfully, to keep a foot in each camp, like Marty Klausner, World War II unquestionably changed the lives and outlooks of many gay and lesbian people. How could it not?

When Fleischer returned to New York from Germany with his Bronze Star, his parents tried to set him up with "the most eligible Jewish girls in New York." Finally, he stood up at a family picnic and said, "Listen. Enough!" It was his combat experience, Fleischer told historian Allan Bérubé, that enabled him to announce his homosexuality at a barbecue in his sister's backyard. After rowing across the Main River under heavy rifle fire and laying mines, even a matchmaking Manhattan Jewish family didn't look scary to Fleischer.

Klausner wrote angry letters. Maxwell Gordon, a veteran who later recalled that he just could not turn back to his old life, did the obvious thing and moved to New York, where he quickly found work at the legendary Sloane YMCA.

Analysts speculate that the extraction of millions of men and women from their rural families and communities might have sped up the migration process so crucial to the formation of gay community. They think that exposure to other gay people in the huge ingathering of recruits at the various bases might have been revelatory to people who thought they were alone. Maybe the male bonding that always accompanies war legitimated some homosexual feelings.

There is no gay census. It is impossible to know how many gay veterans just stayed where they disembarked. During and just after the war, the lights went on at a bunch of gay bars, such as DC's Chicken Hut, for instance, in all the major cities. The Chicken Hut boasted a pianist, Howard ("Miss Hattie"), who serenaded his clientele with special songs, like "Why Oh Why Oh Why-O, Why Did I Ever Leave Ohio?" for the guy from Cincinnati and "St. Louis Woman" for the queen. On a more somber front, a record number of men were arrested for disorderly conduct, often a code for homosexual behavior, in DC after the war, rising from two a day in the late forties to a thousand a year by the fifties.

We Will Surely Each Hang Separately

Except for speaking roles in the histories of homosexuality during World War II, the Robert Fleischers and the Marty Klausners disappeared from history. They formed no organizations, they made no waves. They did not organize to fight back. Briefly, it looked like they might. The New York Veterans Benevolent Association (VBA), the first significant gay organization in America, was incorporated in 1945, being approved without apparent controversy by the state incorporation authorities, which later strongly resisted certifying gay groups. The one hundred or so members of the VBA tried to help gay veterans deal with the military and other matters. They had a legal committee and a program of social dances.

The homosexual soldiers even had a prophet, the poet Robert Duncan. In 1944, Duncan, a central figure in the California Beat scene, founder of his own small magazine, and friend to sexual radicals Anaïs Nin and Henry Miller, signed his name to an article in Dwight Macdonald's monthly, *politics*, laying out the platform for a gay revolution: "What can one do . . . both those critics and artists, not homosexual, who are, however, primarily concerned with dispelling all inhumanities, all forces of convention and law that impose a tyranny over man's nature, and those critics and artists who, as homosexuals, must face in their own lives both the hostility of society in that they are 'queer?'" Duncan asked. And, as always with a rhetorical question, he gave the rhetorical answer: "*They must recognize homosexuals as equals, and, as equals, allow them neither more nor less than can be allowed any human being.*"

Duncan took direct aim at the silence of the Left: "Although hostile critics have at times opened fire in attack as rabid as the attack of Southern senators upon 'niggers,' critics who might possibly view the homosexual with a more humane eye seem agreed that it is better that nothing be said."

One of the unknowns of gay history is what would have happened if Duncan had picked up his pen right there. But, instead, he went on to rip into everything that passed for community in the homosexual world. It's understandable that their allies are so laggard, he continued, because a large part of the fault was in themselves (that they were underlings). Where later historians would see a noble and necessary pre-political community in the previous half century, Duncan saw a fatal flaw. A self-conscious homosexual community was nothing more than a "ghetto," Duncan suggested portentously as the actual Warsaw ghetto burned—cozy, but ultimately deadly. Where historian George Chauncey would see a subversive strategy for dealing with the disconnect between men's assumption of their entitlements as men and gay men's experience of their punishment for acting like girls, Duncan saw a suicidal separatism: "Almost coincident with the first declarations for homosexual rights was the growth of a cult of homosexual superiority to heterosexual values; the cultivation of a secret language, the camp, a tone and a vocabulary that are loaded with contempt for the uninitiated." And as a result, he suggests, "there is in the modern American scene no homosexual who has been willing to take in his own persecution a battlefront toward human freedom."

Macdonald had warned Duncan not to sign his name to the article, but Duncan thought that his broadside in favor of homosexual rights as human rights would be meaningless if he himself was afraid to step forward. After he published his manifesto, John Crowe Ransom, editor of the prestigious *Kenyon Review*, returned one of Duncan's poems, which he had accepted for publication. Ransom wasn't going to run a poem that seemed, now that

Duncan's "secret" was out, to be an argument in favor of homosexuality. Duncan's career as a poet had been at takeoff. Although he was ultimately recognized as one of the main Beat poets in the fifties, he washed dishes for a living for much of the rest of his life.

Although Duncan's article led nowhere, his critique of gay "New York" (and California and all the rest) sets the terms of the argument ever since. Duncan's assertion that homosexual rights are human rights is absolutely necessary to make a revolution and squarely in the American tradition that fuels so much of the great civil rights movements. The humor, the drama, and the defiant assumption of the mantle of inferiority that constitute the camp culture he decried, have all too often offered an escape from the hard work of breaking into boring old straight society, which still monopolizes much of what passes for the goods of a flourishing human life. When, in 1947, the government interpreted the general discharge policy explicitly to exclude homosexuals, there is no evidence of effective protest from the VBA. The VBA dissolved in squabbling. The communities of gay New York and all the other gay cities that developed from 1890 to 1945 did not produce one guy willing to stand up when the armed services pinned the blue rectangle on the sleeves of tens of thousands of its members.

But Duncan was also terribly wrong. His invitation to dismantle such community as there was in favor of the radical individualism of liberal and universal rights was a recipe for paralysis, and paralysis is indeed what it produced. Equal rights for all may be the goal, but, for a despised and marginalized minority, individualism is never the way to equality. Its members must recognize themselves as an oppressed class and act collectively.

First a Community, Then a Movement

Even while recognized as a category unto themselves, "homosexuals" face every imaginable challenge to organizing. They are frequently strangers to their biological families. Too often, gay family experiences resemble the story young Ryan Kendall told to the horrified audience in the California marriage trial in January 2010: "I wish I'd had an abortion, or a child with Down's syndrome," his mother had said, when she discovered his boyhood journals. Martin Luther King Jr. had a black man for his father. Gloria Steinem's mother was a dysfunctional schizophrenic, but she was still a woman. Even with every scientific advance, babies are still the product of heterosexual something, usually the heterosexual, reproductive family. No matter how loving their families are, most gay people grow up surrounded by strangers. Growing up thinking you're the only person in the world with sexual desires for your own sex doesn't immediately generate confident identity, much less confident identity politics. One of the few unchallenged leaders of the gay revolution, Harvey Milk's right-hand man, Cleve Jones, was saved from suicide, he says, only by finding a book about people like him ("homosexuals") in his high school library.

Unlike religious, ethnic, or racial minorities that start out from an established history of tribal or religious identity, the orphaned immigrants to gay New York and other cities first had to construct a political identity that others are born with. Nobody had to tell the seventeenth-century Puritan Oliver Cromwell that he was God's chosen or the twentieth-century Irish nationalist Gerry Adams that he was the representative of a "risen people." But the only group identity homosexuals started out with was a disease label from the censorious sex "doctors." With only the fragile tie—that their sexual desire was directed toward people of their own sex—gay urban migrants created strong neighborhood enclaves, widely publicized dances, bars, cafeterias, and restaurants. Gay New Yorkers organized male beauty contests and drag balls, gay clubs, and cultural events. They had a sexual underground in the parks, streets, bathhouses, and saloons. They had a secret language. But although the "homosexuals" claimed a territory and created safe havens, they did not have a political identity. Cromwell's claim that the godly should rule goes back to the Old Testament. Adams's call to nationalist self-governance dates back to the creation of the European nation-state in the Renaissance. Even the racial civil rights movement, which most resembles the world Duncan desired for gays, got its start out of the community of African Americans, who lived in segregated areas in both the North and the South and who were served by institutions like the black churches and civic clubs. No one had ever suggested that people could make a collective political claim based on their sex life.

But African Americans, whose differences from the dominant majority are arguably only skin deep, always had the option of rejecting their communal identity, as Duncan advised for "homosexuals," and demanding only to be admitted to the society of white individuals they otherwise resembled. Indeed, the option to leave the "ghetto" was one of the forces that ultimately split the racial civil rights movement and stopped it short of achieving its full goals. The women of the feminist movement differed more dramatically from politically and socially dominant males if only by virtue of their tie to childbearing. They, too, however, had a path to integration by virtue of their value as sexual companions and mothers. And many women, too, eventually split from the movement, leaving it well short of meaningful equality.

But homosexuals were lucky. They never had any of those options. Homosexuals differ from heterosexuals in their orientation to and usually also choice of sexual partners. If there was ever to be a gay revolution, gays could not walk away from the differences that divided them from the majority into some imagined paradise of universal human rights. They had to contend that Gay Is Good. Once the revolution got going, the assumed superiority and the community-building institutions of camp culture helped the movement to assert its goodness. And that made all the difference.

Better Red

It took a Communist to start the revolution. After 1914, it almost always has. Martin Luther King Jr. probably wasn't ever a party member, despite the Right's fondest fantasies, but Bayard Rustin, his right-hand man, was. Feminism's Betty Friedan spent a lot more time writing for the fellow travelers' news service, the Federated Press, than leading the life of a suburban housewife as she claimed. Gay veteran Chuck Rowland tried garden-variety New Deal activism when he got out of the service, joining the lefty, but noncommunist, American Veterans Committee in 1945. When he noticed that the Communists, accused of infiltrating the organization, were the only ones who got anything done, he signed up. Three years later Rowland answered the call to action of a homosexual comrade, Harry Hay, and the first real gay-rights organization was born.

2

Red in Bed: It Takes a Communist to Recognize Gay Oppression

It's been a long time since many Americans looked up to Joseph Stalin. But from the time gay-movement founder Harry Hay joined the Communist Party in 1934 to his departure sixteen years later, he did. Hay even got married to satisfy Uncle Joe, which was a real tribute, because Hay had been an active homosexual since he was nine.

Stalin didn't much like homosexuals. Although the Bolsheviks decriminalized homosexual acts in 1918, sixteen years later, the dictator acted personally to reverse that liberal development. After 1934, the Soviets treated homosexuality as the decadent product of bourgeois culture, punishable by years at hard labor.

When Harry Met Willy

Hay the homosexual Communist was a traitor to his class. His father was a successful mining engineer and his mother was born to a mining family with a long military tradition and exalted social contacts. Hay never lost the willful, patrician manner he learned as a boy. Even cross-dressing decades later, he always wore a proper string of pearls.

When Harry was four, his father had a bad industrial accident and had to retire. The family settled on some land he bought in California. Not having a large industrial-mining operation to boss around wasn't great for Harry's father, whose disposition quickly led to conflict with his strong-willed, smart offspring. For years, Harry's father whipped him to cure him of being . . . left-handed. One night, Big Harry said something at dinner about Egypt that contradicted what his nine-year-old son had been reading. The kid disagreed and his father dragged him off to the garage for a whipping with a razor strop followed by bed without dinner. Some hours later, Harry's mother crept into his room with a tray of supper to find her unrepentant son, surrounded by his reference books, looking up quotations on being true to yourself no matter what.

When Harry got to high school, he added to his father's woes by taking a deep interest in drama class. Although their son grew tall early in youth and had a Californian's love of hiking and the out-of-doors, the senior Hays, perhaps sensing something, sent him off to his cousin's farm to "toughen him up." Unbeknownst to Harry's establishment family, several of their field hands were members of the super lefty union, the Industrial Workers of the World ("Wobblies"). Soon Harry was riding on the hay wagon with copies of Marx's "Wage Labor and Capital." Bringing in the hay with the workers of the world quickly captured the idealistic young man's attention.

After a year at Stanford, Harry left school for Los Angeles to try to become an actor. He found a left-leaning community there, too. Apparently California Communists didn't take quite as hard a line on sexual deviance as the Muscovite branch, because Harry was recruited to the party by a lover, Will Geer. Geer, a homosexual and lifelong radical, later immortalized as the all-American Grandpa Walton on *The Waltons* television series, took Hay to San Francisco during the General Strike of 1934. While they were there, the state militia killed two of the strikers and sent eighty or more to the hospital. There was a big political funeral, and young Hay was hooked.

Communism and the Homosexual

Some of the elements of revolution were there before Harry Hay appeared on the scene. There were crowds. Sometimes the benches in New York's Central Park were so crowded with gay men, cruising and schmoozing, that there was no room for anyone else to sit down. Every time there was a gay ball, there was a crowd. When the performer Beatrice Lillie (kind of an early Judy Garland) appeared, there seemed to be no one but gays in the audience. They were subjected to a universe of indignities. Police were spying on them in the subway bathrooms and throwing them into jail on the easily provable charge of disorderly conduct. But they had money to spend. When apartment houses started to spring up in New York, gay men moved into them. They gave great parties—liquor flowed freely throughout Prohibition. They went to Europe on great steamer lines. They never missed a play or a concert.

When like-minded people come together, sometimes they are liberated to act to release their underlying feelings in ways they would never do alone. Terrified French aristocrats called it madness. But as revolution became more common, theorists realized that crowds are actually a convergence of like-minded individuals. Gathering on the streets, abused by the dominant society, tied by bonds of desire, and possessed of resources and a secret language, the gay men of New York, San Francisco, and Los Angeles were a crowd. But crowds do not always or even usually produce a social movement. For that to happen, a community must develop a rebellious state of mind, what the theorists call oppositional consciousness. The crowd of the gay community lacked pretty much all the possible social-movement triggers. It had no ideology, no organizational strategy, and no leader. Until Harry Hay.

Early in his dual career as a homosexual and a Communist, Hay figured out that the revolutionary tenets of Communism could be applied to homosexuals. When he made a tentative suggestion to Geer that they form a "team of brothers" along the communist model, Geer replied that the theater was enough of a homosexual brotherhood. The theatrical brotherhood doesn't talk politics, Hay objected. There was nothing political to discuss, Geer said.

Technically, Geer was right. With communist glasses on, what we now call identity politics, like the homosexual association Hay suggested, were indeed invisible. Marxism teaches that only economic relationships matter. Once the relationships of class are straightened out, the other oppressions will disappear in due course. The oppression experienced by homosexuals, or blacks and women, simply does not matter in the inexorable march to the triumph of the proletariat. When Hay's homosexual commitments finally overwhelmed his communist loyalties in 1950, he was graciously allowed to resign from the party, his political family for sixteen years. And when the House Un-American Activities Committee (HUAC) came after him anyway, the lawyers who usually defended party members left him to depend on the kindness of strangers.

But whether the party liked it or not, communist theory, filtered through the fertile brain of Harry Hay, did indeed apply to the situation of homosexuals. Hay would find a support for this thinking in, of all things, Stalin's own writings. Despite identity politics' invisibility to Marx, Stalin was moved to address the subject, because, as the Communists rose to power in the early twentieth century, they had to compete with national-liberation movements, like the ones threatening to break up the Austrian and Russian Empires. In 1913, Stalin wrote a description of people who qualified as "nations" for purposes of self-determination. A nation is a historically stable community of people, according to his definition. It has a common vernacular language. It occupies a single piece of territory. It has an integrated, coherent economy. It possesses a community of psychological makeup (a folk-psychology, or national character). And it is "a historical category belonging to a definite epoch, the epoch of rising capitalism." Despite Stalin's rather narrow definition of a nation, under his tutelage, Communism did make common cause with some insurgent ethnic groups.

Hay considered his appropriation of the homophobic Stalin's writing to be his finest act. Homosexuals did not exactly fit Stalin's description of a suppressed nation. True, in the epoch of rising American industrial capitalism, gay and lesbian people gathered in large cities and colonized similar pieces of territory. They had developed a common vernacular language. They had something of a coherent economy. And they had a community of psychological makeup. Hay believed that "language and culture were enough to make a minority." But its sites were scattered, its economic institutions were primitive at best, and it encompassed a wide range of psychological attitudes. Conceiving "Gay New York" as a colonial nation in revolt was a stretch to say the least.

Hay had some help making the connection. In 1930, after the Communists had become a serious international force, the body charged with giving direction to Communist parties everywhere—the Comintern—put out a flexible definition of "nationhood." The Communists wanted to attack America in its treatment of its "12 million Negroes." American Negroes, a historically stable community with its own economy, vernacular language, and psychology, were concentrated in the Black Belt of the American South. The Comintern and the American Communist Party first advocated the establishment of an independent Negro state there. The aforesaid Negroes, however, had already begun a substantial migration that would scatter them throughout the North. The Communists wound up supporting Negro struggle everywhere it occurred. And they made a difference: when the Communist Party took up the cause of the Scottsboro boys, nine black youths arrested and eight convicted of raping a white woman in Alabama in 1931, they gained a foothold in the emerging movement, much to the chagrin of the mainstream NAACP.

Once the Communist ideology machine recognized the special place of the oppressed Negro minority in the human liberation project, the way was opened for other American identity groups, such as Hay's team of brothers, to use the idea of a national minority for their own liberation. When Hay joined the Communist Party in 1934, then, the ideas that he would use for the liberation of homosexuals—collective identity and moral claim to equality—were in place. For the next fifteen years he would devote himself to mastering them.

Better Red Than Bed

There's a fabulous head shot of Harry Hay in the thirties, with a natty ascot tie and a flat cap covering his premature bald spot. Level, intense gaze and cleft chin: it's understandable that his early years as a card-carrying Communist involved as much rolling in the hay as remembering the Haymarket. After comrade Will Geer, Harry had a fling with a Brazilian FBI stooge and spent months in the arms of a seventeen-year-old jail bait. All the while he was screwing around, he went to ideology school at the various Communist Party centers. But no matter how Harry tried, he could not reconcile his two worlds. None of his homosexual lovers was the least bit interested in politics. When he came to a gay Halloween party one year around 1936 dressed as the "demise of Fascism," no one could figure out what his costume meant.

Harry finally gave up on his conflicting passions after his most deeply felt homosexual love affair went south. His beloved, Stanley Taggart, had appeared one night at the stage door of a play Harry was in, *Clean Beds.* Six blissful months later, Taggart's mother, the matriarch of the Kansas Taggarts, took her wayward son to England for a spell of reparative therapy. The next thing Harry knew he was opening a wedding announcement. When Taggart returned a year later—repentant, but uninterested in politics and, indeed, still dragging his wife after him, Harry finally confronted the gulf between his life in the closeted gay world and his political commitments. His internist referred him to a psychiatrist—the only time in his ninety-year life he ever saw one—who suggested that a mannish girl might be just as good as the girly men he seemed to prefer. Six months later, in 1938, Harry Hay married Jewish fellow traveler Anita Platky and told his local party officials that his wandering days were over. They adopted two children. He went to work at the Leahy boiler factory in Los Angeles to support the family.

Before the marriage was a year old, Hay was cruising in Los Angeles's Lafayette Park. But during his decade as a purported heterosexual married Communist, Hay devoted himself to learning and teaching every aspect of Marxist thought. He taught political economy, he taught how to run a meeting, and he taught courses on imperialism and, his great love, "Music, the Barometer of the Class Struggle."

Bachelors for Wallace

Just as Hay was putting the finishing touches on his music syllabus in 1948, Bill Lewis, one of the gay men at the Leahy factory, brought his friend "Chuck" to lunch. Chuck was visiting from DC, where he was one of the top secretaries at the Department of State, and Lewis thought Hay should hear what he had to say. "Everyone in his department was terrified," Chuck reported to Hay. A "dreamboat" named Andrew had shown up at State one day from an assignment somewhere else and the lucky guys who slept with him were called in and lost their jobs.

In 1947 President Harry S. Truman had already set up the first security investigations in the executive branch. In February 1950, Senator Joseph McCarthy would tell the good citizens of Wheeling, West Virginia, that he had a list of 205 card-carrying Communists who were working in the State Department. A few months after the Wheeling speech, the State Department's deputy undersecretary for administration, John Peurifoy, went to Congress to represent the department in a security investigation and proudly announced that, although there were no Communists in the State Department, the department's security apparatus had unearthed ninety-one homosexuals, who had been separated from their posts.

Red and lavender, the scares began.

As usual with Hay, the warning about the dangers of trying to organize homosexuals had the opposite effect. "The country, it seemed to me," he remembered thinking, "was beginning to move toward fascism and McCarthyism; the Jews wouldn't be used as a scapegoat this time—the painful example of Germany was still too clear to us. The black organizations were already pretty successfully looking out for their interests. It was obvious McCarthy was setting up the pattern for a new scapegoat, and it was going to be us—Gays. We had to organize, we had to move, we had to get started."

A few weeks after his friend warned him about the dangerous new order in Washington, Hay went to a signing for the new Progressive Party. The party was fielding FDR's very liberal ex–vice president, Henry Wallace, as a third-party candidate for president. Hay was pleasantly surprised at how many people added their names to his candidacy petitions. At dinner on the night of the signing, his wife, Anita Platky, who'd had just about enough of the Communist Party and her homosexual husband, was singularly uninterested in his Progressive Party—and in the party he was going to after they finished eating. Just as well: the invitation for the evening came from the handsome guy Harry had picked up cruising one of Los Angeles's gay parks.

When Hay walked into the party near the University of Southern California that night, he found a gathering of seminary and music students all of whom seemed to be gay. A young seminary student from France opened the conversation. Had Hay heard of the Kinsey Report, *Sexual Behavior in the Human Male*, published just months before in 1948? In this first purportedly scientific study of human sexual behavior, zoologist Alfred Kinsey had reported that 37 percent of American men had had at least one homosexual experience. Hay lit up: Kinsey's report, contested though it was, suggested a substantial population of "brothers." If the Democratic Party could spawn Wallace's Progressive candidacy, what else might be possible?

As the beer flowed, Hay played out how such a group might organize. They could call their organization Bachelors for Wallace. In the midst of relentless mockery (guests proposed campy, derisive names like Fruits for

Wallace), Hay laid down most of the elements of a social movement in the liberal state. Homosexuals might organize gay votes for the liberal presidential candidate, participating in collective self-governance. Then, in a classic political move, they would cash out their efforts and their votes, demanding a plank in the party platform. Their platform would include another hallmark of the liberal state—the right to be left alone—in the form of a "privacy" plank, which was code talk for letting them engage in sodomy without putting them in jail. But Hay didn't stop there; as would characterize the gay movement whenever it succeeded, he demanded respect. Maybe someone of serious social standing might take up their cause and speak for them, dare they think it, at the Democratic National Convention? When he got home, he wrote it up as "International Bachelors Fraternal Order (sometimes referred to as 'Bachelors Anonymous')."

The next day Hay called the guy who gave the party and got names and phone numbers of the other attendees. But all anyone wanted to talk about next morning was how hung over they were. From 1948 to 1950, as homosexuals were fired or driven from the service of their government by the score, and Peurifoy's "ninety-one" came to be smarmy code talk for the love that dare not speak its name, Hay could not find one person to join him in his Bachelors Anonymous.

Hay, always thinking, took the time to figure out a plan of action and a framework derived from his long-held views about oppressed minorities. Unlike the other two great movements, which were identified by race or sex, first, "What we had to do was to find out who we were." Once that big task was behind them, "What we were for would follow. I realized that we had been very contributive [*sic*] in various ways over the millennia, and I felt that we could return to being contributive again." Homosexuals didn't have their own land or economy, but they had a unique culture and a kind of language. He set out the crucial demand that has fueled and refueled the gay revolution ever since: to "be respected for our differences not for our samenesses to heterosexuals. Our organization would renegotiate the place of our minority into the majority."

As with all identity movements, "who we were" would prove to be much fuzzier than the orderly Hay anticipated. At the very moment Hay was drafting his manifesto, a few male cross-dressers gathered in clubs like Los Angeles's Hose and Heels, whose founder, Charles, would one day become Virginia. George Jorgensen went to Denmark for sex-reassignment surgery and returned transformed as the camera-ready Christine. Who were we? Hay himself liked to dress in women's clothing.

Still, however permeable the boundaries, through Hay, the gay movement is rooted in a concept of identity that had flared up only once before, in black separatist Marcus Garvey's short-lived Universal Negro Improvement Association: not the same, but equally to be respected. Recognizing the distinctive gay minority with its own language and culture was crucial to the success of the movement. Any other starting place would have been a lie and likely to fail. Worse, if gays based their claim to proper treatment on sameness to nongays, they would have been conceding that their difference was a drawback or a failing. Decades later, scholars would call this refusal of minority cultures to evolve into heterosexual white Protestant suburban Americans "beyond the melting pot," after Nathan Glazer and Daniel P. Moynihan's book published in 1970. Stalin's definition of a minority, derived from the indigestible ethnic minorities—Hungarians, Serbs, Georgians—of the waning days of the Russian and Hapsburg Empires, would find a whole new life in the anonymous bachelors of Southern California.

The Red Golden Age of the Mattachine Society

On July 6, 1950, one of the products of the old Hapsburg Empire, Viennese Jewish refugee Rudi Gernreich, arrived as usual for a rehearsal of his dance performance at Los Angeles's avant-garde Lester Horton Dance Company. Family man Harry Hay was there watching his talented dancer daughter, Hannah. Across a crowded rehearsal room, he spotted the face of the gorgeous Gernreich, who would one day be one of America's leading avant-garde clothing designers, dressed, as usual, in his sexy black turtleneck and trousers. Harry could not believe Rudi was staring back. They arranged to meet.

It's hard to take the sex out of homosexual. Of course, no human being is defined by what he or she does, as one of my gay friends says, twice a week for fifteen minutes if they're lucky. But the gay revolution was both strengthened and weakened by the sexual connections that were possible among its makers. An amazing amount of the gay revolution turns on those ties. Hay brought a copy of his Bachelors Anonymous manifesto to his first date with Gernreich. "We were in love with each other and each other's ideas," Hay remembers.

Before Gernreich had left Vienna in the nick of time in 1938, he had known about the German Magnus Hirschfeld's Institute for Sexual Research, a pioneering effort to identify the extent of homosexuality and study the subject scientifically. He thought the Nazis identified homosexuals for prosecution from the records they found there and was suitably respectful of the dangers in the McCarthyite prosecutions that were now well under way.

Harry and Rudi went to a Malibu beach famously colonized by gay bathers and got five hundred signatures on a petition to pull the United States out of the Korean War. But not a single peacenik would agree to come to a covert meeting to discuss Kinsey's new findings about social deviancy. Hay was powerfully disappointed. Homosexuals were willing to take on the entire United States military-industrial complex but not to discuss *Sexual Behavior in the Human Male*?

Understanding why people would be reluctant to come forward, Rudi was undeterred. You're teaching progressive music classes, Gernreich observed a few months later in November. Why not try that little blond guy you think is homosexual? Nervously, Hay proffered a copy of his manifesto to his student, Bob Hull, at the next class. Shortly after that, Hull phoned to ask if he and a friend could come to Hay's to discuss what he had provided. As Hay and Gernreich anxiously waited, they caught sight of Hull's roommate, the very Midwestern Chuck Rowland, with his buck teeth and rimless glasses, running up the hill to the house waving the thing "like a flag." "I could have written this myself" were Rowland's first words. Four gay men—three Communists and one closeted would-be fashion icon—the gay movement in America was officially launched. Another sexual connection brought the fifth founder, Hull's then-lover, Dale Jennings. After a stint as a carnival roustabout, the macho Jennings was writing for a living.

Hay may have read Robert Duncan's call to homosexuals to abandon the destructive campy bar talk, because he, with Rowland, pushed hard for the new organization to develop "an ethical homosexual culture." They wanted to discuss how the gay culture could enable gay people to lead well-adjusted, wholesome, and socially productive lives. For a while, Harry and Rudi and Chuck and Bob and Dale and a shifting group of others just talked about their lives, finding comfort in their familiarity and creating their own normalcy through shared experience. They called their relationships "homophile"—loving friendship of men—to replace the clinically tainted term "homosexual."

At first the group took the name Society of Fools. From his extensive researches into the history of music, Hay knew that, in many European cultures, fools were more like jesters than crazies. They were privileged by their clownish disguise to speak truth to power. There were even societies of fools, revelers who used the ancient festivals—the Feast of Fools, which we now know as a range of prankish holidays from Halloween to April Fools' Day—to mock the otherwise untouchable rulers of church and state. Hay concluded—not without support in the scholarship—that some of those societies known for a warlike dance, the *mattasin*, were called, in translation, the Mattachines. Mindful of the negative associations of "fools," the group adopted the name Mattachine Society: masked revelers bearing a message of insurrection. Coincidentally, just before Hay's bachelors organized themselves as revelers, gay men routinely had started calling each other "gay." Unlike, say, "queer," which had been the most common description, meaning, strange or not the norm, "gay" had a happy sound. By the fifties, "homosexuals" had made an important move to call themselves something positive.

Each of the original five Mattachines brought in their acquaintances. They even tried again with the antiwar closeted beach gays from the prior summer's busted play. Within a year, the last two of the essential founders, and, fatefully, the first members without ties to the Communist Party—joined. When one of the newbies saw a copy of the *Daily Worker* on Bob Hull's couch, he thought it was a joke.

Hay and the other founders recognized, crucially, that gay people had a mighty task of self-invention on their hands, because most people learn their values and form their consciousness in their heterosexual families. The Mattachines rejected what they considered the sick and perverse imitation by gays of heterosexual values, with their grounding in rigid gender roles. Thus, long before any modern feminist movement came on the scene, the first months of Mattachine meetings were devoted to what the groups of liberation-seeking women would later call "consciousness raising."

Hay even had a theory for the structure of the organization: like the Communists and the Masons, another subversive group, the Mattachines would be organized in cells, called "guilds." As the discussion groups flourished, the founders selected representatives from the bottom-level groups to join the guilds. Only the guild members knew the names of any other members of their own guild. Altogether, the guild members were the first level of governance. Had they attracted enough people, representatives from the guilds at the first level would come together to form the second level, and so on up a pyramid of increasing hierarchy until they reached the fifth level, which the founders assigned to themselves. Since they never attracted enough people to make it to the third and forth levels, the pyramid mostly consisted of discussion groups and their representatives in first-level guilds. The founders continued to run the show.

The Mattachine Society manifestly tapped into a latent social need.

Within a year or two of the founding, there were discussion groups of as many as 150 people and a first level of guilds populated by handpicked representatives. Wow! The beautiful Rudi returned from an abortive effort to start his designing career in New York. Harry divorced his wife and resigned from the Communist Party. It was 1952. He was at the top of his game.

The People v. Dale Jennings

Mattachine founder Dale Jennings, on the other hand, was feeling like shit. He and his longtime lover, Bob Hull, had just broken up. Dale decided to run over to Westlake Park and see who was around. There was a man in the toilet. I'll follow you home, the man said; can you make me a cup of coffee? When they got to Dale's home, Dale was going to the kitchen when he noticed the toilet guy fussing with his window blind. One minute later, he heard knocking and saw the flash of handcuffs as another policeman came through his door.

At two a.m., Harry Hay's phone rang. Fifty dollars' bail later, Hay and Jennings were sitting at the Brown Derby eating breakfast. Hay had one of his moments. "We're going to make an issue of this thing. We'll say you are homosexual but the cop is lying."

Hay called an emergency meeting of the Mattachine founders for that very night and made an impassioned plea for the group to "press the issue of oppression." Rudi Gernreich, who was always a little different from the rest, had already fought back against similar police tactics, insisting on going to trial when he got caught years earlier. To his amazement, Gernreich was convicted. But not discouraged.

Perhaps emboldened by the unexpected success of their burgeoning organization, everyone agreed that Jennings should fight. The young Mattachine group created a pseudonym for his defense: Citizens Committee to Outlaw Entrapment. The committee hired one of the leading liberal lawyers in Southern California, a straight criminal defense and labor attorney, George Shibley, and prepared to go to trial.

When the establishment media would not carry news of the trial, the committee summoned the gay community into political action. They cranked out leaflets, "Are You Left-Handed?" and the unprecedented "Anonymous Call to Arms." Claiming common cause with the nascent civil rights movement, the gay pamphleteers of 1952 argued that police brutality against minorities was also being applied to them. They distributed their propaganda at gay beaches and bars, in the bathrooms, benches, and bus stops of gay LA. They even got supermarket clerks to put their fliers in their gay clients' grocery bags. They held dances and beach parties and raised thousands of dollars to pay their lawyer and get transcripts for distribution. For at least six decades, American cities, including Los Angeles, had included a minority community with its own coded language, traditions and geography, bars, baths, beaches, and balls. The Mattachine Society and the Jennings trial offered the gay community, at last, politics. In two years, Hay's efforts had gone from talk at a "bachelor" party that no one could remember the next morning to a major civil rights initiative.

And they won! Shibley opened by arguing that the only true perverts in the courtroom were the cruising policemen intent upon entrapment. Forty hours into deliberation, the jury declared itself hung, because one juror wouldn't agree with the other eleven that Jennings should be *acquitted*. "Victory!" crowed the pamphlet the committee sent out when the establishment media refused to run a word about the unprecedented decision.

Many-parented Victory also had a thousand sons. Gay Angeleno Dorr Legg was working in his city-planning job as usual when one of his coworkers walked up to his desk. "Have you heard about the guy here who has fought the police and won?" "No." "Well, he has, and there's an organization about it." One year after Jennings's trial, two thousand people were talking about homosexuality at a hundred Mattachine-sponsored discussion groups from San Diego to San Bernardino. A San Francisco peacenik, Gerry Brissette, started a San Francisco chapter.

As the chapters proliferated, they became more diverse. The San Francisco chapter actually attracted female members in noticeable numbers, while the chapter around UCLA undertook a project of scholarly research. Mattachine applied to incorporate as a foundation with Hay's matronly mother, Margaret Neall Hay, as treasurer. They thought they could get heterosexual allies to support them with research and funding.

Fun-loving Martin Block, legendary for his female impersonation of a garden-club chair at the Mattachine meetings, nearly lost his fur piece at a meeting at Al Novick and Johnny Button's house that spring. "I'm tired of talking," Button blurted out. "I want to do something! Why don't we start a magazine?" The first issue of *ONE* magazine (out of many, one), January 1953, was devoted to Jennings's story. Soon the magazine had sales of two thousand copies a month and a circulation of many more. Fortunately, as it turned out, Jennings, Legg, and the other *ONE* editors organized the magazine separately from the Mattachine Society. The independent Jennings did not want to be bossed around by bossy Harry Hay.

The Mattachines were on a roll. When it came time for the elections for Los Angeles City Council early in 1953, they sent a questionnaire to each and every candidate, demanding to know their positions on questions of interest to the homophile organization, such as, what did the candidates think of police harassment of homosexuals and sex education in the public schools? It was the first time homosexuals in America tried to call their elected representatives to account. It was almost the last.

Better Dead Than Red

A few days later, the nascent activists opened their afternoon copies of the *Los Angeles Mirror* to read "Well, Medium and Rare," a column about their "strange new pressure group" by the paper's columnist Paul Coates. Now look who thinks they can hold their legislators to account, Coates crowed. He easily unearthed the unfortunate fact that Mattachine corporate lawyer Fred Snider had refused to answer questions from the House Un-American Activities Committee (HUAC), invoking his Fifth Amendment right against self-incrimination. Homosexuals had been "found to be risks in our State Department," Coates reminded his readers and told the Mattachine members they had reason to worry about who was in their new club.

In hindsight, the confrontation was inevitable. While the Communist-inspired homosexual organization had been crowing about its victory before one Los Angeles criminal jury in the Jennings case, homosexuals and Communists were everywhere under fire. As Bill Lewis's friend from State had warned Harry Hay in 1948, the search for Communists in American institutions had exploded across the American scene. HUAC, the FBI, the Senate Internal Security Subcommittee—actually headed for a time by the eponymous McCarthyite Senator Joseph McCarthy—were all issuing subpoenas, taking testimony, asking for names, and prosecuting for everything from treason to perjury. The foreign-policy establishment was a particular target for the red hunters, as some of their activities were a response to the victory of the Chinese Communists, an event inexplicable to some as anything but a product of American treason. "Who lost China?" became a watchword of their inquisition.

The search for traitors quickly turned to the institutions of American culture as the obvious place for undermining the great republic. HUAC was particularly feared in California; it had been investigating the Hollywood movie industry almost since 1947. (In an unfortunate coincidence, HUAC was holding hearings in LA when the Coates article appeared.) The government was somewhat constrained by the constitutional right against self-incrimination, and a lot of the people HUAC targeted invoked the Fifth Amendment rather than testify against themselves or incriminate others. Senator McCarthy, with his acute ear for demagoguery, called people who invoked their constitutional rights "Fifth Amendment Communists." The film business, not constrained by the niceties of constitutionality, agreed to blacklist anyone who admitted to being or who was accused of being a

Communist. Scholars estimate that hundreds of people went to jail and tens of thousands lost their jobs.

As Hay astutely figured out, once the forces of inquisition—rural, anti-intellectual, insular—were unleashed, homosexuals would be the obvious targets. After all, Jews had been persecuted and killed only recently; blacks could look for support to the visibly activist NAACP, which had just recently obtained upgrades for the disproportionately black blue-discharge victims while homosexuals got nothing.

The scene for focusing on homosexuals was actually set a little earlier, when, as luck would have it, the perfect symbol of everything the McCarthyites hated—New Deal President Franklin Roosevelt's wealthy Boston Brahmin undersecretary of state Sumner Welles—got caught with a Pullman porter one drunken night in 1940. By 1943, even FDR's loyalty (as a boy, Welles had carried Eleanor Roosevelt's bridal train) could not save Welles from being fired. Thanks to the fuss over Welles, once the witch-hunting for Communists got going after the Communists conquered China and the Soviet Union exploded its atom bomb, the problem of homosexuals in the State Department was teed up. Lost China and too interested in china: the gossip about the gay State Department became so dire by 1950 that a DC newspaper carried a cartoon portraying an anxiously heterosexual former diplomat boasting, "I was fired for *disloyalty*!"

The nature of homosexuality, being behavior and feelings, made it uniquely vulnerable to persecution and much harder to defend than the congenital, morally neutral characteristics like race and gender. The inquisitors did not usually argue that homosexuals were more likely than others to be Communists. They did argue that gays might be blackmailed into treason, although a decade and a half of inquiry never produced a single instance of such a thing. Mostly, though, the prosecution and discharge of homosexuals from the government was justified on the grounds that their behaviors were immoral and their feelings were crazy or both. Someone who was already immoral (or crazy) might do other immoral (or crazy) things like betray their country, the gay hunters argued.

Despite much speculation, no one really knows why longtime bachelor Senator McCarthy was significantly uninterested in the problem of homosexuals in the United States government, but the task was left to North Carolina Democratic senator Clyde Hoey and Nebraska's Republican senator Kenneth Wherry. In 1950 Wherry, using his position as head of the Senate Committee overseeing the District of Columbia, brought DC vice cop Roy Blick to testify about how many homosexuals must be working for the federal government. Considering how many homosexuals his division had arrested, and what that said about how many homosexuals there were in DC altogether, divided by the percentage of DC residents employed by the federal government, Blick concluded that there must be 3,750 homosexuals working for the feds as of 1950. The exact number had an oddly convincing quality despite Blick's admission that he had mostly made it up. Senator Hoey's investigations produced the "finding" that homosexuals threatened national security. A scant seven years later, a Navy Department report concluded that the Hoey report was, well, hooey, but after 1950 the homosexual security threat was a legislative fact. In April 1953, President Dwight D. Eisenhower signed Executive Order 10450 barring "sexual perverts" from federal employment.

And the consequences were scalding. Departments that did keep records indicate that a hundred employees a year resigned or were fired for sexual perversion, rising to four hundred a year between 1953 and 1955. By 1960, the State Department reported firing one thousand homosexuals. Historian David Johnson estimates that the numbers from State imply at least five thousand firings in the government as a whole. Government contractors took their cue from their biggest customers. Congress, which at that time legislated for the District of Columbia, passed a tough new sexual psychopath law and leaned on the DC police to enforce it in order to smoke out individuals who were also federal employees. Jeb Alexander's old flame Dash lost his job at State when he refused to sign a loyalty oath, and Jeb spent the McCarthy years "terrified that the hideous spotlight will land on me." "The only thing I regret," Peter Szluk, head of security for the State

Department until 1962, told historian Griffin Fariello about his job firing gays, "was within minutes and sometimes maybe a week, they would commit suicide. One guy he barely left my office and . . . boom—right on the corner of Twenty-first and Virginia."

That the lawyer who helped incorporate the Mattachine Society in 1953 was a "Fifth Amendment Communist" came as a surprise to Marilyn "Boopsie" Rieger of one of the LA discussion groups. As the cell-like structure of the guilds reflected, the Mattachine founders had gone to some lengths to keep everyone's identity a secret. The groups didn't know who was behind their gratifying new liberation machine; even the first "order" delegates from the groups to the guilds knew only their fellow guild members. Once she found out that the system was concealing people who might be Communists, Rieger attacked the whole system. "To continue working for the cause," Rieger told her group, "she needed faith in the people setting the policies."

Had the founders been more experienced, they would never have called a meeting. But, idealists that they were, Hay and the rest of the founders acknowledged that the explosive growth of the Mattachine Society after the Jennings trial required a new structure with more openness and accountability, as Rieger and others demanded. At the founders' request, two delegates from each guild in California came to the First Universalist Church of Los Angeles. Once everyone got over the amazing sight of some five hundred organized gays and lesbians in one room, the two factions at the 1953 Mattachine convention laid down the terms of argument for the gay revolution from that day forward.

Homosexuals, the founders told the delegates, are different. Because they have been excluded from conventional society for so long, they have a different culture and different interests. Most tellingly, Hay reminded the assembled representatives, they could not protect their marginalized group by distancing themselves from other persecuted people, like the Communists that Coates was attacking. The people coming for the Communists, Hay said, would also come for them. Homosexuals had an interest in a society governed by due process of law. The conservative members might be anti-Communist, but when the interests of homosexuals and the members' other interests come into conflict, it is the homosexual interest that must prevail, not the others.

Wrong, said Rieger and her allies, Kenneth Burns, a conservative corporate type, and Hal Call, an insurgent from San Francisco. Homosexuals are not like Communists, they argued. Homosexuals are just like mainstream heterosexuals except for what they do in bed. The insurgents thought that people should be judged not by the specifics of their sexual choices, but by the content of their character. And the opportunity to be treated just as ordinary individuals would never come as long as they kept doing uppity things like asking the cops to stop following them around the toilet. Instead, according to Burns, their greatest contribution "will consist of aiding established and recognized scientists, clinics, research organizations and institutions . . . studying sex variation problems." The new homosexual order of sameness would hold no place for what would later be called the transgendered minority either. As it happens, at about the same time, the doctors like Harry Benjamin who were doing sexual-reassignment surgery were developing a regime of complete changeover followed by disappearance into the heterosexual society, accompanied, presumably, by a new sexual interest in people of the (now) opposite sex.

The sameness approach had enormous appeal. Unlike Hay's Communist Party, the Mattachines had not come together because they shared common beliefs in the inevitability of the dictatorship of the proletariat or some such thing; their commonality was their same-sex attraction and practices. Put to a vote, they would probably all have wished to stop being entrapped and discharged from their jobs, but how to get there—into the melting pot or beyond the melting pot—was the difference that could not be bridged. The Mattachine convention also introduced the practice that was to bedevil gay organizations for decades: governance by charisma. Hay's communist idealism had saddled the society with the curse of unanimity, rather than the bourgeois conventions of majority rule and rules of order. Absent such orderly procedures, whoever spoke last always seemed to carry the day.

At the end of that day, it was Senator McCarthy who won (again). One of the insurgents proposed that all members sign a loyalty oath of noncommunist affiliation. Although they probably still controlled the majority of the delegates to the convention, Hay and Rowland and the other past or present party members knew that they and their membership could never withstand the scrutiny of the McCarthyite investigations, which were at that point at their height. The founders met and agreed they had to step down. Six months later, corporate sales manager Burns opened Mattachine's November constitutional convention as the new head of the organization. From then on, there would be no political questionnaires. Hay and the others left. Hull and Jennings and other activists like Don Slater took refuge in the independent *ONE* magazine to fight another day. Hay was as close to suicide as he ever came in his long, productive life.

The new Mattachines provided something rare in social history—a controlled experiment. They tried advancing the homosexual cause without hewing to the principles of a successful social movement. Instead of putting forth their own ethics, the new Mattachines promised to conform as much as possible to the ethics of the existing society. Instead of characterizing themselves as a culture, the Mattachine members were to accept the characterizations of others, especially the members of the psychiatric establishment and other medical professionals. Instead of advocating their own interests, the Mattachines would work only through persons who commanded the "highest possible public respect." The last thing they wanted, one such individual advised them, was to make special pleas for themselves as a "minority." Stripped of its charismatic and driven founders, after 1953, the Mattachine Society almost ground to a halt. Discussion groups deteriorated into group therapy, membership plummeted, and the society referred calls from jail to a list of outside lawyers.

As the Mattachine Society hit bottom, in 1955, a tiny group of San Francisco lesbians started a social club, the Daughters of Bilitis. Phyllis

Lyon and Del Martin had met and become lovers a couple of years before. Moving to San Francisco, they shyly ventured to the only place they knew to meet other lesbians, a lesbian bar, hoping to make friends they didn't have to pretend with. When they stumbled across the grand total of five other lesbians who wanted to start a group, they offered their little house high on the hills above the city for meetings. Soon they were borrowing the mimeo machine from the local Mattachine chapter ("we didn't think men were good for much," Phyllis recalls, "but we could borrow their mimeo machine") to put out a little newsletter, *The Ladder.* When the Daughters wanted to start dancing together at their meetings, they asked Phyllis and Del to put up curtains across the picture windows looking out at the bay. Someone might see them, the women feared.

Howl (Against the Dying of the Light)

The conventional faction of the Mattachine Society couldn't have chosen a worse time to cave in. In 1954, one year after the Mattachine members drove out their visionary leaders, Senator Joseph McCarthy made the fatal error of turning his crusade against a real armed force—the United States Army. The army, ably represented by a Boston lawyer, Joseph Welch, took the senator down in a legendary confrontation fueled by what then passed for viral media, television. After repeatedly trying to deflect McCarthy from attacking a young lawyer in his firm as a former member of the left-wing National Lawyers Guild, Welch finally blew up: "You've done enough. Have you no sense of decency, sir, at long last? Have you left no sense of decency?"

Carried by three major television networks, Welch's defiance of McCarthy began to wake the nation from its fevered dream. A few months later, the Senate censured McCarthy and he died in disgrace shortly thereafter. Within thirty days of McCarthy's downfall, African Americans, asserting their status as a discrete and politically isolated minority, won a unanimous victory from the Supreme Court of the United States, ordering the end to segregated public schools. In 1956, Congress took up the first civil rights legislation since Reconstruction.

Ignorant of his lack of stature, a humble government clerk-typist formed a little Mattachine chapter in DC, called the Council for Repeal of Unjust Laws. The handful of men in the DC Mattachine Society had noticed that the civil rights bill under consideration by Congress did not include homosexuals and that some of the most avid advocates of racial civil rights were among the biggest homophobes. They wrote to the national Mattachine Society about their plans to agitate to repeal unjust laws; the national office wrote back telling them to stop. The Mattachine charter, national said, only allows its chapters to engage in research and education. At about the same time, Philadelphian Barbara Gittings found a copy of *ONE* magazine and took her next vacation in California. By the time she left Del Martin and Phyllis Lyon's living room, she was hooked. "You want to do something?" they asked. Start a New York chapter.

Just as the San Francisco headquarters of the Mattachine Society was telling their Washington members not to bother with unjust laws, a mile away, at San Francisco's City Lights bookstore, Beat poet Allen Ginsberg was reciting his poem "Howl." The Beat movement was at first a collection of young poets and writers who had migrated to the cheap galleries and bookstores and raffish reputation of San Francisco. There they gathered around an advocate of modernist poetry, Kenneth Rexroth, and inexplicably began to change American culture. Within a few years, the ragtag group of impoverished bohemian poets were immortalized in the pages of the *New York Times Magazine*. It says a lot about the political impotence of the fifties that poets would make a revolution. But they did.

Consistent with San Francisco's long history of sexual libertinism, gay and straight, the Beat movement was both gay and straight. The Black Cat Bar, whose straight owner, Sol Stoumen, had fought a twenty-year battle with the government liquor police, was, according to Ginsberg, the "best gay bar in America." The atmosphere of freedom drew rebels and poets to San Francisco for decades, including, in 1972, a young gay man named Cleve Jones. The emergence of San Francisco as a gay mecca is due, in no small part, to the Beats and their bookstore, City Lights.

A paean to "the best minds of my generation . . . who let themselves be fucked in the ass by saintly motorcyclists, and screamed with joy," "Howl" aroused the police to arrest and the state to prosecute the bookstore owner, Lawrence Ferlinghetti, for obscenity. As luck would have it, three months later, the United States Supreme Court decided *Roth v. United States.* Books were only obscene under the US Constitution, the court suggested, if the "dominant theme taken as a whole appeals to the prurient interest" to the "average person, applying contemporary community standards" and is "lacking in the slightest redeeming social importance." The court found that Roth's product met even this difficult standard and still upheld the defendants' jail sentences, but the opinion, which set new standards for obscenity, had immediate repercussions in San Francisco. Invoking *Roth*, a local judge acquitted Ferlinghetti, calling the poem a work of "redeeming social importance."

The "Howl" case hinted that under *Roth* the presence of homosexual material didn't automatically remove a publication from the protections of the Constitution. Just in the nick of time. The last remnants of the radical Mattachine Society, which had stayed at *ONE* magazine after the conservative takeover, were turning out some pretty confrontational stuff. In August 1953, the US Post Office held up mailing of *ONE* for three weeks before it passed up the opportunity for a showdown. *ONE* responded to the government's act of tolerance with a cover essay in its next issue titled "*ONE* Is Not Grateful."

Despite the bravado, the editors of *ONE* asked their young heterosexual lawyer, Eric Julber, for a list of rules to avoid censorship. In the October 1954 issue, they published Julber's rules under the cover "You Can't Print It." In a classic act of camp, the "You Can't Print It" issue contained several items that violated the prohibitions on what to print: a story, "Sappho Remembered," that ended with the heroine choosing her lesbian lover

over a conventional life and a poem, "Lord Samuel and Lord Montagu," that mocked the English prosecution of prominent homosexuals such as Sir John Gielgud ("some peers are seers / but some are queers"). When the post office took the bait and seized the October issue, *ONE* sued the postmaster in Los Angeles, Otto K. Oleson.

ONE lost both at the trial court and the court of appeals. In its opinion, the court of appeals acknowledged that it faced a rising tide of protection for sexually explicit material:

> Much is now presented to the public, through eye and ear, which would have been offensive a generation ago, but does not today merit a second thought as to propriety. None the less, so long as statutes make use of such words as obscene, lewd, lascivious, filthy and indecent, we are compelled to define such expressions in the light of today's moral dictionary, even though the definition is at best a shifting one.

Taking direct aim at the self-conscious moral claims of the ungrateful *ONE* magazine and its homosexual constituency, the court said, "An article may be vulgar, offensive and indecent even though not regarded as such by a particular group of individuals constituting a small segment of the population because their own social or moral standards are far below those of the general community. Social standards are fixed by and for the great majority and not by or for a hardened or weakened minority."

Turning to "Sappho Remembered," the court ruled that anything that ends happily for homosexuals must be obscene: "The climax is reached when the young girl gives up her chance for a normal married life to live with the lesbian. This article is nothing more than cheap pornography calculated to promote lesbianism."

So there it was—a clear invitation to the United States Supreme Court to rule that anything positive about homosexuality was automatically obscene and not entitled to the protection of the Constitution. In 1958, the Supreme Court

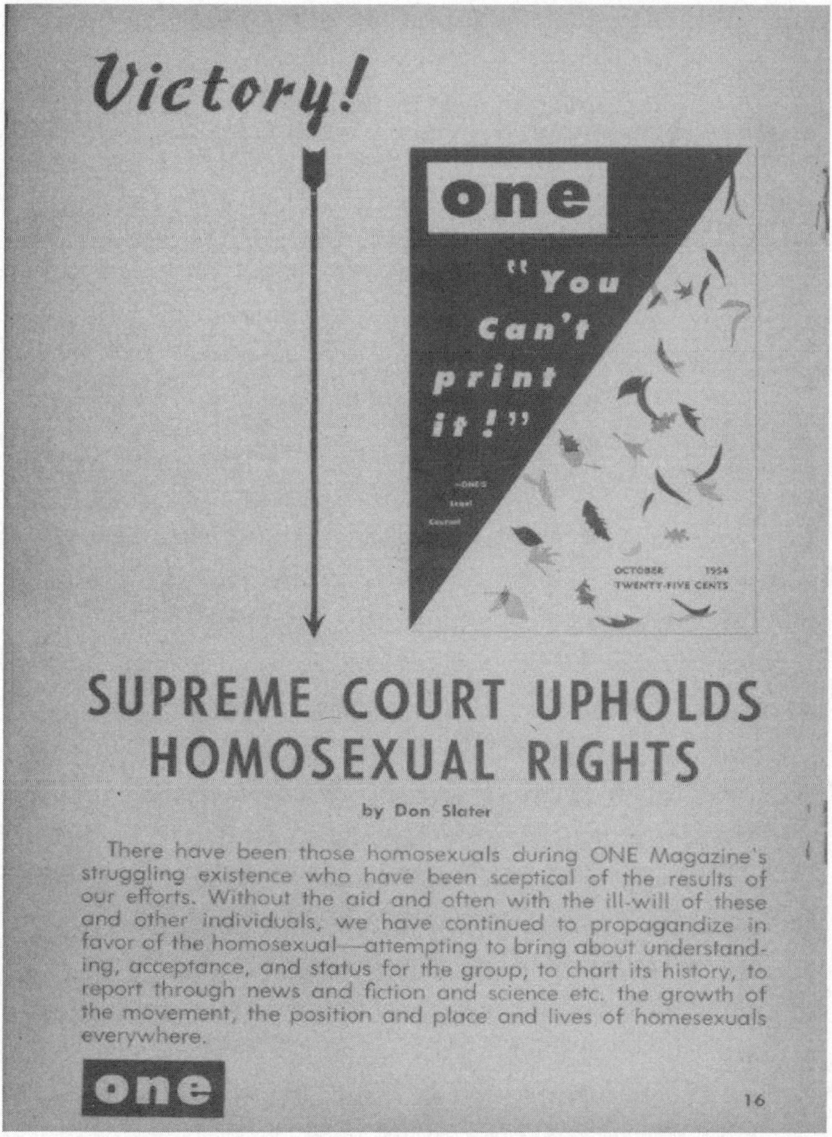

Victory!

one

"You Can't print it!"

OCTOBER 1954
TWENTY-FIVE CENTS

SUPREME COURT UPHOLDS HOMOSEXUAL RIGHTS

by Don Slater

There have been those homosexuals during ONE Magazine's struggling existence who have been sceptical of the results of our efforts. Without the aid and often with the ill-will of these and other individuals, we have continued to propagandize in favor of the homosexual—attempting to bring about understanding, acceptance, and status for the group, to chart its history, to report through news and fiction and science etc. the growth of the movement, the position and place and lives of homesexuals everywhere.

one

16

Cover of *ONE* magazine proclaiming the first-ever homosexual Supreme Court victory, 1958 (Courtesy of the ONE National Gay & Lesbian Archives at the University of Southern California, ONE Incorporated records, Collection 2011.001) turned the invitation down: "The petition for writ of certiorari is granted and the judgment of the United States Court of Appeals for the Ninth Circuit is reversed. Roth v. United States, 354 U.S. 476." It is impossible to express the meaning of *ONE v. Oleson* better than *ONE* did on the issue that followed: "By winning this decision *ONE* Magazine has made not only history but law as well and has changed the future for all U.S. homosexuals," Slater exulted. "Never before have homosexuals claimed their right as citizens."

The Homosexual Citizen

The editorialists at *ONE* couldn't have known how quickly after their Victory an actual homosexual would claim his rights as a citizen. Frank Kameny was, he says, innocently taking a piss at the San Francisco bus station bathroom when the guy next to him made a pass. Maybe so. Of course, Kameny, a little over thirty, tall and thin with dark eyebrows over blue eyes, wasn't someone you'd throw out of bed either. The two cops watching the men's room through a ventilation grille that summer day in 1956 arrested him. The next morning they offered him the chance to plead guilty and leave town when his astronomers' convention ended. He wouldn't even leave a record, the probation officer at trial told him, if he petitioned the court to dismiss the charge after his probation was over. Sure enough, after Kameny completed his six months' probation, the court entered a plea of not guilty and dismissed the complaint. When Kameny applied for a job as an astronomer with the federal government later that year, he admitted having been arrested, but said it had been dismissed.

Within a year, his bosses at the Army Map Service in Washington noticed the disorderly conduct arrest on his job application and called him in to ask if he had "engaged actively or passively in any oral act of coition, anal intercourse or mutual masturbation with another person of the same sex." Although he was clear about his sexual orientation by the time they asked, Kameny refused to answer. "This was a personal matter with no relation to my job performance." The commander of the map service fired him for not describing his offense adequately on his application form, and the Civil Service Commission followed with a ruling that he was immoral and thus unsuitable for federal employment.

By the time the army fired Kameny in 1957, other sections of the federal government, like the State Department, had logged several years of discharging a homosexual a week, without provoking a murmur from the ruined ex-bureaucrats, unless you count the occasional sound of gunshots to the temple. They had no idea what they were starting when they picked on Kameny. Brilliant, geeky, with a penchant for pure reason, and an uncanny memory for numbers, Kameny was one of those New York Jews who goes to Queens College at fifteen and winds up with a PhD from Harvard. No corporate sales manager or executive secretary, like the conformist leaders of the Mattachine Society, Kameny has always judged the world simply according to the extent to which it conforms to what he thinks. "If the world and I differ on something," he says, "I'll give it a second look and I'll give them a second chance to make their case, if I still differ, then I am right and they are wrong and that is that." No one could have invented a better character to represent the movement at its turning point than this man.

As a boy, Kameny had spent years going to the Hayden Planetarium in New York every month, each time it changed the exhibits. Before his arrest in a San Francisco toilet, he had quit school to fight the Nazis, seeing combat repeatedly in the American push across the Rhine. He came back from the war to get a PhD in astrophysics. During his postdoctoral year at the observatory in Tucson, Arizona, he met seventeen-year-old Keith, "who actively seduced the very willing" young astronomer on his twenty-ninth birthday. During his "golden summer" with his first love, Kameny used to drive up to Keith's family cabin in the cool heights of Mount Lemmon every morning as dawn broke and ended his nights looking at the stars. (The two never completely lost touch. In May 2004, Keith, then married under the Dutch same-sex marriage law, called Kameny to note the fiftieth anniversary of their meeting.) Kameny settled in happily at the map service, even entertaining a dream of being an astronaut until someone noticed his admission of a disorderly conduct arrest on his job application.

The conservative paladins of the Mattachine Society may have shunned any comparison to Negroes or any other minority, but Kameny thought it through and decided to make the United States government recognize that homosexuals were no more deserving of persecution and discrimination than "those against Negroes, Jews, Catholics or other minority groups." He immediately began to appeal his discharge, filing every conceivable motion with the administrative agencies within the civil service. When the civil service rejected him, he took it to federal court.

Although he had managed to convince the local office of the national American Civil Liberties Union (ACLU) of the injustice of his treatment, by the time his case reached the Supreme Court in 1961, his ACLU lawyer told him he could not win. The lawyer quit, leaving him to represent himself in the final, predictable defeat. Nationally, the ACLU had a policy treating homosexuality as conduct raising legitimate security concerns, a policy that would not change for almost a decade: homosexuals were subversive, and so not eligible for an equal share in the liberal state. In the hand-made brief to the Supreme Court that finally ended his unsuccessful legal quest for reinstatement, Kameny wrote, "It is in the public interest that many questions and issues relating to homosexuality be dealt with . . . realistically, civilizedly, and directly."

Kameny doesn't remember how he found out the court had rejected his petition, ending his life as an astronomer forever. Oh well, he says, there was nothing he could do to retrieve his professional life so he just moved ahead and took control of the gay movement. Many of the people interviewed for this book have said that at one time or another they contemplated suicide rather than face the reduced lives their homosexuality condemned them to. Not Kameny: "Oh no no no no no no no no, never. I never thought about what I had to give up. I am right and they are wrong and if they won't change I will have to make them."

With no other legal avenues available to him, he started gathering his friends to found a political organization to address the issues the court would not take up. After all, he had to do something to make the other guys change.

Earlier, when he realized he had been caught in the career-ending, life-altering federal discharge machine, he got in touch with the tiny gay movement of the time, and the Mattachine Society had given him fifty dollars. Kameny certainly wasn't a Communist, and he didn't know much about Harry Hay or the coup of 1953 at the time. But he knew fifty dollars wasn't going to do it. At his instigation, on November 15, 1961, a new Mattachine Society with no ties to the national group—the Mattachine Society of Washington—opened its doors.

"Nobody was doing anything," Kameny recalls. So the Mattachine Society of Washington commenced doing everything. He made a lifelong alliance and friendship with New York Daughters of Bilitis's Barbara Gittings, who kept finding herself on the radical edge over at the Daughters. Eventually the handful of little societies formed a confederation, the Eastern Conference of Homophile Organizations. Where the other homophile organizations looked to the clergy and to psychiatrists for help, Kameny realized that "if we were going to be granted the equality we were seeking it was not going to be given to a bunch of loonies." Anyway, as a scientist, he had long resented being analyzed by people he knew to be unqualified to speak to the subject of their supposed expertise.

Instead, Kameny helped found a DC chapter of the ACLU. The two organizations were so closely related that the Mattachine Society of Washington delayed its founding meeting a week so its founders could attend the founding of the new civil liberties organization. Stalin's championship of the Negro minority had inspired Harry Hay, and now the Negroes were making the case for the rights of minorities, what we now call civil rights. Kameny had seen the litigation that had fueled the civil rights movement; knowing he was starting a civil rights movement, he too lined up with the ACLU.

But if litigation wouldn't do it, he was prepared to try other techniques. He was not alone. The year was 1961. Buses full of Freedom Riders were just coming back from the South. A little band of unhappy students at the University of Michigan thought they should work toward a more democratic society.

3

It Was the Sixties That Did It: Gays Get Radical, Radicals Get Gay

Tom Hayden and his comrades in the Students for a Democratic Society (SDS) had been up the whole night drafting the mission statement for their new radical movement. When they walked out of the bunkhouse at the Port Huron resort just before dawn on June 17, 1962, the Michigan sky erupted in light: green, blue, silver bars of glimmering brilliance. It was the aurora borealis. The materialists in the New Left didn't believe in signs, but they took it as a sign anyway. They had seen the pictures of the civil rights workers being pulled off their lunch stools, dragged out of their buses, and beaten and assaulted with fire hoses. The northern lights seemed to signify their determination to illuminate America.

Formally, the New Left lasted little more than a decade—from the freedom rides and the founding of the SDS in 1961 to George McGovern's failed presidential campaign in 1972. Albeit brief, the Sixties were an explosive coincidence of every imaginable social disruption: a revolution in beliefs, led by youth, and fueled by grievances of race, war, and sex. When gay movement founder Franklin Kameny saw his little band of properly dressed gay protest marchers from 1965 swell to thousands in bell bottoms and ruffled shirts in Central Park in 1970, he said, "It was the Sixties that did it." Kameny wasn't talking about Jackie Kennedy's pillbox hats. It was the movement Sixties that did it. In hindsight, once the Sixties heated up, the ignition of the gay revolution was inevitable.

What happened? No one said it better than Bob Dylan:

> *Your sons and your daughters*
> *Are beyond your command*
>
> —"The Times They Are a-Changin'" (1963)

All Orphans Now

Jim Fouratt, a blue-eyed, long-haired, slender hippie and antiwar activist, came to New York in 1960 when he was barely out of his teens to go into the theater. Fouratt says he always thought he was passing for straight. He was wrong. Good thing for him the New York avant-garde theater in the early 1960s was a place where he didn't need to pass. The theater manager at the experimental Living Theater where he worked even took him to a gay bar.

Being who you were was big in the Sixties. Like the thousands or tens of thousands of gay men and lesbians who had moved to New York over all the decades that went before to live their lives as gay people, the movement youngsters, gay or straight, saw themselves as embarked upon a project of self-invention.

Unlimited self-creation sounds awfully ambitious, but no generation had ever been so powerful. The economic boom from 1945 to 1973 was the longest in American history and made America the richest society humanity had ever known. Rich Americans also had lots of babies—from 1945 right into the early 1960s. In 1963 and after, the newly rich and fecund Americans sent their multiple offspring to college, also in unprecedented numbers, up to six million by the end of the decade. Numerous, entitled, and separated from all parental restraints on campuses around the country: the new generation was a crowd, the founding element of a social movement.

The youthful idealists who gathered at Port Huron were determined above all to produce their own values. Not for them the collective wisdom of the Western political tradition, much less some antiquated religion or musty German ethical tract. Self-expression was in the cultural water, and they regarded the entire world as a stage on which they would write and direct their life story.

They sure didn't want to learn from Mom and Dad. As the Sixties generation was growing up, their parents seemed to vacillate between the terminally boring and the terrifyingly terminal. Books like *The Organization Man* and *The Man in the Gray Flannel Suit* described a society that would destroy the soul, and the nuclear bomb promised destruction of the body as well. More than a half century later, former movement journalist Allen Young still remembered the day he realized that no one in the school bomb drill was going to survive a nuclear attack, under the desk or on top of it.

Like the conservatives who pushed Harry Hay out of the Mattachine Society in 1953, a lot of the older liberal parents of the new activists were found under their desks when Joseph McCarthy came after them. Young's parents never gave up on the Communist Party, but one day young Allen found them throwing their lefty publications onto a bonfire. Burning books. The FBI was coming, they had heard. Whether they knew it or not, their children were watching them cave. In 1954, SDS president and Sixties chronicler Todd Gitlin's family got one of those new TVs, and Gitlin watched Joseph Welch ask red-baiting Senator Joseph McCarthy if he had no sense of decency (at long last). Once someone pulled the curtain on McCarthy, the Old Left's surrender to McCarthyism seemed like simple cowardice.

That so many of the original new lefties, gay and not, were Jewish, explains a lot. To their children, in the way the Old Left buckled to McCarthyism, purging their unions and denouncing one another to the House Un-American Activities Committee (HUAC), felt like not standing up to Hitler. Tall, imposing intellectual Gitlin, whose family story runs from Lithuania to the professoriate in little more than a generation, reports the haunting presence of his grandmother's late brother and sisters, left behind when the family departed and murdered by the Nazis. Left icon Meredith Tax tells the childhood tale of checking her bedroom for Nazis every night before going to bed. The Sixties actually opened with the first concerted look at the sins of the Holocaust in the form of the trial of Adolf Eichmann in 1961. In her explosive reports from the trial, public intellectual Hannah Arendt suggested that some of the blame for the genocide rested with the victims themselves. The Jewish children of America's Old Left were not about to open themselves up to that accusation.

When the time came, the Sixties activists brought these commitments to stand up when called to the gay revolution. Pale-skinned, dark-eyed young Carol Ruth Silver tied her brown hair up in a plain black scarf, knotted it behind her neck, and climbed on the bus for the Freedom Ride to Jackson, Mississippi, in 1961. Like all the Freedom Riders, Silver had been told to make her will and notify her parents. She went, she explained, because "I am a Jew, and I come from a background that says it is your responsibility to fix the world." Not gay herself, in the seventies she became number one ally of gay San Francisco supervisor Harvey Milk. Sixties movement and lesbian activist Martha Shelley remembers going berry picking with an older woman in the Catskill Mountains. The tomboyish young Shelley saw her companion shaking her head as she bent over the berry bushes, muttering, "Subvoisive, subvoisive. Whatever you say they call you subvoisive." In the early 1960s, the attractive, dark-haired Shelley was working as a secretary at Barnard College when she got the chance to be on TV speaking about the Daughters of Bilitis. Even though she thought she would be fired, she boasted, she did it anyway, because "for years I was thinking what would I have done if I'd been GERMAN?"

Alienated from their parents and determined to create their own values, the movement revolutionaries became, for a brief period, orphans—just like the gays and lesbians who had abandoned or been abandoned by their ancestral families for decades. Instead of taking it as rejection, as so many generations of gays and lesbians had done, the Sixties youngsters, gay and straight, seized their status. "We thought we were the first ones," Shelley says, "that we were going to liberate the whole world."

I wish, I wish, I wish in vain
That we could sit simply in that room again
—"Bob Dylan's Dream" (1963)

Being and Becoming

When gay activist Dick Leitsch came to New York in 1959, "New York was a police state. They just harassed us all the time, there was no place you could go where you felt safe." Although the conventional explanation for the crackdowns was that the city was cleaning itself up for the 1964 World's Fair, Leitsch says the administration of Mayor Robert F. Wagner Jr. was so hard because Robert Jr. (the mayor's son, Robert Ferdinand Wagner III, later called Jr.) was rumored to be gay. Leitsch found "all these people who are older than I have better educations, more money and more prestige, why the hell didn't they do something about it?"

"Other people were speaking up," Leitsch noticed. In 1960, a spontaneous coalition of Berkeley students invaded what had been a routine HUAC visit to San Francisco. HUAC had, as usual, laid a scary blanket of subpoenas on the progressive community in the city it was about to visit, and dozens of the summonses were directed to Berkeley faculty. When the federal commie hunters opened their hearings in San Francisco City Hall, hundreds of Berkeley students were waiting to watch the proceedings, acting just like admission was open to any American. When they were denied entrance, the would-be witnesses sat in on the stairs leading to the hearing room and sang "The Star-Spangled Banner." The police chief swept the protesters down the marble stairs with fire hoses. The next day the longshoremen showed up to support the students. HUAC would never come to San Francisco again.

On February 1, 1960, four black students left North Carolina Agricultural and Technical College for the Greensboro Woolworth Store. They sat down at the lunch counter, where only whites were permitted to eat. White citizens of Greensboro began to spit at them and throw eggs. The next day seventy-three A&T students sat down expectantly at the lunch counter. Soon there were hundreds. When Martin Luther King's Southern Christian Leadership Conference saw what was brewing at Greensboro, they gave Ella Baker, one of their most effective organizers, eight hundred dollars to call a meeting of the new activists and the Student Nonviolent Coordinating Committee (SNCC) was born.

That fateful week in February, James Pepper, sixteen-year-old homosexual scion of a fine old white Southern family, came home to Greensboro, North Carolina, from prep school. When Jim Pepper saw what the "rednecks" were doing to the students, he thought, you just can't treat people that way, and plunged into the fray. The next thing he knew, he was looking up at the very high desk of the local police sergeant, who addressed him as "New York Jew Boy." The cop saw the fancy local address on Pepper's driver's license and tossed the youthful activist out. Pepper never told his socially well-connected southern parents: "How would they have explained it at the cocktail party?" Sitting by the pool on the deck of his luxe Fire Island home in 2010, Pepper was still reluctant to tell the story (it "sounds so boastful"). By 1970, Pepper *was* living in New York (although he never converted to Judaism). Another decade on, he helped found Gay Men's Health Crisis. Today he is one of the most prominent philanthropists of the gay movement.

Five years later, Leitsch and a little band of homosexuals sat down at a bar. "We're homosexuals," they told the bartender. "And we'd like to order a drink."

He shook the land like the rolling thunder
And made the bells of freedom ring today

—"They Killed Him," Kris Kristofferson

Marching

DC gay activist Frank Kameny had not been idle. Following the legalistic, incremental strategy of the NAACP, he had been methodically litigating the discharges of homosexuals from federal employment. But he had yet to see a glimmer of hope from any tribunal. His chief adversary, Civil Service Commissioner John W. Macy Jr., would not even meet with him and the new US Commission on Civil Rights didn't do anything to help. While fruitlessly trying to throw sand in the civil service discharge machine, Kameny watched the various movement marches: "Day after day, every single day marching by the White House."

On August 28, 1963, 250,000 people went to Washington to join the March on Washington for Jobs and Freedom on the National Mall. By the time Martin Luther King Jr. stood up to speak, the crowd had been standing in the sun for hours. King had a dream, he told the gathered multitudes, a dream of the day "when *all* of God's children, black men and white men, Jews and Gentiles, Protestants and Catholics, will be able to join hands and sing in the words of the old Negro spiritual: *Free at last! Free at last! Thank God Almighty, we are free at last!*"

The roaring crowd didn't pay much attention to the graying, dapper, middle-aged man standing at the side of the stage as King preached. But without Bayard Rustin there would have been no march at all. If King was the messianic preacher of the civil rights movement, Rustin was its John the Baptist. The march on Washington was just the culmination of a long career.

As the March on Washington was about to step off, segregationist senator Strom Thurmond found out that the de facto leader was the homosexual ex-Communist Rustin. Dispensing with the smarmy coded accusations usually leveled at homosexuals, Thurmond took to the floor of the Senate and accused the movement leader of being . . . a homosexual. This time—maybe for the first time in history—something different happened. Instead of backing away from Rustin as they had in the past, the march organizers rallied around him. Some of their motivation was self-interest. Every agency of the civil rights movement, even the litigation-oriented NAACP, had committed its future to the march on Washington. The attacker was their open enemy, a racist from the segregated South. Legendary head of the Pullman Porters' Union, A. Philip Randolph, now in his seventies, called a press conference and affirmed his full faith in the moral character of Rustin and castigated Thurmond for violating the basic precepts of human decency. A prominent homosexual was attacked and survived. One of the witnesses said afterward, "it was like a boil being lanced."

On April 17, 1965, Kameny and his Mattachine sidekick Jack Nichols led ten homosexuals to their places in front of the White House with their signs: "Fifteen Million U.S. Homosexuals Protest Federal Treatment."

Girls' faces formed the forward path

—"My Back Pages," Bob Dylan (1964)

Breaking Out of Sex Roles

By 1964, gay SDS leader Carl Wittman had had it up to here with Tom Hayden's sex life. When Wittman arrived in Newark to help organize the impoverished black residents for SDS, Hayden announced that there would be no drugs or homosexuality in the SDS project and then, Wittman says, "he proceeded to borrow my room to bed down with his latest women," leaving Wittman, who had been having same-sex relations since he was fourteen, stunned and terrified.

Wittman was apparently not alone in being radicalized by Hayden's sex life. At almost that exact moment, Hayden's ex-wife, Casey, then at work in SNCC, sat down to write an anonymous memorandum about the position of women in the Sixties movement.

In hindsight, the eruption of women from the Left was inevitable. How long would women go on making coffee for the leaders of a liberation movement? The whole idea of the New Left was that everyone should create an authentic life for themselves free of any socially ascribed status. Civil rights activists Casey Hayden, a blond fourth-generation Texan, and dark-haired Mary King, descended from six generations of Virginia ministers, had already started the process of Sixties self-creation, just like the men who started the SDS and so many of the homosexuals who migrated to the cities. The two came to SNCC after apprenticeships in the liberal programs of the YWCA and the National Student Association. Although they were more powerful than most women in SNCC, they were still mostly working behind the scenes, at administrative and clerical jobs.

Hayden and King wrote what they called a "kind of memo," "Sex and Caste." The memo, which Todd Gitlin describes as a "slow acting time bomb," called the treatment of women a caste system of "assumed subordination from which women cannot escape." It accuses the movement of assigning women subordinate roles, like cleaning the "freedom" house, and asserts that the caste system permeates even private relationships. King and Hayden questioned the institutions that prescribed women's roles, including fundamental arrangements like marriage and childrearing, and suggested that people were starting to talk about experimenting with new forms of relationships. In 1966, the two published their "kind of memo" in the left magazine *Liberation.* After reading "Sex and Caste," women started meeting separately at the SDS gatherings, enumerating their grievances and discussing their lives.

King and Hayden purported to be surprised by the men's mocking and defensive reactions to their manifesto, given men's stake in upending the "socially determined straight-jacketing of both sexes." But they didn't mention the one group of men, which above all others, should have seen the advantage of breaking the straightjacket right away: gay men. For a century the psychiatrists had advanced the idea that "homosexuality" involved the wrong choice of sexual partner and a failure to act in a socially "normal" gendered way.

The straightjacket, which the feminists used as metaphor, was all too often actually applied to gay men in psychiatric wards, when their families or, worse, the legal system, tried to tie them into proper gender roles. So when King and Hayden suggested that the rigid, presumably "normal" gender roles were actually a matter of social caste, the gay activists, who were coming to political consciousness throughout the Sixties, should have been the women's first disciples.

They were not. Men who lived through the era of rising gay consciousness during the Sixties *now* say that feminism was one of the social movements that paved the way for gay liberation. Yet, there is almost no contemporaneous evidence of this in their diaries or correspondence before 1969. In thousands of pages, the many magisterial histories of the gay revolution discuss feminism only in the context of its effect on lesbians—the women of the "gay" revolution. Sixties gay militant Randy Wicker really did not like most women, particularly his mother. (One of the reasons he was never sorry to be a homosexual is it freed him up from having to deal with women.) Dick Leitsch thinks "women took over the gay movement. The feminist movement started and the lezzies all moved in and Betty drove them out and next thing you know the gay movement had become the LESBIAN and gay movement," he says regretfully.

Jim Fouratt was one of the few men who featured prominently in the antiwar movement and the gay revolution. He was a hippie, hung out with Abbie Hoffman, was in Chicago demonstrating against the 1968 Democratic National Convention, and was at the watershed uprising at the Stonewall bar in New York in 1969. He claims to be a feminist and his political history supports him. Yet he has never read "Sex and Caste."

Outside the New Left, Fouratt remembers, most gay men had no politics at all and, if they did, it was simply a desire to sit at the straight man's table. "Frank [Kameny], for example," he volunteers, "to this day does not understand feminism." The one male gay activist who apparently got it was Wittman. As he prepared to leave the movement and turn his energy to his own liberation, he wrote a farewell address, "A Gay Manifesto." Wittman's manifesto, published just before Stonewall, called feminists "our sisters in struggle": "They are assuming their equality and dignity and in doing so are challenging the same things we are: the roles."

If feminism didn't liberate gay men in the Sixties, it certainly aroused lesbian women. When in 1963 Betty Friedan issued her clarion call to the underutilized graduates of Smith College to get to work, lesbians, most of whom did not have the luxury of dependence, had already experienced much of the sex discrimination the feminist movement would ultimately focus on. They were as victimized by gender roles as any straight woman or gay man. By 1968, a radical feminist, Rita LaPorte, had taken over the Daughters of Bilitis and their newsletter, *The Ladder.*

> *Old lady judges watch people in pairs*
> *Limited in sex, they dare*
> *To push fake morals, insult and stare*
>
> —"It's Alright, Ma (I'm Only Bleeding)," Bob Dylan (1964)

Sexual Revolution, Homosexual Revolution

A poem by one of the original founders of Mattachine DC, Jack Nichols, describes Randy Wicker in the 1960s: "*His, a swift gait, His, a loud mouth.*" Tall and thin as a whippet, Wicker had one of those nails-on-a-blackboard voices and a propensity to overshare, but he was prescient and indefatigable. Wicker was an everything activist. He had been an atheist since childhood. When he was a student at the University of Texas, his homosexual relationship with his roommate got the roommate expelled. He came to New York in 1959, the same year as Dick Leitsch, and set about radicalizing the local Mattachine Society. One day a few years later, one of Wicker's straight friends knocked up his girlfriend. "Two weeks later I found out, he gave her huge doses of quinine and she had a miscarriage." His voice rising in indignation even after all these years, he recalled, "This guy met her parents, the parents of this girl he had been living with for two years, over a bed in Bellevue Hospital, because this girl had nearly died, having a miscarriage."

Wicker made the connection: "Society is not just screwed up about homosexuals, this society is screwed up about sex in general." He was dead on. The law against abortion that landed his friend at Bellevue was a tiny piece of a whole regime of criminal laws governing people's sexual practices. The criminal penalties for sodomy, which contributed so heavily to the misery and oppression of homosexuals, were just one example. Abortion, birth control, adultery, fornication—all were illegal to some degree in almost every state.

This body of law, which seems so inconsistent with the principles of the liberal state, had simply been adopted, with little thought, from the illiberal institution of the church in most cases centuries before. The roots of the injunctions against nonreproductive sex go back to the story of Sodom in the Old Testament (that's why they call it sodomy). At the critical juncture just after Christianity became the official religion of the Roman Empire, theologian Augustine of Hippo loudly repented his failure to confine his unruly sexual desires to marriage, which at least could be justified by the goal of procreation. But the prohibition really got traction in the thirteenth century, when the great Catholic theologian Thomas Aquinas said that reproduction not only justified the otherwise sinful act, but was the natural purpose, or goal, of sex. Aquinas also revived the idea that childrearing was the natural goal of marriage. Anything else, including extramarital sex, was unnatural.

Aquinas did not think this stuff up on his own; he was writing to try to reconcile Christian theology with the writings of the ancient pagan Greek philosophers like Aristotle, which had just been rediscovered by the Latin-reading West. Aristotle believed that everything that existed had to have a purpose, usually for the well-being of mankind. A knife is to cut, a horse is to ride, and so forth (Aristotle did not take a position on the purpose of sex). The Christian church had been humming along for centuries on the assumption that God created the world for his own purposes, including the limited range for legitimate sexual desire. No big surprise, Aquinas concluded that God's purposes and the natural law were the same. Since God created the natural world, anything unnatural was also sinful. That's why so many laws call sodomy—and all the other sex acts that don't lead to the supposedly natural "purpose" of reproduction—"unnatural." For years, the religiously based prohibitions were enforced, appropriately, by the church. But when the nation-states of Europe started taking enforcement of criminal law away from the church, they just swallowed the whole regime of sex sins whole. Presto, sins against nature became crimes against nature.

Charles Darwin's theory of evolution, coming many centuries later, should have driven a stake into this "natural" philosophy. In his theory, there is no God and no man for whose benefit the natural world is ordered. Things mutate and the fittest survive. Even something like nonreproductive sex, which seems crudely not to be a great survival mechanism, obviously has some connection to survival (or is harmless), because organisms with an orientation toward nonreproductive sex do, in fact, survive. In the Darwinian world, anything that exists, bad or good, is by definition "natural." But even after Darwin, the Catholic Church never got around to changing its thirteenth-century position on the purpose of sex. So Randy Wicker's friend wound up in Bellevue Hospital and Wicker, the homosexual activist, "went out and joined the Sex Freedom League."

He was the third founding member. The other founders included Jefferson "Fuck" Poland, an itinerant student with a commitment to the free-love movement, and Tilli Kupferberg, an open-marriage anarchist follower of the renegade psychoanalyst Wilhelm Reich. (It was Reich who coined the phrase "sexual revolution.") Historian David Allyn reports that one of the liveliest meetings of the league centered on a discussion of whether public masturbation was illegal if no one was actually struck by flying semen. Difficult as it is to believe, this group of activists actually foresaw and helped precipitate one of the most powerful cultural changes in the 1960s—the sexual revolution. Their seemingly outrageous list of demands—the decriminalization of interracial marriage, fellatio, cunnilingus, bestiality, and transvestitism—is now, except for the legally protected sheep, the law of the land. Even if the church would not change, sex would finally be uncoupled from crime.

Of course, they were riding a wave. Exactly as Reich foresaw, sexual freedom and political freedom were an explosive combination. In the early 1960s, the political protests at Berkeley turned into protests against the limits on political speech on campus, the Free Speech Movement. Once the free speechers got wind that campus speech rules also prohibited obscene speech, a local radical, John Thomson, put up a sign that said, simply, "Fuck." The "filthy-speech" protest movement was born, and the whole apparatus of regulating sexual expression in public was recast as a matter of free expression.

The Sixties also completely rewrote the rules for the private consumption of sexual expression. Forget Jefferson "Fuck" Poland; the biggest change came from the marble halls of the United States Supreme Court. In its decision in *Roth* in 1957, the Supreme Court had replaced the centuries-old test for obscenity, but the court still upheld time in the slammer for nude-picture merchants Samuel Roth and David Alberts. In 1964, the Supreme Court revisited the obscenity issue, this time incorporating Justice William J. Brennan Jr.'s language about redeeming social value from the 1957 opinion in *Roth* as the basis for an actual decision in favor of the publisher of the scandalous eighteenth-century novel *Fanny Hill.* What book is without redeeming social value? A year later, the Supreme Judicial Court of Massachusetts even protected William Burroughs's *Naked Lunch*, described by the dissenting judge as "literary sewage." The business of banning books was banished from the American scene. *ONE* magazine had been protected since *Roth*, but now periodicals and pulp fiction with gay themes could be distributed anywhere the market demanded. For an isolated teenage gay boy or lesbian girl, the book or magazine that tells them they are not alone was now protected by the United States Constitution.

Talking about sex and doing it are, of course, two different matters. As the Sixties opened, sexual conduct was supposedly still confined to heterosexual reproductive marriage between any man and a chaste female. In his second volume, *Sexual Behavior in the Human Female*, published in 1953, Alfred Kinsey reported that 50 percent of those supposedly chaste American women had actually had sex before marriage and a quarter had sex after marriage with men other than their husbands. Regardless of the accuracy of his statistics, as with Kinsey's first "report" about a 37 percent homosexuality rate, the suggestion itself began to generate the social change it was supposed to be reporting.

Although Kinsey got unbelievable heat from the fifties establishment at the time, by 1960 three unpredictable events conspired to make his report a reality: a biologist attended a dinner party with two uppity women, a nudie-magazine publisher convinced himself that he was Nietzsche, and one ambitious middle-aged copywriter actually married the boss.

The biologist, Gregory "Goody" Pincus, was another one of those Jewish immigrants' kids who went to Harvard. Pincus was interested in biology, specifically mammalian ova. "I'm an egg man," he used to say. He was working on the role of hormones in ovulation when someone he met at a dinner party one fateful night in 1950 turned out to be birth-control pioneer and founder of Planned Parenthood Margaret Sanger. Sanger saw the relevance of Pincus's research right away. She started sending Pincus money. When Planned Parenthood's funds did not produce the results Sanger sought fast enough, she called on her friend and fellow feminist Katharine McCormick to direct some of that reaper money to the cause of female contraception. In less than a decade, Searle's Enovid began rolling off the assembly lines: the Pill had come to the barricades of the sexual revolution.

Once Goody Pincus's pills made the rabbit test for pregnancy obsolete, the little furry creatures found employment serving drinks at the Playboy Club in 1960. There were ultimately many clubs and many magazines, but the *Playboy* operation fairly represents the creeping social acceptability of nonmarital sex. Taking a leaf from the *Roth* opinion, *Playboy*'s publisher, Hugh Hefner, embedded his nude *Playboy* centerfolds in material of redeeming social value—stories, interviews, and culture. He even had a philosophy, the Playboy Philosophy, which held that "this nonsense about the body of man being evil, while the mind and spirit are good, seems quite preposterous to most of us today. After all, the same Creator was responsible for all three and we confess we're not willing to believe that He goofed when He got around to the body of man (and certainly not when He got to the body of woman). Body, mind and spirit all have a unique way of complementing one another, if we let them, and if excesses of the body are negative, it is the excesses that are improper rather than the body, as excesses of the mind and spirit would also be."

Hefner targeted young men. But the sexual revolution would never have succeeded if it had not also included women. Just as Pincus empowered women to control the most feared outcome of sexual activity—unwanted pregnancy—and Hefner gave their male contemporaries a philosophical argument for sex, Helen Gurley Brown told her female readers to defy the double standard. She should know: on her way to the gold medal of sexual Olympics, marrying the boss, she liberated a lot of other girls' husbands from their marital constraints. *Sex and the Single Girl*, which appeared in 1962, had a single moral: watch out for yourself and get what you can. The young Helen Gurley's first lover had the good sense to buy her earrings after they finished dispensing with her virginity.

The philanthropic arm of *Playboy*, the Playboy Foundation, was one of the first funders of the American Civil Liberties Union (ACLU) Sexual Privacy Project, which, in 1973, first brought that powerful and prestigious civil rights organization explicitly to the cause of gay rights. (It would not be until 1986 that the ACLU had an explicit focus on gay and lesbian issues, the Lesbian and Gay Rights Project.)

Liberated, secular, hedonistic, nonreproductive, nonmarital sex: everything about sex changed in the Sixties culture. The only people who had not found out about the sexual revolution were the lawmakers. Ground zero in the battle over government control of sex was the battle over birth control, which had been going on at the state level for decades, as the forces of Sanger's Planned Parenthood organization fought the long-standing opposition of the Catholic Church and a rural, fundamentalist Puritanism. As recently as 1965, Connecticut, for example, had a century-old law that made the use of contraception by anyone, including married couples, a criminal act.

The sexual revolutionaries turned to the shining guardians of individual freedom in the Sixties, the federal courts. Perversely, the legal campaign for consequence-free sex had started earlier with a 1947 decision guaranteeing people's right to have babies! *Skinner v. Oklahoma* was not a self-conscious sexual-freedom case. It arose in the revolt against eugenics in the aftermath of the Nazi atrocities of World War II. In a now-notorious case, *Buck v. Bell*, in 1927, the US Supreme Court had approved a Virginia statute that called for sterilizing "the feeble-minded." The Nazis invoked the decision to defend their practices at the war-crimes trials in Nuremberg after the war and many American states still engaged in sterilization. In Oklahoma, for instance, certain felonies were punishable by sterilization after repeat convictions. When an Oklahoma chicken thief challenged his sterilization in 1947, the Supreme Court struck it down, ruling, in *Skinner v. Oklahoma,* that reproduction is a basic liberty protected by the Constitution. Consequently, any law allowing sterilization would be subject to the strictest scrutiny by the court and the state would have to present a compelling interest to justify its enforcement, an almost impossible standard for a state to meet.

Although the court decided in *Skinner* that the government could not take away people's right to reproduce, the court did not decide whether the government could force people to risk having babies if they did not want to, the birth-control issue, which was the real link to the sexual revolution. While the court was ducking the birth-control cases, the sexual revolution transformed the culture. After a decade of skirmishing the court finally confronted the Connecticut prohibition of birth control in *Griswold v. Connecticut* and found it unconstitutional in 1965. The problem the court faced in *Griswold* is that unlike, say, speech and race, which are explicitly addressed in the Constitution, the founding document is silent about condoms, and the federal judiciary is generally supposed to confine itself to enforcing what federal law says. The court could have grounded its decision in the history of prohibiting otherwise harmless behavior based on religious beliefs. But the constitutional restraints on the establishment of religion had never been interpreted that ambitiously.

Struggling to find a justification for their decision without completely uncoupling criminal law from religious morality, the seven-vote majority striking down the Connecticut law produced four opinions. For purposes of the gay movement, the most influential opinion is Justice William O. Douglas's opinion for the court, which found a right to "privacy" in the penumbras or emanations of various provisions of the Bill of Rights like the protections against unreasonable searches and seizures (hence the word "privacy" in the ACLU's Sexual Privacy Project). In finding privacy rights implicit in the Bill of Rights, *Griswold* not only abetted the sexual revolution, but also pushed the boundaries of constitutional interpretation. It was *Griswold* in part that gave birth to the conservative campaign for strict construction of the Constitution. But, much as they like to bray about strict constitutionality, people sure don't want the state rummaging around in their bedside table for condoms. Since *Griswold*, decisions about contraception are covered by one of the three basic principles of the liberal state—that certain core aspects of human life cannot be dictated by the state. They belong solely to the individual.

The line of Supreme Court decisions directed to protecting people from reproducing if they don't want to turns out to be the primal spring of rights for gays and lesbians, even though they are the least likely candidates for unwanted pregnancy. Once sexual practices became a matter of individual decision making protected from the regulatory agency of the government, the inexorable logic of the precedent should have dictated the demise of the laws against the private practice of sodomy, generally understood to mean anything other than heterosexual genital intercourse.

The happenstance that the Connecticut law applied to married couples also started the line of cases treating marriage as an arena of special constitutional importance. (In striking down the Connecticut law, *Griswold*, amusingly, includes a paean to the sanctity of the marriage chamber from the oft-wed Justice Douglas.) As of late 2011, the court is still out on what that will mean for the gay movement, but for people with logical minds the implications are obvious.

> *Hey! Mr. Tambourine Man, play a song for me*
> *In the jingle jangle morning I'll come followin' you*
> —"Mr. Tambourine Man," Bob Dylan (1963)

Homosexuals Get Radical, Radicals Get Homosexual

Randy Wicker came to New York after an abortive first year of law school. Jim Fouratt followed a lover who promised him a job in theater. Dick Leitsch came to New York on vacation and decided he had to return. They seemed no different from any other gay or lesbian people who had migrated to big cities for decades. But they were different. *They were the children of the Sixties.* Just like the kids who gathered at Port Huron to lay out the program for the SDS.

In 1953, when Harry Hay's Mattachine Society sent a questionnaire on gay issues to the candidates for Los Angeles City Council, a single hostile newspaper columnist, the senator with no shame, and their own terrified membership brought the entire effort crashing down. But by the time the radical homosexuals started gathering in New York—and LA and San Francisco—less than a decade later, the forces of social order had been weakened to the point where the establishment could no longer simply impose its will. The racial civil rights movement, challenging the authority of the white power structure in America, had already begun to bubble up as the organized African American community greatly increased the pressure on the segregated South. Anticolonial movements across the globe were challenging the rule of old white men. The invention of the birth-control pill, which uncoupled heterosexuality from reproduction, undermined the authority of the reproductive nuclear family and, ultimately, of straight men as a class, to rule. Revolutions don't happen when the forces of social order are at their most confident. They happen when the order is wavering.

One sign that the order is faltering is that people are willing to forgo being part of it. Because of the availability of the closet, gay individuals are always subject to the temptation to give up their sexual politics to join the establishment, so the rise of the gay movement is a particularly effective barometer of how vulnerable the establishment was. Even though the youthful Leitsch still looked like a balding Madison Avenue "Mad Man," and to this day speaks with a gentle Kentucky accent, he was a hippie, an anticapitalist, and a Kennedy baby. He never wanted to make money by working in business and was happy tending bar after he moved to New York. Wicker had embraced civil rights at the University of Texas, and Fouratt went to San Francisco to play with the Beats as soon as he had the chance. After he made a few bucks writing this and that, Wicker went to work "at a titty magazine." Weird, marginal, and defiant, the Sixties New York gay radicals were different in kind, and not just in degree, from the homophiles, even their ally, the older Franklin Kameny.

Children of the Sixties, they knew that media mattered. Leitsch volunteered to edit the Mattachine newsletter. Wicker found out that the Mattachine Society had invited a lawyer to talk about how to deal with the police. He made up a hundred fliers and distributed them around the bars. When he arrived at a Greenwich Village antiques shop, the owner, a straight old lady, said, "It's about time." It's about time. The usual Mattachine crowd of thirty swelled to three hundred after Wicker tried elementary media tactics to publicize the cause.

Being children of the Sixties, they were not afraid. In 1963, Wicker got on a soapbox that some anarchist from the League for Sexual Freedom set up at MacDougal and Third Street and, with his legs trembling, said, You know right down this block there's a club and it's run by the Mafia and I think that homosexuals have the right to have their own club and the police should not be corrupted by being paid off. And he got a smattering of applause. It was the first time he ever got up in public and spoke out as a homosexual and he suddenly realized he had an advantage that no one else had. He learned they wouldn't knock you in the head the minute you stick your head out.

Leitsch arrived in New York with a rather sophisticated understanding of the workings of the American Constitution: "The US Constitution and the First Amendment," he says, "say that everybody has the right to assemble and the Fourteenth Amendment says the state can't stop us." Armed with that knowledge, Leitsch and a handful of fellow militants "decided I'm not going to take this any more." "They'd raid bars, they'd raid STREET CORNERS," Leitsch says. "People hung out on the corner, and the newspapers, the *Journal American*, which was the Irish Catholic paper, and they'd say 'nest of undesirables' so that meant that a church or social club could not welcome gays because they were afraid they'd be raided." Leitsch fulminates, "The nuns were gay, the priests were gay, and there was no place to go, bars were just about the only place you could go."

Media-sensitive and emboldened, Leitsch and Wicker and a handful of similarly inclined New York homosexuals began to stick their heads out further and further. The ever-obliging psychiatric establishment jump-started their campaign by providing left-wing New York radio station WBAI with a panel of doctors in 1962 to opine that homosexuals were mentally disturbed. Wicker immediately saw an opportunity and pressured the station to air a program in which homosexuals spoke for themselves. Not surprisingly, the homosexuals Wicker provided to WBAI did not think they were mentally ill. When a right-wing newspaper columnist for the *New York Journal American* attacked the program, it became the most requested offering WBAI ever had. Wicker took the column and ginned up the first real coverage of the homosexual population in decades, maybe ever, generating stories in *Newsweek*, *Harper's*, and even the *New York Times*.

Not everyone was pleased with the campaign. The Mattachine landlord, who owned an Irish bar on the ground floor, was horrified at Wicker's homosexual hundreds. "You have been perfect tenants," he told the homophiles, "but you have to go. I have a liquor license. I cannot have these people in my building." The tension in the New York Mattachine Society between the holdovers from the conservative period and the Sixties activists was already heating up in 1964, when the New Yorkers made the mistake of inviting Kameny to give one of their monthly lectures. Kameny chose for his theme the psychiatrists, their "loose reasoning, poor research, nonrepresentative samplings, and circular reasoning." Everywhere Kameny spoke in those years, his words were the catalyst for the radicalizing of the homophile movement, and the New York Mattachine Society was no exception. Fired up, the new activists set about ousting the incumbents in the 1965 election. President-elect Julian Hodges (who had gone over to the radicals under Kameny's influence), Leitsch, Wicker, and Kameny (who was technically not a New Yorker and already the head of Mattachine in DC) ran for the board and won.

The new radicals of the New York Mattachine and Kameny's DC group embarked on four years of activism. Most of their achievements would be lost in the smoke from the Stonewall uprising. But in the few years between 1965 and June 1969, the Mattachine activists went a long way toward achieving what the gay revolution set out to do.

In 1968, seven years after the Supreme Court shut down Kameny's crusade against the civil service, the US Court of Appeals for the District of Columbia Circuit opened the door a crack. Bruce Scott, who had seen the small notice of Kameny's defeat in a Washington newspaper and called him, had become the secretary of the DC Mattachine. When he applied for federal employment, the civil service turned him down on grounds that he either was a homosexual or had engaged in homosexual conduct. He and Kameny appealed from the civil service to the federal courts. For the first time the DC circuit court reversed the civil service, ruling that its reasons were not specific enough to deny Scott federal employment and stigmatize him, as such a denial would do. On remand from the court, the civil service then turned Scott down for not answering their questions about his homosexuality. The court reversed again.

Worried about the precedent, the government settled with Scott. But just behind him came a NASA employee, Clifford Norton, who got caught cruising in Lafayette Square. Poor Norton picked up some guy while the police were watching, then drove around the park with the pickup once and let him off. It later emerged Norton's overtures had been rebuffed. Even though Norton never even got laid, the once around the park still cost him his job. The DC circuit court ordered him reinstated, on grounds that homosexual conduct off premises and on the employees' own time was not related to the "efficiency of the service" and so violated both the civil service laws that governed federal employment and the Constitution, which requires the government to deal fairly with its people. Although the victories were imperfect—not being Supreme Court decisions, they were not national, and they did not exclude homosexual conduct categorically from being considered—*Scott v. Macy* and *Norton v. Macy* were huge steps toward protecting homosexuals from one of the things they feared most, losing their livelihoods.

Meanwhile, Leitsch, who was "mostly interested in drinking and getting laid," was concentrating on getting the police out of the bathrooms and the bars. The constant fear of encountering an undercover policeman and the inability to gather peacefully in any commercial place were two of the biggest hurdles to any mass organizing of the homosexual community. For all their meetings and conferences and newsletters and contested elections, the Mattachine organizations never attracted a membership of more than a few hundred. Kameny's last march before Stonewall involved an all-time record of fifty-five participants.

Leitsch credits the outing of Lyndon B. Johnson's chief aide, Walter

Jenkins, during the 1964 election campaign with getting the ball rolling for his campaign to clear some space for gays to meet in New York without police interference. Jenkins, who got caught by the police having sex in a YMCA bathroom, lost his job immediately. During the inquiries that followed, however, the Johnson PR machine worked pretty hard to rebut the accusation that every homosexual was a security risk and Lady Bird Johnson came out defending Jenkins. Barry Goldwater is quoted as saying that there are some things worse than losing an election and he refused to use the Jenkins incident. It wasn't what Stonewall would be, but like the response to the attacks on Rustin, the culture began, subtly, to shift. The New York ACLU had gradually swung over to advocating for homosexuals. A liberal Protestant church in the Village, Judson Memorial, began to take their side. The *New York Post*, then a liberal paper, had sent a reporter to the Mattachine Society, where Leitsch put him on an extension to listen in as hysterical, frantic men called, night after night, facing ruin because they had picked up an undercover policeman in the bathroom. The *Post* ran the stories and editorialized against the sodomy laws that made it all possible.

Rumor had it that the new "liberal" Republican mayor of New York, John Lindsay, was not unsympathetic. But in 1966, right after Lindsay took office, his administration provoked the homosexual community by ordering a police sweep of "homosexuals and prostitutes" around Times Square and then in Greenwich Village. Judson Memorial Church called a community meeting. Lindsay sent his chief inspector, Sanford Garelik, who took a verbal beating from the audience and said something that sounded like denial of police entrapment.

As luck would have it, that night a heterosexual Episcopalian priest sat down at the counter of Julius'—then a mixed gay-straight bar—for one of their famous hamburgers. The next man at the counter and the rector started talking, but at midnight the priest was expecting a phone call from a friend in England, so he asked his new companion if he'd like to finish their conversation over coffee at his place. When the two hit the sidewalk, the agreeable barfly arrested the priest for homosexual solicitation. So, just as the police commissioner denied there was such a thing as entrapment, his undercover cop entrapped a straight Episcopalian (who happened also to be a good friend of the Episcopalian mayor). The media were ecstatic.

Lindsay promised that from then on the police would stop trying to drag unsuspecting homosexuals into nocturnal invitations. More establishment help arrived when the Mattachine guys picked up legendary civil rights lawyer William Stringfellow, who sent lawyers from his fancy law firm to defend the gays arrested despite the orders against entrapment. When the sleazy judges at the morality division looked up and saw a lawyer who had just come from representing Procter and Gamble getting ready to cross-examine the cop, they began dismissing the charges at an unprecedented rate. From the mayor of New York to the lowliest night-court judge, the establishment blinked.

Leitsch and the newly radicalized Mattachine leadership immediately turned to the bars. As it had since Prohibition was repealed, the New York State liquor law said that the bar owner must keep the place orderly. The New York State Liquor Authority took the position that the presence of a homosexual meant ipso facto that the place was disorderly. So the gays went to their movement lawyer, Stringfellow, for instructions about how to challenge the prohibition. He told them that they had to have an orderly protest, with no cameras or anything that might be construed as disorderly. Leitsch and a couple of his buddies (and Wicker, who "invited himself") went into a bar. They carried a piece of paper that said "we the undersigned are orderly," announced that they were homosexuals, and asked for a drink. After a couple of smart bartenders refused to play the role of test-case defendants, they finally got the guy at Julius' to say no. Following the mayor's lead, the head of the state liquor authority denied that his agency forbade license holders to serve liquor to homosexuals.

Leitsch and his same-sex bar liberators continued to push the envelope on disorderly conduct. In a series of cases, they got the New York courts to forbid the state liquor authority to pull a bar's license if gays gathered there. After the bar owners showed the courts clips of Orthodox Jews and Greek men dancing with one another and a picture of Charles de Gaulle smooching General Eisenhower, the court ruled the gay patrons could do anything short of criminal solicitation.

At this point, the gay activists were following the fairly conventional script of the early-Sixties movements. The self-invention at the heart of Sixties radicalism, particularly the sexual radicalism, allowed a handful of leaders to boldly come out. Combining litigation with direct action, they set about exploiting the divisions in the existing order that was oppressing them. The increased radicalism of the late-Sixties racial and antiwar movements was just manifesting itself, and the distinctions that would soon set the gay movement on a different, and ultimately more productive, path were still latent.

As the homosexuals were becoming radicalized, the radical movement became gayer. Hippie stalwart and Abbie Hoffman pal Jim Fouratt remembers his first real identification with gay politics. "I didn't want to be a Mattachine kind of homosexual." Fouratt was on a trip to San Francisco around 1966, when he met the Vanguard, a pre-hippie group that rose up to protest a police raid on a gay cafeteria. When the Vanguard protested, they all put on wigs, in solidarity with the cross-dressers busted at the cafeteria. That was the kind of gay movement a self-dramatizing Sixties hippie could love.

Tom Hayden's roommate, movement stalwart Carl Wittman, had a harder time with the New Left than the sunny Fouratt. Like the young Harry Hay, Wittman struggled to reconcile his homosexual desires with his deep and long-standing commitment to a social movement that was so reflexively homophobic. Wittman, the son of Communist parents, was a radical from his college days with the Swarthmore chapter of SDS. The consummate talent spotter, Hayden, elevated the tall, eloquent, blond Wittman to leadership early and took Wittman with him to start an antipoverty project in Newark. But, according to David Mungello, briefly Wittman's lover in the late Sixties, Wittman left Hayden's Newark project to start his own effort in Hoboken in 1966 in order to get away from Hayden's homophobia. That same year, three decades after Hay married Anita Platky to try to pull the conflicting halves of his life together, Wittman decided he'd been fighting his shameful homosexual desires long enough and wed his college friend and coworker Mimi Feingold in the backyard of movement grand old man David Dellinger.

Somehow the hippie potluck nuptials did not offset the falsity of Wittman's sexual commitment. One year later, he and Feingold took the step guaranteed to break up a homosexual's heterosexual marriage—they moved to San Francisco. Wittman, always and to his core an activist, took up with the Bay Area War Resistance. He also, Mungello reports, took up with him and with numerous other gay men in the Bay Area in the priapic California sunshine. Wittman was a blond, Mungello remembers, not a hairless, Scandinavian blond, but a hairy, masculine, tall blond. His Swarthmore yearbook picture looks like a young Tab Hunter.

California had always been a kinder, gentler place, but by 1967, San Francisco was, as Wittman would later describe it, a "refugee camp" for "homosexuals" from "Amerika." As the Sixties succeeded the Beatnik phase, the Black Cat Bar remained the touchstone. Litigious straight Sol Stoumen owned it, gay waiter José Sarria still nightly acted out the opera *Carmen* with himself in the title role, and the performances always ended with the gay patrons linking arms and singing "God Save Us Nelly Queens" to the tune of "God Save the Queen." In Los Angeles, a young landscape gardener, Steve Ginsberg, turned his youthful aspirations to gay militancy as early as 1966, naming his new organization PRIDE. One of the first members of PRIDE, Richard Mitch, had access to the print shop at ABC Studios, where lots of the men were gay. Presto, a "newspaper," the Los Angeles *Advocate*, now the oldest continuous gay publication in America.

In 1962, well before the New York "sip-in" orchestrated by Leitsch and his cohorts, the San Francisco gay-bar owners and managers assembled a Tavern Guild and started doing the grunt work of political organizing. They hired a lawyer and a bail bondsman to represent the patrons arrested in the bars and they started fighting the state liquor authorities. Every time there was an election, the Tavern Guild registered voters. Because San Francisco did not have a population the size of New York's, sooner or later the registered voters of the Black Cat were going to show up on some politician's radar. In 1961, Sarria ran for the San Francisco Board of Supervisors and got a fair number of votes.

Wittman didn't like the Tavern Guild. He wrote in his incendiary 1969 "Gay Manifesto" that the bar owners overcharged the denizens of the gay ghetto and kept them down so they could make money from them. A refugee camp, Wittman wrote, is better than where the refugees came from; otherwise they would not be there in the first place. But it was still a ghetto and not a free place. Wittman wanted gays to make their refuge into a place where they could govern themselves—"set up their own institutions, defend themselves, open a gay dance hall, rural retreats, food cooperatives, a free school"—the whole Sixties litany.

Wittman seems unaware that, to a surprising extent, the Bay gays already had done the deed. In 1964, the supposedly extortionate bar owners and managers from the Tavern Guild helped form an explicitly political gay organization, the Society for Individual Rights (SIR). Although the homosexual rights society was predictably uninterested in the free schools and food cooperatives, they did register voters, canvass politicians, and hold candidates' nights.

Sixties San Francisco even managed to produce a vindication for the prim and proper Daughters of Bilitis and the scared-rabbit late Mattachines. The clergy and professionals became their allies after all. To be sure, it was a very different ministry that gathered in Mill Valley,

California, to meet with the homosexuals in May 1964 from the one the conservative leaders had in mind ten years before. The clergy did not come around because the homosexuals were so "normal" and middle class as the old Mattachine had hoped. Glide Memorial Church, a Methodist outpost in the downtown down-and-out Tenderloin, came around because it cared for the lowest and most desperate of the community—the disproportionately homosexual runaways. When a clergyman with a heart, Ted McIlvenna, tried to get some handle on the orphaned street kids, he ran right into the war between the church and the gay community. It being the Sixties, the Glide ministers tried to make a little love. They brought in a dozen liberal Protestant clergymen, including a few from across the country, to the Mill Valley meeting. The assistant to the Episcopal bishop of Northern California attended. A representative of the liberal but hoary old National Council of Churches came from New York. A United Church of Christ minister came, and a Lutheran, as well as the Methodists.

Under the leadership of the Glide group, the Mill Valley meeting generated a Council on Religion and the Homosexual. It probably wasn't exactly what the socially conscious men of God had in mind, but the next thing they knew they had caused a riot at a gay ball. They intended the gay ball—it was to be a fund-raiser and kickoff event—but they did not intend the riot, although they caused it by behaving like Goody Two-shoes and telling the police of their plans. The police showed up in force, shining klieg lights on the entrance and photographing the terrified participants. When lawyers, gay and straight, tried to stop the police from entering the hall without a warrant, the police arrested the lawyers and some poor anonymous woman who was just there to take tickets. Witnesses report the "ball" turned into a chaotic, scary scene.

Some people have called the 1964 New Year's ball San Francisco's Stonewall, but that is to misread the differences between the communities. There were no nights of rioting following the San Francisco New Year's ball bust. At the same time that Robert Wagner's administration was turning New York into what Leitsch called a police state, the gay-friendly ministers of San Francisco called a press conference, on January 2, 1965, to denounce what the authorities had done, and the mainstream press joined the outcry. God—and the liberal legal community—did save the Nelly queens. When the New Year's ball lawyers came to trial for their criminal misconduct, twenty-five of the most prominent lawyers in town had signed on as "counsel." Who are you going to believe, the vice squad or the men of God? The judge tossed out the charges before the accused lawyers even put on a defense. The police agreed to stop busting the bars, and SIR met with the first candidate for supervisor ever to seek its endorsement. By all accounts, San Francisco was a long way toward becoming the free society Wittman sought before he arrived.

Although it opens in San Francisco, Wittman's "Gay Manifesto" is not about San Francisco. It is about the gay revolution anywhere in "Amerika," the most ambitious statement of the principles of the gay revolution since Harry Hay called out the bachelors in 1950—and a lot better written. "A Gay Manifesto" makes the argument for the three core principles of a successful movement: admit you're different, demand respect, and take care of your own interests first.

"We'll be gay until everyone has forgotten that it's an issue," Wittman advises. "Stop mimicking straights, stop censoring ourselves." Gay Is Good: "We have to learn that our loving each other is a good thing, not an unfortunate thing, and that we have a lot to teach straights about sex, love, strength, and resistance." Wittman even resists the siren song of the universal brotherhood of man from the New Left, which had made him a made man: "A lot of movement types come on with a line of shit about homosexuals not being oppressed as much as blacks or Vietnamese or workers or women . . . talk about the priority of black liberation or ending imperialism over and above gay liberation is just anti-gay propaganda."

As Wittman's manifesto reflects, the gay movement, which had risen powerfully on the currents of the Sixties, exploded in 1969 just as the Sixties movements were showing the flaws that would ultimately take them down. The racial movement had taken a stab at black separatism, with the direct-action Student Nonviolent Coordinating Committee voting to expel all their white allies; in 1968 the long-integrated Congress of Racial Equality followed suit. At the other end of the spectrum, Martin Luther King Jr. remained committed to integration and nonviolence, dividing the movement along pro- and antiseparatist lines. At all levels of separatism or integration, the racial movement took on the burden of opposing the Vietnam War, powerfully diverting it from its original agenda.

The feminist movement suffered from the outset from the defects of its virtues: the potential membership, consisting of more than half the population, was rent by every conceivable division. In 1967, the signature organization of the movement, the National Organization for Women (NOW), could not even achieve unanimous approval of the proposed equal rights amendment and then split off a conservative faction, the Women's Equity Action League, over abortion. By 1969, the poisonous feminist slogan, "The personal is the political," characterized a strong movement of younger, Sixties-influenced women's liberationists. Personal performances like publicly cropping one another's long hair were characterized as political actions. Predictably, once the movement took down the worst of the formal sex segregation, many women transformed their politics into a concern with their individual well-being. The personal is the political after all.

Although the same stresses—an ineffective separatism, dilution, and co-optation—would quickly surface in the gay movement, at the beginning, the nascent movement really had no choice but to adopt Wittman's cautionary principles. Co-optation was not an option. When King asked the nation to judge black Americans not on the color of their skin but on the content of their character, few would have argued that skin color reflected character or that being black should be criminal. For the thing that mattered to King—character—black Americans were the same as the white majority. But the gay revolutionaries' difference from the majority—sexual behavior—ran right into the heart of American moral judgment. Indeed, it sometimes seems that in modern America sexual morality is the only morality. So the gay movement was stuck with two choices. They could ask the society to ignore or tolerate their behavior, immoral or not, in the interests of higher values like freedom or privacy. Or they could argue that their sexual practices were not wrong ("Gay Is Good"). The real danger came from the other two temptations, separatism and dilution. For the moment, however, the homophobia and selfishness of the rest of the Sixties movements ("line of shit about Vietnamese or workers," as Wittman put it) meant that the new movement would be somewhat inoculated against the temptation to dilute its efforts by taking up every left-wing cause. By insisting on prosecuting them for sodomy and busting the places where they sought to gather and meet, the dominant society had also closed off the avenue of separatism, which so strongly tempted the racial movement.

Probably because he had lived through the disintegration of the Sixties movements, Wittman was able to warn his new-movement colleagues against some of the worst pitfalls. And Wittman is a thread that links the gay activists who emerged from the Sixties movement, or from the milieu the movement created, and entered gay politics to change them forever. Fouratt, who would write the epitaph to the Mattachine era at the first meeting after Stonewall, read Wittman's manifesto, he thinks as early as 1966. No one else remembers "A Gay Manifesto" before 1969, but Fouratt's memory is a tribute to its influence on him. Allen Young, the big-deal journalist from the lefty Liberation News Service who came over to the gay movement, describes his Sixties self as "totally compartmentalized." "The first time I really made the connection," between his political self and his gay self, he remembers, "I was reading Carl Wittman's piece." Fouratt had been after Allen to go to a gay meeting and this time he agreed.

On June 28, 1969, four months after Wittman's manifesto appeared, cars filled with policemen rolled up to the front of the Stonewall Inn in Greenwich Village. The gay revolution woke up to its jingle jangle morning. For the next decade, Wittman's words played the song for them.

4

Stonewall Uprising: Gays Finally Get Some Respect

"The Only Language the Pigs Understand"

The rocks had been removed, the glass swept away, and the windows of the Stonewall Inn boarded up when Mattachine president Dick Leitsch gave in to the pressure to schedule a meeting. By the second Mattachine meeting, on July 16, 1969, there were several hundred people crowded into the Episcopal church on Waverly Place in Greenwich Village. The Mattachine secretary, heterosexual matron Madolin Cervantes, proposed that "we ought to have a gay vigil in a park. Carry candles, perhaps. A peaceful vigil. I think we should be firm, but just as amicable and sweet as—"

Long-haired, leather-clad hippie celebrity Jim Fouratt jumped to his feet: "Sweet! . . . Sweet! Bullshit! There's the stereotype homosexual again, man! Soft, weak, sensitive! Bullshit! Be proud of what you are, man! And if it takes riots or even guns to show them what we are, well, that's the only language that the pigs understand!" Wild applause.

Leitsch tried to answer, but Fouratt shouted him down. Leitsch screamed for order again and again but to no effect.

What had happened to the movement?

The Uprising

We'll never really know. The events at the Stonewall Inn in the early morning of June 28, 1969, are the most contested hours in gay history. People who were there dispute each other's accounts and people even dispute who was there at all. Famed gay historian Martin Duberman, who wrote one of the first histories of the event, elicited scathing criticism that he placed people on the scene who were blocks or miles away. Reunions of the Stonewall participants only trigger renewed arguments about whether the person who acted out first was a queen, a lesbian, or no one at all. Only a couple of reporters, from the *Village Voice*, down the street, were present, and their stories were so inflammatory they ignited an additional day of rioting when they were published on July 3. Whatever the details, Stonewall is a genuine American revolution: the authorities took on men in wigs in a bar and all hell broke loose.

One thing no one disputes: what a dump. The now iconic Stonewall Inn did not have running water. As in most Mafia establishments, the liquor was so watered down it wouldn't even kill a germ. Yet the black-painted, plywood-boarded, dirty, overpriced bar with the Sixties black lights was what passed for a good place to go in the last years of New York's gay repression. The corrupt and avaricious owners let the gay guys dance together, and the music in the back room was especially appealing. The bouncers admitted transvestites in makeup. All in all, Stonewall was a place with an unusually wide slice of gay life, from men in suits to men in drag: black, white, rich, not so rich. (Women not so much. Historians and the remaining participants still quarrel about whether there were many, some, or no lesbians at the Stonewall Inn, on the night of the riot or any other night.)

Located in the middle of the densest concentration of gay New Yorkers, Greenwich Village, Stonewall was almost a stage set for the next act of the gay revolution. The Mafia owners had set it up as a "bottle club" with "members"; apparently they thought that such a ruse would delude the New York State Liquor Authority, which was still regulating gay bars for "orderliness." The Mafia, not being inclined to wishful thinking, also took the precaution of heavily bribing the police from the local precinct, who raided only early in the evening, before the fun began. The raids had a ritualistic quality—the employees knew they'd be out in a few hours and the patrons knew they'd get a suspiciously well-connected lawyer and usually never even see a jail cell. That's why, when midnight rolled around on June 27, the mob guys who ran the Stonewall thought the warning phone call they had gotten earlier in the day must be mistaken.

There were always a bunch of runaway street kids in Sheridan Square park across the street from the Stonewall Inn, some of them hoping to get in and have someone buy them a beer. Gay street kids, then and now, are, typically, involuntary orphans, born into heterosexual families and orphaned when their parents find out about their differences. They are often as young as thirteen or fourteen, and frequently from middle class or educated backgrounds. Although traumatized by the treatment they have received at the hands of their families or communities, desperate, hungry, hustling, and thieving, they are still functioning, resourceful adolescents. They were capable of becoming a crowd. As thinkers have known since the French Revolution, a crowd is filled with possibility.

The area was crowded. By one a.m., there were hundreds of patrons in the bar dancing, drinking, and socializing. Local residents, many of whom were gay, were on the street and hanging out on the stoops because it was Friday night and because it was so hot. The kids were in the park. If things had gone as usual, the police would have lined up the patrons, taken some IDs, arrested some of the employees, loaded the cars with booze, and driven to the precinct house. The raiding police had some icky practices, like ordering the transvestites to the bathroom and examining them for their biological gender, then punishing them if they weren't wearing three gender-appropriate garments. (New York law, unbelievably, actually required this.) Usually just threatening to probe the queens' genitals was enough to cause them to admit their transgression without the cops actually having to strip them.

But late June 1969 wasn't a usual time. A mayoral election was looming, never a good time for New York gays, and incorruptible Lieutenant Seymour Pine had been transferred to the Manhattan vice squad with orders to clean up the Mafia bars in Greenwich Village. The police had raided five gay bars in three weeks and closed several for good. Four days before, on June 23, they had raided the Stonewall. Stonewall's mob owners mouthed off to Pine that night and Pine was spoiling for a rematch.

From the moment the police entered the bar, the atmosphere was different. People gave them lip when asked for their IDs. The transvestites refused to be taken to the bathroom to be "examined." The police began hauling the reluctant cross-dressers to jail. But the patrons they had let out earlier didn't leave, as gays in a raid always had. They hung around to see what was happening to their friends, swelling the crowd outside. As the police wrestled the transvestites and other unlucky prisoners into the paddy wagon, the crowd cheered and jeered, and the exiting homosexuals started camping it up. Gay onlookers went to the pay phones in the neighborhood and called their friends. As Pine remembered it decades later, "Instead of the homosexuals slinking off, they remained there, and their friends came, and it was a real meeting of homosexuals." A cop shoved a transvestite, she hit him with her purse, and he clubbed her. A crowd started to boo and shout, "Flip the paddy wagon."

Most accounts pin the eruption of real violence to a person, who may or may not have been a big lesbian, resisting arrest. When the police put her in a patrol car she came out the other side, repeatedly trying to walk away. Finally a cop picked her up bodily, heaved her inside, and locked the doors. A lot of witnesses remember her saying to the crowd, "Why don't you guys do something?" The kids started throwing pennies ("coppers") at the police, and the crowd rushed the wagon full of prisoners, which drove away. The hail of coins increased, and the crowd pounded on the three police cars accompanying the wagon. The police drove off with the imploring voice of Lieutenant Pine in their ears, "Hurry back! Hurry back!" Some surge drove the kids back to a construction site, where they found a pile of bricks and began to throw them at the police. As bricks followed coins, Pine herded his tiny corps of eight policemen into the bar and barricaded the door.

All successful protests have some element of luck. At Stonewall, the police radio broke down, so the police could not call for help. Finally, they found a vent to the roof and sent the smallest policewoman up it with instructions to run to the firehouse around the corner to call for help. For what seemed like an eternity to the police barricaded in the bar, no help came. The crowd launched a full-fledged assault on the Stonewall. They threw rocks through the windows and pulled a parking meter out of the ground to use as a battering ram. They began to break down the doors. They emptied their cigarette lighters into cans and made improvised Molotov cocktails.

Not until the riot squad arrived did the mob begin to back off. And even then, for several hours, the riot police had to chase the gay crowd to drive it away. The police would take the street and the gay protesters would go around the block and came back behind the tactical forces, throwing bottles and chanting. When the tactical policemen lined up in the traditional phalanx formation to clear a street, the gay street kids lined up opposite them in Rockette formation performing high kicks and singing mocking songs: "We are the Stonewall girls, we wear our hair in curls." The tactical cops went nuts, clubbing the dancers, which, of course, only reduced them to the level of the people they despised. New York's finest backed down by the queers. They were murderous with rage.

Not Passive Resistance: Resistance

By the time Stonewall erupted, Bayard Rustin's Gandhian passive-resistance teachings had long been abandoned by the Left. The gay-movement types and the vaguely left antiwar marchers at Stonewall came out of a very different movement from the one that watched the aurora borealis over Port Huron, Michigan, eight years before.

The turning point probably came in October 1967, when the antiwar protesters shut down the induction center in Oakland, California, before being beaten back by the police. The same week, protesters at the Pentagon moved from nonviolent demonstration to an actual invading force, a small number of protesters pushing into the building itself. Although they were repulsed, the protesters skirmished with the guards and hundreds of people were arrested. By the end of 1967, the ghettos of Newark and Detroit had erupted in riots and scores of people were dead. After October 1967, long after the blacks had thrown whites out of the Student Nonviolent Coordinating Committee (SNCC), Students for a Democratic Society (SDS) leader Todd Gitlin wrote a friend that he had heard that "some [black] SNCC guys were saying 'OK boys, you've become men now, we're ready to talk.'"

The radical movement came to a head, legendarily, in the protests at the 1968 Democratic National Convention in Chicago. On August 28, 1968, as the convention was grinding away, the police fought with protesters all afternoon and evening across from the convention hotel. The crowd pelted the police with whatever they could dig up—food, rocks, bags of urine, and chunks of concrete. The battle between the police and the protesters in front of the Hilton itself took place, like the McCarthy-Army hearings, on live TV. "The whole world is watching," the demonstrators chanted.

The radical gays and street boys of the park across from the Stonewall were watching. When hippie Jim Fouratt arrived on the first night of the riots on his way home from a late night at work, he tried to call some of his straight activist buddies to come and help. None of them did. But whether the Sixties counterculture movement acknowledged it or not, Stonewall was its child. John O'Brien, gay veteran of the Alabama civil rights marches and the SDS takeover at Columbia, was there. When the riots started, he followed the gay crowd, telling them what to do from his long experience in the movement. Go against traffic to force the police to chase you on foot.

Take this street, not that one. Bob Kohler, gay veteran of the Congress of Racial Equality (CORE), from the early, nonviolent days of the civil rights movement, was there. Even seventeen-year-old cross-dresser Steve (Yvonne) Ritter "knew a lot about the peace movement when the bar erupted. I did march in some peace demonstrations. I was enraged at some of the civil rights demonstrations when I saw African-Americans being hosed down in Memphis, and it was just one of those things." Street kid Danny Garvin, too, knew what was happening: "We had been in war demonstrations and things like that. We wanted the bar back open."

Early in the events that night, gay bookstore owner and activist Craig Rodwell shouted the movement slogan to the crowd of angry homosexuals outside the bar. "Gay Power!" But all happy movements aren't the same. "Gay Power" sounded too sincere for the gay rioters, and no one took him up on it. A chorus of "We Shall Overcome" also fizzled out. By Stonewall, the "We Shall Overcome" phase of the Sixties—passive resistance, moral suasion—was over. Real violence had displaced nonviolence.

Young queen Martin Boyce remembers, "When it was over and some of us were sitting exhausted on the stoops, I thought, My God, we're going to pay so desperately for this, there was glass all over. But the next day we didn't pay. My father called and congratulated me. He said, 'What took you so long?' The next day we were there again. We had had enough. Every queen in that riot changed."

What Had Changed

> *For as to the strength of body, the weakest has strength enough to kill the strongest.*
>
> —Thomas Hobbes, *Leviathan*

Sooner or later political players have to be willing to fight back. Long before Stonewall, the Mattachine Society in New York and its allies had succeeded in getting a ruling from the New York Court of Appeals that the presence of gay men in bars, even men close dancing in bars, was not illegal. The whole Stonewall Mafia setup was technically unnecessary. But despite the ruling from New York's highest court, as long as the police kept raiding the gay bars, no legitimate business people would open one. As happened with the Interstate Commerce Commission's 1962 order to desegregate interstate buses, society simply does not obey the order to treat people as citizens until they show their willingness to die for their rights.

The willingness to kill or be killed as a condition of social membership has been a reality of Western politics since people like Thomas Hobbes started thinking about politics just about four hundred years ago. Why do people make a political society, in modern words, a "social contract," at all? Hobbes asked. For one thing, he answered, in their natural state rational people are afraid of each other. In order to have a life that is not, as he famously put it, "solitary, poor, nasty, brutish, and short," with everyone going around killing each other, they set up a government to protect everyone, including all the dangerous people. (Later thinkers amended this to include the principle that the government people set up could not be more dangerous to the citizenry than they would be to each other without a government.) There are kinder, gentler standards for citizenship: that all men are created equal and that they are capable of free will and so must have a say in how they are governed. But the history of social movements in modern Western societies is a history of groups showing they are willing to throw their bodies into the maw of the social machinery if they have to.

When gay men were closeted, before people started thinking about them as a class of people ("homosexuals"), they were just as potentially scary as any other men. But once identified as a group, gay people, men especially, were not even as scary as the weakest heterosexual. They just ran and took what society dished out and hid and paid up. Not being scary, they were recognizable outsiders to the social contract. Stonewall rebel and sometime transvestite Martin Boyce described what it felt like to live in the homosexual state of nature: "Every day the police would beat you when they wanted to, they could attack you when they wanted to. *We would look down a block and see who would be danger, how we could be safe.* This was going on for years." One day, Boyce remembers, he was taking his dressed-up self to the Metropolitan Museum of Art. "I wore a six feet scarf that would go around my neck, and a low cut dress, and there were police in plain clothes taking down the horses (there had been a parade on Fifth Avenue). And the cop said a campy, 'Hi-i-i-i' and I said, 'Oh I didn't know you could be in the police and be like that.' Nothing happened," Boyce continues. "I was walking along, the breeze was blowing my scarf. As we got to the museum all of a sudden the scarf tightened around my neck and I was thrown against the car. This policeman had followed me five blocks and he twisted it into a tourniquet. I was blue as a smurf. And [there was] this crowd of middle class, decent people, good citizens, outside the Museum, and they were praising the police for keeping the city safe." Six months before Stonewall, an off-duty transit cop killed two gay men who were at the popular gathering place near the trucks parked along the Hudson River. No action was taken.

The patrons of the Metropolitan Museum of Art did not want to protect gays. The police, the guardians and enforcers of the social contract, beat them and killed them. And then a lesbian did (or did not) scream at the crowd, "Why don't you guys do something?" and the gay men outside the Stonewall Inn stepped into the social contract. As activist Arthur Evans puts it: "We said, 'You are going to have to live up to your democratic principles, or you are going to have to kill us.'"

Every Queen in the Riot Changed

The next night, Saturday, thousands of gay people from all over the region gathered on Christopher Street to see what would happen next and be part of the action they had missed. Despite their experience the night before, there still weren't enough police to clear the streets, so they again had to call in the tactical police force, the riot squad. And the gay demonstrators again fought the riot squad to a standstill on the streets around the Stonewall Inn. The gay demonstrators, who had now come deliberately to protest against the way they were treated, hit on the stratagem of "taking" Christopher Street, blocking it off and only letting through who they wanted. Instead of peeking down a block to see whether they would be safe, the gay crowd forced other people to get permission from them. Hours later, the crowd dissipated and the police left.

Sunday, Craig Rodwell did what any lefty activist would do: he wrote a manifesto: "Get the Mafia and the Cops Out of Gay Bars." Rodwell's manifesto did not have the stylistic brio of Mattachine leader Dick Leitsch's memo, "The Hairpin Drop Heard Round the World," but Rodwell deployed teams of gay activists around the neighborhood on Sunday afternoon to pass his manifesto out. Leaned on by the mayor, Leitsch put a sign in the east window of the boarded up Stonewall Inn: WE HOMOSEXUALS PLEAD WITH OUR PEOPLE TO PLEASE HELP MAINTAIN PEACEFUL AND QUIET CONDUCT ON THE STREETS OF THE VILLAGE—MATTACHINE. With that sign Mattachine began its journey to the dustbin of history.

For all the good the sign did anyway. After two days of R and R, on Wednesday the gay protesters decided to burn down the nearby offices of the *Village Voice*. That morning, the *Voice*, a weekly, had published its report of the Stonewall riots, two side-by-side articles by Howard Smith, who had been in the bar with the police on Saturday, and by renowned author Lucian Truscott IV, then a cub reporter. Unlike the mainstream media in San Francisco, who rushed to the aid of the gay community when the police broke up their New Year's party, Truscott, whose love of language sometimes overcomes his common sense, reported:

> The sudden specter of "gay power" erected its brazen head and spat out a fairy tale the likes of which the area has never seen. The forces of faggotry, spurred by a Friday night raid on one of the city's largest, most popular, and longest lived gay bars, the Stonewall Inn, rallied

> Saturday night in an unprecedented protest against the raid and continued Sunday night to assert presence, possibility, and pride until the early hours of Monday morning.

When the aroused gay protesters saw themselves described as the "forces of faggotry," they turned their newfound force on an old enemy: the media.

Truscott says today, "Some of my best friends are gay. I used 'forces of faggotry' as alliteration and it didn't occur to me in the least that anybody would be offended by it. The gay people I knew used the word 'fag' and 'queer' among themselves and with straight people that knew them. And the *Voice* was one of the most gay-friendly places to work in New York. The staff must have been half gay," he contends, "and you could bring your boyfriend to work and hold hands."

Months before Stonewall, the supposedly gay-friendly *Voice* had refused to take a paid classified ad for a very popular manual, *The Homosexual Handbook*. But in the heady days after Stonewall, the gay protesters were not about to give their liberal "friends" a pass. After the Wednesday riots, they demanded a meeting with editors Dan Wolf and Edwin Fancher and the two liberals agreed that if gay people thought that "faggot" was a derogatory term they wouldn't use it anymore.

The third and final day of the Stonewall riots also involved something new: Fouratt's lefty straight friends finally showed up, along with Black Panthers, street gangs, and a general sampling of the rebellious in the New York area. The word was out: the last great twentieth-century movement was happening.

I Would Kill for Those Kisses

The last thing Mattachine president Dick Leitsch wanted after Stonewall was a protest meeting. Mattachine had a relationship with the authorities and progress was slowly being made. Just a few years earlier Leitsch got the New York licensing authorities to abandon the rule against gay hairdressers. He went to a function the Democratic Party was holding and had a chat with the wife of the New York secretary of state. "You know, if you're a homosexual you can't be a hairdresser," he told her. "That's ridiculous," the politico's well-coiffed spouse responded. "Do you mean my Mr. Rodney?" "You'd better not tell your husband about Mr. Rodney or he could lose his license," Leitsch replied. "And so they changed it," he concludes proudly.

Fatally for Leitsch, he listened to a handful of newfound allies, such as self-described countercultural socialist Michael Brown. After all, Brown had spent the weekend passing out copies of Leitsch's "Hairpin Drop." At the insistence of the new activists, Leitsch scheduled a meeting for July 9. Leitsch had no inkling that once again a lesbian was going to take over the situation.

This was not any lesbian. When Martha Shelley had her first lesbian experience, she came away from it a changed woman. "I would kill for those kisses," she avowed. Only in her twenties, Shelley had already been an official of the New York Daughters of Bilitis (DOB). "DOB was not the sort of organization that went marching anywhere. I was involved with the peace movement," she explains. Although she happened to be in Greenwich Village that Friday night and Saturday morning, she thought the noise from Sheridan Park was just the usual New York ruckus. When she realized what had happened, she says, "It was like falling in love. You don't think about it intellectually, the time is right, the right person comes along, you're young, you're hot-blooded and there it is and you know in your heart that it's the right thing to do. You just go with it, you jump. I didn't have enough sleep, got up next morning, I found out what had happened . . . and it occurred to me that we should have a protest march." Shelley, too, was ready to die for her place in society: "I was tossing and turning and I thought, 'They'll shoot us,' and then I thought, 'We have to.'" She called the women who were running the Daughters and they sent her to Leitsch's Mattachine meeting. Leitsch was not interested in marching. But he told

Shelley to bring it up at the July 9 meeting and see if anyone was interested.

There were hundreds of people at the July 9 Mattachine meeting, Shelley remembers, and, when she asked if anyone was interested in planning a march, a "forest of hands went up." Leitsch sent the march committee to meet in a back room, never a good idea, and the next thing he knew Shelley was shouting, "That's it, that's it, we're the gay liberation front!" Leitsch practically had a fit. "Are you starting another organization here?" he demanded. "Oh no," Shelley answered, "we're not starting another organization, that's the name of our march committee." "But of course," she admits, "we were starting another organization," and of course it was the Gay Liberation Front (GLF). They set the march for late July. When Mattachine met again on July 16 to consider the content of the march, Madolin Cervantes proposed that the committee's march take the form of a sweet candlelight vigil and the troops rose up.

By chance, John O'Brien had reserved a meeting room at Alternate U., the counterculture free school at Fourteenth Street and Sixth Avenue, just in time for the revolution. O'Brien had been a radical since he was fifteen and sneaked out of his white working-class house to sign up with the NAACP. Muscular, independent, and proletarian, O'Brien was no one's notion of a homosexual. He had never been a fan of Mattachine, having failed to qualify for Kameny's picket line in 1967 because he was only twenty years old and not wearing a suit. A few weeks before Stonewall, one of the SDS radical homosexuals, Bill Katzenberg, approached O'Brien in his role as board member at Alternate U. to help him with a proposed homosexual discussion group. After weeks of recruitment on the stoops and in the diners of Greenwich Village, Katzenberg had scared up five people and O'Brien used his place on the board of Alternate U. to get them a place to meet. They put an ad in the underground newspaper the *Rat* and sent out leaflets.

Then came Stonewall. Instead of five, around forty people showed up. Many of them were from the radical Mattachine march committee. When well-connected young street guy Jerry Hoose walked into the meeting at Alternate U., he says, 95 percent of the men and women in the room were total strangers to him. "They became a community really fast," Hoose says, "because we were so angry. We were treated like garbage, and it was an experience most of us had shared. The unity that came was because of the shared experiences of the last decade." By the end of the first meeting, the forty insurgents had set an agenda, picked a name, Gay Liberation Front, and agreed to meet again.

Hoose's story, like all stories of spontaneously erupting social movements, is partly a myth. New identities don't just spring up from nowhere. Although the dramatic young hippie Jim Fouratt and the like never would have admitted it, some of the new "gay liberation" movement really did grow out of the now-discredited and unfashionable Mattachine Society. Even though Leitsch was ultimately behind the curve, in the few years before Stonewall, he had moved Mattachine in a much more radical direction. Fouratt and Shelley went to Mattachine to organize the first political action after Stonewall—the rally. Craig Rodwell, the man who would dream up the legendary 1970 Stonewall anniversary march, had been one of the most visible militants in the new Mattachine. It was under the protective shelter of the old organization that the new identity "radical homosexual" began to form.

At the same time, the homosexuals in the radical organizations of the New Left had begun to take ownership of their homosexuality, often after years of suppressing or hiding it in the interest of their radical politics. The existing movement organizations—SDS, the broader antiwar movement, and a myriad of Sixties institutions—were implicitly and often explicitly homophobic. On January 9, 1969, the Young Socialists Alliance kicked John O'Brien out because they had found out he was a homosexual. While working at a left-wing bookstore in the late Sixties, later GLF stalwart Steven Dansky remembers being given instruction in how to cross his legs and hold his cigarette so as not to appear effeminate and lose his chance at going to Cuba to meet his revolutionary brothers. Around the time of Stonewall, Dansky was working as a substance-abuse counselor. His director called him in before the whole staff and told him that they had found out he was a homosexual. Get treatment, his bosses told him, or get fired. Within weeks, Dansky went to his first GLF meeting and soon became one of its most active members.

Yet the homophobic New Left, too, gave birth to Dansky's and O'Brien's identities. "The women's movement and the civil rights movement are all about human rights and the moral struggle that's necessary for the evolution of humankind," Dansky says. "As a member of these movements, these political formulations that I spent my early life trying to understand, something internal was happening to me and I was understanding the world differently. And that's where I was able to draw the strength to say, yes, I'm going to proceed ahead to investigate a movement that's about me." As leftist believers in human liberation, once gay leftists made the connection, participation in the new gay-liberation movement was essential to Dansky's, and others', larger identities. Movement homophobia catapulted the newly formed homosexual radicals out of the New Left rather more abruptly than their common belief systems would have predicted and the GLF was the beneficiary.

GLF was the most fun most of its founders had ever had. Street guy Hoose and college graduate Dansky both used the word "chills" when describing their memories of that revolutionary period. The July rally, which they planned with the people who remained in the Mattachine Society, was neither as ladylike as Cervantes had wished nor as radical as the breakaways had in mind, but it was a rally, with speeches and attendance in the hundreds.

They rallied . . . and they danced. Arguably, the dances were their greatest accomplishment. Alternate U. had been renting its space to countercultural organizations that wanted to hold dances. Hoose and a couple of the other GLF members who wanted to concentrate on fund-raising for the front saw a golden opportunity and asked Alternate U. if they could hold a dance. "Alternate U wasn't all that excited about having *us*," Hoose remembered forty years later, smiling the smile of a satisfied fund-raiser, "but our first dance was packed and they made more money from our dances than all the other fund-raisers put together." The little movement capitalists at GLF had found a formula that would appear and reappear wherever the gay movement organized—until the AIDS virus appeared and the dancing stopped.

The GLF's most successful political action actually came from the dances. They had tried to put an ad in the *Village Voice* to advertise their "Gay Community Dance," but the *Voice* told them it wouldn't run an ad with the dirty word "gay" in it. So the GLF, now a month old, threw up a picket line. When the *Voice* gave in, Hoose says, the activists knew that Stonewall was not a one-off. They could go on pushing back.

The GLF lasted barely nine months. The new organization was probably doomed the minute the first member said, "No one is free until everyone is free." Just as their dance stash got big enough to fight about, O'Brien proposed giving five hundred dollars to the Black Panthers and all hell broke loose. O'Brien to this day does not wall off his loyalty to the gay cause. "What was 'my cause'?" He asks. "There are gay people of color and women who are just as much a part of my community as Rock Hudson. The Panthers were the vanguard of the black community."

O'Brien's stance is superficially appealing. Since some gay people are black, their interest overlaps with the interest of people defined first as black. But of course O'Brien wouldn't take up the interest of, say, black conservatives. They would hardly qualify as the "vanguard of the black community" to him. What O'Brien is really saying is that the movements he lists—the Black Panthers and women—share a common aspiration. But on closer examination, they don't: their aspirations are actually not the same. Being categorized as sinful, crazy, criminal, and subversive, gays would have to fight for moral acceptance and respect. Not being categorized as crazy or the rest, women and people of color—and their "vanguard" movements—could move directly to claim the goods of the liberal state: security, freedom, and equal self-governance. The particular social change required for gay women or gay people of color was different from and more difficult than the social change that would fully satisfy nongay women or people of color.

And, as Carl Wittman had warned not a year before, O'Brien's strategy is generally fatal when put into practice. Social movements arise in large part because they enable people to act on a new identity formed under the wings of older institutions and then to stand alone with that new identity. A movement may at some point benefit from making an alliance with other movements, but "I'll scratch your back if you'll scratch mine" is a world away from "No one is free until everyone is free." At its stand-alone moment, the identity is at its most fragile. When a movement is at that point, the more inclusive it becomes of other identities the weaker it gets. A movement that wants to advance gay liberation and Black Panthers does not attract gays and Black Panthers. It attracts only people who want to advance both gay liberation *and* the Black Panther cause, a much, much smaller group than either group alone. Instead of growing by alliance, the front actually shrinks. "No one is free until everyone is free" also completely sidesteps the only important question for alliance politics: priorities. Alliances create political surplus. Who's first in line to get the surplus put to their freedom and how much do they get?

Since the GLF had no leaders and ran by consensus, meetings never ended before midnight and nothing was ever put to rest. Although John O'Brien originally lost the divisive motion for the Black Panther donation, the proponents simply reopened the matter at the next meeting and that time it passed. Stripped of any regularized means to campaign against the decision or to protect themselves against further unwelcome decisions, a handful of the GLF members—Arthur Evans, his lover Arthur Bell, and some other single-issue members—did what newcomers to a social movement always do when the movement does not fit their newfound identity: they left.

A Lesbian Is the Rage of All Women Condensed to the Point of Explosion

The gay and lesbian alliance was the next casualty of the centrifugal force of "front" politics. For years, lesbians had closeted themselves in order to find a place in the feminist movement, which spoke so powerfully to their experiences of discrimination and oppression. Hiding your identity in an identity movement was hardly a stable strategy, so when the gay liberation movement erupted in New York after Stonewall, a little band of sisters thought for a while that they might find their liberation through that route.

From the day she arrived in New York in late 1969 until she left for Boston two years later, brilliant and beautiful lesbian feminist "Artemis March" (née March Hoffman) went to meetings every night. "We thought we were going to change the entire world," she reminisces, "from top to bottom." March barely had time to run home to her broom-closet-sized apartment in Brooklyn between meetings.

And yet none of the causes was, like Baby Bear's porridge, just right. The women's loyalty to feminism was stretched thin when feminist leader Betty Friedan left the Daughters of Bilitis out when she convened the First Congress to Unite Women; her remarks about the media turning lesbianism into a "lavender herring" against the feminist cause didn't help much either. Feminism was just too cold. The New York lesbians began attending meetings of the newly born Gay Liberation Front. They even went to some of the dances. But the dances, crowded with men jammed up against one another and reverberating with deafening music, had scant appeal to the women. The meetings were almost as noisy as the dances. The gay men's movement was too hot.

At a typical GLF meeting in January 1970, a twentysomething unpublished writer, Rita Mae Brown, got up on a chair. Brown, a slender brunette with killer cheekbones, was the kind of woman who could always command a room. "Enough already," she announced. "We can't be out in NOW, the guys dominate this, we need a lesbian feminist civil rights movement. Come to my house on Wednesday night." That Wednesday, Brown anxiously waited to see if anyone would show up. Thirty women came, and the radical-lesbian movement was born. Recognizing no limits on their power to change the world, they decided to take on both the homophobic feminists and the sexist gay men. They planned the controversial first all-women's dance.

But the lesbians really had their eye on the women's movement. The feminist Congress to Unite Women (CUW) was about to have its second meeting in the spring of 1970 and the radical lesbians intended to precipitate a confrontation. When the congress met in the usual high school auditorium the first night, the lights suddenly went out. When they went up again, seventeen women in purple T-shirts were standing on the stage holding signs. "Lavender Menace," they proclaimed, and "Take a Lesbian to Lunch." The lesbians pitched the assembled hundreds to let them into the women's movement without closeting or discrimination and passed around Artemis March's mimeographed proclamation, "The Woman Identified Woman" ("lesbianism is the rage of all women condensed to the point of explosion"). Clapping and cheering, the audience applauded the Menace and turned the meeting into an extended ritual of reconciliation and unity. Feeble efforts of the CUW organizers to take back the mike were soon extinguished. It was, after all, a Congress to Unite Women.

Later that year, the lesbians on the GLF fund-raising committee went into the lockbox and took half the treasury for their dances. In the uproar that followed, the lesbians finally left the GLF and officially formed their own organization. The new organization, the Radicalesbians, seems on its face to follow all of Carl Wittman's prescriptions: it acknowledged that lesbian women were different from the larger society, advanced their cause with pride, and resisted diluting their message with the claims of other oppressed groups. Still, it did not last. In a poignant article years later, photographer Ellen Shumsky, who had abandoned her studies in France to come to New York when she learned about Stonewall, remembers. The new organization, the Radicalesbians, would have "no entrenched leadership hierarchies." They drew lots to see who would speak, run the meeting, or go to represent the organization, if invited. It turns out that there were people who were more articulate and more comfortable speaking. Less-articulate women started feeling resentful and protested. In response, people felt they were being hounded out of the organization because of their leadership skills. Once again, people just started leaving. This organization that started out with so much hope turned into a desultory group of people who were trying to solve problems they couldn't solve.

Shumsky comforts herself that the organization fell apart but the consciousness didn't. In the wake of the Radicalesbians, she notes, there were all kinds of self-help groups and lesbian artists groups and lesbian martial-arts groups. It was not all for naught.

You Can't Get More American Than That

There was no way Arthur Evans was going to make any of those mistakes trying to solve everybody's problems, getting agreement on everything, letting everyone talk. Even in the Sixties, he rarely had long hair and his immensely becoming mustache was always neatly trimmed. He even looks tidy marching in a T-shirt with the newly minted gay-rights lambda symbol on it. The anarchic procedures of the Gay Liberation Front "drove me crazy," he recalls. "There was no continuity, so they would adopt a position at one meeting and at the next meeting they would debate the entire thing all over again. There was no structure of responsibility, and also there was no thought-out program. For example, something would happen and then we'd go out and demonstrate, which was great, and then there would be this pause until something terrible would happen again."

Evans, by then a philosophy graduate student at Columbia, and his lover, Arthur Bell, a publicist at Viking (the "Arthurs"), were a great loss for the GLF. Although middle class and educated, they were not uptight establishment types. Evans set his life course while still a student at Brown in the late fifties, organizing a protest against compulsory chapel. Once he realized he was gay, he left college one term short of graduation in 1963 to move into a filthy single room in Greenwich Village, working as a clerk typist for a film company and looking for sex at gay restaurants like Mama's Chicken 'n Ribs. Since Evans was on full scholarship at the time, his parents were not too thrilled with his self-emancipation, but he was ecstatic, because he had his own place and, "thanks to New York City," he was surrounded by gay people, including, eventually, Bell. The couple had tried one meeting of the jacket-and-tie Mattachine Society and, as Evans said, found it "too much like Sunday school" (Bell, who was Jewish, had never been to Sunday school and said he was not about to start).

In August 1969, the couple took a walk in Greenwich Village and stumbled across a GLF meeting. "It was quite wonderful," Evans recalls. "For the first time in our lives we were around these gay people who had an exuberant sense of gay pride, that it was something to be proud of. Many of us had been active in the student movement, and we felt this great energy, this great uprising of the Sixties had finally come to us! Now it was our turn to take to the barricades." Arthur Evans says he will "always be grateful to the GLF for making that happen."

But the ideology, rhetoric, and open structure at the GLF gave them no avenue to contend for their beliefs. When they resisted giving money to the Black Panthers, "We were denounced as being racists," Evans remembers, "so we were really bucking our heads against a stone wall. Because the sentiment in the GLF was almost totally against what we wanted to do. We were a small minority, we were viewed as counterrevolutionary for even suggesting not sharing the wealth, so we were constantly defending ourselves."

Evans and Bell and the other two critical renegades, Marty Robinson and Jim Owles, were the living manifestation of the dangers of GLF's demand that its members spread their identity across multiple causes. Although Evans and Owles had been in the peace movement, they were by no means shaped by the New Left, as so many GLF leaders were, and, by late

1969, Owles was working on Wall Street. Robinson, a self-styled proletarian from a wealthy and prominent family, was never involved in any other cause. Too modern and too young for the fifties-inflected Mattachine Society, they were too focused and too disciplined for the Sixties gay "liberation front." Anticipating the decade about to dawn, they wanted to take to the barricades all right, but only for their "turn."

They were not inspired by the Parisian mob. "We decided," Evans says, "we had to have institutional continuity and revolutionary energy. You don't want to create a bureaucracy, [but] on the other hand you don't want to become victims of revolutionary hysteria. You have to find an intelligent middle ground." For Evans, being a trained philosopher, this was not a hard problem. "So I in particular thought about the American revolutionary experience; that was the thing that inspired me because they did that. They combined the rationality of the enlightenment with the vigor of a popular uprising. We had a historical precedent right in our own country. So based on the models of the US constitution we wrote a preamble to the constitution. You can't get much more American than that."

And so the constitution and bylaws of their new organization, the Gay Activists Alliance (GAA), begins, "We" as in "We the people of the United States": WE AS LIBERATED HOMOSEXUAL ACTIVISTS. But because the gay activists were not yet a nation, the preamble actually reads more like that other American classic, the Declaration of Independence. The GAA demanded:

> Freedom for expression of our dignity and value as human beings through confrontation with and disarmament of all mechanisms which unjustly inhibit us: economic, social and political.

They even mimicked that most establishment of Thomas Jefferson's moves—invoking a decent respect for the opinions of mankind—by placing their demands "before the public conscience."

After all the years of sexual revolution, it would be fair to expect the new activists to simply adopt the language of sexual privacy from the long line of constitutional decisions. As those decisions reflect, however unattractive they are to the majority, the protection of intimate and personal aspects of life from an intrusive state is one of the founding principles of a liberal state.

Perhaps in recognition of the political reality that toleration is really not as blind as it pretends, the GAA constitution frames the demand for sexual privacy in the language not of tolerance, but of approval. The first right on the GAA's constitutional list of rights is "the right to our own feelings," including the right to feel attracted to the beauty of members of their own sex and "the right to express our feelings in action through making love." Regardless of the reason for the choice of words of moral approbation—love, beauty—the implicit claim for approval in the language further embedded the moral grounding of this new movement. As it turned out, the moral framing that was useful in getting same-sex "lovemaking" to the level of liberal tolerance catapulted it well beyond what formal liberal politics had to offer.

Clearly, the line between transgender people and the rest of the gay movement was not as harsh as it would later become; the founding document of the GAA also includes a potent claim for all kinds of transgender behavior, demanding the right "to treat and express our bodies as we will, to nurture, display, and embellish them solely in the manner we ourselves determine."

Only then does the preamble turn to the universal language of human rights, familiar to students of the American Revolution and the centuries of political thinking that justified it, demanding their individual rights under just laws and to be full citizens of the republic that so long ago extended that promise to other Americans.

Having made their declaration, the Gay Activists then construct their more perfect union. Just as the US Constitution was shaped by the colonists' unhappy experience with the disarray of the Articles of Confederation, the founding principles of the GAA start in direct repudiation of the GLF's commitment to freedom for all in alliance with all. The GAA new order was explicitly dedicated only to gay rights and committed to move forward on the actions of oppressed homosexuals themselves. The GAA constitution includes every principle Carl Wittman had set down two years before.

After the endless disarray of GLF meetings, the gender-bending body-embellishing homosexuals of the GAA set up a structure so orderly and conventional it would make the Daughters of the American Revolution look like hippies. Prospective members had to attend three meetings within six months of joining; no more people wandering in from the street and competing for who could be most disruptive. There was even an entrance fee of a dollar. There would be an annual election of officers by secret ballot, and the meetings were to be run by *Robert's Rules of Order.* The constitution forbade any alliance with any organization not directly related to the homosexual cause. The date was December 21, 1969. By March they had forty members. They bought an abandoned firehouse and started holding dances.

If the State Wouldn't Protect Gays, Gays Wouldn't Protect the State

As he helped give birth to the GAA, philosopher Arthur Evans said, "Existentialist philosophers inspired me because they took concrete situations over theory: existence precedes essence. All the existing essences rejected us: the church, the politicians, our fathers, we didn't fit into anybody's essence. And yet my feeling was let's exist, let's be, express our being, and our cognitive realities." The floodgates of gay direct action were about to open. The channel had been cut—by the black students who sat down for lunch in Greensboro all those years before, by the clever, clownish hippie Abbie Hoffman, with his theatrical yippies and by . . . Jean-Paul Sartre. The New Lefties succeeded in part because they acted with their bodies rather than arguing about their beliefs.

Their first target was the mayor of New York, John Vliet Lindsay. After Stonewall, whoever was mayor of New York would be central to the gay revolution: the New York police made gays' lives miserable, the mayor was formally responsible for the police, and the media were heavily concentrated in New York. But Lindsay, a liberal convert whom gay voters had supported, was a natural target. For almost a decade at that point, the gay organizations had been eliciting official statements of what constituted lawful behavior. The New York State Liquor Authority denied it had a policy of forbidding bars to serve liquor to gays, yet no one would risk establishing an openly gay bar. The police commissioner told an audience at a community meeting right before Stonewall that it was not police policy to entrap gay men, yet that same night a cop arrested a straight deacon innocently having a burger at Julius'.

In its early, innocent days, the GAA marched on City Hall, in the time-honored fashion, to present its demands on job discrimination and police harassment, and, in time-honored fashion, Lindsay's representative promised them that someone would get back to them. The next night, in an act of astonishing folly, New York vice cop Seymour Pine raided another gay bar, the Snake Pit. Trapped inside the illegal bar and desperately fearful of deportation, illegal Argentinian immigrant Alfredo Diego Vinales made a panicked bid to escape the police by jumping out a window. He landed, impaled, on the sharp point of an iron fence below. As he lay near death at St. Vincent's Hospital, every gay group in New York called out its troops to march on the police station. This time the incident got some serious press.

More important, it attracted the anger of the indefatigable Marty Robinson. If Evans was the existentialist philosopher of the GAA, Robinson was existentialism incarnate. Young Stonewall denizen Tommy Lanigan-Schmidt describes Robinson's political technique as sex followed by politics. Before you even knew what he was doing, Lanigan-Schmidt reports, his sexy charisma and muscular good looks had swept you in and you were passing out leaflets. Robinson didn't march in antiwar parades and never joined SDS, or any other New Left group. He just caught a young man's eye at twenty, came out, and started living the life of a gay man. After Stonewall, he lay awake all night and got up the next day committed to the movement. Evans says Robinson was the smartest man he ever met.

When Lindsay's deputy mayor and a police representative finally met with the GAA, the deputy mayor assured the gay delegation that "it was not the policy of the police department to harass homosexuals per se." This may have been technically true. By 1970, some courts were starting to invoke basic constitutional rights of association to limit what could be done to gatherings of people not otherwise engaged in criminal conduct, so New York State probably couldn't formally enforce gay harassment and entrapment. Anyway, for years gays had been assumed to be so worthless that they didn't even warrant a formal policy of oppression; the police were just set loose on them, creating anarchy, as the early philosophers imagined life was like before there was a liberal state.

Evans had had enough. His people lived with lawless arrests, name-calling, and intimidation. They weren't even getting the first promise of the liberal state—that their government would provide them with a secure life and certainly never make it less secure for them than if they had no government at all. Seeing Diego Vinales's terror at being deported taught them that their persecution was not limited to the police raid itself. When they were caught in an illegal bar, they not only risked arrest: they lost their jobs, got deported, got reported to their parents.

Unable to get the officials to call off the police, the GAA determined to bring lawless disorder to the officials. Robinson came up with a new tactic, the zap. As in "Zap! You're dead," the children's game. But instead it became "Zap! You're alive." Zaps were extremely vocal, nonviolent confrontations with homophobes, combining a great deal of energy with very articulate and intelligent speech and a queen's sense of camp. "The idea," Evans says, "was these are like little theatrical productions. The other side came across as looking really oafish, stupid, and boring and people on our side were exciting and wonderful and theatrical and inspiring and sexy and energetic. And television is so perfect, we knew we could create these little scenes for TV, so we'd go out and get arrested and then we'd come home and watch it on TV." They decided to zap Mayor Lindsay every time he appeared in public.

Martin Boyce, whom the policeman tried to strangle in front of the Metropolitan Museum of Art the year before, must have felt a thrill on April 13, 1970, when he saw GAA activist Marty Robinson appear next to the mayor right on the museum steps. It was the hundredth anniversary of the Met and Lindsay was there to open the ceremonies. As the city's chief executive smilingly commended the museum patrons on their love of the arts, Robinson meandered up the museum steps and spoke into the mayor's microphone. "When are you going to speak out on homosexual rights, Mr. Mayor?" GAA activists were waiting everywhere in the museum to ask Mayor Lindsay when he was going to help them. Robinson remembers that it took three of the mayor's bodyguards to get a GAA zapper to let go of the mayor's hand.

They infiltrated the operagoers awaiting the mayor's arrival in the perfect zap setting at the bottom of the Metropolitan Opera's grand staircase (filled with patrons and journalists); they disrupted a theatrical benefit chaired by Mrs. Lindsay; they trashed the mayor's presidential fund-raiser at Radio City Music Hall, handcuffing themselves to the balcony railing and setting off personal antimugger alarms, while blanketing the audience below with leaflets.

The campaign was often illegal—it included trespass and disorderly conduct—just as were the harassment arrests and bar busts against the gays. The gay activists were acutely aware of how much heterosexual authorities benefited from enjoying their rituals and public spaces without having to patrol the boundaries all the time. They would show them what it felt like. The zaps disrupted their ribbon-cutting ceremonies and their opening nights, their fund-raisers, and their television appearances.

Histories of the gay revolution often compare the GAA zaps to the early days of the direct-action civil rights movement, like the Greensboro lunch counter sit-in, but they are not the same. The racial civil rights movement was attacking a formal system of segregation, embodied in the openly acknowledged laws and policies of the state. They started their direct action on the premise that they were going to disregard the formal structure of inequality and act as if black people's lives were as good as the lives of white people, eating away peacefully at their lunch counters. Leitsch's "sip-in" was self-consciously a sit-in. The zaps were not.

When the racial movement moved north it found the informal structure of de facto housing segregation much harder to tackle. When the feminists turned from attacking the formal segregation of the help wanted ads into "Male" and "Female" and tried to address the unspoken gendered division of labor in the family, they were met with mockery and derision. Similarly, the gay movement could not get the traction to mount a formal challenge, because the New York authorities would not even acknowledge what they were doing to their gay citizens. Their persecution took place without warning, in secret, in the dark, on unpatrolled streets, in helpless, illegal bars.

GAA zaps, occurring without warning and in vulnerable spaces, were intended not to make their lives as good as the lives of their oppressors, but to make the lives of the authorities as miserable as the lives the gay citizens were living. In trying to impose pain, the GAA was involved in an exquisite balancing act the civil rights movement didn't have to face in its crucial years. After the Stonewall uprising, and similar actions in California, gays had taken on some of the dangerousness necessary to be taken seriously in the liberal state. But they were so despised and marginalized—their fundamental act of identity a crime and a sin and their character categorized as crazy and subversive—that they had to do the work of establishing moral legitimacy at the same time they were engaged in illegal and disruptive acts.

Hence the genius of the zap. The zaps were potent political ammunition for the new gay movement. Consciously or not, they adapted some of the most useful aspects of the camp culture—the use of mockery and the humorous inversion of roles, as when the "invaders" brought coffee and cake to their oppressors. While disrupting their activities, the zaps also forced their victims to be witnesses to gay humanity. When *Harper's* magazine published an article by intellectual heavy hitter Joseph Epstein, expressing his wish to "wipe homosexuality off the face of the earth," GAA activists brought cakes and a big coffee urn to the offices of the magazine, interrupting publication to demand equal time to reply. As each of *Harper's* employees walked into work that morning, he or she was greeted by a GAA demonstrator: "*I'm* a homosexual," the activists said. "Have a doughnut." As decades of ensuing activism would prove, again and again, it's hard to wish someone off the face of the earth when he's offering you a doughnut. Even if he's trespassing.

With just the right degree of gentility and humor, the GAA carried out its disruptions, so that clearing them out of any besieged public space made the enforcers look like brutes. GAA zaps were, at bottom, no different from Martin Luther King's march in Cicero and feminist Alix Kates Shulman's "Marriage Agreement" dividing the household chores. They were all strategies for getting at the hidden structures of oppression. The homosexuals at the Metropolitan Opera in their tuxedos and the nice young men with the doughnuts for the staff at *Harper's* might be deliciously amusing, but the game they were playing was for the highest political stakes.

The Birthday Party of the Gay Movement

Exactly a year after Stonewall, Craig Rodwell and some of the other Stonewall insurgents threw themselves a birthday parade. As it turns out, the celebration may have been more important than the birth itself.

After all, there had been other bar riots. In San Francisco, the gay and straight allies resisted the police incursion on their New Year's party in 1964. A year later, the transvestites at San Francisco's Compton Cafeteria responded to a routine sweep by throwing cups, saucers, and trays at the police, breaking all the cafeteria windows and those on the police car, too. There was a big street protest in Los Angeles in 1967, after the LAPD beat up New Year's revelers at the mostly gay Black Cat/New Faces party. Yet none of these salient events marked the so-called birth of the gay rights movement. Only Stonewall did. Because only Stonewall was followed by a parade a year later.

When the bottles started flying at the Stonewall Inn on that first night, Rodwell remembers shouting, "Gay Power!" His outburst was met with a big shrug. The street kids and would-be Rockettes were not ultimately going to be the fount of gay power. But Rodwell, as always, was undeterred. Raised off and on by a single mom, he'd been an out homosexual since he was thirteen. He came to New York from the Midwest because he heard that there was a group there advocating for homosexual rights. (Rodwell never lost that Midwestern look, though. The pictures of him from the time always show a neat haircut and a white button-down shirt.) When he arrived in New York at nineteen in 1959, he was so young the Mattachine Society, ever mindful of its virtuous reputation, would not even let him join. But they let him volunteer.

Within five years, allied with the Mattachine activists Dick Leitsch and Randy Wicker, Rodwell had basically taken over the place. But Rodwell's genius did not lie in the machinations of the myriad gay organizations, before Stonewall or after. Typically, when Mattachine did not live up to Rodwell's radical expectations, he simply founded a new organization, Homosexual Youth Movement in Neighborhoods (HYMN). Rodwell was the only member. Nonetheless, at crucial junctures, he "represented" HYMN at regional and national meetings like the Eastern Regional Conference of Homophile Organizations (ERCHO), pulling the discussion and resolution of important issues his way.

By Stonewall, Rodwell had perfected the two other activities crucial to social organization but not requiring consensus: the bookstore and the march. Unlike other gay bookstores, the bookstore Rodwell founded did not sell pornography. As a result, the store could have big, open windows that admitted the light and made the place a warm and welcoming destination. There was a gay bulletin board. Organizations could come and distribute their literature or sell it. Professors sent their students there for everything from literature to counseling on how to tell their parents they were gay. When it finally closed in 2009, Rodwell's Oscar Wilde Memorial Bookstore, founded in 1967, was the oldest gay bookstore in the country.

At ERCHO in the Sixties, Rodwell had found a natural ally in the godfather of homosexual militancy, Frank Kameny. So it made perfect sense for him to join Kameny in his mentor's first gay protest march in Washington in 1965. In an eerie prefiguring of his role in the Stonewall myth, Rodwell proposed that they have a march every year. He suggested that it take place in Philadelphia, before Constitution Hall, on the Fourth of July, as an annual reminder that gays and lesbians still did not have full political rights. Thereafter, every July, a subdued ring of forty or fifty perfectly dressed homosexuals presented their claims to a mostly empty sidewalk.

The fifth annual reminder, a week after Stonewall, attracted a rowdier crowd of mostly young recruits from Rodwell's bookstore. When two women at the march had the effrontery to hold hands, Kameny started yelling, "None of that! None of that!" and broke their grip apart. Rodwell was apoplectic. He publicly berated Kameny for his stuffy, retrograde attitude and quarreled openly with his old allies. On the bus going home to New York, there was much talk about how outdated the Mattachine annual reminder had become. Rodwell proposed that they move the event to New York and have a parade about Stonewall instead. A commemoration. Maybe even an annual one.

Kameny may have seen Rodwell and his bookstore band as unwashed upstarts, but as the New Left was fond of saying, "We are your children." Like the Mattachine Society and the Gay Liberation Front, the preexisting annual reminder marches had provided the sheltered seedbed for the new movement to grow. Certainly, the West Coast cities, which had had three incidents of police abuse and homosexual resistance in the late Sixties, never generated anything like it.

Although the gay-pride parade was a logical extension of a familiar idea, it was also a bombshell. Rodwell had already begun the process of inflating Stonewall the week of the riots, calling it "world famous." Mattachine's Dick Leitsch, too, had invoked the universal signifier, titling his leaflet "The Hairpin Drop Heard *Round the World*." To advance his cause Rodwell turned to the distinctly unrepresentative ERCHO, which in November passed his proposal to move the time and location of the annual reminder from Philadelphia on July 4 to New York in June. The motion, too, was drastically more ambitious than anything that preceded it, calling on individuals and organizations all over the country to produce a nationwide show of support to commemorate this life-altering event. ERCHO ordered the formation of a Christopher Street Liberation Day Umbrella Committee.

Which of course turned out to consist mostly of Rodwell and his friends meeting in the bookstore. But Rodwell cannily, and, by all accounts, sincerely, invited all the ever-proliferating gay organizations in the area to participate in planning and sponsoring the event. And they all had agendas. The Gay Liberation Front wanted to cement their ties to other radical New Left organizations. The Gay Activists Alliance wanted to make homosexuals aware of the need to confront politicians and public officials. Rodwell wanted to affirm liberated gay lifestyles. Fortunately, unlike almost any other activity, a parade does not require reconciliation of competing agendas, especially if there is not a speakers' roster to select. It is the ultimate existential activity. Just showing up is a political statement.

A similar laissez-faire approach worked wonders with the other regional organizations. Foster Gunnison, another of the Mattachine activists in Rodwell's circle, wrote an exquisite memorandum to the midwestern and western "regional homophile organizations" to "encourage their support and participation," but not proposing any particular content. He, too, frames Stonewall as the "famous . . . first time that homosexuals had taken massive street action in open battle with offending institutions in the social order." Gunnison's and Rodwell's power grab for the New York event could have failed, surely. But both Los Angeles and Chicago had men of enormous goodwill and increasingly radical outlooks at the crucial power centers. Morris Kight, one of the founders of the Los Angeles GLF, had started the first gay and lesbian community center in history years before and probably did not feel threatened. Troy Perry, the founder of the gay Metropolitan Community Church, was also a uniquely inner-directed individual, and he had been advocating adoption of the techniques of the New Left in LA for years. Jim Bradford in Chicago, too, was ripe for more activism than the Mattachine Society had been offering. The offer of an occasion to march was perfectly timed for their political needs, standing, as they were, at the cusp of an identity-based liberation movement to replace the old, elite-oriented, political gradualists of the Mattachine era. A parade is an excellent vehicle for identity formation. And they grabbed it.

As the months before the march passed, Rodwell had repeated panic attacks featuring an empty street. And it did feel sort of empty in front of the Stonewall at two o'clock that first year. Young gay lawyer Michael Lavery thinks there could not have been more than twenty-five at noon. If there were a thousand people after all that work, it was a lot. As they marched up Sixth Avenue, however, the march grew. First it doubled; then, most observers think, it doubled again. Somewhere between two thousand and ten thousand people marched through the streets of New York. When they got to the Sheep Meadow in Central Park, the first marchers climbed a little rise and looked back to see gay people filling the entire space and still pouring down the street. Frank Kameny remembered the forty-five people at the last annual reminder and now he saw thousands. He was there with his good friends Jack Nichols and Lige Clark. We were, they wrote in the new New York weekly, *Gay*, "awestruck by the vast throngs of confident humanity wending their way into a promised land of freedom-to-be."

5

The Good Gays Fight the Four Horsemen: Crazy, Sinful, Criminal, and Subversive

Richard Socarides, fifteen years old and gay, had his family's Manhattan town house at Seventy-eighth Street and Third Avenue to himself the last weekend in June 1970. Richard brought his high school boyfriend to spend the night. After making love Sunday morning, they decided to go to Central Park. As they crossed Fifth Avenue, they encountered a vast throng of people holding up signs and chanting about gay rights. Smilingly, Richard said to his lover, "Well, I think we did our little bit for gay rights this morning." Twenty-five years later, Socarides took his place in the White House as the first official adviser to an American president on gay and lesbian matters. Socarides still remembers his chance encounter with history: "It was great foreshadowing about how my life just accidentally crossed the movement at the very beginning. I march in that parade every year now no matter what."

The euphoria of Stonewall gave way to the realities of the battle for real social change. By pushing back, gays showed they were scary enough so that the society had to include them in the social contract, agreeing to protect them in exchange for their not making war on other citizens—the first principle of the liberal state. But the four horsemen of the gay apocalypse—Crazy, Sinful, Criminal, and Subversive—still blocked their passage to full social equality.

In the next few years, the newly empowered movement created an infrastructure of institutions to earn the badges of social membership for gay people. They took on the mental-health profession, started churches of their own, challenged the criminal sodomy laws, and pressed the government to stop excluding them from the civil service. Sometimes the institutional agendas overlapped: being classified as sane helped the argument that gay diplomats were not likely to be disloyal. But regardless of whether they proceeded together or independently, pretty much everyone in the newly hatched mass movement understood that establishing their sanity, sanctity, sexual legitimacy, and loyalty were the tasks at hand. The big story of the post-Stonewall years is how they did it.

Trying to change a society with such a broad array of resources available to hate and fear them, in the early hard years after Stonewall, American gays and lesbians enjoyed nearly every advantage any social-movement theory required for success. As classical theory predicted, the social changes of the Sixties, chiefly feminism, had reframed gender behavior as a matter of social convention, rather than natural order or biblical imperative. Gays and lesbians were thus able to see their oppression as a decision society made rather than as an inevitable consequence of their "deviation" from a gender behavior commanded by nature or God. The sexual-liberation movement of the Sixties had split the establishment on the subject of what constituted good sexual behavior, weakening the resistance. In new social movement terms, as the radical movements had become more gay and the gay movements more radical, the new gay activists saw themselves as aggrieved even before they came out and broke away. They had what sociologists call "oppositional consciousness." Coming out engendered a powerful group-based interest binding the participants into the movement. The new identities rewarded participation: in years to come, the annual Stonewall parade would feature marchers with a banner, "Marched in 1970 Parade." As the proud and happy marchers left Central Park, they had all this going for them. The movement could not have succeeded otherwise. They were so few and the tasks were so great.

Crazy: "Faggot! Get Out of Here!"

Gay stalwart Frank Kameny had had his eye on the first horseman—Crazy—for years. Driven by the primal scene of his political life—being fired from the civil service—he was painfully aware of how the psychiatrists enabled the politicians and bureaucrats to banish homosexuals from their own government. Kameny, the scientist, knew the assertion that gays were crazy was totally unscientific, and he knew it was harmful.

The gay movement was not the only social movement to resist the psychiatrists. The feminist movement waged epic battles with the "scientists" who assumed that women were naturally passive actors with foundational penis-envy problems. Yet, unlike gays, women were not crazy by definition. There was no *DSM* (*Diagnostic and Statistical Manual of Mental Disorders*, the American Psychiatric Association's quasi-official classification of mental disorders) category for uppity females who asked for pay raises, which could be used to fire them if they were caught working while female. Feminism battled Freud in elite journals, in academic seminars, in literary magazines, and in a thousand private battles. It was a culture war. The gay activists had to attack the institution of the APA head on, as if it were the government itself, yet without being able to invoke any of the arguments like equality and privacy that constrain the actual liberal state.

Before Stonewall, as Kameny went around trying to radicalize the homophile organizations, he had always made the psychiatrists' treatment of homosexuality as a sociopathic personality disturbance the centerpiece of his presentation. But until Stonewall turned their little band into an angry, acting-out liberation front, the movement did not have a lot of ammunition. Not six months after Stonewall, a band of activists disrupted the San Francisco meeting of the American Psychiatric Association. In response to the demonstrations, the chair of the program committee for the next meeting in DC agreed to let some nonpatient homosexuals speak for themselves.

The gay activists picked Kameny and several other pre-Stonewall veterans of the fight to represent them. Unknown to the cooperating docs, however, the panel members were also involved in plans to zap the DC meeting. The proper, educated Kameny was the last person you'd expect to see hanging around the commune with the group of DC hippies, hitherto unknown to the homophile movement, who made up the Washington Gay Liberation Front (GLF). Craig Rodwell's story of Kameny ordering the lesbians to stop holding hands a week after Stonewall makes him sound like all the other middle-aged homophiles. True, Kameny wasn't crazy about the Gay Liberation Front. "People talked endlessly, there was no way of coming to a vote, nothing really got accomplished, and there was no way of defining what we were doing." But once the DC front got organized, he attended virtually every one of the endless meetings. And the rebels rewarded him by turning out in force to zap the shrinks at the DC meeting.

The psychiatrists gathered only once in one place at each annual meeting, at the convocation. The 1971 convocation was scheduled for the Regency Ballroom in Washington's Shoreham Hotel. Thanks in part to Kameny's spadework, the importance of defeating the psychiatrists was so patently obvious to anyone in the gay community that all the fractious factions of the DC gay movement—the fading DC Mattachine Society, the Gay Liberation Front, and the Gay Activists Alliance of DC, which had just formed a few weeks before—cooperated to plan and execute the attack.

The zap followed the basic script Marty Robinson and the others had developed in New York. The gay activists scouted out the Shoreham Hotel and designated a speaker to present their position once the invading gay troops had secured the microphone. They placed wedges underneath the fire doors at the back of the room so they could get in unannounced.

Kameny and his copanelists were officially in the Regency Room sitting in the audience, when the demonstrators stormed the room. As Kameny tells it, "There sitting offstage were all these psychiatrists wearing gold medals, and the psychiatrists beat our people over the head with their gold medals and they drove them out the door. We had designated one person to seize the microphone but he had been beaten off by the psychiatrists." Perry Brass, a GLF stalwart from New York who came to DC for the big May Day antiwar rally but stayed to zap the shrinks, describes the scene in the Regency Room as something out of Dante's *Inferno*. In the brief moment before someone slammed the fire door shut on him he heard voices shouting, "Faggot! Get out of here! We don't want any more people like you in here."

Kameny saw the designated speaker shoved out the door. "For a few moments nothing was happening at all. Our people were just sitting there. I saw the whole thing was going to disappear and I realized that something had to be done. I marched across the room, stepped up on the stage, and the psychiatrist in charge said, 'What are you doing?' and I said, 'I'm going to speak.'" Some of the psychiatrists had pulled the plug on the microphone. "I've never needed a microphone to be heard," Kameny says, "and I'd made the speech many times." The angry shrinks paused, and Kameny told the assembled professionals that they "may take this as a declaration of war against you." With that, the 1971 APA meeting broke up.

The War Against the Psychiatrists

By the time the gays formally declared war on the psychiatrists in 1971, all the conditions for a classic successful social action on the psychiatric front were in place. The sexual revolution created an unrelated change in the social norms of "normal" sexuality, the act of coming out inherently involved recognition of their sexuality as healthy and normal, Frank Kameny's circle provided strong leadership, and the psychiatric elites were divided.

It had been a long process. The assault on the "crazy" designation started, like so much of the gay revolution, with the Kinsey Report. If homosexuality was a sociopathological mental disease when, in 1947, sex surveyor Professor Alfred Kinsey supposedly found that 37 percent of all adult males had had a homosexual experience at some point, it meant there were an awful lot of crazies around. Slowly, after Kinsey's report, the gay challengers gained allies.

In the early fifties, the movement attracted the attention of heterosexual UCLA psychologist Evelyn Hooker. This was not entirely an accident. Hooker's best grad student, homosexual Sammy From, had gone out of his way to be her friend, hanging out after class and driving her home. One day he took her to a drag show and, observing her open and amused response, put his real agenda on the table. It was her professional duty to study homosexuals who were not in therapy or in prison. He knew, he told her, a whole world of gay people living happy, productive lives. It was an academic's dream, as one of her colleagues in the psych department said, "A whole area of research no one has touched. Ask for a grant right away!"

The psychiatrists' data almost without exception came from their patients, by definition a skewed sample. For fifteen years, Hooker collected histories of nonpatient homosexuals. Her survey yielded a detailed picture of people leading lives of average or better adjustment. When she gave the subjects and a heterosexual control group the contemporary standard psychological tests, reviewing psychologists were unable to distinguish between the two groups. Published in 1957, Hooker's pioneering study suggested that "homosexuality as a clinical entity does not exist, homosexuality may be a deviation in sexual pattern which is within the normal range, and the role of particular forms of sexual desire and expression in personality structure and development may be less important than has frequently been assumed. It may be that the disturbance is limited to the sexual sector alone."

Empirical research was not common in psychiatry. Because, in a crude Darwinian sense, without heterosexual intercourse there would be no humans at all, Sigmund Freud, the father of psychoanalysis, assumed that heterosexuality was the natural and desirable end of human sexual development. He speculated about whether homosexuality was biological or involved the usual suspects—the mothers—but his general pessimism about the possibilities of therapy and his Evelyn Hooker–like observation that homosexuals were not otherwise functionally impaired led him to conclude that his profession should leave homosexuals alone. Nonetheless, by the 1940s, Freud's prudent skepticism had been supplanted by an ambitious faith in treatment. In 1952, homosexuality was listed in the first *DSM*. That so many homosexuals seemed so well-adjusted to their condition that the psychiatrists had to classify homosexuality as sociopathological—a disorder without distress or anxiety—might have raised a red flag.

Instead, having categorized homosexuals as crazy, the New York Society of Psychoanalysts began studying its homosexual patients for signs of "cure." In 1962, the society published the results in a study, *Homosexuality*, authored by Irving Bieber. According to Bieber, homosexuality is presumed to be pathological, it's probably Mom's fault, and there's a good chance it can be cured. Psychoanalyst Charles Socarides (Richard's father, unbelievable as that seems) upped the ante, attributing homosexuality to a toddler's pathological attachment to the mother and characterizing its practitioners as schizophrenic, paranoid, and obsessive. Happily, he reported, his practice produced a 50 percent cure rate. As psychiatric reformer Robert Spitzer would later admit, "In terms of evidence that is acceptable to most scientists [the evidence for homosexuality as a mental disorder] was very limited." Unlike their colleagues in the medical profession, Spitzer says, psychiatrists at that time operated on an "intuitive sense that males and females adapted to each other . . . [so] from an evolutionary standpoint one can argue that if a man is unable to be attracted by a woman something is not working."

For gay men and, to a lesser extent, lesbians, this was not just another battle of the intellectuals. In the years when psychoanalysis dominated social thinking, homosexuals were subjected to every weapon in the psychiatric arsenal. Horrifyingly, those treatments included electroshock therapy and shock-based aversion therapy, sometimes at the insistence of their families, sometimes through the coercive power of the state. Although hormone and surgical treatment had existed for decades to enable them to alter their gender to some degree, transsexuals were subjected to a veritable psychiatric gauntlet in order to get what they wanted from the university-based clinics that dominated the field. Eligible transsexuals had to report a devastating degree of psychological suffering and propose to transform themselves into unidentifiable members of the other gender with accompanying heterosexual desires. Unlike the happy homosexual, transsexuals, who wanted something from the medical establishment, didn't have the option to just walk away. There's a reason Kameny called it a war.

Unfortunately for the psychoanalysts, modernity was about to intrude on their cozy realm. First, health-insurance companies and, after 1965, Medicaid, which were being asked to pay the bill, were unconvinced by psychoanalysts' just-so tales and pushed the APA for some scientifically defensible diagnoses and provable treatments. In 1960, one of psychiatry's own, Thomas Szasz, of the State University of New York, published *The Myth of Mental Illness*, charging his colleagues with putting a cloak of unproved medical language over what was merely disapproved behavior. Few in the profession were willing to adopt the prescriptions of Szasz and the other "antipsychiatrists." Still, the empirical challenges to psychiatry's unscientific explanations for something as important as mental illness set the stage for a radical revision of their diagnostic and therapeutic claims.

Gay activists rapidly adopted the growing skepticism about the judgment of mental health professionals. When the conservatives had taken over the Mattachine Society in the early fifties, they had, for a period of time, considered the psychiatrists their allies. After all, the gentler Freudian treatment of their condition as an ailment seemed vastly preferable to being put in jail for criminal sodomy. But as the psychiatrists' claims of illness and cure grew more ambitious and the gay population experienced more and more aggressive attempts to "treat" their "illness," the alliance frayed.

It is difficult to overstate the effect of Kameny's leadership. His standard speech heavily focused on the unscientific circular reasoning that passed for medicine in the psychiatric treatment of homosexuality. So obviously unjust was the psychiatric treatment of homosexuality that his speeches, for example to the New York Mattachine Society in 1968, not only radicalized the chapter on the issue of gay pathology, it radicalized the chapter in general. Even before Stonewall, gay militants started disrupting "scholarly" presentations of the evidence that they were crazy. In 1968, Charles Socarides met with the first of such protests directed at him specifically, when he spoke to a convention of the American Medical Association in San Francisco.

The worst was yet to come. If Stonewall-era liberation meant anything, it meant, as the GLF paper was called, *COME OUT!* Nothing was less compatible with coming out than going to a psychiatrist to get yourself changed. The psychiatrists' insistence that homosexuality was pathological was a threat to the very foundation of the liberation movement. As the great chronicler of the conflict between homosexuality and American psychiatry, Ronald Bayer, puts it, going to a psychiatrist was considered collaboration. Not surprisingly the post-Stonewall liberation groups produced a limitless supply of protesters to take the psychiatrists on. The gay protesters were particularly visible at the meetings of behavioral therapists, because those specialists were the most aggressive in using aversion therapy like electric shocks (the protesters called it torture) to try to cure homosexuals. The gay activists used the disruptive techniques like the DC zap to empower the "good cops" like Kameny and the Gay Activists Alliance's Ron Gold, who were negotiating with sympathetic APA insiders to get them heard at successive meetings.

Propelled by all these advantages, the victory came quite quickly. It was the Sixties, after all. Dissent over the treatment of homosexuality was but one of the divisions within the profession. A group of young psychiatrists, the Committee of Concerned Psychiatrists, had already begun to defy the cozy APA old-boy network, especially on opposition to the war in Vietnam. By 1971, the young Turks had made declassifying homosexuality one of their planks. After garnering 40 percent of the votes for APA president in 1971, the insurgents' next candidate, Alfred Freedman, a professor at New York Medical College, slid to victory by two votes the next year. In the election after the 1972 meeting, the young psychiatrists ran a whole slate and swept the election.

The gay protesters also gained a valuable ally in Robert Spitzer, a very smart academic psychiatrist who sat on the Nomenclature Committee, the group that named the disorders. Spitzer, an intellectual gadfly and relentlessly energetic individual, met the protesters at a meeting of the association for the advancement of behavior therapy: "They had a panel on the treatment of homosexuality and there was a speaker who came all the way from England but he never got to give his talk because the meeting was broken up by some gay activists. I went up, and spoke to the gay activists later and said that wasn't a very nice thing that you did. And they found out that I was on this committee on nomenclature and they asked me if it would be possible for them to make a presentation to that committee." Spitzer went to the head of the committee and told him that the group wanted to make a presentation; the chairman agreed.

By all accounts, the gay activists' presentation to the committee was a triumph. The presenters, Spitzer says, made the irrefutable argument that there was no scientific evidence for classifying homosexuality as a mental disorder, that the arguments were all based on a preexisting prejudice, and that the classification does terrible things to gay people. "Something had to happen; we could not just ignore their protests anymore."

Spitzer realized he had a political problem with his colleagues, when, after the gay presenters made their case, the head of the Nomenclature Committee said, "Okay, Bob, you got us into this mess, what do we do now?" Spitzer decided to have a symposium on the issue at the 1973 APA meeting in Hawaii. There, for the first time, the assembled doctors heard gay people debate the question among themselves, instead of the psychiatrists offering a solid front against demonstrating activists.

Still, gay activists, like Gold, were uncertain of Spitzer's commitment to them. Gold knew there was a covert caucus of closeted gay psychiatrists. When he appeared in Hawaii, he made a pitch for them to come out. Although they did not do that, they invited him to their off-site soiree at the Bamboo Bar, and, in a risky and dramatic move, Gold took Spitzer with him. The largely closeted group, whose members rightly feared for their jobs, were not pleased with the unannounced appearance of one of their most powerful colleagues, but Gold convinced them to tell him about their lives and how the reconsideration of the issue would help them. One gay psychiatrist, who had just come out of the army, where he was forced to closet himself every minute, cried as he explained how important the change was. Spitzer says it humanized gay men in his eyes, made him identify with their suffering, and convinced him to be helpful to the extent that he could. The gay movement's political strategy of the tragic anecdote was born.

Spitzer figured out that what he had to do was propose a policy that would give therapists the option of treating homosexuals for *something*. So he wrote a statement that homosexuality by itself, while an irregular sexual development, is not a psychiatric disorder unless the homosexuals are distressed by their homosexuality. For the next six or seven months, Spitzer's compromise wound its way through the many levels of the psychiatric bureaucracy. Bolstering the series of votes on the proposal to change the treatment of homosexuality in *DSM* was the firm commitment of Freedman and the insurgents at the top to seeing this get done.

Finally, on December 15, 1973, the Spitzer proposal was presented to Freedman's liberal board of trustees. Freedman knew that he had the votes. But Freedman wanted this profound social and professional conversion to be as close as possible to unanimous. To gather more support, Freedman agreed to weaken some of the pro-homosexual language. Thus, the original statement that "homosexuality in itself does not by itself constitute a psychiatric disorder" was changed by the board to say that "homosexuality in itself does not *necessarily* constitute a psychiatric disorder." This was no small change, but, at the end of the day, the first proposal in history to withdraw homosexuality from the list of psychiatric disorders passed unanimously. "Victory for Homosexuals," the *New York Times* proclaimed the next morning.

Twenty-six years later, on December 15, 1999, Alfred Freedman woke up to see that the *Washington Post* had chosen as the most important December 15 of the twentieth century, December 15, 1973, the day the Board of Trustees of the American Psychiatric Association announced that homosexuality in itself did not necessarily constitute a psychiatric disorder, for its "This Date in History" feature.

The gay movement did not just change America for gay people. Because of the challenge to psychiatry by the well-adjusted homosexuals, academic psychiatrist Spitzer and his colleagues were forced to address a question central to the treatment of mental illness for everyone. What is the status of behavior that society doesn't like but that the people who practice the behavior think is fine? Rightly or wrongly, to this day, Spitzer thinks there's something not optimal about homosexuality, a behavior that does not lead to survival in a simple Darwinian world. He figured out right away that in order to protect the homosexuals whom psychiatry had hurt so badly and with no defensible scientific proof of treatable illness, he had to distinguish between what he calls less than "optimal social functioning" and disease. From there, the entire diagnostic machinery had to be re-engineered from the ground up, with a big effort to avoid pathologizing behaviors that are just socially unfamiliar. The process eventually produced the famed *DSM III*, an attempt to frame mental illness as a medical condition, not just some analyst's intuition or interpretation of the work of Dr. Freud.

Spitzer was the chief draftsman of *DSM III*. He says it was the gay challenge that started him down the road of rethinking the whole procedure of identifying mental illness. In an article about *DSM III* and Spitzer, the *New Yorker* concludes that, "In the course of defining more than a hundred mental diseases, he not only revolutionized the practice of psychiatry but also gave people all over the United States a new language with which to interpret their daily experiences and tame the anarchy of their emotional lives." And so the gay revolution changed America for everyone.

Sinful: God Does Not Have Any Stepsons and Daughters

Troy Perry started his campaign against the classification of gays as sinful by trying to commit an old-fashioned sin: suicide. Fortunately, his roommate came home unexpectedly to their little apartment in LA that night in

1969 and found Perry with his wrists bleeding into the bath. A couple of years earlier, after decades of denial, Perry, a Pentecostal minister, husband, and father of two, had finally recognized the truth: "Troy Perry, you're a homosexual." He left his wife and children and his successful ministry, moved to LA, found a boyfriend, and had the best six months of his life. But when the lover broke it off, Perry decided to die.

As he lay in his room at the LA County General Hospital, waiting for the doctor to come and sew him up, an African American nurse walked into his room. "What's the matter with you?" she demanded. "Don't you have somebody you can talk to? Can't you just look up?" She used all the tenets of his faith, he recalls, and left him crying uncontrollably, when the doctor walked in. "Well," boomed the doctor, "Do I need to lock you up for seventy-two hours? I'm not going to be responsible for you. Are you going to be OK?" He would be, Perry answered, because for the first time in six months, he had prayed to his familiar God, asking for forgiveness. So the doctor let him go home. The next morning, his roommate asked him the same question: Can I leave you alone today?

"I'm laying in bed," Perry says, "and in the middle of this something happened and this has been my testimony for forty-two years: I prayed and I felt good after my prayer, but I said, 'God, I know you don't love me,' and all at once there was that joy of our salvation in my heart, and I said, 'Oh God, wait a minute, this can't be right, [that] you can't love me, the church has told me that.' And I tell people to this day that God spoke to me. A still small voice. That's one of the few times I heard the authentic voice of God. God said, 'Troy, don't tell me what I can and can't do, you're my son. I don't have stepsons and daughters.' And with that I knew I was a Christian and I knew that I was still a gay man."

From the beginning, Perry's revelation was both religious and liberationist. Inspired by his divine moment of free consciousness, Perry knew he was not sinful and he was going to take that horseman on. He figured out that if God loved him, he must love the others too, and "that was the message to my community." It's hard to imagine a more potent consciousness-raiser than hearing the voice of God. Once God says, Gay Is Good, then the arguments against homosexuality are not just mistaken—they're heresy.

Perry's revelation was the more potent because it came against a backdrop of almost uniform hostility to homosexuality by all the institutions of Western monotheism. (Some of the most liberal San Francisco churches had started supporting the gay movement a year or two before, but that alliance was a tiny first crack in the long-standing, remorseless clerical condemnation.) Not only is the sex act that separates gays from the heterosexual majority stigmatized as sinful, but, centuries ago, the church prohibition on sodomy got absorbed into secular law, a crime with no victim in any earthly sense. The entire apparatus of criminal law—such as police sweeps and bar raids—rested on the back of the sinful horseman.

In many modern social movements, the strategy for dealing with religiously based oppression is to walk away from the sinful argument and just say, well, it's my private behavior; you may think it's sinful, but in the liberal state you hold your nose and tolerate it. The government has no more business criminalizing sodomy, the argument goes, than requiring everyone to eat only kosher food. Indeed, that's the argument the gay lawyers made when they took on sodomy in the years after Stonewall.

Perry's position—that God loves gays just like everyone else—is much stronger than the thin claim for "tolerance" and "privacy." Perry said there must be something wrong with the way you're reading scripture if it conflicts with God's love. If gay sex isn't sinful by definition, by the way, it follows that the police in the bedroom are a threat to all people's private sex lives. And he started a Christian church, Pentecostal no less, right in the face of the most committed opponents, to stake the claim. Perry's church was not some wishy-washy universalist kumbaya circle; belief in the Trinity is the first principle of Perry's Metropolitan Community Church (MCC).

Maybe only Perry could have pulled it off. In 1982, Dennis Altman, one of the major theorists of the gay movement, called Perry "perhaps the most charismatic leader yet produced by the American gay movement." Perry comes from a family of southern preachers. He heard the call to the ministry at thirteen and had been actively pursuing the Christian gospel all his life. It is typical of this mold-breaking homosexual that he thinks his character was defined by his years in the military. "Once they send you where people are shooting you, you get pretty brave," he says. A tall, handsome, muscular, and charismatic individual, all his churches, before his coming out (and defrocking), had grown with beanstalklike speed.

After getting the Word, Perry took out an ad in the *Los Angeles Advocate*, announcing the first service, to be held at his home. He had a plan for people who had been thrown out of religious groups, who said they weren't loved. Twelve people came—nine friends to comfort him when his effort failed and three new churchgoers.

Perry told the little flock that there was no such thing as hell and that God loved them. He had a simple, obvious message, which is the basic gospel of the MCC to this day. He believed, first, in Christian salvation. Second, in Christian community: if someone is hungry, feed them. Third, and more predictably, that the church strongly advocates Christian social action—go downtown with me and hold demonstrations.

Perry had some things going for him: The gay community was filled with spiritual people who had been forced out of their churches and totally without any place to turn; many of his early congregants were defrocked clergymen like himself. They were ready to believe God loved them, too, and Perry was an inspired leader. Christian salvation and Christian community seem like obvious steps.

But while Perry was explicitly modeling his effort on the inspiration of Martin Luther King Jr., gay Christian social activism was hardly a foregone conclusion. Perry's first demonstration—in support of a man who had been fired for being homosexual—attracted ten people. In spite of Perry's exhortation to remember the Christian position on death and resurrection, they were afraid. This was not paranoid; in early 1970 vice cops dragged a hapless homosexual from his room at LA's Dover Hotel and beat him to death. But Perry's first ten marchers included the militant activist Jim Kempner, the mainstay of the incomparable *ONE* magazine during the darkest years of the fifties, and Kempner brought, out of the past, Harry Hay. It was nine months before Stonewall.

As Perry's church was getting off the ground, his polar opposite, the lefty union organizer and antiwar activist Morris Kight, founded the third chapter of the Gay Liberation Front in the country—GLF/LA. A few weeks later, Kight showed up at Perry's office with the letter from the Stonewall March committee. "Troy," Kight said, "I got this letter from New York. Maybe we could do something to celebrate this." "They wanted a march," Perry says, "but this is Hollywood. We have to have a PARADE!" When the odd couple went to the city to get a permit, the police chief said he'd rather have thieves and burglars marching in his town. They had to get the ACLU to file a lawsuit. The permit came just forty-eight hours before the day, so they got on the phone to all their flock. "Build floats. Bring your cars. Bring your pets!" the organizers exhorted. Twelve hundred marchers came, and tens of thousands to watch the spectacle on Hollywood Boulevard. It was the first gay parade to close the street.

The Metropolitan Community Church spread like early Christianity. From the beginning, unlike almost any other organization of the gay revolution, they met weekly; it was Sunday services after all. "First there were twelve and then twenty-four and then three hundred," Perry remembers. Two years after Perry started, in 1971, the Metropolitan Community Church held its first service in its own building. A thousand people attended. Jews came and decided to start the first gay synagogue. By 1970, there were MCC churches in Los Angeles, San Francisco, San Diego, Chicago, and Honolulu, and enough leaders for a "federation, the Universal Fellowship of Metropolitan Community Churches." Within a few years there were MCC congregations all over the world.

The MCC had the first gay-rights lobby in Washington, with an office right down the street from the Supreme Court. For two years, they were the only gay lobby in DC. During the AIDS epidemic, the MCC made buttons that read GOD IS STRONGER THAN AIDS. The church buried five thousand of its members. And then, "We ended up preaching funerals for people who were not members of MCC," Perry says. "The parents would come to me and say would you preach my son's funeral. We're from Alice, Texas, and our Baptist Church wouldn't understand." MCC pastors went in and washed the bodies before the morticians would touch them. Today there are forty thousand members in three hundred congregations. In towns that are not obviously gay friendly, like Jacksonville, Florida, churchgoing gay people, often southerners and African Americans, find a welcoming home in the local MCC. Yet Perry still says, "If you had told me that the largest organization touching the gay community should be a church I would have called you a liar."

Churches matter. They are part of the unofficial apparatus of social approval, so central to the gay revolution. When the movement needed resources beyond what the formal language of legal equality could provide, the MCC was there. Perry was the protester who demanded to be arrested in order to challenge California's sodomy law. He was the plaintiff in the state same-sex marriage case. When someone had to debate fundamentalist Southern Baptist preacher Jerry Falwell, Troy Perry went. After all, he could go chapter and verse with the other reverend.

An early congregant had suggested that Perry elevate the modest surroundings of his first gatherings by wearing clerical robes. His presence in his beautiful clerical garb added a note of ritual and respectability to his most radical enterprises. For decades, when a gay delegation was invited to the White House, Perry was there. The image of the upright gentleman in his clerical collar in the White House Red Room makes arguments that no formal claim of reason can make.

Troy Perry at the White House (Photograph by Phillip De Blieck)

Criminal: Of Course, No One Wants to Defend Homosexuals

In 1963, Michael Lavery was in that temple of reason, law school, when he heard a knock on his dorm room door. Two postal inspectors were standing in the hall. Had he received a copy of *ONE* magazine? Or joined one of the "correspondence clubs" (a sort of early matchup service) the magazine was advertising? The post office had put a mail watch on his PO box and the inspectors knew he had.

By chance that day, Lavery's constitutional-law class had been discussing censorship. Yes, he said and suggested to the two men in brown shoes standing in his hallway that there was a Supreme Court decision to the effect that there was nothing wrong with his receiving *ONE* magazine. Well the correspondence club was illegal, the postal inspectors suggested. Would Lavery like to give them any information he received by way of correspondence? Lavery, an unprepossessing-looking guy with a shy air and thin dishwater hair, said he would not. In that case, how, one inspector asked, would Lavery like his law school to know about what he was reading?

But it was 1963, not 1953. Unbeknownst to the feds, their bashful victim had already joined the antiwar movement and was appealing the denial of his status as a conscientious objector. "Well," Lavery said, "if that's the way it is, that's the way it is." But nothing happened to Lavery.

In 1969, Lavery, who was practicing law in New York, and his lover, Rob, went to a demonstration in Berkeley while on vacation in San Francisco. They ducked into a bookstore to escape the tear gas and picked up a copy of the alternative paper, the *Berkeley Barb.* There had been a riot in New York. "Something's Happening Here," Lavery remembers thinking. From the song. When he got home he ran right over to the first rally after Stonewall, joined Martha Shelley's Mattachine Action Group and then the GLF and then the GAA. There, another young lawyer, Carrington Boggan, started a legal committee and then a law partnership with a third gay lawyer, Bill Thom.

The three GAA lawyers thought that their movement needed a legal arm. By 1972, the idea of a legal defense fund was hardly a brilliant insight. With its carefully structured series of escalating attacks on the Jim Crow regime in the South in the 1950s and '60s, the NAACP Legal Defense Fund had transformed the face of America. The ACLU had played a major role in achieving legal equality for women. The third horseman of the gay apocalypse—that by virtue of the sexual desire that defined them as a minority, gay people were criminals under the sodomy laws in forty-nine states—seemed an obvious candidate for the conventional civil rights approach, asking simply to be let alone.

For some reason, the young gay lawyers took their inspiration from the Puerto Rican Defense Fund. They just scribed their incorporation papers, putting "homosexuals" wherever "Puerto Rican" appeared, and sent them in to the New York courts for approval to practice law as a benevolent or charitable corporation, as New York law allowed. They would be the Lambda Legal Defense Fund.

The New York judges didn't think "homosexual" was a synonym for "Puerto Rican." In a classic example of how the gay activists had a different—and harder—task than their counterparts in modern activism, the judges ruled that the homosexuals were not the same as any minority with a history of oppression. They weren't just the wrong skin color; they were doing something wrong. Representing homosexuals was neither "benevolent" nor "charitable," the judges ruled. Puerto Ricans couldn't help it if they were poor and no one wanted to represent them. But if no one wanted to represent homosexuals, the court said, it was probably because they made reprehensible choices no one wanted to defend. Although there is no mention of the church, the opinion rests clearly on the clerical history of benevolent and charitable corporations. In the church-inflected world of benevolence and charity, gay sex was sin. There would be no homosexual legal defense fund in New York.

Fortunately for the gay lawyers, the higher courts had a somewhat more worldly vision of what the secular state of New York should require. Even in 1972, turning down the gay lawyers just months after approving the Puerto Ricans, and in a constitutionally sensitive area like the right to legal representation, was a recipe for reversal. The New York Court of Appeals reversed and ordered the judges below to reevaluate Lambda's application. On reconsideration, the original judges made Thom strike from the list of the fund's purposes the goal of encouraging more homosexuals to practice law. Their behavior was still wrong and the court did not want more of it. They let the gay lawyers incorporate, but the fight over it illustrates how far they had to go just to qualify as a garden variety . . . insurgent social movement.

For many years, Lambda was a sorry bunch. They worked out of Thom's apartment. They had no money. The liberal foundations would not touch them. New York lawyers were scared to death to be identified as gay, so it was almost impossible to get volunteers. They could do only the most basic cases—representing people who were arrested, kicked out of their homes, losing their children, or being deported. They could mostly only take cases in the New York metropolitan area; they had no money for travel. Often they did not even find out about a crucial case until it had gone up on appeal and all they could do was file an amicus brief.

At that very moment, the Orthodox, Jewish, heterosexual female, improbably blond and blue-eyed Marilyn Haft had just gotten a job at the national office of the ACLU in New York. Haft was determined to make a name for herself. "Who needs me?" she thought. There was no shortage of lawyers for race cases, and Ruth Bader Ginsburg seemed to be doing a pretty good job at the Women's Rights Project, but the gay movement was just getting started. They did not have lawyers, she noticed, just people "walking around with torn legal briefs." She admits frankly it was not because of her passion for the gay issue—she was just trying to find a group who needed somebody to make the law for them. But she called a meeting. Carey Boggan came from Lambda, which was in its very earliest days. She also attracted Bruce Voeller, the controversial president of the GAA. Maybe the New York courts didn't think homosexual lawyers were pure enough for incorporation, but Haft correctly figured out that the militantly secular new Playboy Foundation would be open to funding something called the "Sexual Privacy Project." And so they did.

From the standpoint of the young gay legal movement, the ACLU was establishment. And Haft played its establishment credentials to the hilt. She used the ACLU's legitimacy and longevity to make the next move into the establishment, appealing for help in reforming the law to the establishment institutions that governed the legal profession, the American Bar Association (ABA) and the Practicing Law Institute.

Like the American Psychiatric Association, after the Sixties, the prestigious and stodgy ABA had become the target of its younger members. The insurgent liberal lawyers were concentrated in the section of the ABA that focused on individual rights, so Haft and Boggan politicked the committee to pass a resolution saying that gay people are entitled to be protected against employment discrimination. This seemingly innocuous position was as radical as it got at the ABA in the early 1970s—Haft and her crew had to lobby the committee repeatedly to get the resolution adopted. She believes her success was due in no small part to the fact that she was a straight woman and coming from the ACLU. "There was all this women's rights stuff going on," she recalls. "I made a comparison to the women's movement, I always did and I always talked about equal protection of the laws. The women's movement was something they could understand and they could justify." Haft and Boggan got a straight-male white-shoe lawyer from DC to coauthor their volume in the ACLU rights series, *The Rights of Gay People.*

An antidiscrimination resolution was okay, but the name of the game was getting rid of criminal sodomy. The Lambda lawyers knew it, Haft knew it, and the bold activists at GLF/LA knew it. As long ago as 1950, Harry Hay knew it: repealing the sodomy laws was the first campaign he imagined for his Bachelors for Wallace. If the very sexual act that distinguished gays and lesbians from the heterosexual population was criminal, everything else followed, from arresting them on the street to refusing to hire them for jobs.

Despite the threats to "out" Lavery to his law school and the gratuitous slap at Lambda for trying to recruit new gay lawyers, the days when people could be fired from their government jobs because homosexuals were believed to be inherently disloyal—the fourth horseman—were coming to an end. In 1975, the civil service lifted the prohibition on employment of gay people, which had been in effect since President Eisenhower bowed to the force of the McCarthyite storm. But as long as homosexual sex was criminal, the movement was always on the defensive. The first wave of gay activism against the regime was to separate the criminal from unassailably constitutionally protected conduct like speech and assembly in the 1958 *ONE* magazine case. Even if sodomy was criminal, a series of cases dealing with gay bars established that employees who might engage in criminal sodomy still had the right to gather in bars in the hours when they weren't at work.

Sooner or later, however, the issue was going to have to be attacked directly. As usual, California led the way. In May 1974, LA's Morris Kight and Albert Gordon, a straight lawyer with a gay son, organized the Felons 6—a gay male couple, a lesbian couple, and a heterosexual couple (the sodomy law there, as in many jurisdictions, applied to everyone, gay or not)—to confess that they recently had committed sodomy. Kight made a citizen's arrest and took the criminals to the local precinct, where the police refused to arrest them. Finally, the whole crew went to the district attorney, who issued a statement that "it is the policy of our office not to file criminal charges where consenting adults, in private, engage in sexual acts which might be considered violations of the penal law." (The district attorney thus saved himself from throwing one of the self-described felonious gay men, the Reverend Troy Perry, Pentecostal head of the thousand-plus member Metropolitan Community Church, in the slammer.) In 1975, the California legislature repealed the sodomy law.

The Felons 6 strategy, like much American social history since the sit-in at the Greensboro lunch counter, worked by forcing the establishment to enforce its discriminatory laws—or to back down. It was a media-based strategy; the Felons 6 had a posse of media with them at every stage of the sodomy-in. California was much further along in the process of treating its gay residents like citizens than New York was. Instead of dancing away like Mayor Lindsay's police commissioner did and then raiding their bars, the Los Angeles police just didn't enforce the sodomy laws, period. By 1975, California gays had enough muscle to get a repeal enacted through the agency of representative government, the legislature.

At about the same time as the Felons 6, a rising Lambda Legal found a courageous individual to defend himself against New York's manifestly unconstitutional loitering statute, one of the superficially neutral laws the police used to regulate gay public life. When the prosecutor realized he was going to have to go to trial, he dropped the charges. Undaunted, the young legal-defense fund sued the state to declare the statute unconstitutional, but the court declined to hear it on grounds that the plaintiff was in no danger of being prosecuted. Although the authorities denied the gay activists a clear-cut victory in both cases, the tactic was working to force the authorities to keep attesting to the fact that they would not enforce the antigay laws.

In 1980, the highest court of the state of New York struck down the New York sodomy laws as unconstitutional. Lambda, by then ensconced in an office at the New York Civil Liberties Union and beginning its ramp up to a big national law firm, led the friends of the court in shaping the argument. The New York decision came five years after sodomy-law repeal in California and a court decision is never as politically weighty as a legislative act, but the decriminalization of homosexuality seemed to be under way.

Subversive: The Time Had Come for Mainstream Politics

But the hardest job still lay ahead. In a democracy, no conversion of psychiatrists, establishment of churches, or even court victories is ultimately enough. Calling gay people traitors—the fourth horseman—meant more than just keeping them out of the State Department. By 1969, "McCarthyism" was a political dirty word. But Communists or not, gay men and women were still treated as unfit to be full citizens of the American democracy—their elected governments paid no attention to their needs; unless they were closeted, they were not officeholders—they were not even candidates. When Stonewall erupted, no governing body in the nation included a publicly gay member. Yet the gay revolution needed more from the government than simply to be left alone. Gays were going to need affirmative protections for the basic human enterprises—love and work. Sooner or later, the dramatic and amazing new gay movement was going to have to stop parading around and zapping and start acting like any other participants in the democratic process—raising money, electing their friends, and punishing their enemies. Protected against violence and with private sex lives, they were still going to have to claim the third principle of the liberal state, democratic self-governance.

In 1969, as movement polemicist Carl Wittman was putting the last touches on his jeremiad on San Francisco as a refugee camp from "Amerika," the refugees began to take over the camp. Ladylike California state senator Dianne Feinstein, Jewish, conventional, daughter of a doctor and wife (serially) of several wealthy men, was the improbable game changer. Feinstein ventured into politics back in the late 1960s when she ran for San Francisco's city council, the Board of Supervisors. In those days, the eleven-member board was elected citywide, six in one election and five in the next. Such a system put a high premium on coalition building, as there was no one group in San Francisco large enough to carry an election by itself. Feinstein had two unenviable support groups—Jews, who were not numerous, and women, who were not reliable. So, at the advice of Morris "Mo" Bernstein, fight promoter and classic political wheeler-dealer, the refined Mrs. Feinstein sought out the assistance of the new gay organization the Society for Individual Rights (SIR).

And did she get it! Money, volunteer workers, votes; not since gay waiter José Sarria had temporarily abandoned his role as Carmen to run for office in 1961 had the gay community turned out in such numbers. Once they turned their attention to politics, they were really smart about it. Jim Foster, head of the SIR political committee, knew that to succeed in a multicandidate election, you concentrate all your votes on the candidate you really care about. Forget the other five. The gay movement didn't have five candidates who had sought their support in 1969. They had Dianne Feinstein. Feinstein was elected with the most votes of anyone running and thus became, in her first term, the powerful president of the San Francisco Board of Supervisors. (In 1992, Feinstein became a United States senator.)

Foster was one of the many socially privileged guys who landed in the gay revolution after being radicalized by the gay-hunters in the army. Halfway through his obligatory stint in 1959, Foster, a Brown University graduate from a Republican family, got the full military treatment: interrogation, demand for names, dishonorable discharge. In San Francisco, Foster joined forces with Rick Stokes, who was making a fortune as the owner of the city's most popular bathhouse. In 1971, they were joined by Wall Street star David Goodstein, whom Wells Fargo bank had recruited to California only to fire him when they found out he was gay. In 1974, Goodstein used some of his Wall Street money to buy the *Advocate*, the largest gay publication in the country. As San Francisco transformed itself from a largely manufacturing and port city, educated gay men came pouring into town, taking jobs in the new service sector that was emerging. The San Francisco gay community recognized that they had a collective grievance against society, they threw up strong leaders like Jim Foster, and they gave him sufficient resources, such as Goodstein and Stokes could command. All the elements of a successful social movement were in place.

Winning the supervisor race for Feinstein was just the beginning for the angry gay men. Foster's next idea was to organize a gay Democratic club. California was fertile soil for clubs, because, as in most western states, the turn-of-the-century Progressive Movement had weakened the power of formal political parties. In 1953, energized by Adlai Stevenson's presidential run, a group of California activists established a formal structure for such clubs, the California Democratic Council. The CDC quickly became a kind of parallel Democratic Party, convening, cheekily, when the formal state Democratic Party had its convention. And they began to win elections, putting a Democrat in San Francisco City Hall in 1964 and launching the career of the inimitable Willie Brown, the first African American speaker of the California State Assembly.

On February 14, Valentine's Day, 1972, the Alice B. Toklas Democratic Club held its first meeting. The dues were two dollars a year. Schoolteacher Gary Miller, later club president, but then just a grunt, remembers thinking, "What? We can join the Democratic Party?!" Having two statewide organizations—the regular party organization and the club council—was a crucial element in the success of the San Francisco gay movement. Stokes ran for office unsuccessfully, but finished respectably and, perhaps more important, the club ran at least one person for the board of the Democratic Party organization. The Foster troika immediately plucked counterculture favorite, lefty, antiwar, civil rights advocate Richard Hongisto from the police force, where he was, to put it mildly, languishing, and pushed him for sheriff. In 1972, the city passed an ordinance forbidding people holding contracts with the city from discriminating against gays and lesbians.

For many years, no liberals ran for office in San Francisco without a stop at the Alice B. Toklas Democratic Club. The California club structure also explains in part why the gay revolution in California took such a different path from its counterpart in New York. There were Democratic clubs in New York, and they had substantial success in organizing against the old New York party machine. But the New York clubs were organized according to the districts represented in the New York State Assembly. So New York gays had a much harder time generating identity-politics special interest clubs.

The myth of Stonewall, so powerful in New York, is but a faint presence in this idyllic setting. Carol Ruth Silver, later a supervisor herself, but then working for the newly elected Sheriff Hongisto, tells a story of being assigned to take special care of the homosexual people who happened to be jailed in his jurisdiction. The last thing they wanted was another Stonewall. They didn't even want to go to the Stonewall birthday party. On June 28, 1970, there were a few hundred people in Golden Gate Park for a "gay-in." "We knew it had happened," Gary Miller remembers, "but it was not part of our consciousness." San Francisco gays were already moving to claim the benefits of the liberal state through conventional politics. They really didn't think they needed a parade.

When the presidential primary rolled around in 1972, Foster mobilized his new organization for the liberal George McGovern. Knowing that California rules rewarded the top spot on the primary ballot to the person who got his nominating petitions in first, Foster organized gays to register voters and sign McGovern petitions at bars all over San Francisco the night before the petitions were due. When the secretary of state's office opened the next morning, gays had secured McGovern enough signatures to score the top line on the ballot. On July 12, 1972, Foster became the first openly gay person ever to address a national political convention.

New York Makes Politics Outside the Liberal State

Without a structure for penetrating the Democratic Party like the California club movement, the New York gay activists faced the much more daunting task of mainstreaming their liberationists. In 1973, the GAA elected property-owning, previously married father of two, Rockefeller University biologist Bruce Voeller to be their next president. Voeller must have been more than a trifle alarmed when he looked around at a GAA meeting right after he took office and saw one of the loudest of the liberation front founders, leather-clad provocateur Jim Fouratt. When the Gay Liberation Front imploded shortly after GAA broke off, it unexpectedly catapulted the loose activists right into the organization formed to escape them. In no time, GAA was arguing over everything and meeting until the wee hours.

GAA barely made it into 1973 when Voeller and a handful of other bourgeois professionals abandoned the increasingly disorderly mass organization to organize a new group—open this time by invitation only. They had had it with the cross-dressing queens whom the sensation-seeking media quickly elevated to representatives of the gay movement. Despite his long blond hair and beard, Voeller wasn't all that interested in liberation. He just wanted gay people not to be fired from their jobs. And he didn't think the costumes were helping.

Transgender activists, three decades later leading their own militant identity movement and demanding the support of the gay and lesbian establishment, attribute the divide to this development. How did it come to be, they ask, reasonably, that a movement revived in part by the queens at the Stonewall Inn in 1969 found them unpalatable allies so soon afterward? As soon as the formerly despised gay men got a little power, they developed a heavily masculine presentation of self, leaving little space for their comrades who also challenged norms of gender.

Like their garb, Voeller's new organization, the National Gay Task Force, was boring. Members were expected to pay dues, not just show up at the firehouse for a dance and the occasional protest. The organization was going to be run by its board, which, like most boards, would be expected to raise money. Voeller and his establishment cronies intended to hire a paid staff, and to lobby for legislation in New York; for the first time the new movement also set its eyes on Congress.

The gay social movement thus began to enact the most conventional movement script. The early charismatic leadership like the Gay Liberation Front ("Sweet! Bullshit! [Force is] the only language that the pigs understand!") gave way to conventional qualifications for office—education and money. People called the Task Force the "doctors' group" and Voeller and his colleagues were indeed doctors, the PhD being soon joined by Mayor Lindsay's former public health commissioner, the newly outed Dr. Howard Brown, and the original gay PhD, Franklin Kameny. Being educated or wealthy or both, such new leaders occupied an elite status that separated them from their membership. The *Advocate* accused the new group of "aping high class values." Arthur Evans told the new leaders they should just call their group the Gay Professional Association. One by one, the old activists drifted away—Arthur Evans moved to San Francisco, where he took up with a spiritually oriented group, the fairy circle, and devoted himself to neighborhood politics; attendance at GAA meetings went way down; someone set fire to the firehouse.

The Task Force was not clearly destined for survival. Despite singular and repeated efforts, the city council of its own liberal cosmopolis kept rejecting the proposed gay civil rights ordinance. Its fund-raising efforts were anemic; the larger society was experiencing a robust and hostile conservative revival. It didn't even have a proper lobbying office in DC, using the Metropolitan Community Church's Washington office when it came to town. The New York group did not have the comfortable model of political organizing the Californians stepped right into.

Yet the Task Force limped along. People gave modest contributions. New York congresswoman Bella Abzug introduced a gay civil rights bill in Congress. It wasn't the most popular bill to say the least, but a marker had been laid down. Whenever "official" gay representation was required, people turned to the Task Force. They connected with activists in other cities, as the title "national" implied. It was—briefly—the only national game around.

And it managed to achieve that rarest of accomplishments: a long-term political alliance between gay men and lesbian women. One day in 1975, former nun and lesbian activist, the small but feisty Jean O'Leary showed up in Voeller's office. Voeller had had little good history with O'Leary, who had led the lesbian women out of the GAA during his tenure as president and into a splinter movement, Lesbian Feminist Liberation (LFL). After two years with the LFL movement, O'Leary was ready for a little coalition politics.

The feminist lesbians who came back to the Task Force were not your Stonewall-era Radicalesbians. They had now had five or six years' experience successfully fighting the homophobia in the feminist movement. Feminist mother of us all Betty Friedan, who had called lesbians the "lavender menace," had been pushed out of National Organization for Women (NOW), and the lesbians were firmly ensconced in the formerly hetero-only institution, maybe the first nongay political organization in history with lesbians firmly ensconced. Voeller and O'Leary shared an office. Within a year, she was cochairing the Task Force with Voeller and the group had passed a resolution that their board would always be fifty-fifty male and female.

The Task Force was by no means an edenic exception to the constant strain of gender politics. Many of Voeller's male board members objected strenuously to the quota system on the board. (Let the best man win, they said.) The lesbian feminists immediately began holding angry potluck suppers in Brooklyn to plot strategy for greater influence in the organization. Still, the conventional social behavior and agenda of the Task Force men removed a real source of strain with the women, most of whom did not like the rowdy promiscuous male sexuality of the liberation movement. For an important stretch, the alliance held.

And the lesbians helped the men move toward the mainstream. O'Leary was lovers with Democratic activist Midge Costanza, not publicly out, who became the president's assistant for public liaison when Jimmy Carter won the 1976 election. Thus it was O'Leary who arranged for the first homosexuals to present their political demands at a White House meeting. (As O'Leary told it, "I rolled over in bed and said, 'So, when are we going to the White House?'") The president was not there and none of the issues the Task Force delegation presented got anywhere during Carter's only term. But it was a photo op: Homosexuals at the White House. And just seven years before, the New York police had been carting them off from the Stonewall and tossing them in the slammer. The Task Force was doing pretty well.

The Ultimate Mainstream: Taking a Lesson from the Republicans

By the late 1970s, the American "mainstream" had moved so far to the right that acceptance by the Democratic Party was getting the gay movement no traction; nobody really wanted a meeting with Jimmy Carter. And the gay movement had just the character to take it further to the right: California's David Goodstein. Goodstein had long been a voice against the people he called "spoilers," meaning the weirdly dressed, angry spokesmen the media loved to feature when any gay issue was on the table. Goodstein did not play well with others. The preeminence of the National Gay Task Force (NGTF), which he did not control, was a real thorn in his side. Since he couldn't buy the Task Force, in 1976 he called an invitation-only conference of gay activists, putting them all up at a fancy hotel at his expense. When his handpicked troops were gathered, Goodstein proposed something new, the Gay Rights National Lobby (GRNL), to be located in Washington, DC, like a proper lobby, and targeted at law reform. No more perching on a desk at the Metropolitan Community Church DC office for Goodstein's group. No more costumes. Good plan, the gathering concluded. After the conference voted to establish the lobby, however, the uniquely ungrateful invitees organized it to be just the kind of radical organization Goodstein despised, with a huge, unmanageable board and all kinds of democratic accountability. In a heartbeat, Goodstein decided not to fund it.

With this inauspicious beginning, the Gay Rights National Lobby was launched. Within a couple of years it was pretty broke. But luckily for the gay revolution, one of those natural young political operatives who fuel all political movements, Steve Endean, was at loose ends. Endean, a slight winsome collegiate type, had come out of the gay-friendly precincts of the University of Minnesota to spend a couple of frustrating years trying to get some local gay civil rights law passed. In 1978 he had about given up on Minnesota possibilities and agreed to take on the defunct GRNL. Living hand to mouth in DC on donations from anonymous donors and from the brochures he put around dirty-book stores, little by agonizing little, Endean actually began to build a lobbying operation. The Task Force, which by then was in the hundred thousand dollar budget range, did not see the competition coming. After all, there had been no breach, which was the usual pattern for the gay revolution, just this Minnesota kid and some unreliable donors. But little by little the more establishment lobby began to occupy the rich soil on the right.

In 1980, Endean decided to imitate the Republican election machine and start a gay political action committee (PAC). If the gay lobby couldn't convince the existing legislators to support gay rights, maybe they should start electing people who would. After all, that's what the Republicans had just done in the 1980 election. By then Endean knew some gay millionaires other than Goodstein (whom he loathed). Together, Endean and his gay plutocrats founded the Human Rights Campaign Fund (HRC-F), a gay PAC with no mention of homosexuality in its title. And so in a decade, the gay movement went from the leather-clad SDS alums of the Gay Liberation Front to an elite club of the richest gay men in America—what San Francisco social chronicler Armistead Maupin called the "A-gays"—meatpacking heir James Hormel, the impossible David Goodstein, even a Republican, beer heir Dallas Coors. A-gays in LA had been meeting at one another's fancy homes for several years now. A handful of courageous California pols even stopped by to make speeches (and raise money). HRC-F took it national. The blockbuster black-tie gay fund-raiser was born.

The Milk Machine

As Goodstein and the others were tying the ties and setting out the champagne buckets, a very different phenomenon was developing in San Francisco's Castro District: the rise of Harvey Milk. As happens so often in America, the course of events was ultimately determined by a madman with a gun; in 1979 fellow San Francisco supervisor Dan White shot and killed Milk, the first out gay member of San Francisco's city council, the Board of Supervisors. Had Milk lived, gay politics might have transformed America for everyone. But he did not live. So we must be content with what he did achieve.

Milk was more than an elected official. He was a phenomenon. His election put a genuinely charismatic gay figure squarely in the public spotlight just as California felt the full impact of the religious attack on the new gay movement. Forty-six weeks after being elected he was also a martyr, gunned down, alongside San Francisco's liberal mayor, by a conservative, disgruntled ex-colleague. Memorialized by the premier chronicler of gay life in America, Randy Shilts, in his book *The Mayor of Castro Street,* Milk then became a martyred phenomenon. His martyrdom accelerated the process of gay political participation exponentially. "If you had given Harvey the choice of living long and thriving or being martyred to advance your cause like the suicide bombers," his friend and political ally, Carol Ruth Silver, says, "he probably would have said dying was worth it."

No one better exemplifies the transformative power of charisma—the elusive quality of outsize spiritual and rhetorical leadership—than Harvey Milk. Charisma fell out of fashion in social movement theory with the rise of economic analysis of politics in the 1960s. Thinkers tended to emphasize the mobilization of resources like Goodstein's money and changes in the cost-benefit analysis of acting, as when the Sixties fractured the self-confidence of the governing elites. But the role of the charismatic leader with a powerful relationship to his followers reemerged in the scholarship with the appearance of movements, like the gay revolution, that could not be explained by the cold-blooded calculus of economics alone. The charismatic leader fit comfortably with the emphasis of new movement theory on emotional motivations and the role of common identities in motivating people to act, and Harvey Milk was charisma incarnate.

Milk, a tall, dark-eyed New York Jew with a nose job, arrived in San Francisco in 1972 as part of the flood of gay men in the seventies, drawn by the city's long history as an open city and by the growth of the service and tourism economy. Many of them wound up in the Castro, a formerly Catholic ethnic working-class enclave somewhat removed from San Francisco's glamorous downtown. The Castro was the perfect gay colony—cheap housing, left behind as the working class fled the newly white-collar city, and a dense commercial central corridor, perfect for meeting and greeting. Always a theatrical personality, before coming to San Francisco Milk had tried on a number of roles: navy man, teacher, financial analyst, and theatrical producer. Being really smart, he was successful at most of them, so when he decided to chuck all convention and move to Castro Street, he had a little cushion. Milk, at fortysomething, was almost twice as old as the other cool gays walking down the newly colonized gay Castro neighborhood in their tight jeans. But he did bring his current lover, the perennially younger man of the moment, Scott Smith. Scotty and Harvey opened a camera store in an old Castro storefront, just to do something, not that they knew anything about cameras.

By the time Milk surfaced, historians estimate that somewhere between 20 and 25 percent of the population of San Francisco was gay. As the gay migrants flooded in, they were greeted with every imaginable inducement to register to vote. The bars were registering gay voters; the Alice B. Toklas Democratic Club was registering gay voters. As Carol Ruth Silver puts it bluntly, "Gays were the most reliable liberal voters in town."

Milk was, by all accounts, the best natural politician the gay revolution has ever produced. Before a year was up, streams of local residents were stopping into the camera store for help with potholes of every stripe and for advice on their personal lives. Never the soul of patience, Milk, the newcomer, unknown and unsupported, decided to run for supervisor. He ran on a genuinely liberal platform—protecting the neighborhoods against the increasingly rapacious San Francisco real estate developers, getting enough money to the schools, and legalizing marijuana.

The upstart candidate soon attracted the attention of the power brokers at the Alice B. Toklas Democratic Club. The cautious, reform-minded lawyers and media moguls had a somewhat more gradual plan than Milk did—cultivating liberal allies and slowly infiltrating the political process by running for tiny obscure offices. The wealthy establishment gays at Alice were comfortable with the limousine liberalism of someone like Dianne Feinstein, then president of the Board of Supervisors, and cozy with the real estate developers and the like. If someone was going to break the heterosexual barrier, it wasn't going to be a guy who still sounded like the New York upstart Harvey Milk. Milk, Jim Stokes explained to him, you can't join a church and expect your first job to be pope. Milk lost. Within two years, in alliance with the Teamsters, Milk got the gay bars to support the union boycott of Coors beer and founded the merchants association of Castro Street—and a rival Democratic club, the San Francisco Democratic Club. In 1975 he ran again and lost and ran for state office and lost.

Then Milk caught a break. All eleven supervisors had always run citywide, an arrangement that benefited the most well-funded coalition builders and the establishment interests like the downtown developers. In 1976, a coalition of more liberal forces pushed through a referendum to divide the city into geographical districts for board elections. In 1977, on his fourth try, Milk, who had always carried the Castro neighborhood, won the election to represent the new Castro district. At every stage of his political rise, Milk broadened the reach of the Milk Machine, particularly with the still robust representatives of organized labor in that longtime labor town, but also with the environmentalists, the dope smokers, and the prostitutes' union, Call Off Your Old Tired Ethics (C.O.Y.O.T.E.).

Milk's life and brief tenure mark a shift in the story of the gay revolution, particularly in California. First, because he had the nerve to run for high office as an out gay candidate, he greatly accelerated the process of gay participation in San Francisco elections. From the midseventies, the votes were there, but the Alice folks were too timid to take advantage of the change, and their old-fashioned culture—hillside mansions, suited professionals—would never have made a mass movement out of the blue-jeaned throngs cruising the Castro. It took a leader like Milk—old enough to be serious but hip enough to be relevant—to mobilize the electoral power of the new San Francisco gays. His club, renamed the Harvey Milk Democratic Club after his assassination, claims to be the largest Democratic club in California.

Second, because Milk was in office, the gay community had the advantage of his charisma, energy, and political skills when California faced its first challenge from the surging forces of the newly energized religious right. It was a scary moment. In an unrelated development in 1978, President Jimmy Carter's Internal Revenue Service suggested stringent regulation of the formerly tax-sheltered all-white private schools, affectionately known as "segregation academies," that had sprung up after the Supreme Court ordered the desegregation of public schools in 1954. The religious right sprang into political action almost overnight. Once on the political scene, the believers found many things not to like: abortion, the curtailment of school prayer, and the handful of gay antidiscrimination ordinances passed in liberal cities or college towns where the Task Force had gotten a little traction. The right found its antigay voice in the person of singer and evangelical Anita Bryant, who started an organization called, effectively, Save Our Children. In short order, Dade County, Florida; Wichita, Kansas; and the college town of Eugene, Oregon, all repealed their gay civil rights laws. The morally grounded gay revolution met another movement of moral certainty and the battle was joined.

California state senator John Briggs thought an antigay initiative would be just the thing to advance his gubernatorial ambitions. Since there was no gay civil rights act for him to repeal in California yet, he decided to go on the offensive and get the gay teachers tossed out of their jobs. Had Briggs succeeded in California, the gay revolution, already staggering under the force of the recent religious revival, might have been set back for decades. But he did not. The successful fight against the Briggs initiative had the proverbial parentage. Former antiwar activist and just-out political guru David Mixner and David Goodstein ran a perfect conventional fight, involving a heterosexual campaign manager and the invaluable endorsement of ex-governor Ronald Reagan. But Milk gets a big piece of the credit, too. He deployed his now signature volunteer-based door-to-door precinct machine in San Francisco, arguing that nothing would be worse than losing a gay fight in San Francisco. The precinct-working Milk strategy set the pattern for any successful resistance to popular antigay initiatives from then on. It might not guarantee success, but, as gay activists would learn and relearn, they cannot win without it.

Milk's death, like his life, too, changed the story of the gay revolution. The night the jury let Dan White off for Milk's murder with a trivial sentence for manslaughter, the gay community erupted in a bloody and violent march, culminating in a siege of San Francisco City Hall and hand-to-hand combat between the police and gays swinging tree branches and parking meters. By daybreak there was not an intact pane of glass in the symbol of civic governance. Smoldering police cars lined the streets. "Avenge Harvey Milk," the signs said. Once again, almost exactly ten years after Stonewall, gay citizens had to resort to violence to stake their claim to the social contract. If the state did not protect their lives by punishing their killers, they would take revenge themselves. No state can survive if a significant segment of its population does not agree to yield private vengeance to the promise of public justice. It's the oldest political lesson in the book.

But unlike the angry Stonewall rioters, San Francisco gays were registered to vote. They turned their political wrath on the politicians they held responsible for White's light sentence: they retired the district attorney who unsuccessfully prosecuted White as well as every member of the Board of Supervisors except Milk's gay successor, Harry Britt. The liberal establishment had to pass the first big-city gay civil rights law in the country. Thereafter gay candidates and balanced tickets were synonymous in the city by the bay.

In death, Milk became an icon. Randy Shilts chronicled his life. He was immediately the subject of a documentary. Eventually he ascended to the realm of the Hollywood biopic with *Milk*. Milk was so charismatic and hardworking and clever and energetic, it is not a stretch to imagine him as the mayor of San Francisco, and thus the first gay mayor of any American city, large or small. Had Milk lived, the genuinely populist coalition he started could have transformed that city and been a model for a revived liberal politics everywhere.

Instead, the Alice Club's reform-minded gradualists, funded and to some extent dominated by the wealthy David Goodstein, recaptured control of the important San Francisco branch of the gay movement. The substance of their agenda moved to the right—they just wanted to be included in the gentrification of San Francisco instead of being allied with labor and other marginal groups to make the process more just for everyone. As America moved to the right and the seventies drew to a close, gays were not idealistic insurgents, but part of the California political establishment. Maybe it's just as well. They were soon going to need every weapon they had.

6

Dying for the Movement: The Terrible Political Payoff of AIDS

Before

When Steve Endean arrived in Washington in 1978 to run the Gay Rights National Lobby, the telephone was disconnected for nonpayment. To get the gay PAC, then called the Human Rights Campaign Fund (HRC-F), going in 1980, he had to send a gorgeous young man to entice the semicloseted Tennessee Williams to sign the group's first fund-raising letter and, even then, the gay politicos had to wait until Williams was mostly in the bag to get his assent. Chicago's Howard Brown Clinic for gay men shared a room over a grocery store with a coffee bar. The only overtly gay-themed play to have run on Broadway was the historical drama *Bent*, about the Nazi persecution of homosexuals in Germany.

Roscoe Willett Browne, Robby Browne's favorite brother, was running Pan Am's Asian operations out of Sydney and living with his lover, Craig. Closeted lawyer Dan Bradley, head of the US Legal Services Corporation, was praying he would not get caught at the bathhouses he frequented. Randy Shilts had just become the first openly gay reporter at any major American newspaper, the *San Francisco Chronicle*. Harvey Milk's right-hand man, activist Cleve Jones, was working for California state assemblyman Art Agnos and making lifelong friends out of the men he casually picked up for sex on the street and in the baths.

After

In 1996, the gay lobby Human Rights Campaign (HRC) had a full-time staff of sixty, a budget of $10 million, and 175,000 members. The president of the United States spoke at its 1997 fund-raising dinner. The AIDS service organization Gay Men's Health Crisis (GMHC) was spending $30 million annually. Tony Kushner's play *Angels in America* had run on Broadway for two years, winning both the Tony Award and the Pulitzer Prize. Cold sober and with no boys in the picture, legendary actress Elizabeth Taylor had raised hundreds of millions of dollars to cure a disease heavily affecting gay men.

But Roscoe Browne's mother had to pay the funeral home extra to lay his infected corpse in the family plot in Louisville. Dan Bradley was buried in the blue cap he thought made his eyes look blue. Randy Shilts dictated the end of his last book from his deathbed. Cleve Jones was lying alone on the bathroom floor awaiting the inevitable.

A Civil Rights Movement Unlike Any Other

AIDS was the making of the gay revolution. Before the epidemic struck, the gay movement had settled into a predictable pattern. The charismatic period after Stonewall gave way to newborn bureaucracies. The blandly named National Gay Task Force (NGTF) was taking model civil rights ordinances from one liberal city to the next. The Human Rights Campaign Fund, without even the word "gay" in its name, was raising money from millionaires for its liberal political allies, some of whom would agree to have their picture taken with gay leaders only if the PAC promised not to release it until after their election.

True, the liberation period since Stonewall had thrown up a robust cornucopia of private pleasures. The gay Metropolitan Community Church was growing exponentially and so were the bathhouses. But the robust civic sector was not reflected in a similarly robust political movement. Unlike the other major civil rights movements, the gay movement was still saddled with free riders, people passing as heterosexual while the out activists labored to make the world a better place. Like the racial and feminist movements before it, the gay movement was struggling with a powerful backlash, fueled in this case by the revival of the religious right. By 1980, the racial civil rights movement had stopped well short of achieving anything like the radical economic measures that would have changed the prospects of most black Americans. The black communities of the separatist movement were simply not important enough to white Americans to generate any serious political capital and the availability of integration siphoned off the most economically viable movement beneficiaries. While opening up formal opportunities for women in the workforce, the feminist movement had similarly left the structure of the reproductive family intact, marooning its newly employed female workers in the iron grip of the second shift. While the newer mainstream gay organizations were slowly making progress in their conventional ways, the arc of the movement was by no means clear. Then AIDS struck.

AIDS was just the type of emergency public health institutions exist to address—a fatal, infectious disease. And yet, as the protesters would chant when they finally acted up, many years later, "We die/they do nothing." For several crucial years the government of the United States did nothing. Most states and cities did nothing. Often their own families did nothing. The existing institutions of the gay movement did next to nothing. The loudest voices in the community urged them to do nothing. Twentieth-century history was full of examples of people who, when threatened, did nothing, and they might have done the same. Instead they created the most successful social movement of the contentious American twentieth century. They came out. Where their families and their state failed them, they created new institutions to replace the family and the state. When their shadow society still wasn't powerful enough to stop the epidemic, they created yet more institutions, this time, to capture the state itself. What had started when a gay Stonewall patron threw a brick at a policeman in 1969 ended with gay activists leveraging the government to spend billions looking for a cure for a fatal, heavily homosexual, disease.

Getting the government of the United States to help them was a victory that no other movement in modern American history has ever achieved. The racial civil rights movement desegregated the schools and the polling booths. But it never got government resources that would have enabled African Americans to escape the historical legacy of poverty. After the civil rights movement, poor blacks and rich whites alike are free to go to the schools they can afford. The feminist movement decriminalized abortion, the procedure that guarantees women's control of their reproductive fates. But they never got poor women access to the resources of public health for this essential civil right. After the feminist movement, poor women and rich men alike are free in America to pay for their abortions.

Only the gay-driven AIDS movement captured the resources of the government for their needs. The AIDS movement was an inspiration for every progressive social movement of the next quarter century, including—after the worst of the epidemic was over for the gay community—the revival of the gay movement itself.

They Die/the Government Does Nothing

Dr. Alvin Friedman-Kien's tasteful waiting room did not look like the boat dock on the river Styx in 1981. And he didn't think he was in for a trip to the underworld either. The purple spots on his young patient's nose were weird, but the doctor was not immediately alarmed. When the biopsy came back Kaposi's sarcoma, he thought that the lab must have mixed up the test reports. Kaposi's sarcoma was a disease of old Jewish men. The lesions showed up on their legs. In all his years practicing dermatology, Friedman-Kien had never seen them on someone's face. Then he saw a second case. Both patients were gay men.

"So I began to have a creepy feeling," Friedman-Kien says. The doctor, a lively, bald and bearded opera-loving guy, had entered dermatology because he didn't like seeing people die, but he had trained as a virologist and studied epidemiology. He started asking around. Gay doctors in the New York area turned up five KS cases in a week. Friedman-Kien called a friend, gay dermatologist Marcus Conant, in San Francisco. Conant had not seen the cases, but he was going to a dermatology meeting that Friday and would ask. Conant elicited two cases in San Francisco. One of them was dying. When Conant accrued another six cases and the New York docs had twenty, Friedman-Kien called the Centers for Disease Control (CDC).

The CDC doctor told his colleagues that there was a "kooky dermatologist in New York who thinks he's got an epidemic of guess what—nobody in this room will have heard of it—Kaposi's sarcoma." It took them four weeks to send somebody to New York.

At almost exactly the same moment Friedman-Kien saw the purple spots, UCLA immunologist Michael Gottlieb saw his first patient with rampant pneumonia, a kind of lung infection normally seen only in cancer or transplant patients with radically suppressed immune systems. On June 5, 1981, the little-known CDC publication, *Weekly Mortality and Morbidity Report*, reported five cases of *Pneumocystis carinii* pneumonia (PCP) among previously healthy "homosexual" young men in Los Angeles, "probably acquired through sexual contact." Four weeks later, the mortality and morbidity report announced twenty-six cases of Kaposi's sarcoma among gay males.

The United States CDC is the world's emergency squad. It has a proud legacy: when an almost entirely fatal, rampant fever broke out near the Ebola River in Zaire in 1976, the CDC detailed its hot young virologist Don Francis to the World Health Organization to deal with it. Three months later, Red Cross volunteers covered from head to toe were digging graves in open violation of local burial customs that had spread the virus, the infected were quarantined, and the potential victims tracked and followed. The Ebola epidemic came to a screeching halt. When the reports of the gay disease started coming in to the CDC, Francis was working on sexually transmitted hepatitis in gay men. He thought the outbreak might be a virus and he knew immediately that a crisis was at hand. "Normally, CDC notices something happening," he says, "and CDC comes and raises the disease to a level where something has to be done with it." Condoms were good against hepatitis, he thought; the CDC should start containing the disease by warning people to use them now. Not this time: "The White House [the CDC is run by the cabinet-level Health and Human Services Department] told us to 'look pretty and do as little as we can.'" An illness that at first threatened only gay men was the last issue the conservative Reagan administration wanted to spend government time or money to address.

Even in the gay center of New York, Mayor Ed Koch had little time for AIDS. Certainly the disease was not as important as saving the city from bankruptcy, which he believed he had been elected to do. "I did whatever my medical advisers asked," Koch contends. His gay health coordinator, Roger Enlow, notoriously pronounced in 1982 that his job did not include telling gay people how to have sex, so no one in the city would consider closing the bathhouses or any program of public education. New York spent no direct money specifically on AIDS services or education, and there was no increase in general New York social or medical services either.

The CDC's parent agency, the research-oriented National Institutes of Health (NIH), also did as little as it could. When the epidemiologists at the CDC tried to track the disease, using ordinary methods like patient questionnaires, they could get neither the NIH nor the administration to give them money to tabulate the responses. In September 1981, the NIH did convene a small Kaposi's sarcoma conference. The contemporaneous "summary of the workshop" reflects an eerie passivity typical of the government's recalcitrant response in those crucial early years. The government recommended measures like "following patients closely" and hoping for "a revival of the immune system." When the CDC docs presented the cluster of diseases to the researchers at the NIH, the research doctors, including the eminent virologist Robert Gallo, who later claimed credit for discovering the virus, were not interested. "For years," Friedman-Kien says, "some of the best immunologists at NYU weren't interested at all because the NIH gave us no money. The NIH will deny it but they were not interested in a disease that affects gay men."

Seeing that the research scientists weren't going to start looking for the virus he suspected was causing the disease, Francis tried unsuccessfully to get money to look for the virus himself. Almost two years after the CDC docs started hounding the NIH, the august Dr. Gallo put some serious resources into looking for the virus in the tissues of the now numerous fatally infected patients. (He failed; the Institut Pasteur in France ultimately cultured the virus, though they got the idea of what to look for from Gallo.)

Counsel to the congressional Committee on Health Tim Westmoreland was on a routine visit to the CDC in Atlanta in 1981 when he heard about some cases of an odd disease in committee chair Henry Waxman's Los Angeles district. One of only two out gay staffers in Congress, Westmoreland, a cheerful and charming guy with a handlebar mustache and a Yale law degree, was an expert on health law. Westmoreland knew from the day the Reagan administration came in and started slashing the budget for public health that there would be a health crisis. He had been betting that cutbacks on child vaccinations would create an emergency, but the emergency he feared turned out to be AIDS.

When Representative Waxman called a hearing on the new disease the following year, he learned that the CDC had had to steal and cadge money from other research to try to do the epidemiology. Waxman did what he could: at the first hearing he sarcastically announced that "the administration would manage to find the money if the disease particularly affected tennis players." The committee appropriated two million dollars where the NIH had only asked for one. And so it went. At each hearing, the oversight committee asked the witnesses from the executive branch to tell the Congress what they were doing for AIDS, and the witnesses tried to make it look as good as possible for their agency. When the congressmen asked the same witnesses what in their professional and technical expertise needed to be done, sometimes, the witnesses would tell them what they really needed.

The Reagan administration held two meetings on the burgeoning disease in 1983. The first was an informational meeting at Health and Human Services (HHS) between Judi Buckalew, special assistant for public liaison, and two representatives of the Gay Task Force. The second involved public liaison with representatives of the Moral Majority and the Conservative Caucus alone. Two years were to pass before there was a third. Fifteen hundred people died from AIDS in 1983.

They Die/They Do Nothing

Steve Endean, who was, in 1981 and 1982, leading the only full-time gay lobby, was a legend. His colleague at the gay lobby, Vic Basile, recalls that when they traveled around the country raising money together in the eighties, Endean was completely unavailable after ten o'clock at night, because he was in the parks every night in every city pursuing sex partners. Endean was not the only one in denial. For a lot of average, fun-loving gay men, gay liberation and sexual liberation were the same thing. The last thing they wanted was to change their behaviors.

Big mistake, said Dr. Alvin Friedman-Kien. "If I were a gay man," he told his friend and patient, writer Larry Kramer, "I'd stop having sex." Kramer was the perfect recipient for this advice. He had just published the novel *Faggots*, a scathing condemnation of the promiscuous gay male community of the post-Stonewall seventies. One August day in 1981, Friedman-Kien's phone rang. Would the doctor come to Kramer's apartment and speak to some gay men? Great, Friedman-Kien thought, these guys have to know what's going on, most people are just acting as if there's nothing happening. They're losing their friends; they're dying.

Friedman-Kien told Kramer's group that the culprit was a virus, but it would be a few years until the scientists could prove it. "You're not going to change your behavior until it's official," he speculated despairingly. They had no one to help them but themselves, he told them. Stop having sex. Or use a condom at least.

Many of the men who stayed to help were outraged at what the doctor had said.

Some, like Paul Popham, the closeted businessman whose Fire Island housemates kept dying, were persuaded or frightened enough to stay at Kramer's apartment and try to figure out what to do. On Labor Day weekend, the group set up a table on the dock where all the boats came to Fire Island and tried to collect money for Friedman-Kien to do his research. People shunned the group. The only thing they were angry about was being told they had to give up the sexual freedom they had fought so long to get.

For a long time, most of the official and visible gay community fought changing their sexual practices. When legendary San Francisco activist Cleve Jones was reported to be advocating closing the bathhouses, people spat on him in the Castro. When Kramer's group, then called Gay Men's Health Crisis, had its first fund-raiser in 1982, they had a disco group close its set with a number about having only one sex partner at a time. The men in the audience quickly formed a gay men's chorus to sing back. "NO WAY," they caroled merrily. "NO WAY."

With no authoritative voices from their own community, gay men were left to their own devices. When Roscoe Browne told his brother that he'd just pop over to St. Marks baths after running the New York City Marathon in 1984, Robby tried. "You're going to go to the bathhouse," he said. "Don't you think you might get AIDS in the bathhouse?" And Roscoe said, "Well, I don't know." "I think maybe it's a possibility," Robby replied. And Roscoe said, "You don't know how I feel in a bathhouse." So Robby said, "Okay. I don't know how you feel there."

For fifteen years, curtailing sexual behavior was the first, last, and only way to stop the fatal disease. Still, from a movement standpoint, the demand to curtail sexual activity was profoundly offensive. First, as a matter of simple equality, who else would be asked to give up sex as a solution to venereal disease? After all, heterosexuals had been getting syphilis since

Columbus discovered America. No one suggested that straight people rein in their sex lives. Given the gay right to gay sex, the only legitimate answer was to get the scientists working and get some drugs.

Second, what would the gay revolution have achieved if gay men had to give up their unrestricted sex practices? In a survey, the San Francisco AIDS Foundation found an astonishing 69 percent of men who'd had three partners in the prior month agreed with the statement that "being gay *means* doing what I want sexually." In their piece in Boston's self-consciously left *Gay Community News,* activists Michael Lynch and Bill Lewis made the political connection clear. The gay male community, they asserted, is "knit together" by the "promiscuous fabric, that, in its democratic anarchism, defies state regulation of our sexuality." Even the leading proponents of safe-sex practices, Michael Callen and Richard Berkowitz, conceded in 1982 that "ultimately, *it may be more important to let people die in pursuit of their own happiness than to limit personal freedom* by regulating risk." These arguments put a very different frame around the refusal to limit sex. Maybe the guys didn't, as Kramer accused them, "love their asses and dicks so much" they wanted to die for them. Maybe, like martyrs since biblical times, they were willing to die for the "fabric" of their movement.

The personal-freedom advocates should have been alarmed when they saw who was on their side—and who was not. Time and again, as the preventative role of condoms became scientifically incontrovertible, the religious conservatives in the White House—Gary Bauer, William Bennett, and Carl Anderson—stopped the public-health agencies from informing the homosexual public about the dangers and how to avoid them. In their analysis some years later, sociologists Charles Perrow and Mauro Guillén concluded that substantial numbers of nongay Americans prefer to let people die of AIDS to discourage homosexual sex than teach them how to have limited, but safe homosexual sex.

Doctors, who are professionally unenthusiastic about martyrdom, went crazy over the suggestion that gay liberation required unprotected sex. Gay or not gay, the professional morality of medicine completely obscured all other considerations, even in the lives of people sympathetic with or personally liberated by gay liberation. Powerful head of the National Institute for Allergy and Infectious Diseases Anthony Fauci told people to use condoms. Friedman-Kien said it to Kramer's guests in 1981. Dr. Marc Conant was damned for saying it. Epidemiologist Dr. Don Francis aborted his career at the Centers for Disease Control in 1985 because the Reagan HHS wouldn't let him add his voice to the chorus. He did not want to spend his life with blood on his hands.

They Die/Their Own Groups Do Next to Nothing

Congressional staffer Tim Westmoreland rarely found himself in the position of educating interest groups in how to lobby him, but that's what he found himself doing in the early years of the AIDS epidemic. He had to be on the phone with gay organizers almost from day one. They didn't even know how the government worked, he remembers.

The ignorance and recalcitrance of the existing gay organizations to recognize the emergency before them must have taxed even Westmoreland's good nature. The Gay Rights National Lobby's Steve Endean says in his memoir, "Most of us still didn't have a clue as to the magnitude of the health crisis to come. A worst case, we thought at the time, was that it might be similar to Legionnaire's Disease . . . so initially we resisted dropping the rest of our agenda to focus full attention on AIDS." "To make matters worse," he continues, "GRNL was a very young lobby without either the number or quality of staff that would be necessary to meet the challenge."

When Lambda Legal started a regular conference call among lawyers around the country in 1983 it was dubbed the "sodomy call" by participants, reflecting the high priority that important institution of the gay revolution gave to challenging the criminal sodomy laws. There was no "AIDS call," although Lambda did find its docket increasingly filled with AIDS-related calls for help.

AIDS was a triple threat: as a disease it required the caring services conventionally found in the biological family; as a sexual disease it threatened the bedrock norm of privacy-based sexual freedom; and as an epidemic it could only be resisted with all the resources of a paternalistic state. Public health was a living manifestation of two principles of the liberal state: people living together needed a government authority to stop them from killing each other, in this case, with their germs, and the institution of collective self-government exists so that citizens can leverage their communities to help them. But there was no place in an epidemic for the third principle—an arena of life where the individual must be left alone. No response could both preserve sexual freedom from the state and also leverage the resources only the state possesses. No wonder the existing institutions were paralyzed.

It was a lesbian, National Gay Task Force executive director Ginny Apuzzo, who, among the organization officials, first recognized the magnitude of the peril. Gay lobbyist Endean remembers Apuzzo castigating him for denial of the disease in light of his "active sex life." Apuzzo started the first direct-action AIDS group, the short-lived AIDS Action, in 1983, and hired Washington activist Jeff Levi to lobby for action on AIDS.

Apuzzo is but the most visible of the legions of lesbian—and heterosexual—women who stepped up to the crisis, from San Francisco dermatologist Marc Conant's nurse, leaving her cushy job to run the AIDS clinic, to the garment-business heiress Leslie Fay Pomerantz, the oldest surviving volunteer at Gay Men's Health Crisis. The NGTF had women leaders early on. But for the decade from the time the women took their dance money out of the Gay Liberation Front (GLF) cash box to the epidemic, most lesbians and gay men followed very different political paths. Women took on the cause of AIDS for many reasons—because the homophobia it triggered threatened them as well, because their friends were dying, and because they really are just good human beings. As Apuzzo's leadership symbolizes, AIDS was the remaking of the alliance. Despite many rocky moments, it has lasted to this day.

Apuzzo's lobbyist Jeff Levi recognized that he was asking the gay movement to make a bedrock change. As he told journalist John-Manuel Andriote,

"The traditional gay and lesbian agenda is [for government] to stay out of our lives. Now we're saying we need affirmative programs that will save our lives and that we need a much closer relationship with the government." As Apuzzo, the rare activist known for her careful utterances, put it, "Getting people to change their perspective was like trying to turn a ship around."

New York: AIDS Without Politics

If the task is turning a ship around, there's no tugboat like Larry Kramer. If the existing organizations weren't going to step up, he'd start his own. The first AIDS-specific group, New York's Gay Men's Health Crisis, was born when the men gathered in Kramer's living room in 1981 to hear from Alvin Friedman-Kien. Gay men and lesbian women have been meeting in one another's living rooms since people began building apartments in the nineteenth century. From the earliest years of the gay urban migration to the outbreak of the disease, gay men generated shared assumptions, norms, values, and ideas about a good life. That's what people do when they have no political power. The living-room culture produced everything from enormous, elaborate drag balls in the 1920s to the Gay Activist Alliance (GAA) zappers who ended John Lindsay's presidential ambitions in 1972. Cleve Jones remembers, "When I was a little kid and came to San Francisco, the old queens took me in, sheltered me, taught me to watch out for the cops, learn the secret language, how to forage for food, how to make fire."

The men who started GMHC had been shaped by their experience of participating in the gay community. Even the closeted ones, though they didn't march, had made a community, partially in isolation (Fire "Island"), which inherited the long tradition of gay men and lesbians creating institutions the gay population needed. GMHC turned out to be a throwback to life in Gay New York. They turned in on themselves, and raised money for their own cure. They created an alternative information network outside the normal channels of mass media and medical systems. They re-created the ancestral family from which so many of them had fled or been flung, walking each others' dogs and visiting the sick. Constituted as they were by their closeted gay life, GMHC must have felt comfortably familiar.

It made Kramer, who had originally called them together, nuts. He wrote furious hortative essays in the *New York Native* ("1,112 and Counting") and plays like 1985's *The Normal Heart*, exhorting the gay men to make the government do the work of public health and social support. As Kramer continued to pound on them, the founders of GMHC threw him out and handed the reins over to Rodger McFarlane, the large, athletic former hospital administrator, who became its first paid staff member. Born and raised on a chicken farm in Mobile, Alabama, McFarlane joined GMHC within months of its founding, and essentially started all its programs. The original GMHC hotline rang in McFarlane's apartment. McFarlane set up the volunteer-driven organization with an elaborate bureaucracy, which probably helped it survive when other institutions faltered. McFarlane not only took care of generations of his own friends; he tenderly ministered to his own baby brother who tragically died of AIDS in 2002. Care was Rodger McFarlane's middle name.

By 1985, GMHC had volunteers answering the hotline, sometimes at the rate of a hundred calls a day. What funeral homes would take AIDS victims? Where could they rent a wheelchair? The ranks of volunteers swelled daily. Real-estate heiress and socialite Joan Tisch stuffed envelopes. The organization bought a building, the Tisch Building. GMHC's first fund-raiser set a record for gay fund-raising. Although GMHC never became a civil rights movement, the group framed the threat to fit its communal norms and produced social institutions to meet the threat as they had framed it.

In the early years of AIDS, the gay community had none of the psychological or political resources to make a contentious social movement. Gays did not feel aggrieved, because they didn't know how much the state was at fault. The illness, whatever it was, was seen not as the product of a political decision by an oppressive government, but both as a fact of nature, which it is, and as a sexually transmitted disease, which spread as the result of individuals' personal behavior. Since the responsible public officials outside of California uniformly resisted addressing the epidemic, gays saw no chink in the establishment armor that might allow them to get some traction. The Reagan administration, the Centers for Disease Control, and the New York City health commissioner were all in agreement: ignore AIDS.

GMHC and the rest of the gay-care revolution were heroic. In the long run, even the most heroic alternative universe of care was not going to solve the problem. Eventually the New York activists were going to have to turn to politics. Meanwhile, however, the gay-care revolution transformed the gay revolution. First, in order to care, the closeted gay population, infected or not, had to come out. GMHC brought wealthy and successful gay men like money manager Jim Pepper out. Pepper had been leading a gay social life for years, but, he says, "Everyone at work just socialized separately. I felt no need to share my sexual orientation." Pepper was not sick. But with AIDS he saw caring for those who were as his moral obligation. When Pepper decided to go on the GMHC board, he had to ask permission of the partners; board work took time away from business. He told his partners he would resign from the board of his college to make up for his new commitment. And they said, incredulously, you want to join the board of a gay men's health crisis and drop your board position at your college? And Pepper said, "Yes, I have a moral obligation." And they said, "Well, maybe you can get them to change the name." Pepper said he didn't think Gay Men's Health Crisis was going to change the name. But there was unanimous approval anyway.

The incident speaks volumes. Before GMHC Pepper's boutique money-management firm had, unspoken, confined him to a kind of closet at work. In forcing rich, successful gay men out in their powerful circles, AIDS challenged the myriad hidden institutions of society. In 1986, Pepper agreed to sponsor the first New York AIDS walk, a GMHC fund-raiser. Unbeknownst to him, the walk and its sponsors were promoted on posters all over the New York subways. So Pepper came the rest of the way out on the New York subway.

Pepper's "moral obligation" didn't arise in a vacuum. For at least a century gays had been constructing elaborate networks of sex, family, and friendship that existed in parallel with their closeted lives at work or in their families of origin. They were embedded in the AIDS community and had to help. In order to help, they had to come out. Outing oneself is powerful and perpetual. Once someone was out to his family and his workplace there was no going back; his fate was then inextricably tied to the fate of the movement.

In addition to coming out, they created institutions that met the deep moral standards of the larger society: love thy neighbor as thyself or, in secular terms, act in a way you'd want everyone to act. For a long time, the larger society had conflated morality with sexual convention and used the weapon of "sexual morality" to beat up on gay people. When the thin morality of sexual convention was posed against the deep morality of the gay IV-changing, shit-wiping, food-delivering, dog-walking care revolution, the moral calculus shifted, silently, to the gay side. The moral revolution was situated in the most contested arena of gay politics: family values. Coming out and caring was a virtuous cycle. As gay activists cared, they grew in their moral self-regard. As sociologist Deborah Gould describes it, pride in their caring community produced a "heroic narrative of early AIDS activism." Seeing themselves as morally upright caregivers, gay activists were poised to rise up.

San Francisco: AIDS with Politics

New York is always the center ring, but it's not always the model. From the beginning the San Francisco gay community responded to the epidemic with contentious politics: revolution, not just care revolution. But San Francisco was always different.

Don Francis's longtime friend and colleague Marc Conant calls Francis "about the most heterosexual person that exists on this earth." But when Francis fled the CDC in 1985, the very hetero Dr. Francis joined the flood of men who had been migrating to San Francisco, the "gay refugee camp," as Carl Wittman called it in 1969, from "Amerika." He got himself deployed to the AIDS public-health empire Marc Conant had built, courtesy of the city of San Francisco and the state of California.

By the late seventies, around one-fifth of the city's 335,000 registered voters were gay. Many powerful gays in San Francisco were already out. Thanks in part to Harvey Milk, San Francisco gays were concentrated, organized, and allied with powerful nongay political players. San Francisco's gay men were not left to their own devices to counsel one another about how to avoid the fatal, sexually transmitted disease. When Alvin Friedman-Kien first phoned in 1981, Conant, who had been a volunteer in the Haight-Ashbury VD Clinic for years, had the improbable combination of experience and training that allowed him in his own words "to become hysterical almost immediately." Every new sexually transmitted disease that could spread, he had observed, spread like wildfire in the gay population.

By 1982, Conant's San Francisco AIDS Foundation already had a big chunk of a half million dollar AIDS grant from the city of San Francisco. When, a year later, the CDC surveyed AIDS prevention in nine American cities, only San Francisco had the public-private collaboration with any chance of succeeding in educating about prevention.

Conant knew where the money was. When the NIH, which had not even started looking for research proposals, turned down the first round of proposals from the eminent scientists from the California medical centers, Conant went to his man on the city council, Harry Britt, the gay San Francisco supervisor who succeeded Harvey Milk, and a friend, lesbian activist Carole Migden. The gay activists called San Francisco's representative in the statehouse, California assembly speaker Willie Brown.

The first year, California provided the doctors with $3 million. In ten years, almost $100 million flowed to AIDS research and treatment from the state of California. Don Francis came and did what he could. But Conant and Francis both knew that California could only mount a holding action. Any real solution had to come from the feds. California couldn't do it alone. What was to be done?

7

ACT UP: Five Years That Shook the World

When the curtain rose on Larry Kramer's AIDS play, *The Normal Heart*, in 1985, the audience saw a wall of names. Each person named had died of AIDS. "We're being treated like shit," Ned Weeks, the Kramer character, screams, "and we're allowing it. And until we force them to treat us otherwise, we get exactly what we deserve!" Social-movement thinkers would have told Kramer/Weeks to save his breath. AIDS was mysterious, and people were in denial. Where would their critical consciousness come from? Governments were killing by inattention, their responsibility for the spread of the terrible illness largely invisible. Act up? Who was going to act up? And who would they act up against?

Suddenly conditions changed. In 1985, the United States Patent Office issued a patent for a test to detect the AIDS virus in the human bloodstream. Any American in any stage of denial could find out if the illness had infected him. Up until this point, there was no way to know if a person was infected. And even in 1985, it was not yet clear how many months or years would pass before symptoms of the disease would appear, so even seemingly healthy people could be infected and spread the disease unknowingly. Then, countless gay men learned that their life expectancy had just been reduced to a handful of years. Sexual promiscuity without precautions now carried the risk of suicide for those who were not HIV-positive or homicide for those who were. AIDS was no longer mysterious, and no one could rationally be in denial.

In 1986, the federal government took affirmative action against gay people. In the long-awaited federal challenge to the criminal sodomy laws, the Supreme Court of the United States ruled in *Bowers v. Hardwick* that gays and lesbians were immoral actors, unworthy of the protections of the United States Constitution. For them alone, there was no privacy principle in the liberal state. In more than half the American states, they were committing a crime every time they had sex. Any other conclusion, Justice Byron White wrote for the court, would be "facetious." In the face of this decision, no one could say that the government's inattention to AIDS was innocuous.

Piled on top of five years of living in a society perfectly willing to let them die, the Supreme Court decision radicalized the gay movement. Gay people had come out. They had re-created the caring family. And they were still not citizens. If they were going to do something to save their own lives, they needed power and they had to act collectively to get it. The AIDS Coalition to Unleash Power (ACT UP) was born.

Out Gay People Were the Tinder

Thirty-nine-year-old Victor Bender, privileged son of a family of Jewish doctors, watched his doctor shut the hospital room door behind him.

"I have bad news," the physician said.

Once Bender's spots turned purple in 1985, he couldn't protect his midwestern sister from knowing he was gay. His sexual orientation made her uncomfortable in her heartland town, but in his world, the time for discretion was over.

Coming out is the central element of the gay revolution. There's an old gay thought experiment from way before AIDS. What if every gay person woke up one morning and found he had turned green? No more closet, the exercise concludes, and the gay revolution is accomplished. The purple lesions of Kaposi's sarcoma made the green thought experiment a horrible reality. As time went by, the spots came out, and the society learned that everyone from Rock Hudson to Joseph McCarthy's right-hand man, Roy Cohn, was gay. In 1982, Dan Bradley, head of the Legal Services Corporation, became the highest-ranking federal official to come out. By 1985 his HIV infection was public information. Time and again during the crucial years to follow, FODs (Friends of Dan), like Senator Lowell Weicker's wife, Claudia, and First Lady Hillary Rodham Clinton, made important decisions to fight AIDS and help the gay revolution along.

Social movements are almost always preceded by changes in the background conditions. When the cultural changes called "the Sixties" changed the background norms of open gender identity, Stonewall ensued. For the gay revolution, part of what brought change was the technology of the blood test for AIDS. Before the test, AIDS victims like Victor Bender were often at death's door when they found out they were sick and came out. They had little time to act politically or in any other way. After the test, they could learn they were infected long before they even felt sick.

As the illness and the technology recruited newly outed troops for the movement, they had a general just waiting to lead them. He'd been waiting for a long time. In 1983 the CDC reported AIDS deaths of "1,112 and Counting," and Larry Kramer's article of the same name appeared almost immediately in the gay newspaper, the *New York Native*. "1,112 and Counting" was reprinted in practically every gay newspaper in America. Like Carl Wittman's "Gay Manifesto" just before Stonewall and "Woman Identified Woman" right after, "1,112 and Counting" was one of those inspired documents that both captured and transformed the movement.

By 1983, Kramer knew that the only way this epidemic was going to be stopped was through the power of the United States government. In order to command its attention, gay people had to constitute themselves into a political movement. It would have been nice to get a few thousand dollars from the revelers at Fire Island to help Alvin Friedman-Kien look for a virus, but the Centers for Disease Control (CDC) needed two hundred thousand dollars just to rewrite their questionnaire: "The country, President Reagan, and the National Institutes of Health, [and] Congress," Kramer wrote in "1,112 and Counting" are "the most important ears of all." Even his attack on Mayor Koch, who had been eerily silent as the epidemic raged in his city, concludes with the assertion that if Koch had spoken up, the national administration would have had to listen.

Although demanding an extraordinary response from the government, Kramer invoked very conventional activism. You are victims, he told the reader, this is a civil rights movement, come out and push back, using the techniques of direct action. By 1983, Kramer had gathered a new group from the activists he once scorned—the Gay and Lesbian Task Force, Lambda, and the rest. He hoped they wouldn't have to conduct sit-ins or tie up traffic, he said, but, just in case, his new group, the AIDS network, had been taking lessons from an old-time aide to Martin Luther King.

Kramer was not alone. Ginny Apuzzo, the prescient and gifted lesbian head of the Task Force, was trying to, in her words, turn her ship around. Kramer's and Apuzzo's first try at mobilizing the anger, what he called the AIDS Network, failed in 1983. But the memo, like the crowd of newly out gays and lesbians, was everywhere, like tinder, waiting for the spark.

Social Change Was in the Air

All the elements for social movement were present. By the end of 1986, people didn't see the disease as their fault so much. They knew that even if they had limited themselves to one partner, as the GMHC chorus warbled, many had still been exposed to AIDS. Warnings about what they had to do had been too slow or too ambiguous to save them. As Victor Bender said, "They said limit your partners, not have no partners." Even if they adopted the strict and explicit safe-sex guidelines that people like Callen and Berkowitz had developed, it was often too late to save them. So when the test brought bad news, the mortal danger seemed less a matter of something they had done and more a medical condition that the official health authorities were not heeding fast enough.

And they had hope, which always makes for a dangerous combination. Once the basic science identified the retrovirus that caused AIDS and, thanks to Congress, after five long years, a reasonable amount of money started to flow from the National Institutes of Health (NIH) to researchers, talk of possible treatments increased exponentially. There was AZT, an old failed cancer treatment that pharmaceutical giant Burroughs Wellcome had taken off the shelf. There was word of other drugs, like ribavirin. But the new drugs were proceeding through the legendarily glacial process at the federal Food and Drug Administration, which approves drugs for use. The FDA gave the newly aroused victims a target.

Their adversaries were showing weakness. The governing elites were no longer so united on the subject of AIDS. In 1984, someone leaked to congressional staffer Tim Westmoreland the futile request that assistant secretary for health Ed Brandt had sent, urgently demanding $55 million in AIDS funding from Reagan's secretary of health and human services, Margaret Heckler. Brandt denies that he was the leaker, but that year the money for AIDS went up 60 percent. A year later, Westmoreland's contact at Health and Human Services suddenly lost patience with the dancing around.

"Pssst," she said. "Do you know the bench by the fountain in Bartholdi Gardens, right in between the Health and Human Services (HHS) building and the House Office Building? Meet me there." When Westmoreland arrived, his contact handed him a plain brown envelope containing a list of every budget request for every AIDS-related program at every level of the process for 1985. Knowing what Heckler was sitting on, Westmoreland's boss, Representative Henry Waxman, chairman of the House Subcommittee on Health, threatened to subpoena the scientists' requests for money. When she finally gave in and turned over the documents, Waxman gave her all the money her scientists wanted.

In 1988, AIDS spending increased $450 million, the largest jump to date. In essence, a handful of gay staffers and sympathetic employers, like California representatives Waxman and Phil Burton and New York's Ted Weiss, started a process of inserting AIDS funding into larger spending bills until the money for research began resembling a meaningful response to the seriousness of the threat. When AZT started looking promising, but still rapaciously unaffordable, for the ten thousand AIDS patients otherwise near death, the five-year-old Human Rights Campaign sent its lobbyists to Lowell Weicker, Republican head of the Senate Appropriations Committee, to ask for money for the drug. Weicker's wife, Claudia, who happened to be in his office, had worked for Dan Bradley at Legal Services. One of the gay lobbyists looked at her and dropped that "Dan Bradley, whom I think you know, is sick." The next day Weicker took the floor and put in $49 million to fund AZT for people who could not afford it. Anthony Fauci, who by then had been head of the division of the National Institutes of Health responsible for AIDS for more than a year, was plotting with congressional staffers at his gay chief deputy's apartment to circumvent his own bosses at the White House. Even Ronald Reagan's surgeon general, the impeccably conservative C. Everett Koop, had let his medical ethics get the best of him and was trying to say "condoms" in public. Victims were angry and hopeful, elites were divided. Any theory of social movement would predict that a critical moment was at hand.

Old activists stirred to life. The still irresistible and charismatic Marty Robinson, whose zaps had brought the civil rights direct-action tradition to the gay revolution in the Gay Activists Alliance (GAA) days, and some old movement chums started a new group, the Swift and Terrible Retribution Committee. The indefatigable Robinson then organized twelve of his swift and terrible demonstrators into the "Lavender Hill Mob." A small group of gay men in the arts started potluck consciousness-raising dinners. They began discussing a poster initiative. Silence? Death? Silence=Death.

Fliers equating silence and death and displaying the pink triangle the Nazis had pinned on homosexuals were pasted all over Greenwich Village.

The artists wanted their posters to tell the gay community they had to act, that silence was tantamount to complicity. The upright triangle symbol, the inverse of the Nazi symbol, is now a proud assertion that gays will not be taken silently to their death.

Many in the movement fiercely opposed the Nazi analogy. But when *National Review* editor William Buckley published a piece in the *New York Times* that year suggesting that HIV-positive men should be forcibly tattooed, the swift and terrible committee had a mob of protesters outside the offices of his conservative magazine the next day. Maybe he didn't mean any harm. Shortly after Buckley's essay appeared the followers of weird political maverick Lyndon LaRouche got a referendum, ultimately unsuccessful, put on the ballot in California to classify AIDS as a communicable disease, with attendant danger of forced testing and quarantine. Overwrought or not, silence being death once, the resurgent activists were out to make sure it never happened again. Several of the Silence=Death Project were Jews; they bore the memory of the Holocaust in their genes, Silence founder Avram Finkelstein says. One thing no one wanted to be in the late twentieth century was the silent dead Jews of Europe.

The Spark: *Bowers v. Hardwick*

Supreme Court justice Lewis Powell's gay law clerk, Carter Cabell Chinnis, saw no reason to share his sexual orientation with his employer. Chinnis, Virginia gentleman, BA Princeton, JD Yale Law School, Supreme Court clerk, was on the fast track. When his boyfriend had come to visit the court, he introduced the man to the Justice as a friend from New Orleans. In June 1986, Justice Powell cast the deciding vote in *Bowers v. Hardwick*, upholding Georgia's criminal sodomy law. Unlike any other sex, gay sex, or "sodomy," the court ruled, was outside the privacy protections of the Bill of Rights.

Bowers was an ugly surprise. For a while the gay legal activists had been looking for a case to test the sodomy laws, and, in a society that values the right to be left alone, *Bowers* seemed like the perfect test case. The gay plaintiff, Michael Hardwick, was actually blowing an acquaintance in his apartment in Atlanta when a cop walked into his bedroom to serve a warrant for an unrelated offense and arrested him for sodomy. Even the relatively conservative federal Court of Appeals in Georgia affirmed that Hardwick had a right to privacy in his own bedroom and struck the Georgia sodomy law down.

When the Supreme Court exercised its discretionary right to review the decision, there was much nervous justice-counting in the gay legal institutions. Going in, the court appeared to be divided four to four, with the outcome resting on Justice Powell. Powell, it later emerged, had voted in favor of Hardwick's claim in the preliminary conference among the judges and then he changed his mind. Chinnis did not have to write the opinion. Powell assigned that task to one of his other clerks, a married Mormon father of three. After retiring a few years later, Powell later apologized for his vote in *Bowers*. He actually didn't know any gay people, he said.

A Supreme Court decision like *Bowers* has the virtue of leaving no room for spin. In the four decades before rejecting the gay claim, the court had extended privacy rights to every single other group in society. In addition to completely disregarding their own precedents, the opinions expressed an unprecedented degree of moral disgust with the gay minority. Chief Justice Warren Burger wrote a special opinion in *Bowers*, taking pains to emphasize the historically negative attitudes toward homosexual sex, "a crime not fit to be named," and concluded that protecting the sex lives of America's homosexuals would cast aside millennia of moral teaching.

The Supreme Court decision triggered street protests all over the country, in some cases for the first time since Stonewall days. Calling for a march on Washington, Reverend Troy Perry said he'd never seen people so pissed. The protest in New York became so angry that movement leaders tried to send the people home, but they would not leave. A month later, at an event honoring Chief Justice Burger, the Lavender Hill Mob appeared where the GAA had stopped the opera all those years ago, marching and chanting.

Once unleashed, the activists were not going to limit their curses to the life-tenured members of the Supreme Court, whose ruling had just come down. In March 1987, the Lavender Hill Mob traveled to Atlanta to protest at the CDC conference on AIDS. No sooner did the Mob get back to New York than they heard that Larry Kramer had agreed to take the place of Nora Ephron as the speaker at the monthly Gay and Lesbian Community Center speaker series in Chelsea. People mobbed the hall to hear what he would say and to see who else was turning up.

Larry Kramer Lights the Fire

On March 10, 1987, Kramer told the crowd at the Gay and Lesbian Community Center that the political moment was ripe. The epidemic wasn't their fault because they had had sex before they knew it was dangerous: "The real tidal wave is yet to come: people who got infected in 1981. You had sex in 1981. I did too." There was hope: "Dr. Mansell has five drugs waiting to be tested." The government was the problem: "One of the top AIDS doctors in the United States can't get protocols through the FDA." And then he called the gay community out: "All power is the willingness to accept responsibility."

The Left, which had been mostly dormant since the antiwar movement fifteen years before, offered little by the way of inspiration. So Kramer used an example from the vibrant social movement of the eighties, the right. A thousand Roman Catholics had recently marched on Albany, the state capital, Kramer said. Now the gay community needed to do the same. As he spoke, someone from the meeting ran up to the center office to book the room for another meeting. An hour later, someone ran up to the office and booked the room for a meeting every week.

Two days later, three hundred people came back to the center for the first meeting, and the AIDS Coalition to Unleash Power was born. Soon there were chapters all over the country.

Shutting Down Wall Street and Pennsylvania Avenue

Before cabbie and artist Michael Nesline's lover died of AIDS, the couple had gone to see *The Normal Heart.* "That Kramer guy really knows what he's doing," Nesline's companion said. "You should try to connect with him." So when Michael heard about the fuss at the Gay and Lesbian Center, he decided he'd go to the follow-up meeting two days later.

Nesline and the others at the meeting were all really upset that they were being ignored. As he recalls, "We're middle class white guys and we're not used to being ignored and so what can we do to get what we want? And what we want is for other people to know what's going on, and we want the *New York Times* to write about it, even inaccurately. We needed to draw attention to ourselves and to our problem. So, we probably should have some kind of demonstration. Tim [the first facilitator, Tim Sweeney of GMHC] solicited suggestions for where would be a good place to have a demonstration. And, I guess, you know, majority rule decided that City Hall–Wall Street would be a really good place to have a demonstration. So, we began to make plans for that."

What is more powerful than a bunch of white guys who aren't getting what they think they deserve? Ann Northrop, the savvy TV producer and old-time activist who often facilitated the ACT UP meetings, says ACT UP succeeded "because gay white men realized they did not have the privilege they thought they had."

White men have contacts. Audience members at Harvey Fierstein's play *Safe Sex* found leaflets for the Wall Street demonstration on every seat. White men ask for what they want. ACT UP threatened an action at the gay men's chorus performance of *Peter and the Wolf* at Avery Fisher Hall if they were not allowed to announce the demonstration to the music lovers. "We're dying," the ACT UP representatives said to the hesitant chorus organizers. "And you're making a distinction between politics and culture?" White men have access. One day before the action, Larry Kramer's op ed piece, "The FDA's Callous Response to AIDS," appeared in the *New York Times.* White men have friends in high places. The prop shop at the Public Theater made an effigy of FDA chairman Frank Young.

The old ACT UP activists remembered from their antiwar days that nothing attracts the cameras like getting arrested. On March 24, 1987, all morning traffic on Wall Street stopped. Hundreds of demonstrators crammed the area, screaming and chanting and hanging the effigy of Young. ACT UP demonstrators handed out an information sheet. Handsomely printed with the Silence=Death fuchsia triangle, the handout demanded immediate release by the FDA of a very specific list of seven drugs, each with its pharmaceutical developer tag attached. The pamphlet listed a series of increasingly broad demands, culminating in demand number 7: "Immediate establishment of a coordinated, comprehensive, and compassionate national policy on AIDS." The 1987 demand list was a perfect snapshot of ACT UP politics—demands for ribavirin and demands for world peace.

Protesters charged the police barricades and lay down in the street. There were only seventeen arrests, but the next day every major newspaper in the country carried pictures of the protesters being put on stretchers and carried away. Suddenly even the most staid members of the gay establishment wanted to get arrested. Three months after the Wall Street demonstration, the normally well-behaved HRC demonstrated across the street from the White House. Led by their board chairman, dying activist Dan Bradley, wearing a large funeral wreath, they blocked Pennsylvania Avenue. The police, wearing bright yellow rubber gloves like the ones people use to wash dishes with, picked them up and carried them to the waiting vehicles. Again the photographs were everywhere. Dan

Bradley, former president of the Legal Services Corporation, carried off like a dirty dish.

ACT UP owes a huge debt to the revived activists of the Lavender Hill Mob and the like, and in turn to the Stonewall-era GAA. But American activists have short memories. After fifteen years of conservative political dominance, ACT UP seemed like a resurrection. Every radical movement, gay or not, that came after—Queer Nation, Lesbian Avengers, GetEqual, protests against the World Trade Organization—identifies its roots in ACT UP. Looking back on it in 2010 Kramer said, "ACT UP was the single most important thing the gay population ever achieved."

Man, the Political Animal

In 2000, Professor Eric Rofes found himself teaching his social activism class at Humboldt State University in California from the writings of Martin Luther King and the music of Joan Baez. "Don't you have anything a little more about us?" one of his students asked. When Rofes started to put together some contemporary teaching materials about the present, he realized the organizing around AIDS was the "starting point" for modern activism.

How did they do it? Part of it was their perfectly pitched structure. Jim Eigo, experimental writer and longtime participant in random political actions—a little antiwar, a little Central America—wandered into the ACT UP gathering at the Gay and Lesbian Center early in 1987 by mistake. He was looking for a panel on the effect of *Bowers v. Hardwick*. The table by the entry was full of literature that everybody was producing themselves. And there was a buzz everywhere.

It was the ACT UP Monday meeting. For five years, ACT UP solved the problem of how to keep order in a charismatic movement. It seems like an insurmountable obstacle. Lefties looking for action flooded into ACT UP. The meetings were so large, they had to be moved from the center to a bigger auditorium. The Gay Liberation Front had lasted six months, the GAA two years. When the Task Force tried to escape the dynamic, it became a bureaucracy with a philanthropic board and professional employees. HRC started that way intentionally.

ACT UP found the sweet spot between bureaucracy and anarchy. Frequent cofacilitator Ann Northrop says, "I ran the show just like I used to produce the news." People who wanted to present something had to get it by the facilitators first. No one could speak a second time until everyone who wanted to speak had had a turn. Whenever people took an interest in doing something—the women, predictably, formed one of the most visible caucuses—they could organize themselves to do it, subject only to the general principles of the organization and submission to the electoral power of the general meeting. "Discussion might provoke a proposal for action," Northrop recalls. For example "This insurance company has rejected claims. . . . Oh we've got to shut down the insurance company. . . . Thursday we're going to picket the insurance company. . . . Let's have a poster party Wednesday night and we'll show up Thursday or we will refer it to the actions committee and come back to the floor with a plan." They had a democratic form of government, but "it wasn't one of those hippy-dippy we-all-have-to-agree things," Northrop says. In a small, but significant, dispute, for example, people started arriving late. The group discussed the lateness; they voted that the meetings would start on time and, says Northrop, "That's what we did."

The process allowed most people who wanted to make their presence felt in the political arena to do so. In the lobbies of the meeting place and on other nights, committees and affinity groups were pursuing much more particularized politics and nonpolitical relationships. The Actions Committee planned demonstrations. The Treatment and Data Committee was studying chemistry. Wave 3, a group of twenty who were arrested together, had a weekly potluck supper.

ACT UP produced probably the most effective visual propaganda since the Bolsheviks. "Who did those Silence=Death signs in the Village?"

people kept asking. At the second or third meeting, Silence=Death cofounder Avram Finkelstein finally stood up. "We did. And we'd be happy to share it with ACT UP."

A few weeks later, ACT UP artists formed an art collective, Gran Fury (for the Plymouth cars the cops drove). Gran Fury is what you get when red-diaper babies like Finkelstein are running an ad agency. Not for them the homemade posters of lefty movements. They wanted their visuals to look like advertising, like Silence=Death did. Because advertising is what people read. Most of the graphics had didactic messages: KNOW YOUR SCUMBAG; THE GOVERNMENT HAS BLOOD ON ITS HANDS.

Gran Fury member Marlene McCarty was very close to the European artist who was making the culturally radical Benetton ads, like the one with the black woman and the white baby. So, when the rumor started that you could get AIDS from kissing, McCarty and artist Donald Moffett made a billboard to tell the world that kissing didn't kill: GREED AND INDIFFERENCE DO. The billboard showed three couples, two men, two women, and one man kissing a woman, all interracial, just like the "we are the world" radical-chic Benetton ads. The Gran Fury members thought it was hilarious that the art world accused them of making propaganda. Of course they were making propaganda! Since the government wasn't telling people what was going on, they were going to tell people what was going on. "It was polemic, flat footed, propagandistic," McCarty says proudly, "everything art isn't supposed to be."

Thrust into a situation where they had to actively engage in politics literally to save their lives or the lives of people dear to them, the activists in ACT UP found the independent rewards of an engaged life. "The group had structured my entire life from 1987 to 1993," direct-action maestro Greg Bordowitz says. "It was my life. It was all I did. Every meaningful relationship I had was with people who were in ACT UP. There was nothing else outside of it."

We Die/They Do Nothing: Seize the FDA

Despite all the talk of the Holocaust, the United States government did not create AIDS to kill gay men. Instead the government failed to act. At a critical juncture after Stonewall, the modern gay movement had formed around a failure to act, when the governments of the cities where they gathered would not rein in their abusive police forces. The old GAA activists whose fingerprints were all over ACT UP knew what to do in the face of a failure to act.

The activists benefited from the fact that the failure to act to stop AIDS arose in one of the few areas where government has an obligation to act and a history of acting to help its population: public health. Despite all these social-movement advantages, government inaction still might not have triggered ACT UP. But it looked like the government was not just failing to act, it was standing in the way of AIDS victims' getting the cures they hoped for. Soon after its founding, ACT UP turned directly to the source of the problem. Seize control of the FDA.

By 1988, the Food and Drug Administration had it coming. Most of the forty-six new drugs approved by the United States in 1985 and 1986 were available five years earlier in foreign markets. While the FDA took its sweet time in 1988, more than twenty thousand people died of AIDS. One of them was Dan Bradley. He had told his best friend that he wanted to be buried in the Kangol hat he thought made his eyes look blue and the sweater she had knit him. When she got to the church, she said, "Will you open the casket?" So the funeral guy opened it, and she said, "Well, where's his cap?" And he said, "We were wondering what that cap was doing in there." And she said, "Well, he needs to wear that cap." So she put the cap on his head, and then they closed the casket.

ACT UP was ready. A committee, Treatment and Data (T&D), that would focus on drug development and approval, had been formed when Dr. Iris Long, a heterosexual pharmaceutical chemist from Queens, walked into an early ACT UP meeting. "You people don't know squat. I'm going to teach you," she announced, "about how drugs come out."

The science wonks on Long's T&D Committee were having a devilish time getting information, much less cooperation, from the FDA. ACT UP had to get the Lambda lawyers to file a Freedom of Information Act suit just to get lists of the drugs the government was considering; but to make an impact they knew they had to get the movement activists over at the Actions Committee to help them. Their eye fell on Greg Bordowitz, a handsome and charismatic activist who had come to ACT UP and gravitated to the lefty Actions. T&D heavy hitters David Barr and Mickey Wheatley invited Bordowitz to lunch and pitched their plan for an action against the FDA. First, and to his surprise, they told him he had become a real force in ACT UP. Then they told him about their idea of targeting the agency, rather than the usual suspects, Congress and the White House. Bordowitz was kind of skeptical; the proposal was so different from the direct-action politics he was used to, but Barr and Wheatley persuaded him to present the idea to the Monday meeting. Directing action against the FDA was a lot like the GAA showing up at John Lindsay's presidential fund-raiser. The activists did not need changes in the formal law. They needed to make inaction more painful for the decision makers than action would be.

Bordowitz had figured out that ideas that seemed to spring full-armed from the mass meetings on Monday had usually already been lobbied in the various affinity groups that met on other nights. He went to a meeting every night, sometimes two, explaining to each group why seizing control of the FDA was good for women, people of color, whatever. He dubbed it "Seize Control of the FDA." The New York FDA activists repeated the process at a meeting of representatives of all the big ACT UP groups around the country, convincing everybody that the FDA was the place for the new activist movement to be. They formed a national group, ACT NOW, for the action against the FDA.

The "Seize Control of the FDA" initiative had all the classic ACT UP hallmarks. The activists had done their homework, analyzing all the drugs the FDA was testing. (ACT UP is surely the first social movement in history to include with its demonstration handout before occupying a

Anti-FDA demonstration, 1988 (Photograph by Rex Wockner)

government building an analysis of the drug Trimetrexate, suggesting its potency and concluding that, nonetheless, "the FDA, out of alleged fear for Trimetrexrate's side effects, limited its use.")

They made a media plan that would have supported a political convention. The media strategy was guided by Ann Northrop; Michelangelo Signorile, who had previously been PR'ing Broadway plays and movie stars; the consummate movement media coordinator, Urvashi Vaid, detailed over from the Task Force; and a cookbook publicist who understood the value of run-up. By the time the demonstrators arrived at the FDA building in Rockville, Maryland, media kits had gone out to every talk show in the country. "The largest demonstration since the storming of the Pentagon," they proclaimed. Groups from each city were assigned a placard with their name on it, because Vaid knew that the media from local markets all had bureaus in DC, and they loved to interview members of their own communities.

On October 11, 1988, a thousand ACT UP demonstrators came streaming across the lawn outside the suburban headquarters of the FDA.

Wrapped in red tape, bearing fake tombstones, sporting black T-shirts with the signature triangles, for eight hours they surrounded the building. They chanted, stickered the walls of the building, lay down like corpses, and got arrested and carted off by the police. The protesters were still lying in front of the FDA at six o'clock at night, because someone knew that drive-time radio shows like nothing more than live events at drive time.

The video "Seize Control of the FDA" captures the demonstrators chanting, "Forty-two thousand dead of AIDS. Where was the FDA? Seize control, seize control. Release the drugs now. Release the drugs now." And, most poignantly, "We die/they do nothing. We die/they do nothing."

Remembering the scene, former theater flack Michelangelo Signorile smiles with satisfaction: "This wasn't like having a bad Broadway show that you have to publicize."

Two weeks later, the FDA announced it was speeding up the process for developing and approving AIDS drugs. Four new drugs were approved in a matter of months. AIDS chief Anthony Fauci says there are two eras in American clinical research: before Larry Kramer and after.

"Stop the Church": The Demonstration That Went Too Far

The perfect movement moment could not last forever. The first sign appeared one freezing Sunday morning in December 1989, when legendary hothead Michael Petrelis stood on a pew in New York's landmark St. Patrick's Cathedral on Fifth Avenue and started screaming, "O'Connor, you're killing us! You're killing us, just stop it! Stop it!"

The St. Patrick's action had all been so carefully planned. The Archdiocese of New York was visibly using its substantial resources to stop both Catholic and public institutions from teaching the use of condoms for AIDS prevention. Since the Catholic hospitals and social-service agencies provided the vast majority of AIDS patient care, paid for with public monies, the church's resistance to safe-sex education had consequences. John Cardinal O'Connor, who presided over St. Patrick's, was a leader even among churchmen in his resistance to the lifesaving message of safe sex. Catholic hospitals in other dioceses, like Chicago, for example, were not forbidden to talk about condom use. Taking on the church had great appeal to interest groups within ACT UP, especially the women, who had longstanding grievances with the church on abortion.

Still, Stop the Church was identified early on as a reach into offensiveness even for ACT UP. "We didn't care if we were liked," Ann Northrop says, "but we had to be effective." It took six months of debate, crying, anger, argument, and back and forth before ACT UP took the vote to act against the church. The planners had the hard job of shining a light on the role of the church's sexual politics in exacerbating the AIDS epidemic while minimizing the insult to the act of faith.

They thought they could control the impact of their actions by controlling the action. They would act during the archbishop's homily, the least prayerful part of the service. One demonstrator was assigned to stand and read something very specific, another to lie in the center aisle quietly, and others to handcuff themselves to the pews, certainly confrontational in the sense of being visible, but very controlled.

When the homily began, the demonstrators went to lie down in the aisle and the designated speakers to read their piece. Then Petrelis started screaming, and the congregation started yelling. Eventually the police took Petrelis out and calmed down the congregation and the police came in with stretchers and slowly and systematically took the demonstrators out. When the service resumed, ACT UP member Tom Keane went to take communion. He took the communion wafer in his hand, crumbled it, and dropped it. The crumbs landed on the front pages in every newspaper in the world.

Northrop loved it. "An entirely appropriate reaction to a life-threatening situation," she says. The media crucified them. Demonstrations against the United States government at the FDA and the establishment of international capitalism on Wall Street were nothing to the media compared to the crumbs of that communion wafer.

To this day, supporters of Stop the Church revel in the attention it brought the protest movement. But the price was high. ACT UP, like all direct-action movements, was constantly navigating the line between being disruptive enough to be effective and too disruptive to be effective. In Stop the Church, they had voted on a very precise set of actions that enough people agreed fell on the right side of the line, but the vote was closer than usual. Afterward, people within ACT UP were, as Petrelis says, "mad" at him for "having been so loud." And he responded, "Well, that's what I wanted to do." With this response, the fragile cooperative structure of ACT UP swayed. People drifted toward the normal human behavior of putting themselves first.

Killing ACT UP . . . with Kindness

One lovely day the following May, in 1990, Dr. Anthony Fauci looked out the window of his office at the usually peaceful campus of the National Institutes of Health and saw the signs: FAUCI, YOU'RE KILLING US. Hundreds of demonstrators, many in leather jackets, earrings, and Mohawk haircuts, were all over his peaceful domain, shouting, waving signs, planting tombstones, and lying down.

Fauci admired the hell out of his accusers.

As the Montgomery County police and the FBI were about to arrest them all, Fauci went downstairs and told the police to get the five people who are the leaders and send them into his office. They would sit down and talk. Born and raised in New York, Fauci, who had spent a lot of time in the Village, had the advantage of not coming to the situation with the kind of aversion to gay people that he saw in many of his fellow scientists and bureaucrats. Jim Hill, his chief deputy and the godfather of one of his daughters, was gay. (Hill was also HIV-positive. Watching him weaken and die, Fauci says, did tend to concentrate the mind on the task at hand.)

The invitation seemed at first like good news. By 1990, Fauci, head of the NIH National Institute of Allergy and Infectious Disease and effectively the AIDS czar since his appointment in 1984, knew ACT UP. He had started doing business with the activists more than a year before, after running into Larry Kramer walking his dog at the Montreal AIDS Conference.

Although a lot of his research scientists thought civilians, much less civilians with twenty earrings, had no place in the hallowed halls of science, most of the things the civilians said made complete sense to Fauci. He understood that they were challenging the general paradigm of how to test drugs. Under that paradigm, he explains, even if you have a disease where everybody dies and there's no treatment, researchers will allow only a certain number of people into the trial and the drug will not be available for anybody else until it's proved to be effective. They were saying, Fauci understood, We don't have time. We're going to die. We can't wait for this. So we want a more expanded, flexible clinical-trial process. We want people who geographically can't get to the place where there's the trial to be able to get the drugs. And we want to be able to test multiple drugs at the same time in an individual, so they don't have to choose between, say, going blind or dying from HIV. The conventional practices make sense from a pristine scientific standpoint, Fauci acknowledges, but if you were somebody who was dying from a disease, they made no sense whatsoever. "So I was listening to what they were saying, and I was saying, if I were in their shoes, I'd be doing the same thing."

"They were very good at it," he notes. "There was a core group of young gay well-connected, well-educated, really smart people who were quick studies in what you need to do to push the system. They beautifully combined extraordinarily dramatic, provocative, and theatrical ways to get attention and once they got your attention they were able to talk to you like they were experts in the field." Little by little, Fauci cajoled or forced the researchers to change the way they conducted their business. He put the ACT UP treatment experts right on the committees of the AIDS Clinical Trials Group, the network of sites doing the actual testing, where they educated the scientists about how to test the drugs in the kinds of real conditions the people with AIDS were living with.

When Fauci offered to meet with five representatives of the screaming masses, he must have seemed like a god. He was. For ACT UP as an institution, he was Nemesis, the god who curses men by granting them their wishes.

ACT UP was always a provisional alliance: dying white guys needing treatment; uninfected gays and lesbians who had learned from the AIDS crisis how marginal they all were; and nongay activists who always wanted to change the world. But as the brilliantly self-educated, mostly white, male treatment experts were invited inside the establishment, they grew apart from the activists who wanted to change society at its root or in its attitude toward homosexuals or even the disaffected Catholics who wanted to yell at the cardinal.

ACT UP Breaks Up

Once the opportunity to participate in the scientific enterprise arose, ACT UP, which seemed the very incarnation of a new way of acting collectively, fell into the conventional movement trap. They had political capital. Once there was capital, people began to compete for it. Soon, every decision presented a conflict. If some in ACT UP pressed for more attention to the people with AIDS who did not fit the gay white male model—women, with different presenting symptoms, or intravenous drug users—others believed ACT UP should use its political capital with the NIH to press for pure research. The newly empowered treatment activists did not think they had the money and energy to do the social-movement labor the traditional lefties desired. An anonymous writer suggested to the ACT UP newsletter that his opponents wanted to use ACT UP to "save the whales."

Nothing revealed the forces pulling ACT UP apart like the split between the men and the women. Although women, of course, were vulnerable to AIDS, few of the women in ACT UP were infected. Thus, ACT UP women presented a pure target for the people with AIDS, who suspected that the uninfected, male or female, would put other political interests before their survival.

From the women's perspective, powerful white men like Fauci were selecting people who resembled them to make decisions that affected women's lives. Women in ACT UP had long been suspicious that their voices were not being heeded, noting that when they were speaking at the Monday night meetings, the buzz of side conversations got perceptibly louder.

Women were important to ACT UP. By 1987, women had been in the trenches in the feminist health-care movement and in abortion rights for more than two decades. Women like Marion Banzhaf, who had run the DC Feminist Women's Health Center for years, brought to the new organization invaluable knowledge and history about how to democratize health care and insert the patients' voices. They also got a lot. The psychologically entitled white men were a powerful machine. When the women's caucus wanted to protest the CDC definition of AIDS that excluded women, ACT UP generated a horde of screaming T-shirted protesters at CDC offices all over the country.

When ACT UP finally got Fauci to schedule a conference on women and AIDS in 1990, the sessions were, to put it mildly, contentious. As luck would have it, Fauci and some of his pals in ACT UP were going to a party together after the conference. As one of the women reported in the organization newsletter *Outweek*, they "collided with members of the Treatment and Data Committee of ACT UP/NY, who were, unbeknownst to us, heading to a social event with these same dreaded government bureaucrats." A few weeks later the women proposed that all meetings between ACT UP representatives and the scientific agencies, either on women's issues or, more threateningly, altogether, be suspended for six months.

Suspend all contact with the scientists? In March 1992, exactly five years after Larry Kramer's speech at the gay and lesbian center, the leading lights of the Treatment and Data Committee sent ACT UP an open letter announcing that they were starting a new organization, Treatment Action Group. Membership would be by invitation only.

We Will Be Citizens

People were still dying in droves when ACT UP broke apart. It would be two long years before the government started testing the multiple-drug treatment that finally slowed the epidemic down. ACT UP did not develop protease inhibitors or drug cocktails, which proved so effective at controlling the progression of the disease, although the activists played a big role in getting the cooperation of the multiple drug companies. But they had done the most crucial social-movement work: they made the victims matter.

A sure sign that ACT UP and the other activists had achieved a political breakthrough for AIDS patients and, by implication, all gay people, was the release of the Hollywood movie *Philadelphia* in 1993. Tom Hanks played the brilliant and unjustly treated AIDS-infected corporate lawyer Andrew Beckett. Although Beckett has a cool loft apartment, he otherwise looks a lot like the heterosexual majority. The audience never sees him in bed with his partner, barely even imagines them kissing, and nowhere sees the rich and resourceful universe of gay communal resources available to people with AIDS by 1993. Still, Hanks won the Academy Award for his performance in the thin and uninteresting role. It was the twelfth-highest-grossing film in 1993.

Had the gay AIDS revolution stopped at *Philadelphia*, it never would have accomplished all that it did. Gay people are not sexless heterosexuals with better apartments. But it had to start there. When gay AIDS patients were faceless, the government of the United States silently watched them die. Even Justice Powell said he ruled to keep their sex lives criminal because he didn't know any gay people. In 1993, a major institution of culture—the popular movie—showed them as human individuals, people the heterosexual majority might know or even have in their families.

Cleve Jones had figured this out. In 1987, he started the NAMES Project, a gigantic patchwork quilt made of patches commemorating each person who had died of AIDS. By making them individually human, he thought, he could not only comfort the grieving but also change the way the society saw the consequences of its indifference. The quilt put the "we" into "We die/you do nothing." The quilt self-consciously imitates the strategy of Maya Lin's famed Vietnam War Memorial, with its list of every American soldier who died during the war, an ascending mountain of grief and loss, each line of engraving a distinct human being.

As part of that project, in 1987, the NAMES Project took the quilt, then two thousand squares, to the National Mall in Washington, DC, and spread it out before the lawmakers they thought could make the United States government do something different. On a mostly sunny day, people came to read from the squares that commemorated their losses.

One of them was for Roscoe Browne. In 1985, Robby's mother, Dixie, called Robby, worried that she had not heard from Roscoe for a long time. Four months later, Roscoe Browne, the godlike brother who had taught Robby to drive and to water ski and whose visits home from camp and school were the high points of Robby's youth, was dead. Dixie Browne paid the funeral home extra to bury her son's infected body. When the quilt came to Washington, Robby thought Barbara Bush could go out and read his brother's square. After all, wasn't Roscoe a Yalie like her husband and her sons? After the quilt had come and gone, Peggy Swift, Barbara Bush's social secretary, sent him a note regretting that Mrs. Bush had been unable to acknowledge Robby's brother.

Just as *Philadelphia* presented a palatable story to the consumers of American culture, in 1993 Tony Kushner's *Angels in America: A Gay Fantasia on National Themes*, opened on Broadway to make a full-throated claim for gay citizenship. From the first scene, a eulogy for the gay protagonist Louis Ironson's immigrant grandmother, Kushner made clear that *Angels* was going to be a play about America—its immigrants, its aspirations, and its gays.

Roy Cohn, in reality the lifelong closeted right-hand man to Senator Joseph McCarthy, appears as a version of himself in *Angels in America*. Kushner's Cohn describes the distance gays have yet to come: I'm not a homosexual, he tells his doctor after he's diagnosed with AIDS, no matter who I have sex with. "A homosexual," Roy Cohn says, "is somebody who, in 15 years of trying cannot get a pissant anti-discrimination bill through the city council. A homosexual is somebody who knows nobody and who nobody knows." The closeted Cohn does not need ACT UP; he blackmails the White House to get him AZT, threatening to blow the whistle on the Iran-Contra scandal (the play is set roughly in 1987). No randomized clinical trials for people like Roy Cohn.

But the character Cohn finds out that he may only be taking a placebo from his cross-dressing nurse Belize, not from his well-connected friends in Washington. The government would even deny Cohn potentially life-saving medicine, Belize informs him, in a line right out of the ACT UP playbook, in the interest of getting results that will satisfy "the *New England Journal of Medicine*."

By the time Cohn gets AZT, it's too late. As soon as Cohn dies, Belize takes the rest of Cohn's ill-gotten stash and gives it to Louis for Louis's former lover, Prior Walter, who is also infected. Cohn dies, but, as the play ends several years later, Walter, possibly because of the purloined AZT, survives. Thus, the out gay community triumphs where the closeted, evil-doing McCarthyite conservative fails. As the curtain falls, Walter, who has some gift of prophecy, looks out at the audience and says, "This disease will be the end of many of us, but not nearly all, and the dead will be commemorated and will struggle on with the living, and we are not going away. We won't die secret deaths anymore. The world only spins forward. We will be citizens. The time has come."

The Time Has Come

"We die/they do nothing" could describe most of human history. A few hundred—at its height ACT UP/NY had a thousand people attending weekly meetings—members of a despised and marginalized minority, just emerged from crazy and disloyal, still sinful and recently reconfirmed as criminal by the Supreme Court, defied that ancient order. The ones who were HIV-positive resembled the victims of the Holocaust in that they had, literally, the freedom of those with nothing left to lose. Positive or negative, they were numerous, they were loud and disruptive, male and female, they were macho. Screaming, dressed in similar uniforms, disrupting public ceremonies, massing, forcing their way into the heart of the shadowy bureaucracy with tombstones as symbols, they could not be ignored. With their advertising-driven laden graphics, they were cool.

And they were hot. ACT UP, which at one point seriously debated whether members should carry firearms, pushed the very limits of peaceful civil disobedience. They didn't kill anyone or destroy any buildings, but they stopped business at St. Patrick's Cathedral once, at the Stock Exchange at least twice, and at the heart of the government science establishment repeatedly. If Stonewall had not been enough to convince the majority society that the gay population would stand up for itself, ACT UP—and its offshoots like the Lesbian Avengers, with a ticking bomb as their symbol—reiterated the message.

After the emergency receded, years later, the image of the booted, leather-jacketed man yelling that the government has blood on its hands and the lesbian women with their bomb letterhead changed the way people thought about gays and lesbians and so changed the gay revolution for good. In their actions, they continued the work that began at Stonewall of pushing gays and lesbians into the social contract. They would be citizens.

By late 1995, when the Food and Drug Administration announced it was approving the last of the drugs in the drug cocktail, the United States National Institutes of Health was spending well over a billion dollars a year on AIDS research. Although gay men were by no means the only Americans suffering from the disease, nor the only people acting politically to mobilize the government to act, they were certainly at the heart of the action. No other social movement has leveraged public resources so effectively. They essentially redefined the content of the liberal state to include spending large amounts of resources to protect a vulnerable minority from a fatal disease. But, as Larry Kramer said, sadly, when asked about his starring role, at what a terrible price.

Two weeks after starting the new medicines, Cleve Jones got out of his deathbed and went down to the little store on the corner. He thought he'd get himself an English muffin.

8

Failed Marriages and Losing Battles: The Premature Campaign for Marriage and Military Service

May 18, 1992, was a gorgeous day in Hollywood, California. A crowd of exceptionally good-looking and well-dressed men (and a few women) filled the courtyard of the bright blue Spanish-style Palace Theatre. As the day turned to evening, Bill Clinton's motorcade pulled up and he and his old friend David Mixner got out. When Mixner, a mainstay of the Los Angeles gay and lesbian scene, took the stage, the people at the Palace erupted. Dressed in an immaculate white shirt and a blue suit, the handsome Mixner looked out at the crowd.

"My brothers and sisters," he said in his customary twang, "we've all come a long way."

The Long Way

What a way it had been. Mixner, raised in the 1940s on a farm in rural New Jersey, like Clinton in Hot Springs, Arkansas, grew up without indoor plumbing. Being gay, he always knew he was different; he thought he was bad and he desperately feared being caught. For a poor rural boy, getting away even to a modest college like Arizona State was like escaping from jail. When he met Clinton on vacation from Oxford at an antiwar retreat in

1969, he had a moment's pause. "If I weren't gay," he asked himself, "would I have thought I could go to a fancy college too? Be a Rhodes scholar?"

As with so many refugees from "Amerika," when the Sixties receded, Mixner took refuge in California. Closeted and well connected from his antiwar activism, he soon got to be a player in Los Angeles, making a living as a political consultant. Little by little, he let people in on his secret, until, finally, in the heat of the battle against the Briggs initiative in 1978, he came out. His friends Bill and Hillary were totally okay with it, they said.

Mixner had come to Los Angeles politics at just the right time: by the midseventies in the city of glamour and power, glamorous, powerful gay men had decided to make their cause fashionable. Not for them the "hippies" of the Stonewall-era gay and lesbian center. In 1976, Peter Scott, a successful lawyer and the love of David Mixner's life, gathered the men in his consciousness-raising group and added a few more A-gays to start the first gay political action committee. The PAC became the Municipal Elections Committee of Los Angeles (MECLA), a nice neutral name like Human Rights Campaign. In a stunning debut, MECLA took down the entrenched, rabidly antigay Los Angeles City Council president John Gibson. Since the presidency of the city council always went to the leading vote-getter in the council elections, MECLA simply gave Gibson's hapless opponent five thousand dollars, and the nonentity took a third of Gibson's vote, relegating Gibson to the relatively powerless position of just another councilman.

Even in the eighties, as AIDS devastated their community, the wealthy, connected gays and lesbians of California were creating the institutions of what would ultimately become the gay establishment. The new organizations revealed their financial power almost immediately. LA gays, led by the omnipresent David Goodstein, had created the Human Rights Campaign Fund (HRC-F), modeled on MECLA, in 1980. A mere two years later, the gay campaign fund gave almost two hundred thousand dollars to Democratic candidates. The same year, Senator Edward Kennedy was the keynote speaker at the MECLA dinner.

The gay political organizing benefited greatly, as it always does, from competition within the Democratic Party, this time in the run-up to the presidential election in 1984. Not only did they have money to spend, but California, the last big primary state, made California Democrats disproportionately powerful in the nominating process. Democratic presidential aspirant Walter Mondale grudgingly signed on to the still small—yet slowly growing—minority supporting the federal nondiscrimination bill, now a decade in the hopper. Leading Democratic contender Gary Hart came to Mixner for the MECLA endorsement, followed by his real goal, a big private gay fund-raiser. Although their candidate, Hart, did not win the nomination, gay Californians began to make demands in exchange for their financial support. The 1984 Democratic National Convention included a record number of gay delegates and produced a robustly progay platform.

In 1987, in response to the glacial, maddening federal drug-approval process, Mixner and his pals devised the successful strategy of getting California to do its own funding and approval of AIDS drugs. A sympathetic state attorney general shepherded the law through the state legislature, and places like California's Salk Institute started doing their own research. Along the long way, Mixner's love, Peter Scott, died of AIDS. Even California could not stop the dying. But the research went on.

The flood of money AIDS unleashed within the gay community overflowed to the political groups. When Michael Dukakis declared his race for president in 1988, Mixner and MECLA calculated they could easily raise a million dollars for him. Mixner says Dukakis's people wouldn't accept money openly donated by a gay group, so the deal fell through. But the candidate's misstep finally motivated the California group to move beyond supporting straight so-called allies and into running its own candidates. MECLA morphed into Access Now for Gay and Lesbian Equality (ANGLE). When Abby Rubenfeld came to Lambda's office in "a closet" at the New York Civil Liberties Union as its second employee in 1983, the lawyers' organization had an income of around one hundred thousand dollars. When she left in 1988, they were running just under a million. In 1989, the Human Rights Campaign took its increasing stream of donations and declared itself not just a PAC, but a federal, state, and local lobby "for the social promotion of the gay and lesbian community." The next year, Vic Basile, just retired from building the HRC Fund, along with some pals from Texas decided that if big women donors could elect Ann Richards governor of Texas, gays and lesbians should start a PAC to fund openly gay and lesbian candidates. In less than a year the Victory Fund had put an African American lesbian on the Seattle City Council.

The newly self-conscious gay power players might have been imitating the women's political action committee, but they certainly weren't going to dress up like women (unless they happened to be women). As the gay establishment began to establish itself, it consciously left the transgendered and other socially radical elements of the community behind. In 1986, strategic compromisers from the New York Civil Liberties Union and the growing Lambda Legal Foundation finally got the gay antidiscrimination city ordinance New York activists had been seeking since Stonewall. In order to win the battle they had to abandon their gender-nonconforming allies. New York political guru Ethan Geto was brutally frank when confronted by angry queens: "Let me just explain this to you. We can't do this. *We can't do this.* This is what we can do." If Ted Kennedy's campaign insisted, as it did, that the same-sex dancing not start until the senator was long gone from the MECLA dinner, they wouldn't dance. The movement that started with the pearl-bedecked Communist Harry Hay in 1948 was going to try the conventional route. Emphasizing their similarity with heterosexual allies and using the most establishment political weapon—money—the new establishment aspired to make a new move in gay politics: respectability.

Clinton Had a Vision and Gays Were a Part of It

So David Mixner was not entirely surprised in 1991 when he got a call from his old friend Bill Clinton. "He called and asked me to support him," Mixner recalls. "I was a friend, and I said I don't know, and he was taken aback because I was a friend, I had worked on his campaigns in Arkansas." But Mixner had a larger purpose: "I said I want to know how you stand on the issues—the military, employment discrimination, hate crimes, AIDS."

Mixner's inclusion of "the military" in his wish list reflects the increased political ambition of the post-AIDS movement. And why not? Being closeted, gays were already *in* the military, and their records were laden with positive reviews and promotions. No one could argue that gays, being gay, would not make good soldiers. There was a long history of resisting the military exclusion. The first stable gay organization in America was the 1945 Veterans Benevolent Association, organized to fight the injustice of the blue discharges issued to World War II soldiers accused of homosexuality. In the wake of Stonewall, numerous soldiers rose up to challenge their discharges, but gradually the challenges, largely unsuccessful, died out. As early as 1988 pressure began to build within the movement to try again. Lesbian activists found out by chance about "lesbian baiting," how the antigay policy was used against women who didn't put out for their male superior officers. Some soldiers started asking Lambda Legal for legal counsel to contest their discharges. Asking for a national declaration of equality in the hidebound institutions of war making was a far stretch from asking New York City employers not to discriminate or electing people to the Seattle City Council. But the issue was so seductive. In addition to the injustice of denying people the opportunities they sought in the military, activists knew that President Truman's integration of the military in 1948 had been invaluable to the racial civil rights movement. All they needed was a Harry Truman.

At first, LA gays did not think it would be Bill Clinton. Everyone in the community was leaning toward Clinton's rival, Massachusetts senator

Paul Tsongas, whose record on gay and lesbian issues was the best in the country. In 1979, when even Ted Kennedy would not sign on, Tsongas became the first "liberal" in the entire United States Senate to step up and sponsor the federal antidiscrimination law Steve Endean and the gay lobbyists had proposed. Tsongas won awards from the Massachusetts Task Force. With his support, Massachusetts had a state antidiscrimination law, while in Arkansas sodomy was still a criminal offense (and when a liberal state legislator tried to repeal it he got no help from then-governor Clinton). But when Tsongas met with the ANGLE group, he just kept pointing to a booklet reciting his record. And he didn't even stay for lunch.

Poor Paul Tsongas. When Bill and Hillary Clinton came to the obligatory candidate meeting with the ANGLE heavy hitters that October, Hillary turned their heads with her encyclopedic grasp of the details of health care and the AIDS epidemic. Bill won their hearts with his intuitive empathy for what he called their "cycle of death" and a very specific list of commitments. He would have signed the gay antidiscrimination bill Republican California governor Pete Wilson had just vetoed, he promised. Obviously lacking any sense of what he was getting into, in response to a question at a student forum earlier in the campaign, Clinton had offhandedly promised to issue an executive order to end discrimination in the military. He repeated the promise in LA. Exiting the meeting, candidate Clinton went public with his commitment to the gay and lesbian politicos and told the *Los Angeles Times* the same thing: he thought the state gay antidiscrimination bill was the right thing to do. The LA group was in Clinton's palm.

And so that May, Mixner introduced his friend Bill Clinton to the biggest presidential rally ever held by the gay and lesbian community. "I didn't think I could allow myself to dream any more," Mixner told the crowd, "until last October I sat down with Bill Clinton and he said he'd sign an executive order banning discrimination against gays and lesbians in the military and I thought of the thousands each year who are discharged and I started dreaming of all of us standing here like this on a lawn in the White House next March and there's this big table and the President of the United

States picks up a pen and with the stroke of a pen we're so much freer, so much freer, I'm allowing myself to dream again and it's because of this man, who's going to be our Harry Truman . . . the next President of the United States, Bill Clinton!!"

The videotape of Clinton's appearance at the Hollywood Palace that May went the 1992 version of viral immediately, copies of the tape circulating everywhere in the gay community. When ANGLE made a three-minute excerpt to use in campaigning, people were already watching the whole thing on the TVs in the gay bars. Anyone who ever doubted Clinton has only to watch the video to see why he was such a phenomenon. It's a short speech. But so was the Gettysburg Address.

Clinton did not start with the interest group before him. He started, like Lincoln, with the founding principles of the liberal state. All Americans are one people, he began, by "our nature, our basic values, and our basic laws." In contrast with the Supreme Court, which had just, six years before, called such comparisons to homosexuals "facetious," he surrounded the movement in the room with all the other movements that sought admission into citizenship in the liberal state: one people "without regard to race or gender or sexual orientation or age or region or income." Inclusion of gays and lesbians in the great national proposition, he continued, is not just doing good; it is also doing well by doing good. Because "you represent a community of our nation's gifted people that we have been willing to squander. We can't afford to waste the hearts, abilities and minds of the gay and lesbian people, for every day that we refuse to avail ourselves of the potential of any group of Americans, we are less than we ought to be." It's a foregone conclusion, then, that we just can't afford to waste such able people when they want to serve in the military.

It would have been unthinkable for a political candidate to speak to this audience in the second decade of the AIDS epidemic without addressing the disease. Clinton selected from the many possible aspects of AIDS the perfect segue from the value of the people his nation has been willing to waste: their virtue. Gay was good:

> When it was dark and lonely you did not withdraw and this nation has already benefited from the courage and sense of community which you practiced. You did the first important work in pioneering AIDS drugs, you sounded the alarm, stood fast in face of government discrimination and killing silence. And I want to give you my thanks for that struggle today.

Many of the people he was talking to had paid extra to the funeral homes to bury their lovers. When Mixner went to a fund-raiser at the home of some straight liberal allies during the worst of it, he had been offered dinner on a paper plate. By May it was pretty clear that this man was likely to be the next president of the United States. And he was thanking them. There was not a dry eye in the house when he concluded, "I have a vision and you're a part of it. I believe we're all a part of the same community and we'd better start behaving as if we are."

After the election, CNN's Bill Schneider said that one in seven votes for Clinton was connected to the gay community, either through direct votes or from families. When Clinton's gay organizers would put out a call for volunteers, thousands turned out in West Hollywood. The campaign had to send buses to take them to other congressional districts because they were too many for their district. Nationally, gays raised four million dollars for Clinton. In 1992. They were a part of it.

Until They Weren't

Six months after taking office, on July 19, 1993, Clinton announced that the regulations governing gays in the military would be changed to eliminate inquiry into the sexual orientation of applicants. The new policy still called for military discharge of a service member for homosexual conduct, including statements indicating a propensity to engage in homosexual acts. The policy, which came to be known by the shorthand don't ask/don't tell, was an unsatisfactory "compromise" that resulted in the pursuit and separation of thousands of gay and lesbian military personnel in the ensuing years. Worse, two months later the policy was enacted into federal law.

President Clinton's initiative on gays in the military was an almost perfect political disaster. After the fact, gay organizations had a field day of recrimination. Whose idea was it to put military service at the head of the agenda? In the middle of the AIDS epidemic? Why weren't their own organizations more prepared for the firestorm? When did Bill Clinton's pledge get to be reliable political capital?

Despite this agonized second guessing, the don't ask/don't tell debacle illustrates the illusory nature of perfect movement rationality and perfect movement control. Just as nothing seemed to move most of the institutions of the gay movement during the early years of the AIDS epidemic, nothing probably could have stopped the ill-considered, ill-timed attempt to reverse the military policy when Clinton reached the White House.

As always, chance played a role. The National Gay and Lesbian Task Force got involved when, in 1988, NGLTF director Sue Hyde, who was touring the South visiting the states that still had sodomy laws, began hearing the stories of lesbian baiting of the women at the Parris Island, South Carolina, marine base. Further investigation revealed a harrowing pattern of sexual harassment of the female marines followed by threats of outing or criminal prosecution for sodomy if they did not comply. Inspired by what they were seeing, Hyde and her radical sidekick Urvashi Vaid started the Military Freedom Project. Their first strategy was to make an alliance with feminist groups to fight the use of lesbian baiting in service of illegal sexual harassment.

Joe Steffan found his voice. When the navy booted him out of the US Naval Academy mere weeks before his graduation in 1991, Steffan seriously considered doing nothing. Someone put him in touch with seventies gay military victim ex-midshipman Copy Berg. Inspired by Berg's story, Steffan went to Lambda Legal and sued the navy. A year later, Petty Officer Keith Meinhold and Lieutenant (JG) Tracy Thorne both went voluntarily on ABC News *Nightline* to announce their homosexuality. Both were discharged and both sued. Before 1992 was out, another militant homosexual soldier surfaced in the unlikely person of fifty-year-old Colonel Margarethe Cammermeyer, chief of nursing in the Washington National Guard. These individuals were all military stars. Steffan was a battalion commander, one of the ten highest-ranking midshipmen at the academy, Thorne was a bombardier-navigator, according to his commander, an "exemplary," "hard-charging lieutenant," and Meinhold one of the best flight instructors his superiors knew. Cammermeyer had won a Bronze Star for her service in a Vietnam field hospital. While Midshipman Steffan was doing discovery for his lawsuit, someone leaked him a study of gays in the military that the Defense Department had secretly requested from the Personnel Security Research and Education Center (PERSEREC) of the Pentagon. The report concluded that there was no evidence showing gays were unsuitable for the military. It was the military's leaked study Bill Clinton was talking about in his speech at the Hollywood Palace.

For months before Inauguration Day, as Americans learned from Clinton's various statements that gay service was on the table, the institutions of the religious right started hammering on it. In an interview with sociologist David Rayside after the fact, astute political observer Congressman Barney Frank explained how legislators think when their phones light up like that: "People's ability to organize mail is a pretty good marker for their ability to organize votes. . . . If you know these people are totally out of sympathy with the overwhelming majority of the public, that lessens their impact. But if you know that the public is divided, what legislators attend to is the public opinion that registers itself. It's not public opinion; it's voter opinion." Public-opinion polling soon reflected the successful campaign against gays in the military, plummeting from an approval rating of 60 percent in 1992 to less than half that a year later. David Mixner thinks that had Clinton simply issued the order rescinding the military policy prohibiting homosexuals from serving, along with a bunch of other executive orders his first day in office, he might have gotten away with it, as when Jimmy Carter pardoned the draft dodgers in 1977. Instead, Clinton had started the process by asking his secretary of defense to start preparing an executive order, and all hell broke loose.

Despite the somewhat limited involvement of the NGLTF, the gay movement was simply unprepared for this fight. There wasn't even an organization of gay service members, past or present. Since the agreement to lift the ban had emerged from the small, wealthy California activist groups, what passed for mass, grassroots organizations, such as the NGLTF and the Human Rights Campaign, had no say so and no plan. When the organizations finally generated a counter campaign, dispatching able movement lawyers like Lambda's Tom Stoddard to stave off the worst outcome, it was beyond too late.

But the problem wasn't only an unprepared movement. A just-elected president, with a majority of his own party in both houses of Congress, might have been able to resist the collective force of the vocal and powerful religious right. The open gay baiting and antifeminism of the 1992 Republican National Convention was widely regarded as one of the causes for the defeat of incumbent Republican president Bush in the election. The problem was that the movement, and also probably Clinton and his liberal allies, had underestimated the extent to which the military defined itself by old-fashioned standards of heterosexual maleness. Monied and connected Los Angeles gays might have thought of themselves as the pillars of the community, but the military establishment had quite a different view.

President Clinton and his besotted gay supporters soon learned that they faced General Colin Powell, the universally revered, Republican-sponsored first African American chairman of the Joint Chiefs of Staff; Georgia Democrat Sam Nunn, chairman of the Senate Armed Services Committee; and white-ethnic big-city Democrat Charles Moskos, eminent academic chronicler of the racial integration of the armed services. Collectively, in their background and politics the three antigay crusaders might be taken to represent as close as you come to a centrist political position in 1993.

None of these men would express their opposition in terms of disobedience of God's law or destruction of the family. Instead, they put forth a defense of the current policy in terms of the troops' entitlement to privacy and the threat of homosexuals to good order and discipline. Powell was the killer. When he went public in opposing President Clinton's plan to admit open gays to the military, then-representative Pat Schroeder wrote him a stinging letter: "I am sure you are aware," Schroeder wrote, "that your reasoning would have kept you from the mess hall a few decades ago." He needed no reminders, Powell wrote back, "concerning the history of African-Americans in defense of their nation and the tribulations they faced." Unlike race, which was "immutable and *benign*," Powell wrote, gays' "sexual orientation, perhaps the most profound of human behavioral characteristics," was inconsistent with the "necessary standards of order and discipline required on the armed forces." According to Powell, for purposes of military service, the "most profound" human behavioral characteristic was not hard-charging or exemplary service, but sexual orientation. A lot of the moral fuel for the gay claim rested on their analogy to the racial integration of the military. Once the first African American chairman of the Joint Chiefs of Staff rejected the comparison, it simply collapsed.

If Clinton tried to lift the policy ban, Nunn, and Clinton's foreseeable 1996 presidential opponent, minority leader Bob Dole, threatened they would pass legislation embedding the complete prohibition into a federal statute. Nunn scheduled "hearings." In May 1993, Nunn took a press road show, with cameras and microphones, into the tight quarters of the USS *Baton Rouge*, listening to the crew explain why they did not want homosexuals in their shower rooms. By the time the Nunn road show left the dock, Clinton must have been grateful to extract any semblance of a change in the blanket discharges of homosexual human beings. In July, he announced that the United States armed services would change their policy to Moskos's suggested don't ask/don't tell. Recruiters wouldn't ask and gays would not be pursued. But they would be separated from the service if they engaged in "homosexual conduct," including statements, which were, weirdly, designated as conduct. Essentially, as before, gays were to remain in the closet. Just in case the gay movement was inclined to ask the executive for more again, Congress enacted the new policy into law. Any further changes would have to come from Congress itself.

Had they been paying attention, the lawyers at Lambda Legal and the feminists at NGLTF and the rich Angelenos at the Clinton rally could have seen the investment of the American military in its heterosexual male identity, which had already manifested itself when women started agitating for gender integration into combat roles at about the same time. The author of don't ask/don't tell, Charles Moskos, was also a critic of adding women to the mix, contending in the *Washington Post* that women's compassionate natures would be a hindrance to combat service. In 1993, the United States military was defined as a gender hierarchy with heterosexual men on top. The gay movement would find no shortcut to equality through sacrifice. In an article published in the middle of the debate, political scientist John DiIulio and former Air Force Academy faculty member Gerald Garvey explained: "by military cultural definition, a soldier can't be gay." Letting gays serve would "change the meaning of who they are."

The gay military activists had made a category mistake. The strategy for using the military as an entry point into civil equality depends, as did the African American and Japanese American claims, on such valuable characteristics as exemplary service trumping the characteristics that make them different. The strategy of volunteering to die for your country doesn't work as a civil rights mechanism if the military is a culture for which the minority is ineligible by definition.

Senator Sam Nunn probably wasn't trying to teach the gay movement a foundational lesson in activism when he took to the Senate floor early in the fight, unleashing a barrage of "questions" intended to paint a picture of uncontrollable—and undesirable—social change. However, Nunn's litany of doubt is a roadmap to the social change the movement had to accomplish before they could successfully take on the military. "What," Nunn asked, "would be the impact of changing the current policy on recruiting, retention, morale, discipline, as well as military effectiveness?" "What restrictions should be placed on conduct between members of the same sex," especially compared to acts allowed between members of the opposite sex? "Should homosexual couples be entitled to the same benefits as legally married couples?" Writing in the *New York Times* shortly thereafter, Ronald Reagan's secretary of the army, John Marsh Jr., was more explicit: what about the Uniform Code of Military Justice ban on sodomy? The Supreme Court had just ruled six years earlier that the Georgia cops could burst into Michael Hardwick's bedroom and toss him in the slammer for giving (or getting) a little head. Why shouldn't the army do the same thing? What did the president propose: to recruit people who would then go directly to the brig?

A quarter century after Stonewall, the gay movement was still in the early stages of gaining any semblance of citizenship in the liberal state. They had no right to be left undisturbed by their government; sodomy was still criminal in half the states and the US military. They had scant equality in self-governance—as Nunn boasted, their "coupled" relationships were not "legal," like "legally married couples'" relationships were. Until they did, instead of dining on the lawn to celebrate the gay emancipation, David Mixner chained himself to the White House fence and was carried off to jail.

What Else Went Wrong: Defending Marriage

At almost the same moment, and without any greater foresight or strategic analysis, the gay movement went after a harder target: marriage. Same-sex marriage guru Evan Wolfson says he embraced the concept of same-sex marriage as a pure intellectual exercise sometime during his years at Harvard Law School in the eighties. What is, he asked himself, "the central social and legal institution in this and any society? Marriage is. In many arenas, like employment where gays are discriminated against, people are just moving their prejudices from the sexual arena into a part of life where they have no place at all. A gay lawyer is a lawyer," Wolfson says. "But barring them from marriage correctly focuses on the core of what makes them different: their sexual and emotional relationships. Challenging marriage discrimination would challenge the core of gay exclusion," Wolfson thought. It would be, in Wolfson's words, "electric." "Radioactive" would probably be more like it. In 1983, when Wolfson first wrote about his plan in a senior paper at Harvard, all fifty states either defined marriage as between a man and a woman or interpreted their laws as if that were the case. In 2003, after twenty years of campaigning for gay and lesbian couples to marry, no states at all had changed their laws to permit same-sex marriage. Although several states and localities had instituted various arrangements for civil union, many in the gay community regarded these nonmarital alternatives as insulting or at best, segregationist, efforts to buy them off with less than full equality.

Gay intellectual Andrew Sullivan must really have a wonderful family. He came to the cause of same-sex marriage very early—just a few years after Evan Wolfson wrote his law school paper and well before any court had so much as glanced their way—with a stunning cover essay in the *New Republic*, "Here Comes the Groom," in 1989. One of his earliest memories of being gay, he says, was the realization that he could not marry and therefore would never be as good as Mom and Dad. When he did finally marry, in Provincetown, in 2007, bringing his family and his spouse's family together was "one of the happiest times in my life." Deploying all the skills of a star Oxford debater, Sullivan lays out the case for marriage in "Here Comes the Groom" in terms so simple, they seem ridiculously obvious today. Yet at the same time, it was regarded as almost unthinkable. And the *New Republic*, where Sullivan was a young writer, was riding a wave of influence among political journals.

Evan Wolfson says that Sullivan's essay, and later his book, *Virtually Normal*, made the ideological case for this tectonic social change. "He was one of the earliest and most sustained intellectual advocates for marriage,"

Wolfson says. "He has made a really important contribution as an advocate who wrote about the moral and familial dimensions. Very personal and how it's about restoring wholeness to people's lives." In a very Catholic-inflected analysis, Sullivan says that marriage is a vehicle to enable weak humanity to embrace virtue. Why should heterosexuals have a monopoly on the institutions of virtue? In the wilderness years, he and Wolfson traveled, often together, arguing and making their case. "In words," Sullivan says, "we had to persuade the majority to agree with us. We are so few. We had only argument to use."

What made marriage so much worth fighting for, in Wolfson's eyes, was exactly what made it, to his opponents, so worth defending. The centrality of the family in Western culture goes back to antiquity. Indeed, at the beginning of Western political thought in Athens twenty-five hundred years ago, Aristotle said the same thing Wolfson says about the importance of marriage. Thinking about how politics came about, Aristotle imagined that people, being individuals first, naturally gravitated to families (households) for the sake of material survival, or life, and only thereafter into the state. Rooted in material survival, this version of marriage is, by definition, reproductive and therefore heterosexual. Sullivan made an interesting decision in his marriage advocacy to duck the whole naturalism argument and just point out that nature's god, so beloved by Aristotle's medieval interpreter Thomas Aquinas, wasted an awful lot of sperm every time heterosexuals had their naturally procreative intercourse. To say nothing of spontaneous abortion. What a careless deity. "Aquinas was a great thinker," he says. "If he were alive today he'd be teaching about Darwin. He just used what he had in the thirteenth century." Like the military, marriage was defined as something for which gay couples were ineligible.

And, like gays serving in the military, gay marriage had been on the table for decades. Right after Stonewall, two activists from Minnesota, Jack Baker and Michael McConnell, had sued for the right to marry. Their defeat was the first of countless such rejections, until, finally, interest waned. The revival of militancy in the wake of the insulting opinion in the sodomy case, *Bowers v. Hardwick*, and the AIDS crisis, gave birth to renewed agitation for marriage equality within the movement. Coming after years of sexual liberation in the gay community, the proposal was hotly controversial. For once, the gay revolution's claim to moral inclusion and gays' defense of their own difference dictated conflicting positions. Lambda Legal witnessed a pitched battle between promarriage executive director Tom Stoddard and legal director Paula Ettelbrick, who resisted the suggestion forcefully. "Since when is marriage a path to liberation?" Ettelbrick famously asked.

Sullivan, a believing Catholic and a professed conservative, was a complicated messenger for the cause in those days. All the resistance to the conventional and historically patriarchal aspects of marriage could easily be focused on this most conventional (and therefore unconventional) gay activist. The Lesbian Avengers picketed his book reading in Chicago; people posted head shots of him with targets on them. "I cannot believe we won this battle on marriage and the military in my lifetime," Sullivan says, combative to this day, "especially since even the gay rights movement opposed this strategy from the get-go and took a decade to reluctantly sign on."

Marriage godfather Evan Wolfson was marooned in a riven Lambda in 1990 when Bill Woods, the founder of the Hawaii Gay and Lesbian Center, got a phone call from Honolulu lesbian feminist Ninia Baehr. She and her partner Genora Dencel could not name each other beneficiaries of their insurance policies, she complained. Woods responded by suggesting they sue the state. Organized gay activists were unenthusiastic. Reverend Troy Perry would not come over and marry the Hawaii couple. Lambda Legal would not represent them. Neither would the ACLU. Champing at the bit, Wolfson got his bosses at Lambda to let him help out behind the scenes. The trial court dismissed the case.

Three years later, in 1993, the Hawaii Supreme Court reversed and Hawaii became the first state in history to rule in favor of same-sex marriage. The ban, the court held, violated the equal-protection clauses of the state constitution. Hawaii is one of the few states whose state constitution explicitly prohibits classification based on sex, the local version of the national Equal Rights Amendment sought by feminists in their prime. The state supreme court found the requirement that men marry only women and vice versa to be an impermissible classification based on sex. The Hawaii court sent the case back to the trial level to see if the state could prove that banning same-sex marriage served a compelling state interest that would justify the inequality.

The opponents of same-sex marriage went ballistic, fearing that two judges on the supreme court of a bunch of islands could impose same-sex marriage in every one of these United States. This was not crazy; the federal Constitution requires that "full faith and credit shall be given in each state to the public acts, records, and judicial proceedings of every other state." States have some leeway to reject a sister state's proceedings if they violate local public policy, but states usually recognize marriage judgments. That's why teenagers from Dogpatch could enforce their marriages in the heart of Manhattan and why people used to fly to Nevada for a few weeks and come back divorced. The country was confronted with the prospect of planeloads of homosexuals returning to Utah from Hawaii with suntans and wedding bands. To make matters worse, another couple, not surprisingly, sued for a marriage license in DC.

Just as the marriage case, revived by the state supreme court in 1993, was about to go to trial in Hawaii, the 1996 presidential primary season opened in Iowa. When antigay Texas congressman Phil Gramm tied frontrunner Bob Dole in the Iowa straw poll that winter, Dole returned the donation he had accepted from the gay Log Cabin Republicans. The Republicans began their race to the bottom on gay marriage. That spring, Republican House leader Newt Gingrich pressed Georgia congressman Bob Barr to draft a law forbidding the federal government to recognize same-sex marriages and allowing states to deny them full faith and credit. In May, Barr's federal Defense of Marriage Act (DOMA) went to the House Judiciary Committee, chaired by Illinois representative Henry Hyde.

The committee engaged in a stunning set of openly homophobic hearings. Reprising the archaic and discredited notion that all things on earth are created for a purpose rather than the purposeless products of the process of evolution, Aristotelian political philosopher Hadley Arkes told the House Judiciary Committee that "reproduction is the 'teleology [purpose or end] of the body.'" Monogamous reproductive heterosexual families, accordingly, were the product of a purposeful natural order and were, in turn, essential to the political order. Hence, their defense by Congress. South Carolina congressman Robert Inglis exploded at Colorado's Pat Schroeder, who was opposed to DOMA, informing her that same-sex marriage would destroy the country: "One of the reasons the Republic has survived so well is that for a long time in this country," Inglis said, "there was a generally accepted view of what is right and wrong. . . . And folks that you associated with for a long time have attempted to now undo that sort of understanding, and that's part of what's happening here."

The report the House of Representatives generated to accompany the bill explains that Congress was acting because the Hawaii state court was about to permit homosexual couples to "marry." (Each time the Judiciary Committee referred to same-sex unions, it put scare quotes around the word "marriage.") The legislators were, they said, "tending and nurturing the institution of traditional, heterosexual marriage," not because they knew how harm would come but because they feared it might. Anyway, same-sex "marriage" cannot *be* marriage, they reported, because, according to conservative pundit William Bennett, "marriage *is* [emphasis added] a socially functional coordination of [male and female] . . . different characters, abilities, inclinations." Representative Inglis needn't have worried about the Republic. DOMA sailed through Congress, with only sixty-seven representatives and seventeen senators voting against.

When DOMA reached the White House in September 1996, Richard

Socarides, who crossed the first pride parade in 1970, was serving as special assistant to the president and senior adviser for public liaison. Socarides says he argued as hard as he could against Clinton's signing the law, but it was now full campaign season, and campaign guru Harold Ickes did not want to have gay marriage to be an issue in the campaign. Anyway, Socarides said, DOMA was essentially a harmless error, because no one could get married anywhere in the world at that time.

By 2003, all that Wolfson had accomplished with his unremitting labor and the help of every major gay movement institution in America was to motivate a bunch of states and the federal government to enact anti–gay marriage provisions, often most irreversibly, into their state constitutions. Where the law had not said opposite sexes it did. Where the states had routinely recognized the nuptials of other states, however bizarre their content (twelve-year-olds, cousins), they now forbade recognition of unions of the same sex. And the federal government told them it was okay. During the height of the marriage wars, a federal study of the impact listed more than a thousand benefits available to couples with recognized marriages. DOMA barred the members of same-sex unions from them all.

No one would ever accuse Wolfson of carelessness. From the beginning of his crusade to clear the aisles for gay marriage, he had a plan. Wolfson believes it was a battle that had to be fought. The gay movement should not be left alone "in a little huddle" by themselves. He didn't want them to have their own church or their own relationships. He wanted them to be embraced and accepted. In this positive vision of the gay revolution, being let into the institution of marriage is the "core." After Hawaii, Wolfson had big winds at his back. The flood of previously closeted conventional individuals who fueled the disastrous military effort also wanted the traditional relationship of marriage. Lesbians, who had ascended to positions of authority in many organizations, had been fighting for family-related rights, like custody of their children from previous marriages, for years. Wolfson, who remained at Lambda, started the Marriage Project, which issued a Marriage Resolution to attract potential allies, gay and not. The ACLU got involved, starting in the Hawaii appeal. After the DOMA battle, the Stonewall-era voices calling for a gay-led liberation of all Americans from patriarchal marriage subsided to a faint hum.

A backlash of this magnitude, however, usually indicates that events got ahead of the canny movement strategists. Since the eruption of the marriage issue, political thinkers have speculated on what it is about marriage that made it so resistant to gay claims. One school of thought is that Wolfson got his wish: marriage directly confronts heterosexuals with the sexual part of homosexuality. And they find it disgusting. Lambda Legal leader Kevin Cathcart calls this response "the ick factor." Certainly the ick factor goes a long way to explaining why Senator Sam Nunn felt he should bring cameras into the close quarters typical of submarines when fighting the battle against gays in the military. But repugnance should have driven a similar response to the gay campaign for decriminalization of sodomy, which was succeeding brilliantly in the legislatures when the marriage and military battles went so badly awry.

What Went Wrong: Marriage, the Military, and Modernity

The gay revolutionaries could never just take the straight path to formal liberal equality by mimicking the behaviors of the dominant political and social hierarchies. They were different, and their difference was the source of formal social condemnation (it was sinful, and so forth). They had to make the more ambitious claim that, despite their difference, they were good. Unable to mimic their rulers in the crucial arena of their difference, the gay revolution had a harder fight than other movements did even for core political rights of the Enlightenment, asking to have sex in private and not be fired from their jobs. But at least in those arenas they were still making demands on the basic liberal bargain. As Arthur Evans put it so long ago, America was going to have to kill the gays . . . or live up to its democratic principles.

When the gay revolution took after marriage and the military, it was making a bid for membership not just in the cold precincts of the liberal state, but in the club of social acceptance. The exact nature of the club was a moving target, but, in a development little noted at the time, the epidemic of coming out that the real epidemic engendered brought many people with otherwise conventional desires to the movement. They wanted to wear uniforms and carry orange blossoms.

They had their work cut out for them. After Andrew Sullivan visited the AIDS quilt in the midst of the AIDS epidemic, he went to mass, as he did every week, and the priest was preaching a sermon about Jesus and the lepers. "We don't have plagues now," the priest announced, "so we just have to think of leprosy as something like cancer." When Sullivan asked the priest if he was aware of the AIDS epidemic raging all around them, the priest responded that he didn't think anyone with AIDS would be in the congregation. "And of course," Sullivan says, "one of the other priests in that very church had AIDS." As, later, would Sullivan.

In these aspirations, they were asking for inclusion in two of the few institutions, formally run by the government but still heavily rooted outside the liberal state. Unlike the liberal state, marriage was a realm of insecurity and inequality. Until relatively recently, the common law had covered married women with a doctrine that disabled them from owning or managing their own property. There was no such thing as marital rape and domestic abuse was rarely punished. The feminist movement began the process of bringing marriage into the world of democratic principles. The first feminists, the suffragists, pushed for married women's property rights. The second wave demanded the criminalization of marital rape and the enforcement of battery laws in domestic cases.

At each stage of the women's long fight to bring some public values into marriage, the opponents invoked gays' old adversaries—Aristotle and his Christian avatar, Aquinas—arguing this time that nature had made men and women "for" different purposes, male rule was natural and godly, and women belonged in the home. William Bennett, the conservative political pundit whose work figures prominently in the legislative history of DOMA, has been a leading voice opposing feminism's efforts to break out of the natural marital roles Aristotle prescribed. The battle to bring liberalism and equality to marriage was still raging when Ninia Baehr and Genora Dencel asked the Hawaii court to recognize their union.

In addition, as in the criminal laws governing sex, the state had long deferred to the church where marriage was concerned. Even though the American colonists did not formally assign marriage to the church when they came to the New World, culturally, marriage was largely immune from basic principles like separation of church and state. For centuries in America, churchmen were authorized to perform the state's function of marrying people. So although it may have seemed a little strange for a witness to testify about Aristotle and Aquinas in Congress in 1996, as Hadley Arkes did, he was actually the mouthpiece for the Catholic Church. And even in 1996, where marriage was concerned, what the church thought mattered to the state. (In a suitable coda to the weirdness of invoking a thirteenth-century thinker on sexual purpose in 1996, Arkés, born a Jew, converted to Catholicism in 2010. It was, he said, the "fulfillment" or natural purpose of his Jewishness.)

The religious underpinnings of the fight over same-sex marriage, however anachronistic, brought out the most resilient horseman of the gay apocalypse—sin. In contemporary political science, sin-inflected issues like gay marriage, drug policy, and abortion have given rise to a whole new category of analysis, morality politics. When issues of morality politics arose, political scientists noted, voters made reference to the very basic principles of their beliefs—things are "right" or "moral," or "wrong" or "immoral." They gave little credence to expertise, such as the studies showing that children raised by gay couples do not turn out worse than other children. The lack of deference extended to their elected officials, as voters strongly preferred to decide such matters by direct democracy. In the marriage issue, as in the military initiative, the gay revolution, grounded in moral belief in its own rightness, met a moral opponent.

So, when considering DOMA, Representative Robert Inglis accused his opponent of palling around with people who would ruin the Republic, congressmen argued about concepts of right and wrong dating back to Aristotle, and they paid no attention to the sociologists who told them existing marriage would not suffer from the incursion of gay couples. Although the federal system has no avenues of direct democracy, half the state DOMAs were the product of direct voting at the state level. When the Hawaii trial court finally unburdened itself of its opinion in 1998, seven years after the suit was filed, the Hawaii legislature sent the voters a defense-of-marriage amendment to the state constitution, which passed by 61 percent.

Similarly, the military has historically been located outside the precincts of liberal democracy. The founding principle of modern politics is that people make a government because they want to avoid the dangerous state where every man is a law unto himself and life is nasty, brutish, and short. But the military asks people to risk exactly what modern liberal government is supposed to protect against: a violent death. The military is an institution left over from a premodern era. That's why soldiers are treated as heroes when they volunteer or risk their lives even when they do not have to do so. They are considered to be doing something extra: a communal or virtuous act way beyond what the democratic government should ask. The Japanese Americans could leapfrog into equal citizenship after their service in World War II: they had done something extra. In exchange for this extra service, the military demands values beyond the distant egalitarianism of modern politics. Soldiers are foxhole friends, best buddies, essential support, back protectors.

Marriage is not the state; it's a congregation. The military is not the state; it's a club.

Like the newly rich since time immemorial, the rich gay Democratic donors thought they could buy their way into the congregation and the club. The smart gay lawyers and intellectuals thought they could argue their way in. But that's not how clubs work.

9

Founding Fathers: Winning Modern Rights Before Fighting Ancient Battles

A few minutes after the Supreme Court issued the first explicit progay ruling in constitutional history, President Bill Clinton's gay advisers Marsha Scott and Richard Socarides met in her office. Should the president comment on the decision? He should not, said some midlevel White House counsel who stopped by to advise. *Romer v. Evans*, the sweeping opinion extending to gay and lesbian Americans the guarantees of the equal protection clause, "doesn't mean a thing." "No?" Richard responded. "All it means is the beginning of the end for people like you."

It was also the beginning of the triumphal last phase of the gay revolution. In 1996, at the very moment that gays overreached and lost in their efforts to join the illiberal institutions of marriage and the military, their decades of slow but steady work for membership in the liberal state began to bear fruit. And so, even for this most unconventional movement, the final push began in the most conventional way. Starting with *Romer*, they achieved the simple goods of the liberal state—participation in collective public self-governance, protection against the state for their private lives, and protection against their violent fellow citizens, to live, period.

I. Public Life

The Successful Gay Ground Game

Romer struck down an amendment to the Colorado constitution prohibiting any government action on behalf of gays, lesbians, or bisexuals. There were many battles left to fight after 1996 before Victory was clear. But *Romer* was surely the critical marker.

For the gay revolution, the Supreme Court was the last, rather than the first, resort. Unlike black Americans, no one had fought a civil war for gay folks. The constitutional amendments the court invoked in the race cases were unassailably written with black folks in mind, even though it had taken a while for them to be enforced. Nor could the gay revolutionaries claim that their treatment was the product of overbroad stereotypes that violate the broad command of equal protection like the feminists could. They were, in fact, different. They had to argue that their difference did not justify their treatment. In the early days of the movement, no one except the singularly inner-directed Frank Kameny thought of claiming that the Constitution entitled them to fair treatment, like the racial movement did in *Brown*. (He lost.) Small minority that they were, they were still going to have to start with the Sixties repertoire of direct actions and conventional mechanisms of electoral politics, rather than the faster route of constitutional litigation.

During the quarter century after Stonewall, the gay revolution focused most of its political efforts at the local level. By the time Stonewall erupted, cosmopolitan cities had long been the centers of gay community life. Long before there was a federal Civil Rights Act of 1964, the gay activists observed, cities with sizable racial minorities had enacted local antidiscrimination laws. Even before Stonewall, gay activists had already started targeting the local police departments and the sweeping disorderly conduct laws they enforced. After the police raid on Stonewall, the focus sharpened. The new activists quickly learned that their city governments, which supervised the police, were the institutions with the biggest impact on their day-to-day lives. Starting in 1971, in little liberal college towns like Madison, Wisconsin, or larger, gay-infused cities like San Francisco, gay activists worked to pass ordinances prohibiting discrimination against them. Asking not to be beaten by your own police or not to be fired from your job for your sex life were easy appeals to the security and privacy principles of the liberal state. And using local political power where your voters were concentrated was a clear invocation of the third principle, self-governance.

Denver, which would ultimately test the access of gay people to democratic self-governance, is a perfect example of the process. Within a year of Stonewall, Denver had a gay-liberation front. When the Denver police parked a bus decorated with a "Johnny Cash Special" sign near the gay cruising area and assigned an undercover agent to entice men on so other cops could arrest them until the bus was full, the new coalition called a press conference and a political movement was born.

Activists succeeded in getting the Denver City Council to repeal its lewd-loitering and cross-dressing ordinances in 1973. The liberal city council in the university town of Boulder about thirty miles from Denver passed an ordinance barring sexual-orientation discrimination in employment in 1974.

But Boulder residents made such a ruckus about their newfound inclusiveness that, immediately after they passed it, the legislators submitted their own enactment to a referendum. The people of Boulder voted to repeal the antidiscrimination law, recalled one of the two supporters eligible for recall, and then denied the mayor reelection. In 1977 pop singer and Christian activist Anita Bryant started a religiously driven movement, Save Our Children, to use the referendum process to undo the antidiscrimination ordinance that had passed in her home area, Dade County, Florida. Buoyed by the contemporaneous rise of the religious right, Bryant's success spawned similar efforts in all the cities where gays had won rights: St. Paul, Minnesota; Eugene, Oregon; and Wichita, Kansas.

With a handful of exceptions, Bryant's strategy blocked state and local progress for gays and lesbians for almost a decade. But for all those backlash years, the gay activists just kept playing local politics, looking for an opening. San Francisco gays organized a Democratic club and registered more voters. After annual defeats in the legislature, in 1975, Pennsylvania activists lobbied liberal governor Milton Shapp to issue an executive order protecting gay state employees. In 1982, a concerted campaign led by one extremely strategic out gay state legislator and heavily invoking Wisconsin's long progressive history finally produced the first statewide gay antidiscrimination law.

The slow but steady local success in Colorado eventually provoked the effort that was the subject of *Evans v. Romer* (as the case was called when it started out in Colorado). In 1975, the coalition that organized the 1973 Denver City Council action, with the lesbian group from NOW, came close but failed to get a statewide gay civil rights bill. Having failed politically both in Boulder and statewide, Gerald Gerash, out, gay, and an all-around-left activist lawyer in Denver, figured out that community had to precede politics. A small but energetic Denver group reorganized themselves into a Unity coalition to build a gay and lesbian center, called just the Center. It would be a place, first Center director Phil Nash remembers, where people could just "be," especially if the bar scene was not their idea of a good time.

There weren't a lot of big gay donors to build a community center in Denver, Colorado, in 1975. But there were the queens. Or more to the point, the cross-dressing and drag-embracing empresses, duchesses, and other nobles of the International Imperial Court System of the United States and its local chapter, the Imperial Court of the Rocky Mountain Empire. The Imperial Court System is older than Stonewall and about the size of the Human Rights Campaign. Started in 1965 in America by the redoubtable José Sarria, opera-singing icon of San Francisco's Black Cat Bar, just for fun ("Why be a queen when you can be an Empress?"), the association soon generated chapters all over the world. Although the Empire's most public manifestation is its yearly "Night of a Thousand Gowns" ball in New York each spring, the real mission of the Imperial Court System is to raise boatloads of money for charity, gay and nongay (the Empire strikes back at breast cancer and domestic violence as well as supporting gay causes). In the early Imperial days, some charities wouldn't even accept their money. But they just kept partying and fund-raising. In 1975, the two-year-old Rocky Mountain Empire was the largest donor to the would-be gay and lesbian center.

Once there was community, politics followed. With little fanfare, in 1978 tourism-sensitive Aspen passed an antidiscrimination law and held onto it. The activists who organized and ran the Center formed the core of the local movement. They met. They planned programs. They squabbled. Change came, as it often does, from the local elites. The newly organized gay community made an alliance with the first Hispanic candidate for mayor of Denver, Federico Peña, who was running against the conservative, antigay incumbent in 1983. Right before Peña's election, *Outfront*, the main gay newspaper, ran a ringing endorsement. "Finally," the Center's Nash says, "someone in city hall returned my phone calls."

Colorado politics on the whole began to change. As in the rest of the country, AIDS activism brought some people out and the community saw gay people start to die and take care of each other. One day in 1987, a bunch of kids too young to have been burned in 1974 started to agitate for another try at a civil rights ordinance in Boulder. They put an initiative prohibiting sexual-orientation discrimination on the ballot. The wife of a philosophy professor from the university ran the group, and some lesbians and feminists raised a little money. After thirteen years of keeping gays out of civil rights protection, Boulder's new law applied not just to employment, but also to housing and public accommodations, and it passed by the same direct-democracy process that had reversed so much progay legislation in the past.

In 1990, Denver policewoman Angela Romero decided she'd had enough abuse from her department. Romero had wanted to be a policewoman since she was a child. After a long and distinguished career, she was caught buying a book at a lesbian bookstore. She was transferred from her specialty—teaching safety in the public schools—and assigned to domestic-violence cases. Duty call became a nightmare of harassment and lesbian baiting. After four years of this, she began lobbying for Denver to pass a nondiscrimination ordinance. Denver gays and lesbians had already ramped up their activism for the 1988 election year. After the election, they held a meeting and decided an ordinance would be a good project. So lesbian feminist organizer Tea Schook and a bunch of the activists from the Center effort started drafting. Inspired in part by Boulder, in 1991, the city council of Colorado's largest city enacted its ordinance and defended it successfully against the predictable rollback initiative. That same year, gay activists even made the mistake of poking a stick into the eye of the religious right by proposing a civil rights bill in Colorado Springs, home to the multimillion-dollar Christian Right powerhouse Focus on the Family.

The Colorado Springs ordinance failed, but one of the activists who worked against it was aroused enough to start a statewide opposition, Colorado for Family Values. A CFV spokesman told Denver newsweekly *Westword*: "And we said no further. This is not going any further. . . . They were just going to go city by city and county by county. And there was only one way to stop it, and that was to do something statewide." The new coalition was determined to repeal the existing civil rights laws and put an end to the local strategy. Denver: meet Colorado.

Colorado was the perfect place to test the statewide antigay resistance. Access to the initiative process in Colorado is easy and wide open, and it takes only a simple majority to amend the state constitution. Colorado for Family Values proposed to amend the state constitution to prohibit any "PROTECTED STATUS BASED ON HOMOSEXUAL, LESBIAN, OR BISEXUAL ORIENTATION." Under the new provision, "Neither the State of Colorado, through any of its branches or departments, nor any of its agencies, political subdivisions, municipalities or school districts, shall enact, adopt or enforce any statute, regulation, ordinance or policy whereby homosexual, lesbian or bisexual orientation, conduct, practices or relationships shall constitute or otherwise be the basis of or entitle any person or class of persons to have or claim any minority status, quota preferences, protected status or claim of discrimination." The proposed constitutional amendment not only reversed all existing protections of any substance, but, under its terms, any gay political movement would be barred from ever trying to come back to any state legislature or local government to get any new protections passed.

The Game Changer

It was a Hail Mary pass. Even in the heyday of the Anita Bryant backlash, the antigay movement had never succeeded in enacting measures to make life radically worse for gays and lesbians. The first time they tried—in 1978, with the Briggs initiative in California to bar gays and lesbians from teaching school—they met their first defeat. Amendment 2 tried to make things as much worse as possible. After two decades of slow but steady progress, gays were to be, as the Supreme Court would later opine, "strangers to the law" in Colorado.

Young Colorado gay activist Pat Steadman was anything but a stranger to the law in 1991 when the Amendment 2 initiative appeared. A slender, handsome young man with a mop of floppy hair, he had just graduated from law school and registered for the Colorado bar exam. Steadman rushed off to the gathering activists had hastily convened in a conference center outside Denver to respond to the new attack. There was no real statewide gay organization, so the group from the Denver ordinance fight, now named the Equal Protection Coalition, quickly took over the movement, rented space in the Center building, hired staff, and started fighting over how to fight the amendment.

The Amendment 2 campaign was a classic of morality politics—a mass electoral action based on intuitive aversion. University of Colorado coach Bill McCartney, founder of the Christian men's group Promise Keepers, called a press conference at the university to announce his support for Amendment 2. "Homosexuality was an abomination of almighty God," the coach announced. The well-organized legions of the Christian Right turned out.

In the campaign waged on behalf of the amendment, proponents taught voters that gays and lesbians were actually after "special rights." "Special rights" has been code talk for civil rights since the racial movements of the Sixties. Marginalized groups using the law to get what the society already offered to the majority—service at lunch counters, for example—was framed as asking for "special" treatment. The special rights talk got louder with the appearance of the remedy of affirmative action. Although none of the gay rights laws in Colorado mentioned affirmative action, the proponents of Amendment 2 suggested that straight people, already "bumped" by blacks and women, would have to now step back again, while homosexuals took their stuff away. Just before the election, Amendment 2 proponents had distributed an eight-page broadside to homes all over Colorado. The last page displays a cartoon of an employer at a day-care center turning a nongay applicant away because the center had not yet met its quota for gay day-care workers.

The Equal Protection Coalition never dreamed Amendment 2, which had never led in the polling, would pass. But Tea Schook started having a very bad feeling when she observed morality politics at work in a focus group of women who were supposed to be sympathetic: "That was supposed to be our voter. We watched how one very poisonous woman turned a bunch of people who really didn't have an opinion into some very rabid, queer-hating people. We didn't know how much of a shoo-in hate really was." Lawyer Mary Celeste was in bed with her partner, Beverly, watching a report on TV about how Amendment 2 would never pass, when Beverly sat up and said, "And if it does? What is our fallback position here?" The next day Mary and Beverly and some other gay lawyers started planning litigation strategy. Their "dream team" was to be led by Jean Dubofsky, the retired first woman justice of the Colorado Supreme Court, then teaching at the University of Colorado Law School. Dubofsky, the brilliant Harvard Law School graduate with a pixie haircut, had cut a swath through liberal legal circles in Colorado from the day she arrived fresh out of Walter Mondale's Washington Senate office. When Pat Steadman, then a green law student, heard Dubofsky speak at the law school, he knew her politics were a perfect fit with the movement. Even though she was not gay.

Amendment 2 passed easily. According to the highest law of their state, Colorado's gay, lesbian, and transgender citizens were cast out of politics.

First Thing Let's Do Is Kiss All the Lawyers

When politics fails to protect fundamental democratic principles—as it did in Amendment 2—the United States Constitution, as enforced by the courts, is the last resort. Even a state constitution amended by a six-point majority has to meet the requirements of the US Constitution.

So the day after the passage of Amendment 2, Steadman called to remind Jean Dubofsky that, in the palmy days of six-point polling leads, she had promised to represent them. Symbolized by lead plaintiff Richard Evans, from the governor's own staff, the gay side's legal team assembled an all-star roster of plaintiffs from cities with antidiscrimination ordinances as well as from a bunch of the cities and local governments targeted. The case so clearly pitted the liberal New West cities like Denver against the narrowly conservative state electorate it might as well have been called *Denver v. Colorado* as *Evans v. Romer*. Amendment 2, the case claimed, violated the Fourteenth Amendment to the US Constitution. It deprived the plaintiffs of the equal protection of the laws.

In no time, Dubofsky was swarmed by the national gay legal establishment: Suzanne Goldberg from Lambda in New York and a team from the ACLU Gay and Lesbian Project, including the experienced and strategic éminence grise from San Francisco, Matt Coles.

The competition for control of the *Romer* case reflects how the legal profession's role in the gay revolution had grown since Marilyn Haft and the lawyers at the ACLU started lobbying the American Bar Association (ABA) for gays in the early seventies. With little fanfare, three years after idealistic feminist lawyers from San Francisco founded Equal Rights

Advocates in 1974, Donna Hitchens, who ended her career as a California state judge, and Roberta Achtenberg, who is a member of the United States Civil Rights Commission, nested a Lesbian Rights Project there. In 1988, the project spun off as the National Center for Lesbian Rights (NCLR). The NCLR is legendary in the movement for its unremitting battle for the rights of lesbians and the families they created or were trying to hang onto after divorce. One custody fight at a time, using the established doctrines of family law, organizations like the NCLR began to weave a web of legal legitimacy around the idea of the lesbian, or gay, family; in 1996 *Newsweek* magazine published an article, "The Future of Gay America," predicting a "Gayby Boom."

By 1989, the ABA, a reliable barometer of the pressure within the legal profession, had endorsed a gay antidiscrimination bill. When the military issue heated up, the law schools started banning the military from recruiting lawyers, because the military discriminated against homosexuals, just as, years before, they had forbidden legal recruiters who said they wouldn't have women in their law firms. In 1992, the ABA passed a resolution supporting the law-school ban on military recruiting.

Once the gay population made the crucial transition to a civil rights movement in the eyes of a critical mass of the legal profession, they benefited from the profession's nostalgia for the heroic role it played during the racial civil rights movement. As the seventies and eighties passed, both the racial movement and the gender movement leveled off, as social movements do, or retreated in the face of the backlash, or both. But the gay revolution was coming on strong. For young lawyers aspiring to be the next Thurgood Marshall, the gay revolution was the civil rights movement of their generation. In *Bowers v. Hardwick* in 1986, men who had had recourse to only two or three suspiciously "connected" lawyers from the hallways outside sex-crimes court were represented by one of the premier constitutional scholars in America, Harvard law professor Laurence Tribe. Where once graduates from fancy law schools, such as Justice Lewis Powell's clerk Cabell Chinnis, were hiding in the closet in order to feed their career ambitions, now, ambitious out A-gay lawyers like Harvard's Suzanne Goldberg were elbowing one another aside for a chance to work for places like Lambda and the ACLU.

The lawyers and the lawsuits came in perfect sync. Litigation like *Romer*, Matt Coles says, does not just happen. It is "engineered" with exquisite attention to every nuance of who the judges were and what they would attend to. When Dubofsky would not hand her case over to the movement pros, the nationals started coaching her, while simultaneously working it through briefs by friends of the court.

Changing the Rules of the Game

Although a constitutional challenge was the only option left, it looked bleak. The Supreme Court, which would ultimately have the last word, had been implacably hostile to the gay movement almost without exception since the movement's legal efforts started in 1950. In 1986, the court had ruled in *Bowers v. Hardwick* that Georgia could make gay sex a criminal offense. By 1992, the federal courts, including the Supreme Court, had been shaped by twelve years of conservative appointments from Republican administrations. For years, the consensus in the gay legal community was that after the devastating defeat in *Bowers*, anything that might trigger a Supreme Court decision should be avoided. Yet everyone—Jean Dubofsky, the Lambda folks, lawyers from the ACLU—agreed that Amendment 2 was too drastic to ignore. They decided to avoid the hostile federal courts for a while by starting the challenge in the state courts of Colorado. (It is a little-known fact that state courts can enforce the federal Constitution, but at the end of the day their decisions on federal law, too, are subject to review by the United States Supreme Court, if the Supreme Court cares to take them up.)

Nonetheless, if ever there was a case to test whether the United States Constitution applied to gay Americans, *Romer* was it. Short of getting Amendment 2 repealed, gays and lesbians were cut off from any prospect of protecting themselves through law. Amendment 2, as Harvard law school's Larry Tribe would later describe it, made them "ineligible" for the protection of the laws. Under Amendment 2 gays would have lived in a kind of state of nature in their own society, all civil rights protections they had achieved repealed and new protections, no matter how harsh their treatment, forbidden.

The Fourteenth Amendment forbids the states to deny to any person "due process of law or the equal protection of the laws." Although the words look fairly straightforward, the contest over their meaning is fierce. For sixty years before the plaintiffs filed their suit in Colorado, the Supreme Court had been interpreting the prohibitions of the Fourteenth Amendment in two ways. One, the states are forbidden to deprive people of fundamental civil rights, like free speech or the right to vote. (Thus the lone gay victory in the *ONE* magazine case all those years before.) And two, the states may not discriminate against a discrete and insular minority with a history of bad treatment, like African Americans. Such classifications are, in Fourteenth Amendment talk, "suspect." If a state does either of these things, it must show a very good reason why.

The suspect-classification argument did not look good for plaintiffs. After the Supreme Court upheld Georgia's right to toss gays in jail for having sex just a decade earlier in *Bowers*, nobody could envision the court assigning gays to a suspect classification like African Americans or even a sort of suspect classification like the court had extended to women. If a group wasn't a suspect classification, the government could single it out for pretty much anything, as long as the government could make some rational argument for doing it. No one wanted to depend on *that* winning.

The lawyers elected to focus on the first argument, the way the law deprived gays and lesbians of the fundamental right to participate in the political process, rather than the second argument of suspect classification. They thought that maybe, although gay *sex* might not be fundamental, gays acting politically would be. After all, the Constitution explicitly protects the right to vote, and politics is the core of America's "democratic principles."

Here, the overreaching sweep of Amendment 2 did the heavy lifting. After Amendment 2, there was absolutely nothing gays and lesbians could do politically in Colorado. No city could protect them against prejudice, no judge could find they had been inappropriately harmed; the Colorado legislature's hands were tied. Unless they got a majority of the people of Colorado to repeal Amendment 2 to their state constitution in a rerun of the election they had just lost, they were helpless.

This strategy was vulnerable, because the Supreme Court had been letting states get away with making a lot of unpopular causes politically harder by amending their state constitutions to tie the hands of their state and local legislatures. So a state constitutional amendment requiring that public housing could only be established by a supermajority of the legislature, for instance, got the nod, even though it clearly nullified the political efforts of people who needed public housing. In constitutional terms, the argument started to look like a debate over how many rights had to be walled off by the state constitution before the general right to vote was implicated.

The legal team also began to sniff around a third argument. Even if the political process could do pretty much anything to any unprotected group, it could not legislate against a group of people on the staple of morality politics—intuitive distaste. There was actually a Supreme Court precedent for disallowing such open hatred. In 1971, at the height of the Sixties social movement, Congress amended the Food Stamp Act to disqualify any household whose members were not "related." The Supreme Court took a look at the legislative history to see why Congress had done that and found septuagenarian Florida senator Spessard Holland explaining that the provision was designed to keep food stamps out of the hands of "hippies" and "hippie communes." The 1973 Supreme Court struck it down: "For if the constitutional conception of 'equal protection of the laws' means anything, it must at the very least mean that a bare congressional desire to harm a politically unpopular group cannot constitute a legitimate governmental interest."

Regardless of what the lower courts found, everything the plaintiffs did in *Romer* was designed to build a record to appeal to the United States Supreme Court on one or more of those theories: the law infringed fundamental civil rights, it did not even meet the low standard of basic rationality much less show a damn good reason, and it was enacted because gay people made the voters puke.

The Home-Court Advantage

In 1993, Jeffrey Bayless, a judge with a reputation as a moderate, enjoined the implementation of Amendment 2 while the case went to trial and the Colorado Supreme Court agreed.

For a social movement, a trial is a chance to replay the drama of the political campaign in a forum with very different ground rules. Once a question gets into the legal system, the answer is constituted by values of the legal system. By constitutional fiat, in America the government may not overtly legislate a religious belief. Law can stop people from harming others and to some extent require them to help others. The Constitution requires, at minimum, that any law must bear a rational relationship to a legitimate state interest, which does not include saving its citizens' souls.

In that system, a social position expressed by a moral bumper sticker—"homosexuality is the end of the American Republic"—is the beginning of the inquiry, not the end. The relationship between the law and the legitimate interest must be proved according to the system's rules for proof. A witness on the stand—or even a person "testifying" through what he or she wrote—must have personal knowledge of the matter or be a scientific, technical, or other specialized expert. The professional habits of thinking in terms of direct evidence and material harm enable the lawyers to see through the easy appeal, so powerful in other realms, to the "natural" or the traditional. Not for the courtroom the lay expertise of unexamined intuitions characteristic of morality politics. The change of frames, in turn, changes the political lesson people learn. They see authoritative figures issuing judgments that people must obey based on secular, rational processes. Not only did *Evans v. Romer* go to trial, it was televised over Court TV to people all over the state.

The Amendment 2 campaign looked very different in a courtroom. During the campaign the public had been introduced to outsider citizens trying to make a grab for extra privileges. Instead of reading about some fictional greedy pedophiliac day-care worker, trial watchers met policewoman Angela Romero. They heard religiously driven junk science offered as expert testimony and debunked. The campaign literature, which is the equivalent of legislative history of a referendum, painted an indelible picture of the proponents' desire to harm an unpopular minority. The trial court ruled that the proponents of Amendment 2 had failed to justify the measure, sending the case again to the Colorado Supreme Court.

The Colorado Supreme Court did not just reject the proponents' arguments; it flayed them. The Colorado court had particularly destructive things to say about that perennial favorite, "special rights": "Defendants offer no authority," the court ruled, "to support the rather remarkable proposition that the government has a compelling interest in seeing that the state does not support the political objectives of a 'special interest group.' *The state exists for the very purpose of implementing the political objectives of the governed* [emphasis added] . . . virtually any law could be regarded as a benefit to a 'special interest group.'" Civil rights laws in Colorado were no different from the laws passed to benefit the ski industry. In what passes for a dueling-level insult in legal circles, the Colorado court concluded, "No citation of authority is needed to make the point." If *Romer* lifted the freeze on political activity, this language would be invaluable to any progay rights forces in the upcoming political battles left for, say, a statewide antidiscrimination law.

Friends in High Places

Jean Dubofsky and her team had been praying the Supreme Court would just let the Colorado decision lie. When, instead, the court exercised its discretion and agreed to review the case, a chill fell on their brief celebrations. The United States Supreme Court had held that gays could be jailed for having sex and allowed state constitutions to preempt all kinds of other political action. Where were five votes to overturn the Colorado constitution going to come from?

States, cities, churches, unions, and the NAACP all wanted to be friends of the court, but Supreme Court lawyers know that to flood the court with briefs is the best way to ensure that they pay no attention to your friends. Cue the cavalry: Harvard con-law *capo di tutti capi* professor Larry Tribe wrote a brief. He then handpicked the five most influential constitutional law scholars in the country to sign their support, deliberately including the representatives of a whole range of thinking about the court's role in interpreting the Fourteenth Amendment. Philip Kurland, who had written the definitive critique of the court's performance in the school-desegregation cases, signed the brief. John Hart Ely, the man who started the campaign to delegitimize the court's abortion decision in *Roe v. Wade*, signed the brief. In essence, the Tribe brief gave the court permission to make new equal-protection doctrine, not just from liberals like Tribe but from all the people who had previously tried to rein it in.

Tribe's amicus brief is now a legend in the rarefied circles where constitutional doctrine gets debated. Maybe only someone who edited the authoritative treatise on constitutional law for decades would have had the chutzpah to tell the Supreme Court that all its existing Fourteenth Amendment precedent meant nothing in this context. I know, Tribe told the court, that you have two avenues of analysis when you see Fourteenth Amendment cases—the suspect classification and the fundamental rights. Cast off those old, tired categories, because "never since the Fourteenth Amendment's enactment has the Supreme Court confronted a law quite like this."

Being in a class by itself, Amendment 2, according to Tribe, raised a problem the court must deal with "prior" to its familiar categories. The problem was whether "a state [may] set some persons apart by declaring that a personal characteristic that they share may not be made the basis for any protection . . . from any instance of discrimination, however invidious or unwarranted?" The answer, Tribe suggested, must be no. Indeed, he contended, to decree that some characteristic precludes a group from ever claiming protection against discrimination previously or in the future is "*by definition* a denial of the equal protection of the laws."

Tribe, who had argued and lost *Bowers*, gave the court permission to preserve that harrowing decision. Even if you are still committed to letting stand the criminalization of gay sex, he implied, that is one discrete penalty that you can perhaps justify as rational. Still, even if the conduct that distinguishes the target group is criminal, you cannot let Colorado make outlaws of a whole segment of its population. Imagine if a conviction of, say, gambling, made all gamblers forever ineligible to receive medical care or protection from assault, he implored.

Finally, Tribe contributed to the Colorado Supreme Court's process of normalizing civil rights. You wouldn't allow a state to exclude a whole group of citizens from protection against robbery, he asserted. Why is cutting them out from protection against discrimination different?

In this heavily precedent-driven system of constitutional law, Tribe turned the plaintiffs' failure to qualify for protection under existing precedents into an advantage. If the court can't find a reason to strike it down within its existing precedents, he concluded, that's not a weakness in plaintiffs' case. It's because no state had ever tried anything as flagrantly unconstitutional as this before.

It Is Not Within Our Constitutional Tradition to Enact Laws of This Sort

On October 10, 1995, Colorado solicitor general Tim Tymkovich stood up to present the argument for Amendment 2. No sooner had Tymkovich introduced himself to the court than the generally conservative justice Anthony Kennedy interrupted him: "Usually when we have an equal-protection question we measure the objective of the legislature against the class that is adopted, against the statutory classification," Justice Kennedy began. "Here, the classification seems to be adopted for its own sake. *I've never seen a case like this.*"

The plaintiffs' lawyers exchanged startled glances. They had assumed the support of the court's four "liberals." Now they had their fifth vote. Justice Kennedy had accepted Larry Tribe's invitation to view Amendment 2 as outside the universe of modern equal-protection jurisprudence.

Justice Kennedy's opinion for the majority of six, issued on May 26, 1996, did not just reject the effort to estrange gay Americans from their own democratic republic. It laid down an authoritative constitutional barrier protecting any movement, however unborn or unforeseeable, that would ever invoke America's democratic principles. It was a high roll. Had the court gone the other way, Tribe says, the next step against homosexuals would have been something like *Dred Scott*, the notorious pre–Civil War decision that categorized slaves as not citizens of the United States, stripping them even of their standing to invoke the protections of the federal courts. In such a regime, no one's rights are safe.

Justice Kennedy started the opinion with a citation of the holy writ of equal protection, Justice Harlan's 1896 dissent denying the constitutionality of racial segregation, which was ultimately vindicated in *Brown*. "One century ago," Justice Kennedy wrote, "the first Justice Harlan admonished this Court that the Constitution 'neither knows nor tolerates classes among citizens.' *Plessy v. Ferguson*, 163 U.S. 537, 559 (1896) (dissenting opinion). Unheeded then," Justice Kennedy continued ominously, "those words now are understood to state a commitment to the law's neutrality where the rights of persons are at stake. The Equal Protection Clause enforces this principle and today requires us to hold invalid a provision of Colorado's Constitution."

Kennedy accepted Tribe's invitation to treat the case as outside the standard categories of suspect classifications and fundamental rights. In an almost verbatim quotation from Tribe's brief he concluded:

> Respect for . . . [the law's neutrality] explains why laws singling out a certain class of citizens for disfavored legal status or general hardships are rare. A law declaring that in general it shall be more difficult for one group of citizens than for all others to seek aid from the government is itself a denial of equal protection of the laws in the most literal sense.

No further analysis was required.

The opinion also adopted Tribe's characterization of civil rights as no different from any other body of law. The court said, "We find nothing special in the protections Amendment 2 withholds. These are protections taken for granted by most people either because they already have them or do not need them; these are protections against exclusion from an almost limitless number of transactions and endeavors that constitute ordinary civic life in a free society." After *Romer*, everyone gets a shot at "ordinary civic life in a free society"—both members of a powerful majority who don't need civil rights protections and everyone else who may.

In passing, Kennedy also warned against excesses of moral rectitude in lawmaking. Amendment 2's "sheer breadth is so discontinuous with the reasons offered for it that the amendment seems inexplicable by anything but animus toward the class that it affects; it lacks a rational relationship to legitimate state interests."

The Rules of War

Any Supreme Court opinion of this magnitude that is not unanimous is to some extent a dialogue between the majority and the dissent, both sides keeping an eye on history. Dissenting justice Antonin Scalia argued that conservative Colorado was legitimately trying to win a decisive battle against liberal, cosmopolitan values they hated. Colorado for Family Values, he opined, were engaged not in a "fit of pique," but in a "Kulturkampf"—a peculiar choice of words, invoking nineteenth-century German Protestant chancellor Otto von Bismarck's campaign that essentially cut the Catholic clergy out of politics and imprisoned the defiant.

Just in case anyone was tempted by the German model of minority relations, Justice Kennedy used Supreme Court code talk to remind his brethren of the bedrock American constitutional prohibition against selecting out a minority for legal death. "It is not," Justice Kennedy concluded, "within our constitutional tradition to enact laws of this sort."

Drinks All Around

The world did not change at once. Homosexual sodomy remained criminal in twenty-four states. Gay progressive campaign consultant Lisa Turner, working for the national Democratic Party as a state organizer at the time, found that there was literally "no presence" from the LGBT community in the state capitals, in Michigan, Vermont, Maine, Oregon, wherever she went. "Whether it was fund-raising, candidate selection, or having a legislative voice, you name it," she says, she "saw every interest group—teachers, women, trial lawyers—at the table. But no gays."

But it was a critical moment. Protected by the decision in *Romer*, the gay revolution could use the political process to gain access to ordinary "civic life." In Colorado, a robust progressive alliance including gays and lesbians grew stronger every year, fueled by the annual battles with the religious

President Bill Clinton leaving the White House for the first-ever speech to the Human Rights Campaign, November 1997. From the left: Richard Socarides; Bill Clinton; Maria Echeveste, deputy chief of staff; Ginny Apuzzo, assistant to the president; and highest-ranking gay appointee to that time, speechwriter June Shih. (Official White House photograph, Clinton Library)

right over some statewide initiative or other. The National Gay and Lesbian Task Force started a federation of state organizations as a place where local groups could exchange information and best practices. In 2000 the Equality Federation left the Task Force nest and became an independent entity, joining the activists from every state. Richard Socarides's boss Bill Clinton became the first sitting president to address a formal dinner of the Human Rights Campaign.

The Transgender Law and Policy Institute was formed in 2000, followed quickly by the first state legal organization for transgender people, in San Francisco, and the second, the Sylvia Rivera Law Project, in New York.

In keeping with its mining tradition, Colorado struck it rich. Twenty-five years before *Romer*, a scared freshman at the University of Colorado had wandered into the student gay group, then called Boulder Gay Liberation. "Hi," he said. Then he shook for ten minutes while the person manning the office tried to comfort him by talking about something like "queer theory." Within a few months he was working at the group's office. By the second semester he was talking to Abnormal Psych classes about what it was like to be gay. Although the people where he worked after he graduated knew he was gay, he wasn't active because he was concentrating on his career. But when Amendment 2 came up, formerly scared University of Colorado freshman Tim Gill, now Forbes 400 founder of the computer graphics company Quark, was the single largest donor to the fight. When his side lost, he took 60 percent of his immense fortune, endowed the Gill Foundation, and started looking around for ideas about what to do.

"Sixty percent of people in Colorado," Gill learned, "didn't know anyone gay or lesbian. That meant they were forming opinions about LGBT people based on stereotypes rather than facts and personal experience." His solution? To "structure a fund, the Gay and Lesbian Fund for Colorado (GLFC), like a corporate-giving program. We wanted to give to important causes in Colorado but we also wanted to make sure the LGBT community got credit for it." Go to any cultural event or anything that's being sponsored by anyone, Pat Steadman, now a state senator, says, "and the program prominently features the distinctive red, white, and blue Gay and Lesbian Fund for Colorado logo. And not just in the Denver-Boulder corridor; they fund events across the state—little theater companies, programs for children. They have very clear expectations that their branding and acknowledgment of his gift is a condition of the gift. It's part of our culture, and that's been going on for so many years here it doesn't offend anybody." Not only are Colorado gays not strangers to the law, they aren't strangers at all.

Perhaps because Gill was first involved in the context of Amendment 2, his efforts have always focused heavily on the state level, which turned out to be where a lot of the action was after 1992. For the gay revolution, states were the new cities. In 2003, a Colorado state representative, Republican Shawn Mitchell, tried to pass a law that would forbid discussion of homosexuality in the classroom. "If Shawn's bill had passed," Gill says, "it would, for example, forbid me to speak at my own high school since I can't tell my life story without mentioning that I'm gay." A year later, Gill and his allies flipped the Colorado legislature from Republican to Democratic, and Gill founded Gill Action for the express purpose of politics and lobbying. Gill calls himself a "genetic Republican," because that's what his parents and grandparents were. But looking back on the 2004 Colorado election, Gill consultant Ted Trimpa describes a nonpartisan philosophy: "Take known antigay elected officials and target them specifically for their past antigay views, actions, and statements. . . . How we win is by creating an environment of fear and respect." If the Republicans choose to take that role, they're in the crosshairs. It's nothing personal. "Heck," Gill says, "One of Gill Action's strategists is a former Karl Rove protégée." With a newly Democratic legislature, in 2005 Colorado amended its law against bias-motivated violence to include sexual orientation and sexual identity and, two years later, passed a statewide antidiscrimination law, a second parent-adoption law, and a designated-beneficiaries law. Colorado politics would never again be a gay and lesbian no-fly zone.

For years, Jean Dubofsky says, she could not go out to dinner in Denver, where she lives, without champagne arriving at her table from some anonymous person in the restaurant.

II. Private Rights

Sodomy May Be Gay but It's Not Funny

John Lawrence was not drinking champagne in Houston in 1998 when police came to his house and arrested him and another man, Tyron Garner, for sodomy. The weapons charge that had brought the police to Lawrence's home turned out to be bogus (another of Garner's lovers had called the cops for sport). But Lawrence and Garner spent the night in jail anyway. Gays and lesbians might have won the liberal right to participate in government in *Romer*, but they were still denied the equally important principle that some things are protected from the government. Homosexual sodomy was illegal in Texas and, as the Supreme Court had said all those years ago in *Bowers v. Hardwick*, that was okay with it. In fact, any other position was "facetious."

Even after *Romer*, the gay legal establishment was not spoiling for a federal fight. Lambda Legal director Abby Rubenfeld remembers the day she found out about the defeat in *Bowers*. "That was one of the moments that made me want to give up my law license. I didn't even want to stay at work." The handful of lawyers at Lambda in 1986 were left to pick up the pieces, dealing with the angry, disaffected gay community. There were street riots in New York.

Anyway, they had found another way to win. Right after *Bowers*, a lowly trial court in Kentucky acquitted defendant Jeffrey Wasson of soliciting deviate sexual conduct. We don't care what the US Supreme Court thinks is funny, the Kentucky judge said in effect, this is private, consensual conduct. Under the Kentucky constitution, it's protected. The Supreme Court of Kentucky agreed. Slowly and patiently, for twelve long years after *Bowers*, the gay litigators' roundtable gathered cases in the states where sodomy was still criminal and brought the number of such states down to little more than a dozen, including, of course, Texas.

When Lawrence's case landed on their doorstep, however, Lambda decided it was time for another try at the feds. *Lawrence* had a lot to recommend it. Rightly or wrongly, the state of Texas convicted the two, and the courts of appeals affirmed, so the pattern of unequal justice across the states was graphically presented. Individual rights and equality were protected in thirty-six states but not in Texas. They petitioned the Supreme Court to review the Texas decision and boldly asked the Supreme Court to overrule its seventeen-year-old precedent in *Bowers v. Hardwick*. Lambda's own out gay board member Paul Smith argued for Lawrence.

When Justice Kennedy took the bench on June 26, 2003, to announce the decision in *Lawrence v. Texas*, they learned they had succeeded beyond their wildest dreams.

Crying for Justice

The Supreme Court always decides all the cases that have been briefed and argued before the term is out. With *Lawrence* still hanging fire in the last week of the 2003 term, pressure began to build. The night before the last remaining day of the term, Lambda president Kevin Cathcart said to himself, Oh the hell with it, and got on the train to Washington. He got up early the morning of June 26 because he knew there would be a big line at the court building. One of the people waiting was Larry Tribe, who had argued another case that term and was waiting for that decision. As Tribe sat in the magisterial courtroom of the United States Supreme Court on the morning of June 26, 2003, and listened to Justice Anthony Kennedy read a summary of the opinion, he felt tears rolling down his cheeks.

The Supreme Court in *Bowers*, Justice Kennedy ruled, had been mistaken from the moment it opened its mouth. The gay claim for membership in the liberal state was not, as Justice Byron White suggested in *Bowers*, laughable. It was in fact indisputable.

Justice White stated the issue, Kennedy said, as the right to engage in homosexual sodomy: "To say that the issue in *Bowers* was simply the right to engage in certain sexual conduct," Justice Kennedy scolded, "demeans the claim the individual put forward, just as it would demean a married couple were it to be said marriage is simply about the right to have sexual intercourse. The laws involved in *Bowers* and here are, to be sure, statutes that purport to do no more than prohibit a particular sexual act. Their penalties and purposes, though, have more far-reaching consequences, touching upon the most private human conduct, sexual behavior, and in the most private of places, the home. The statutes do seek to control a personal relationship that, whether or not entitled to formal recognition in the law, is within the liberty of persons to choose without being punished as criminals."

Kennedy acknowledged that, as Chief Justice Warren Burger so passionately expressed, "The Court in *Bowers* was making the broader point that for centuries there have been powerful voices to condemn homosexual conduct as immoral." The intensity and sincerity of the public's moral convictions "do not answer the question before us, however. The issue is whether the majority may use the power of the State to enforce these views on the whole society through operation of the criminal law. Our obligation is to define the liberty of all, not to mandate our own moral code."

But Kennedy was not content to leave the gay revolution in the cold peace of the liberal state. It was not so clear their actions were always and everywhere immoral, either, Justice Kennedy continued:

> Scholarship casts some doubt on the sweeping nature of the statement by Chief Justice Burger as it pertains to private homosexual conduct between consenting adults. . . . This emerging recognition should have been apparent when *Bowers* was decided.

Bowers must be wiped from the record, a matter of institutional shame like the shameful 1896 decision approving segregation in *Plessy v. Ferguson* that Kennedy so detested:

> When homosexual conduct is made criminal by the law of the State, that declaration in and of itself is an invitation to subject homosexual persons to discrimination both in the public and in the private spheres. The central holding of *Bowers* has been brought in question by this case, and it should be addressed. Its continuance as precedent demeans the lives of homosexual persons.

And with that, the Supreme Court placed the second of the legs of the liberal state under the gay community. Like the chicken thief saved from sterilization in *Skinner* and the married couple who wanted to decide how many children to have in *Griswold*, like the impoverished, desperate single pregnant woman in *Roe v. Wade*, gays and lesbians got a piece of their lives the state could not address. They would be citizens.

III. Public Safety

Nasty, Brutish, and Short

After *Romer* and *Lawrence*, the gay revolution had achieved two of the three foundations of citizenship in the liberal state. The third founding principle of the social contract is that the government exists, at the minimum, to protect its citizens from each other. This seems pretty obvious. But sometimes the most obvious part of citizenship is the hardest to win. More than any other group in society, gay people as a group lived in fear of their fellow citizens. Without the government providing them with physical security, their lives were, too often, nasty, brutish, and short.

As Aaron Kreifels rode his mountain bike on a deserted road outside of Laramie, Wyoming, on the morning of October 7, 1998, Matthew Shepard's short life was ebbing away. Aaron saw what he thought was a scarecrow, lying near a fence. But it was Shepard, a fellow student from the university, beaten, tied to the fence, and left to die.

Matthew Shepard never got to be very big. When he was murdered at the age of twenty-one, he was only five foot two and a little more than a hundred pounds. The oldest son of two ordinary middle-class parents, he spent some time in school in Europe when his father was transferred to work in an oil field in Saudi Arabia. Back in the US for college, he enrolled at the University of Wyoming, where his dad had gone. By all reports, Shepard was openly gay. On the night he was murdered, he encountered two locals, Aaron McKinney and Russell Henderson, in a Laramie bar. He got into their truck, and they drove him to a deserted spot, where McKinney bludgeoned him with a gun butt and tied him to the fence to die. The blood-covered murderers then went home to their girlfriends, who helped them concoct a cover story.

Gay lawyer and politico John Aravosis was sitting at his computer a day later when an alert from one of the early gay e-mail lists pinged into his inbox. AP had a story about a gay kid hung from a fence at the side of the road in Wyoming. Just months before, Aravosis, already an old Washington hand who had worked as an online consultant for the liberal Children's Defense Fund, had been talking to a friend about starting a website. "I'll build you a simple website," the friend said, "and you just keep adding stuff and it shows up at the top. Just keep posting."

Aravosis posted, "The Associated Press reported that a gay student at the University of Wyoming was savagely beaten, burned and left to die, tied to a wooden fence outside Laramie, Wyoming, thirty miles northwest of Cheyenne." A day later, the university called and asked if it could link to Aravosis's website. The story got fifty thousand hits. "As soon as I saw the AP story," Aravosis says, "I knew I was onto something bigger than just another dead gay kid."

From then on, the website posted fifteen, twenty times a day on the Shepard case. Updates from AP, from the college paper, statements from the Human Rights Campaign and the president of the United States, a place to "send a card to Matthew"—Aravosis didn't miss a beat in developing this story. From the first day, he used the Shepard story to drive a political narrative about hate crimes. Within four hours of posting the AP story, he quoted the local ACLU about how the attack proves the need for a law protecting gays against hate-motivated violence, which the Wyoming legislature had defeated recently. Interspersing increasingly horrific revelations from the scene—that the young man begged for his life, that his body was covered with burns—with political analysis and exhortations—the religious right's usage of the issue as a wedge against the Democrats, the comparison of gays to alcoholics and kleptomaniacs—Aravosis tied the death of Shepard to the political agenda of protecting gays from violence with an unbreakable cord.

Five days later, without ever regaining consciousness, Shepard died of his wounds.

Hate Crimes

By the time he first saw reports of the attack on Matthew Shepard, old antiviolence activist Kevin Berrill thought he'd heard everything. Gays tortured, beheaded by serial killers, picked up while walking across a bridge, and tossed into the river below to drown. Still. "God," Berrill remembers thinking, "the kid's been crucified."

Berrill had had his share of violence against gays and lesbians. When he started working as a receptionist at the National Gay Task Force (NGTF) in 1982, he had no clue that he would become the point man on this profound and wrenching issue. Local organizations had started reporting an uptick in incidents, including in New York's heavily gay Chelsea neighborhood, right after Berrill started work. The Chelsea Gay Association held some town halls and started a hotline. Maybe gays had become more visible by virtue of the decade and a half of liberation since Stonewall, or maybe the AIDS epidemic rendered them vulnerable to the label of "diseased," in addition to all the other labels they bore. Whatever the reason, by 1983, the number of reported incidents of attacks was skyrocketing.

The gay antiviolence movement did not have to start from scratch; it was consciously modeled on the feminist rape and domestic-violence programs, developed over the long years of bringing women into full citizenship by guaranteeing the fundamental right of security in their persons. Like their predecessors in gender violence, the gay community produced hotlines, counselors, refuges, and people to press the police and DAs. And there is always money for crime victims. With a grant from the state victims board, the official New York Anti-Violence Project was launched.

But Berrill, promoted from greeting people at the front desk at the Task Force, knew that community-based solutions were not sufficient and that, in order to get a meaningful *official* response to the problem, there needed to be official documentation of it. Task Force lobbyist Jeff Levi asked the United States Justice Department research arm, the National Institute of Justice, if it might have money for a survey of violence against gays and lesbians. "Is there violence against gays and lesbians?" the NIJ contact inquired.

The movement, as usual, had to do the first groundwork itself. Berrill developed a survey to pass out at Pride Week around the country. The first report, in 1983, showed that one in four gay men and one in ten lesbian women had been hit, punched, or kicked. Many studies done since then have produced roughly the same results. Every year the Task Force report got more press. Berrill went on *The Oprah Winfrey Show*. (In a new low point for daytime TV, the teaser for his segment of the show asked, "Is killing gays the solution for AIDS? Stay tuned.")

Berrill had heard that the Anti-Defamation League of the Jewish organization B'nai Brith did an annual audit of anti-Semitic incidents, so he went to the ADL to see what he could learn. Turns out the ADL had been trying for a couple of Congresses to get a law passed requiring the FBI to collect data about anti-Semitic violence. Great, the Task Force folks responded, let's just get them to put us in the Jewish bill also.

The Jewish activists were understandably less than thrilled to transform their essentially uncontroversial bill by adding gays to the mix. But

Berrill began making the rounds of the Jewish organizations—the American Jewish Committee, the American Jewish Congress, groups that were interested in hate crimes—and the Jewish groups came around. "There were people in the ADL legal office," Berrill says, "who were very sympathetic. The data showed there were many more injuries and deaths from antigay violence than anti-Jewish violence." So they formed a coalition, Jews and gays, and began lobbying Congress in 1987 to pass a hate crimes statistics bill.

It took a couple of Congresses, but the gay movement had found a sweet spot at last. They said they weren't asking for a *rights* bill, heaven forfend; the bill was just a statistics initiative to get the FBI to collect the data. "It was so hard for them to say we can't collect the statistics," Berrill remembers gleefully. "We had the moral high ground here and the religious right has such a hard time with that." The Task Force lobbyist, Jeff Levi, organized it and Berrill gathered his alliance: "I got the National Organization of Black Law Enforcement Executives. The once-dreaded American Psychiatric Association brought in its brilliant lobbyist Bill Bailey and Bill brought in [the renowned sociologist] Greg Herek. There was this mass of civil rights groups, professional groups, law enforcement groups and it passed the House." Even the conservative Mormon senator Orrin Hatch supported keeping sexual orientation in the bill. In 1990, President George H. W. Bush signed the federal Hate Crimes Statistics Act.

The religious right was right, Berrill concedes, to fear the law. "It was a crowbar that would give us leverage in other ways. We were trying to enlist the police, who gay people had been hiding from all these years. If the FBI was going to collect data, they would have to train law-enforcement officials around the country to recognize gays, and we would become three-dimensional to them. Organizations like the National Association of District Attorneys invited me to speak to them."

The Task Force was pumped. In a pure ACT UP move, when the National Institute Against Prejudice and Violence, a leading research institution on ethnic violence in all its forms, resisted adding sexual orientation to its antiviolence legislation, the gay activists threatened to have a demonstration at its annual convention. Imagine hundreds of gay and lesbian demonstrators around the *National Institute Against Prejudice* meeting, chanting, "We die/they do nothing." The institute backed down and the two organizations soon became firm allies. Now that they had the government gathering the numbers, they turned to the substance of prohibiting hate crimes altogether.

No Murder They Wrote

They stood on tall shoulders. One hot Mississippi night in June 1964, a dozen white men took three civil rights workers, James Chaney, Michael Schwerner, and Andrew Goodman, from their car and killed them. The two white men, Schwerner and Goodman, were shot once through the heart, but Chaney, who was black, was badly beaten before he was riddled with gunfire. Six weeks later, Congress passed the Civil Rights Act. In 1968, Congress amended the act, making it a federal offense to attack people because of their race while they attempted to engage in federally protected activities like voting or going to school. It was the first federal hate-crimes law.

By making racist motives an element of federal crime, the national government began the process of bringing African American southerners into the social contract that the state will protect its citizens from one another. It passed too late to use on Chaney's killers, whom Mississippi refused to prosecute. (They were prosecuted under one of the federal Reconstruction-era civil rights acts.) But the modern campaign for meaningful laws to protect vulnerable groups, federal at first and then, as the enthusiasm for civil rights waned in Congress, at the state level, was born that Mississippi night.

There are three kinds of substantive hate-crimes laws. Laws like the 1968 Civil Rights Act make racially motivated violence a special crime. A handful of subsequent hate-crimes laws make actions that would not otherwise be criminal, like cross burning, into crimes. (These hate-crimes laws restraining expression were largely declared unconstitutional in 1992.) Still other hate-crimes laws add penalties to existing acts of wrongdoing if the crime is motivated by hate.

California is generally credited with passing the first hate-crimes law addressing hostility based on sexual orientation in 1984. By the time the cops/Jews/gays coalition motivated Congress to gather data in 1990, Oregon, Minnesota, Maine, and Wisconsin had all followed California's lead.

After their success in Congress, the new hate-crimes coalition ramped up its efforts in the states. The ADL had already been working with a model statute. The coalition changed the model statute to include sexual orientation and bit by bit the coalition started persuading state legislatures to amend their existing hate-crimes laws to include sexual orientation or, in states where there was no hate crime-law at all, to pass laws covering all the categories of victims. Ultimately protected by the decision in *Romer* against further initiatives like Colorado's Amendment 2, the gay state groups were engaged in conventional politics, lobbying for legislation to protect their interests.

Throughout the 1990s states and cities enacted some kind of hate-crimes law that addressed actions against gays. Predictable places like Tacoma, Washington, and Washington, DC, and unpredictable places like Utah and Louisiana put laws, either penalizing bias-based harassment and intimidation or enhancing penalties for existing crimes, into place. In 1993, Minnesota passed the first statewide hate-crimes law protecting transgendered people as well. The 1995 murder of anatomically female Brandon Teena, supposedly because of her presenting herself as male, and a case in DC involving the death of a victim whom emergency medical personnel neglected when they discovered she was anatomically male, ramped up the social activism for the physical protection of transgendered people.

By the time Aaron McKinney and Russell Henderson tied Matthew Shepard to the fence, Wyoming was one of only ten or so states with no protections of any sort, while a growing number of more progressive states were including transgendered people in their protections. In what Republicans must have bemoaned as the worst possible timing, they had to put the kibosh on the latest effort to pass a substantive hate-crimes law for gays and lesbians the very week in October 1999 that McKinney's murder trial started. The Democratic Wyoming State Senate had finally passed a bill, after a decade of gay lobbying, and it was up to the Republican House to ensure it would not pass. Which the Republicans did.

When Laramie prosecutor Cal Rerucha began to assemble his case under Wyoming's general law against murder, gays and lesbians from all over the country were watching every move, largely through the portal of John Aravosis's new "bloggy" website. Instantly upon learning that Henderson, the sidekick at the murder, was going to plead guilty, Aravosis was all over the prosecution. Would this Wyoming prosecutor play the role of Mississippi, which had refused to prosecute the civil rights killers, but by the device of just rolling over? Just as the tumult subsided when news emerged that Henderson had received two consecutive life sentences with no hope of parole, the whole thing heated up again. McKinney would defend himself on the ground that Matthew Shepard had made a pass at him, driving him to an uncontrollable rage (the "gay panic" defense). Trial watchers held their breath; would the jury let the killer off with a slap on the wrist, like the jury in San Francisco had done twenty years before for the man who killed Harvey Milk?

As if to justify the Republicans' arguments that existing law was good enough, the Wyoming justice system seemed to be working perfectly. The Wyoming judge scoffed at gay panic and forbade the defense lawyers to use it. In his speech at the sentencing hearing, Matthew's father, Dennis, recognized that by this ruling the judge had opened the social contract to let gays in: "Because of your . . . willingness to take a stand and make new law in the area of sexual orientation and the 'Gay Panic' defense . . . you have emphasized that Matthew was a human being with all the rights and responsibilities and *protections of any citizen of Wyoming.*"

Two weeks later the Wyoming jury convicted McKinney of felony murder. The only thing that stood between McKinney and the death penalty were Matthew Shepard's parents. Dennis and Judy Shepard are a pretty formidable force. The defense lawyers didn't even propose a plea bargain to the prosecutor to save their client's life. They went right to the Shepards. And with that, Matthew Shepard, tiny and gay, became as dangerous and as much a member of the social contract as the gun-toting Aaron McKinney. "Mr. McKinney," Dennis Shepard said, "I'm going to grant you life, as hard as it is for me to do so, because of Matthew. . . . Mr. McKinney, I give you life in the memory of one who no longer lives. May you have a long life and may you thank Matthew every day for it."

The Laramie Project

Then Dennis Shepard announced that the gay revolution was going to gain an invaluable asset—the Shepards. "I can't bring him back," his father said. "But I can do my best to see that this never, ever happens to another person or another family again."

Judy Shepard has a round face with plump cheeks and a little bow mouth topped off with a mop of blond hair. For a few years of her adult life she taught grade school and then took her place as the devoted wife of the tall, take-charge oil-field safety instructor and as mother of two young sons. Family pictures of the Shepards before the murder have a certain Brady Bunch quality to them, except that Matthew was unusually handsome.

In America, the only thing better than a white, middle-class boy with a chiseled profile representing your cause, is that boy with a plump little mother with a vaguely western-southern twang and an oil man for a father. Throughout the decade after Matthew Shepard's death, the Shepards just kept using their symbolic social conventionality to normalize other gay Americans. In 2010, a plainly dressed Judy Shepard posed for a picture when awarding the Matthew Shepard Foundation award to the octogenarian founder of the Imperial Court System, José Sarria, resplendent in red wig, tiara, and yellow chiffon.

José Sarria, founder of the Imperial Court System, winner of the 2010 Matthew Shepard Award, and Judy Shepard (Courtesy of José Sarria)

The Empire had raised one hundred thousand dollars for the Matthew Shepard Foundation in one year. It was the foundation's biggest donor.

It took ten years. By the time Matthew's killers were sentenced, John Aravosis's website already carried statements from Judy Shepard on behalf of the Human Rights Campaign (HRC). The Shepards established the foundation in Matthew's name, and Judy moved back to the United States from Saudi Arabia. For the first five years, it seemed like there was never a single HRC black-tie dinner that did not feature Judy Shepard.

Finally on October 22, 2009, a Democratic Congress handed a Democratic president the Matthew Shepard and James Byrd, Jr., Hate Crimes Prevention Act. Under the new law, any bias-motivated act of violence against a person is in the jurisdiction of the United States Department of Justice. The requirement of involvement in a federal activity is gone and the protected group has expanded to include not just racial or religious minorities but gays and lesbians and people who are transgendered. If the locals cannot or will not pursue the offenders, the Justice Department can step in and do what is required. On October 28, 2009, as Dennis and Judy Shepard looked on, President Barack Obama signed the bill.

The federal hate-crimes bill brought out the usual opponents. A group of preachers filed a class-action suit to have it declared unconstitutional as infringing on their right to call gays the sinners that they are. Straight white criminal law professor James Jacobs wrote a whole book about how terrible the hate-crimes law, and indeed all of "identity politics," were. Powerful gay pundit Andrew Sullivan wrote a long, scholarly essay about how the law was merely symbolic. One month after Sullivan's essay appeared, two men in their twenties attacked forty-nine-year-old gay Jack Price as he came out of a deli in Queens and beat him nearly to death. Prosecutors acting under the New York hate-crimes law, which increases penalties for crimes of bias, sent Price's two assailants to jail for sentences of eight to twelve years.

Andrew Sullivan was partly right about the mostly symbolic value of the law. The number of reported hate crimes is not huge, and the state laws were already effective in many states, as the New York case reflected. The federal law is likely to be mostly of symbolic value. What he missed, of course, is the value of the symbol.

A month after Matthew Shepard died, playwright Moises Kaufman and his Tectonic Theater Project began coming to Laramie. Eighteen months later they premiered *The Laramie Project*, based on the testimony that they gathered. Judy Shepard is often quoted as saying that the play saved more gay lives than all the hate-crimes laws in America.

Kaufman knew exactly what he was doing: "Matthew Shepard's murder was a defining moment in our history—in our history as Americans, in our history as gay people, in our history as people who are in the middle of a social justice fight, and some would say, in the middle of a social justice war. And Matthew Shepard was one of the great casualties of that war." Although Kaufman saw many reasons why the Matthew Shepard murder became that kind of watershed historical moment—he was white, the killing resembled a crucifixion—primarily, Kaufman believed America was, "as a culture, finally able to hear it."

It was time, Kaufman felt, for the theater to do its job in challenging America again to live up to its democratic principles: "We have in America this ideal of equality, we all have the same rights and the same responsibilities and this kind of thing happens and we ask how are we living up to this ideal?" Kaufman the playwright fully understood how art did its job. After telling the story of the town where Matthew Shepard was killed, *The Laramie Project* closes with the students at the local university performing in a production of Tony Kushner's *Angels in America.* As in the original *Angels in America*, it is the hero, Prior Walter, who delivers the political message to the people of Laramie sitting in the audience. "We're not going anywhere," he says. "The world only spins forward. We will be citizens."

Even Matthew Shepard's killers knew about the power of symbols. When Kaufman's people interviewed Aaron McKinney in the tenth year of his prison sentence for a sequel, *Laramie, Ten Years After*, they asked him if he held any hope for parole. "I'm never getting out of here," the convict answered. "I'm the poster child for hate crime murders."

10

Massing the Troops for the Last Battle: The New-Media Gay Revolution

At the beginning of the April 30, 1997, episode of the sitcom *Ellen*, Ellen's friends are sitting in her living room waiting for her to emerge from her bedroom, dressed for a date with an old college friend. She's taking an uncharacteristically long time to appear. "Ellen," says her pal Paige Clark, "are you coming out or not?!" An hour later, network television star Ellen DeGeneres announced she was a lesbian. A few years later she hosted the Oscars.

Starting in 1996, the gay political movement had begun to get real traction. First, in *Romer*, the Supreme Court said gays could use the government for their ends, just like every other group in America. Then in *Lawrence*, it said gays could lead their private sex lives undisturbed, just like every other group in America. Passing hate-crimes laws, legislatures across the nation reminded their citizens that gays were not target practice. And, finally, the United States Congress added its voice to the chorus.

As they took their place in the liberal state, the gay revolutionaries never lost sight of their desire to join the ancient clubs of war and marriage to which entry was still barred. They might be different from the majority, but they would not put on the badge of dishonor offered them in the early Clinton years. Now in the third decade since Stonewall, they methodically organized to fight the last battles.

They were determined not to repeat their mistakes—of being unprepared and of losing control of the time and place of the battles. Without any concerted plan, a few key players also moved quickly to adopt the new techniques that became available to social movements in the Internet age. The movement's success had always been heavily driven by its amazing adaptability, as it morphed from the discreet Mattachines to the bell-bottomed liberationists and the rich array of organizations and strategies that ensued. Black-tie dinners, screaming protests. The contemporary push to Victory involved every imaginable strategy, including some that could not have been imagined when the first street kid threw a penny at the cops in 1969.

Military Justice

By June 1993, the armed services had taken Bill Clinton to the cleaners. The would-be reformers thought it was bad before they started making a fuss? They didn't know the half of it. As the effort to revoke the antigay exclusionary policy faltered, to be replaced with the hated DADT, the military had been identifying the people it thought might be gay and now it was going to get rid of them. When that happened, as activists like retired air force captain Michelle Benecke knew from experience, one day a soldier or sailor would be in his bunk and the next morning he'd be gone, bunk neatly made, all evidence of his existence erased. The activists called them "the disappeared."

The day Congress passed DADT, Benecke—JD, Harvard Law School—and Dixon Osburn, a newly minted JD and MBA from Georgetown, looked at each other across the office that had housed the gay movement's brief and ineffective Campaign for Military Service. The lobbyists the movement had deployed and everyone else were gone. And the phone was ringing off the hook. "If we don't do something now," Benecke remembers them saying to each other, "it will be decades before this comes up again." MBA Osburn went home and wrote a business plan for a new organization. They would reverse DADT and they would represent the service members whose lives were on the line. They would be the Servicemembers Legal Defense Network.

Benecke knew that the whole strategy of fighting for gays' civil rights in the first DADT campaign had been a mistake. "They didn't even think of us as human beings," she says of her former colleagues in the armed forces. "Asking for civil rights made no sense to them at all," Benecke says. "People who disappear in the middle of the night certainly have no accountability and no pushback. Our goal was to be their voice when they could not speak for themselves." Instead of asking for rights for the entire group, they would represent one sympathetic case after another, each apparently isolated, until the accumulation of individual cases undermined the entire policy. Like the gay civilians before Stonewall, gay soldiers had been living in the state of nature in the military; once identified, they became objects, rather than players in the social contract. As such, they were in a free-fire zone, subject to anything their superiors wanted to do to them. Benecke's project was classic social-movement tactics, to push back until the oppressors were forced to recognize their victims as people who would be citizens. As a side benefit, the pushback would, case by case, undermine the justification for the entire policy.

A DC veterans group that happened to be run by a progressive guy from the Vietnam era gave them a room in its offices and four computers. The two-person legal-defense fund and their two volunteer helpers had four hundred cases the first year. Of course they could not act on all of them, but the Servicemembers Legal Defense Network (SLDN) gave gay military people a place to call. Slowly, the gay establishment started to hand Benecke and Osburn some of its Rolodex. Benecke remembers the turning point when, two years after they started, gay philanthropist Henry van Ameringen of New York enabled them to hire a fund-raiser. They got some cooperating attorneys from outside.

In America, one of the key aspects of citizenship in the liberal state is being entitled to a lawyer. So, in the first of many moves to impose on the military the values of the liberal state, the young activists engaged with the military's own defense lawyers. Even the military's lawyers are lawyers and they began to up the ante on their advocacy for gay people. The activists trained the lawyers to get in the minute they got a call for help from someone being targeted instead of waiting until charges were filed and then merely playing a formalistic role defending them.

Usually, the actions against members came in clusters, under a particularly homophobic command or local culture. The gay group called them "witch hunts." (SLDN even had Halloween fund-raisers at which they auctioned off the best pumpkins to raise money.) When they got word that a witch hunt was taking place—members would call, or chaplains or gay groups would complain—they would focus their resources on that particular base or unit. As a premodern institution, the military will always let people from another premodern institution, the church, visit military members, so SLDN would ask the local congregation of the gay Metropolitan Community Church—or a sympathetic nongay church—to send a chaplain to a targeted base or unit. Preach the two commandments of the accused, they implored their clerical allies: Say nothing and ask for a lawyer.

Sometimes the accused really had to ask hard. Seaman Amy Barnes, for example, was at the Norfolk Naval Base fighting her discharge. When she missed her second appointment with her military lawyer, he became worried and started to look for her. He found her locked in a room with navy officials who were trying to get her to sign her discharge paperwork and waive her right to a discharge hearing. They would not let him in. He could hear her saying, "I want to speak with my lawyer" and "I'm not signing anything until I speak with my attorney." Meanwhile, he was banging on the door demanding to be let in and yelling, "She has a right to an attorney. You have to let her go." Frantic, he called SLDN, which got one of their cooperating outside lawyers to run to federal court and fill out a complaint by hand. Shortly thereafter, the judge enjoined the navy from proceeding. The federal judge was more than a little surprised at the navy's "procedures." Maybe the military didn't embrace every nuance of the constitutional order, he suggested, but there were limits. Her lawyer was banging on the door where they were plea "bargaining" with her!

SLDN's client representation morphed into a political initiative when the press started taking the goings-on seriously. In 1994, SLDN began to assemble its myriad cases into a big report, documenting meticulously the skills and honorable records of the people being driven from service. The stories first started getting attention from the gay press, especially from Lisa Keen, editor of the gay DC paper, the *Washington Blade*. Finally, after batting the stories away like a bothersome fly for too many years, the mainstream media started to come to SLDN press conferences. In 1997 Benecke was interviewed by CNN. In 1999 she appeared on PBS. One of their stories made the front page of the *New York Times*. In each case, the coverage made the victims of DADT human to the public.

SLDN also took advantage of the fact that every soldier was also someone's constituent. Congressional inquiries stopped a number of witch hunts. SLDN even worked with conservative senator Strom Thurmond, who had a legendary constituent-services operation, to help South Carolina gay soldiers. Being constituents was another way SLDN framed the gay soldiers as human beings, not just scary shadows in the shower in Sam Nunn's photo op.

Help came from unexpected places. After a harrowing sexual-harassment, rape, sodomy, and adultery scandal at the army's Aberdeen Proving Grounds in 1996, the army took a sudden interest in the treatment of women. As the National Gay Task Force's Sue Hyde had noticed almost a decade before, military women were always disproportionately targeted for accusations of homosexuality; it was a way to keep them in line. A July 1997 secretary of the army's *Senior Review Panel Report on Sexual Harassment* finally recognized that "one particular form of sexual harassment not addressed [in the survey that they had done for the report] but commented on in a few focus groups and by other female soldiers in informal discussions, was the fear of being accused of being a homosexual. Female soldiers who refuse the sexual advances of male soldiers may be accused of being lesbians and subjected to investigation for homosexual conduct. As in the case of men falsely accused of sexual harassment, women accused of lesbianism believe that the mere allegation harms their careers and reputations irreparably." Undersecretary of Defense Edwin Dom issued a guideline to protect such women: "The fact that a service member reports being threatened because he or she is said or is perceived to be a homosexual shall not by itself constitute credible information justifying the initiation of an investigation of the threatened service member." Slowly the environment changed.

Not soon enough for Private (FC) Barry Winchell. One of his fellow soldiers at Fort Campbell in Tennessee, Calvin Glover, had been ragging him about his sexuality, and Winchell punched Glover out. On July 4, 1999, Glover took a baseball bat to Winchell in his sleep. As Winchell's roommate, later convicted as an accessory to the murder, egged Glover on for losing a fight to a "faggot"—Winchell had started a relationship with a transsexual from a local bar and either was or was not gay—Glover killed Winchell in his bed.

When some straight soldiers in Winchell's bunk found out that the army was calling it an "altercation between soldiers," they illegally left the base to get to a pay phone. One of them had an uncle he knew was gay. The uncle called Human Rights Campaign (HRC). "My nephew says there's been a death at Fort Campbell and the military's saying it was a fight and it's not," he told the person who answered the phone. HRC called the SLDN and the SLDN sent its people flying to Tennessee. They made common cause with Winchell's mother and stepfather, and the case went public. Pressed by SLDN, the Pentagon sent an A-level investigative team to the base. The army tried and convicted Glover of first-degree murder and bargained a long sentence with the roommate. More important for political purposes, the army inspector general investigated the base for allowing such a climate of harassment. If there's anything commanders don't want, it's the media, or the inspector general; General Robert Clark of Fort Campbell got a hefty dose of both. As the Clinton administration drew to a close, the Pentagon issued an action plan on harassment and training, a direct response to the uproar over Winchell's murder.

As the years went by, SLDN found a number of officials who were genuinely appalled at DADT. The drip, drip, drip of cases of real soldiers lost to the service of their country and SLDN's painstakingly detailed documentation allowed the military to start seeing their gay and lesbian members increasingly as people. In 2006, Massachusetts congressman Marty Meehan introduced a bill to repeal DADT. He was not overwhelmed with sponsors, but, starting with a respectable 122 colleagues, he began the slow work of increasing the number every year.

The campaign had turned gay and lesbian soldiers into three-dimensional human beings, the movement to change the position of gays in the military was run by people experienced in the military, and the campaign was leveraging internal military values of service and orderly relationships. Things were unlikely to change with a Republican Congress and president, but, as the first decade of the new century began to pass, the movement was lining up its troops to line up its troops.

From Massachusetts

The movement opened a new front in Massachusetts. Massachusetts was the only state in the country to vote for Democrat George McGovern, who lost to Richard Nixon in a landslide in 1972. As the Watergate scandal erupted the following year, people from the Bay State started sporting bumper stickers that said "Don't Blame Me. I'm From Massachusetts." In 2003, the ornery Bay State went its own way again, when the Massachusetts Supreme Judicial Court became the first tribunal in the nation to effectively order the state to marry same-sex couples.

The Massachusetts case was the product of a long, carefully constructed campaign. Hawaii had taught the gay activists a valuable lesson: once the movement turns to litigation, any random lawyer and client can raise political issues with nationwide implications, anytime and anywhere they choose. The gay lawyers' Litigators' Roundtable, which had developed around the sodomy issue, tried to take control of events. They had a roadmap. In 1994, a Dutch scholar, Kees Waaldijk, detailed a strategy, "Standard Sequences," for how to make a successful move on gay marriage, based on the positive experience with the issue in Europe. Take small steps, Waaldijk advised: decriminalize sodomy and get antidiscrimination laws passed before taking on marriage. Do not try to short-circuit the process. (Being a European, Waaldijk's list does not include the most important consideration: how easy it is for the marriage opponents to toss the issue to the people, in a direct vote. It was the referendums in Hawaii and Alaska that reversed both early American court victories.)

So it was no surprise that gay legal activists—this time the experienced and connected New England legal group, Gay and Lesbian Advocates and Defenders (GLAD)—turned to Massachusetts on marriage. Boston's GLAD was, with Lambda Legal and the National Center for Lesbian Rights, one of the oldest gay legal institutions. Founded in response to a police sting operation to catch gay men at the Boston Public Library, since 1990 GLAD had, under the leadership of its legendary Civil Rights Project director, Mary Bonauto, become an institutional leader in high-impact litigation for the gay and lesbian community. The state had a history of stubbornly progressive politics: sodomy was not criminal and discrimination was already forbidden. In addition, it was harder to gin up the initiative process there. On November 18, 2003, four of the seven members of the Massachusetts Supreme Judicial Court took same-sex marriage—an arrangement that had never been enacted into law by any voter in even one American state or city—and enshrined it into the equality provisions of the Massachusetts state constitution.

Massachusetts Supreme Judicial Court chief justice Margaret (called "Margie" with a hard *G*) Marshall, who wrote the opinion in the case, *Goodridge v. Massachusetts Department of Health*, is that rare judge with the Cheshire cat qualities normally found in very successful politicians.

Everyone in Boston has a story about Justice Marshall's warmth and graciousness. A native of South Africa, between 1964 and 1966, Marshall was president of the antiapartheid National Union of South African Students. Sent abroad for her own safety, she spent the years after her radical youth in the most conventional path—going to Yale Law School, then working for a corporate law firm. Recruited to help Harvard hire a general counsel, she somehow wound up getting the job herself. Republican maverick governor Bill Weld put her on the Supreme Judicial Court. When his Republican successor Paul Celucci tried to elevate her to chief judge, the powerful Boston archbishop, Bernard Cardinal Law, stepped in to stop it, arguing that she was anti-Catholic. Marshall so charmed the Catholic speaker of the state House of Representatives, Tom Finneran, that he vouched for her personally and she prevailed.

GLAD presented the Massachusetts court with the predictable marriage arguments. Gays had been the subject of historic discrimination, so the laws fencing them out should be treated as suspect; marriage is a fundamental civil right, as established in the race marriage cases; and sexual partnership is a private decision like birth control. This last argument was hanging fire when GLAD filed *Goodridge*, as the US Supreme Court had not yet decided *Lawrence v. Texas*, the sodomy case.

No one will ever know what went on behind chambers doors after the argument in the marriage case in March 2003, but the Massachusetts justices, who normally issue their opinions within three months of oral argument, fell silent for a record eight months. As they deliberated, they and everyone in the country knew that the US Supreme Court would be deciding *Lawrence* that June. Four months later, in October, Massachusetts handed down its opinion.

Justice Marshall calls *Goodridge* a mere application of constitutional language. Under the Massachusetts constitution, "All people are born free and equal and have certain natural, essential and unalienable rights. . . . Equality under the law shall not be denied or abridged because of sex, race, color, creed or national origin." Although the federal Supreme Court has not spoken to this exact issue, she concedes, the Massachusetts constitution often protects its people better than the nation.

Goodridge laid down the basic pattern of all the same-sex marriage decisions that would follow. Following *Lawrence*, the Massachusetts court wove what Larry Tribe calls the "double helix" of constitutional DNA: one strand of protection of fundamental rights and one strand of protection of equality. As the court protects people in the fundamental areas of human life, like childbearing and marriage, it increases the equality quotient in society, enabling more people to have a normal civic existence. As it increases the equality quotient in society, it spreads the wealth of the elements of a decent human existence. Marriage having long ago been recognized as one such element, the constitutional regime demands it be extended equally unless there's a very good reason not to.

The evidence in *Goodridge* reflected, as it has throughout the constitutional litigation of gay rights, that there is no legally cognizable evidence to support the exclusion of gays and lesbians. The social-science learning all being on the side of the gay plaintiffs, the court declined to follow Justice Scalia's invitation to a Kulturkampf. And then it showed why it had waited for *Lawrence*: "Our concern is with the Massachusetts Constitution as a charter of governance for every person properly within its reach," Marshall opined. As the Supreme Court had just held in *Lawrence*, she continued, " 'our obligation is to define the liberty of all, not to mandate our own moral code.' "

But the court was not content to rest its decision that gays could marry—the first in the country with some chance of survival in the political process—on an invocation to the electorate to hold its collective nose. Like Justice Anthony Kennedy in *Lawrence*, Justice Marshall chose to address the contention that the people think homosexuality is immoral directly. "Several amici suggest that prohibiting marriage by same-sex couples reflects community consensus that homosexual conduct is immoral. Yet," she wrote, echoing Dutch scholar Waaldijk, who had set up the strategy a decade before, "Massachusetts has a strong affirmative policy of preventing discrimination on the basis of sexual orientation." See, she wrote, policies on employment, housing, credit, services, hate crimes, public accommodation, public education, decriminalization of private consensual adult conduct, and child custody law.

Every one of the laws Marshall invokes could be explained by the liberal insistence that "moral code" not be allowed to interfere with the benefits of citizenship in the secular, liberal state. Even people whom some in the citizenry consider immoral are entitled to equal-employment opportunity or protection from violence. This lower standard for citizenship in the liberal state explains why the fights for eligibility to pass civil rights laws in *Romer* and protection of sexual relations in *Lawrence* were easier than battles over marriage or the military. But dishonest as the morality argument is, it reflects a deeper reality: Once people start to participate in the secular state—dating, working, living nearby, and so forth—their moral stock does begin to rise. When marriage (and military service) is the only aspect of civic life withheld from people who are otherwise acceptable co-workers, neighbors, tenants, or café patrons, it increasingly looks like the only explanation possible is not that gays are immoral but just the subjects of the dreaded ick factor, prohibited to lawmakers since *Romer*.

By putting marriage in a category with employment, housing, and the rest, the Massachusetts decision also recognized the process by which marriage has been increasingly digested into the liberal state. Married women have achieved rights of contract, tribal prohibitions against interracial coupling fell to the values of equal protection, and secular protections against violence penetrated the single-family dwelling. The more marriage began to resemble the other institutions of normal civic life, in which equal citizens freely choose their relationships, rather than a naturally prescribed union of two structurally unequal participants, the more vulnerable it became to the gay arguments, like equality, from normal civic life.

With the decision in *Goodridge*, the process, begun centuries before, of bringing marriage into the liberal state took a giant leap forward. Opponents tried—and almost succeeded—in getting the issue to a referendum, which would have been its death knell. But the referendum procedure in Massachusetts requires a majority vote in two successive joint meetings of the whole legislature over two successive years before an amendment to the state constitution can go to the people. Although the proposal passed the first year, the second year it failed. The exquisitely careful planning of the long-sighted, obsessive gay legal establishment paid off.

Perhaps for the first time in history, people began reciting excerpts from an opinion of the Supreme Judicial Court of Massachusetts as part of their wedding vows. EleGala.com, the wedding planning website, suggests one passage to use:

"Marriage is a vital social institution. The exclusive commitment of two individuals to each other nurtures love and mutual support; it brings stability to our society. For those who choose to marry, and for their children, marriage provides an abundance of legal, financial, and social benefits. In return it imposes weighty legal, financial, and social obligations. . . . Without question, civil marriage enhances the welfare of the community." It is a "social institution of the highest importance. . . . Marriage also bestows enormous private and social advantages on those who choose to marry. Civil marriage is at once a deeply personal commitment to another human being and a highly public celebration of the ideals of mutuality, companionship, intimacy, fidelity, and family. . . . Because it fulfills yearnings for security, safe haven, and connection that express our common humanity, civil marriage is an esteemed institution and the decision whether and whom to marry is among life's momentous acts of self-definition."

Marshall thinks all the fuss over her court's venture into the culture wars was vastly overrated. Many great social-change decisions start in state supreme courts, she told an interviewer. The California Supreme Court struck down the law against interracial marriages two decades before the federal courts finally got around to it in 1967. "Nobody ever remembers the state judges who make these decisions," she explained. Marshall, who was raised in South Africa, has one of those plummy British Empire accents that elicits disproportionate respect. Even with the accent, though, it's hard to swallow her assertion that *Goodridge* would not in the long run be the most important decision she ever made.

Republican Backlash, Gay Movement Organizer

President George W. Bush wasn't coming to the wedding. On February 25, 2004, he approached the bank of microphones in the Roosevelt Room of the White House. The United States, he announced, must enact a constitutional amendment to "preserve" this most "enduring human institution" from the gays and their allies on the Massachusetts Supreme Judicial Court. He'd hinted at such an amendment in the State of the Union address and now he was making it explicit. In the months that followed, in states all over the country, antigay activists put up statewide initiatives forbidding gay marriage just in case the federal effort ran aground. Republican strategist and presidential wise man Karl Rove contemplated the 2004 election and rubbed his hands.

Rove might not have been as happy had he known what he would inspire. Listening to the president in his apartment nearby, former fund-raiser and movement activist Michael Rogers got pissed. He knew the Republican Party was riddled with closeted members, and he was "sick and tired of watching the Bushies use marriage to get elected when they were then going out and sucking dick." He didn't have a bank of microphones, but he had learned a lot about direct action years before when he was in ACT UP. That February, he started calling the offices where the closeted gay staffers worked and asking whoever answered the phone questions like, "I want to know why Pete Meachum is working for Ginny Brown and he's a gay man." Tell whoever answers the phone, Rogers figures, and everybody in the office will know. He kept calling around and asking.

Rogers's neighbor, John Aravosis, had the same reaction Rogers did. He was so angry at the president's proclaiming a campaign against gay people he started a website, DearMary.com. Write to Vice President Cheney's openly gay daughter, Mary, it urged, and ask her to stop the campaign for an anti–gay marriage amendment. Then Aravosis started a regular blog, Americablog. Down the street, Rogers saw what Aravosis had done, quit his phoning around, and started BlogActive.com. As he gathered his information about the gay staffers and legislators working against the gay community, he started publishing their names. "No community," Rogers says, "should be expected to harbor its own enemies." And so the List was born.

In the year or two before the president's antigay press announcement, as blogging software became available, tech-savvy gay guys started teaching themselves how to use it. Political journalist Andrew Sullivan, who mixed gay journalism and advocacy in with a myriad of other political interests and subjects, was the quintessential early adopter, starting his immensely successful blog, the Daily Dish, in 2000. Like Sullivan, the Dish attracts an enormous following in the nongay world, because of its wide-ranging subject matter and reliably unpredictable political stances. The Daily Dish is not strictly a gay blog, but it covers and advances the gay issues that interest Sullivan with disproportionate power because of the size and diversity of its audience. Sullivan sees his mission as bridging the gay and nongay world. "We're going to get nowhere," he contends, "unless we convince people who are not gay to support us." (He has never even given up on the Church, although the pedophilia scandal tried his faith sorely.) "I bought a copy of 'HTML for Dummies'," successful blogger Andy Towle of Towleroad (as in "toll road") reminisced recently. Towle had been editing a conventional gay magazine, *Genre*, and was a writer by trade. At first Towle, in California, and another blogger, Indiana farm boy Bil Browning, used the technology as a kind of journal or personal site. Towle posted things like how he went to the beach with his boyfriend and a picture of a cute dog they saw.

Slowly, as the politics heated up, the bloggers turned more and more to gay activism. Browning turned his personal website into the Bilerico Project, a group blog, sort of like the gay Huffington Post, but not as wealthy. Browning just made up a wish list of people he would like to have write for his blog, and almost everyone said yes. Browning is particularly watchful about diversity, and developed a number of contributors from the transgendered population within the community. Towleroad has always included a healthy dose of popular culture. Towle watched his traffic mount steadily as he heavily covered the making of the gay love story *Brokeback Mountain*.

Once there were blogs, news started pouring out. For years, freelance journalist Rex Wockner had been the secret information system of the gay revolution. He started with the technology early, in 1996, to help his editors in the conventional print media. His bulletins on domestic and international news of the LGBT community, including Rex Wockner's List, were a veritable gay AP. But it was an insider's resource, directed to people like the heads of gay organizations. The new blogosphere was retail. It was the logical extension of Wockner's List. No longer did gay people have to scour the mainstream media for a handful of stories about gay subjects; they were all gathered in one place. Although the heavily political gay blogosphere mostly started in response to a Republican president's official insult to the community, once established, the blogosphere belonged to everyone.

Radical activists in apartments in DC's hip Adams Morgan neighborhood weren't the only ones to see the possibilities in the new technology. Since 1996, millionaire philanthropist Tim Gill had spearheaded periodic meetings of an ever-expanding group of other gay philanthropists—the OutGiving conference. In 2005, one of Gill's attendees, another gay computer mogul, Juan Ahonen-Jover, and his partner, Ken Ahonen-Jover, decided that the meetings had no carryover. "The rich ones met every eighteen months," Juan says. "They talked about this and that, and then they went home and nothing changed." Ahonen-Jover started a website and a Listserv, eQualityGiving. "Services for donors," the website proclaims: endorsements, conference calls, all courtesy of the Ahonen-Jovers. We pay for everything, they say. No advertising, no obligations. The Listserv was as exclusive as the blogs were democratic. Big givers—"not just any thousand-dollar donor," as Juan says—and powerful policy makers (legislators and their chiefs of staff, no Indians) were invited to participate. Once the Democratic Party could have told gay donors anything and they would never have known if it was true. No more.

Every single one of the eleven states with anti–gay marriage initiatives on the ballot passed them in 2004. Looking at 2006 coming down the road, medical technologies heir and gay philanthropist Jon Stryker tried to figure out what to do next. He dispatched his adviser, progressive gay political consultant Lisa Turner, who had worked in state capitals as political director for the Democratic Legislative Campaign Committee and for the Victory Fund, to look into the matter. Turner learned something startling: the Democratic Party in the initiative states had done nothing to stop the tide in 2004. Their field offices played no role. Their workers carried no literature. In some of the states, the Democratic Party would not even let the gay opponents to the initiatives have access to the precious rolls of Democratic voters, the voter files.

Former White House gay staffer Paul Yandura, whom Turner knew from the community of rich gay philanthropists and their advisers, was furious. Since the Clinton years the gay community had thought it could buy its way to political power by funding the Democratic Party. Yandura had raised a bunch of gay money for the Democrats. And the dishonest beneficiaries wouldn't even stay bought.

Big, bearded, right out of the Italian working class, Yandura sees himself as unusually free of the Washington status-and-access game. Yandura got his start in politics when he tried to volunteer to work at the Clinton White House in 1996. His first day, he was sitting in the top row of a big bowllike auditorium "wearing a suit and tie for the first time in my life, surrounded by a bunch of Ivy League kids" listening to a Secret Service agent lecturing the would-be politicos about being forthright regarding any past indiscretions. A woman came into the room at the bottom of the bowl and asked the Secret Service guy a question. "He turned white," Yandura remembers, but he dutifully said to the assembled multitudes, "Is anybody out there gay?" Yandura raised his hand. "Come with me," the woman said. So Yandura gathered up all his stuff and took a long walk down the stairs of the auditorium, all eyes on him, the room silent, sweating bullets, and thinking, "I'm dead." The messenger took him to Marsha Scott, a heterosexual woman in charge of Clinton's first outreach to the gay and lesbian community, who took his arm and walked him into the White House and then into the Oval Office and in walks the president of the United States. "This is the guy who's going to help me with gay stuff," Scott says.

Rising from volunteer to a staffer, in 2000 Yandura raised millions for the party. "They were my family," he says of the Democrats. "They gave me a job, they gave me a home." After the 2000 election, Yandura opened a consulting firm with his former boss. When he found out what Turner had uncovered, Yandura decided to see if he could get the story of the Democrats' failure to fight the initiatives in the states out. Yandura sent Democratic National Committee (DNC) chairman Howard Dean a public letter asking why the Democrats weren't doing more to fight for their gay constituents. The DNC responded by firing their employee Donald Hitchcock, Yandura's partner. Bad plan. The blogosphere lit up. The era of the Democratic Party doing anything it wanted to the gay movement was over.

11

With Liberal Friends: Who Needs Enemies?

Senator Dianne Feinstein's guest for the State of the Union address, San Francisco mayor Gavin Newsom, was fuming. He had just listened to George W. Bush call for a federal amendment to ban same-sex marriage in the 2004 State of the Union address. As he listened to the conservative audience members congratulating themselves that someone was finally going to "do something about the homosexuals," he got even madder. How dare the president of the United States use his office to divide the country and instigate such a hateful idea? Newsom, the youngest-ever San Francisco mayor, read the opinion in *Goodridge* and decided that the California constitution, like the Massachusetts constitution, required marriage to be available to couples regardless of their sexual orientation. These were human beings the president was talking about. Newsom was going to order his clerk to start issuing marriage licenses. San Francisco would again be the gay refugee camp—from George Bush's "Amerika."

The Gathering Storm

The smart people who run UCLA's LGBT think tank, the Williams Institute, had been afraid of this. As they had learned in Hawaii and Alaska, the remaining issues, like same-sex marriage, were not winners in the precincts of mass politics. In early 2003, they called a meeting of the heavy hitters in the California gay legal movement—the ACLU, local Lambda lawyers, San Francisco's National Center for Lesbian Rights director Kate Kendell. After much debate, they took the pledge—not to pursue marriage litigation in California. They knew any victory would trigger an anti–gay marriage initiative, which they were confident they would lose. Everybody signed off on the agreement to wait.

Gavin Newsom hadn't signed the pledge. When his aide called Kate Kendell, she immediately went into movement mode and started talking about how risky it was. "We're not calling to ask permission," the aide said. Even in hindsight, though, Kendell asserts, she would not have stopped him. "Having a straight, Catholic mainstream politician embrace the cause of same-sex marriage was a game changer, even if the city he was mayor of was San Francisco. In a single gesture," she says, "it put the marriage movement light-years ahead. It was simply exhilarating."

Once Newsom made his decision, the ultimate confrontation over the law was unavoidable. The only defense San Francisco had for violating California law excluding gay people from marriage was that the California law was unconstitutional. The city officials put forth that defense, their opponents asked the state court to declare the law to be constitutional, a bunch of gay groups like the establishment Equality California challenged the exclusionary law, and before you could say media scrum, Los Angeles celebrity lawyer Gloria Allred had jumped in with a suit of her own. The certainty of a hostile referendum if they won in the state court seems to have disappeared from the calculus. Even political consultant Chad Griffin, who would soon be called in to deal with the utterly foreseeable aftermath of Newsom's decision, defends the mayor fiercely. After all, Kendell says, the victory in Massachusetts had not triggered a referendum. Maybe it would take long enough for the opponents to organize a referendum that people would get used to seeing same-sex marriages. Maybe people had come far enough so that they wouldn't believe the things marriage opponents would say in a referendum campaign.

Maybe. But by the time the California Supreme Court ruled in favor of same-sex marriage by a bare majority of four to three on May 15, 2008, the anti–gay marriage forces were already preparing the campaign to undo the decision by amending the California constitution, with what would become Proposition 8 on California's 2008 ballot. The forces behind Prop 8 were not new. For years before he died in 2004, California state senator William "Pete" Knight of Palmdale, outside of Los Angeles, had led the fight to limit California marriages to opposite-sex couples only. After Newsom's step, Knight's wife and his right-hand man, Andrew Pugno, joined forces with the California Family Council, a local associate of James Dobson's Focus on the Family, to form ProtectMarriage.com in 2007. To run the campaign they hired Schubert Flint Public Affairs, which had played a key role in defeating tobacco taxes for children's health and fighting for corporations against personal injury verdicts, or "tort reform." Before the state supreme court even ruled, the coalition had hundreds of thousands more signatures for the referendum than they required.

The Storm

It looked like an uphill fight for the gay marriage opponents and Schubert Flint. A Field poll in the spring of 2008 showed Prop 8 going down by three to five points. Like Massachusetts, California had long before passed the whole package of laws welcoming gays and lesbians to the secular state—hate-crimes acts, nondiscrimination, decriminalizing sodomy—that Justice Marshall had used to rebut the moral-repugnance argument in *Goodridge*. ProtectMarriage.com's job was to sever the connection between marriage and the liberal state. Just because society had to live with gays and lesbians, Schubert said, did not mean they had to approve of them: "No longer would it be enough for Californians to tolerate gay relationships, they would have to accept gay marriage as being equivalent to traditional marriage. Tolerance is one thing; forced acceptance of something you personally oppose is a very different matter."

The antigay consultants did an almost pitch perfect job. They quickly identified the handful of remaining areas of American life where the democratic values of the liberal state are weakest, and revulsion is still considered a legitimate political posture. According to Schubert, "We settled on three broad areas where this conflict of rights was most likely to occur: in the area of religious freedom, in the area of individual freedom of expression, and in how this new 'fundamental right' would be inculcated in young children through the public schools." Maybe Californians couldn't beat up gays or refuse to hire them, but, ProtectMarriage argued, they should still be entitled to hate them when observing their religion, when engaging in protected hate speech, and when teaching their children to hate what they hated. Two of the three areas Schubert Flint identified—church and family—are the areas of life furthest from the liberal state, and hate speech is an arena where freedom, however hateful, trumps equality in the American system.

Church and hate speech were relative whiffs. Pretty much everyone knew that gay people would not be trying to solemnize their unions in the cathedrals of the religions that hated them when so many appealing alternatives existed. And even Schubert Flint's people could not produce a viable campaign ad extolling the rights of people like the Westboro Baptist Church, who carried a "Fags in Hell" sign at Matthew Shepard's funeral.

But the schoolkids campaign sent the ball clear out of the park. When Schubert Flint laid down the kids card, the support for same-sex marriage dropped like a rock. The argument about the effect on children of legalizing same-sex marriage also had the virtue of being somewhat truthful. Public schools *are* in fact the place where the values of the liberal, secular state and values of the parochial, hierarchical family may come into direct conflict. This has been true at least since the "Monkey Trial" controversy over the teaching of the science of evolution in 1925. Despite a century of religiously driven resistance, by 2008 almost all American public schools taught biology in the form of ordinary falsifiable Enlightenment science. Like it or not, learning about evolution in public school, children learn a lesson about the reliability of the Bible. Similarly, in the rights revolution of the Sixties, families who believed in the superiority of white people had to send their children to school with people who were not white, a powerful implicit message of racial equality. And then they had to stop praying in school, a powerful message of skepticism. Next thing the parents knew, the schools were teaching the kids about sex, including how to have it without its natural justification of reproduction. In Massachusetts—and elsewhere—as part of the diversity curriculum in some public schools, books showing same-sex families were included in public school materials.

People who did not want their children to learn the lessons of the liberal state pulled their children out of public school to pray and teach them biblical science in racially controlled environments with abstinence curriculums. After the Internal Revenue Service briefly threatened the tax deductions for the private all-white "seg academies" in 1978, the option got less attractive. For families that did not believe in Lincoln, Darwin, or Margaret Sanger, rearing children who spent the day in the public schools was a constant Kulturkampf.

As a technical matter, allowing gays and lesbians to marry did not address how the marital household was to be presented in public school. But schoolbooks are full of representations of families—they are most children's primary experience of the wider world. Even story problems in math class have families in them. So if the world was going to contain families formed by same-sex marriage, sooner or later a curriculum devoid of such examples would start to look like biology without Darwin.

The real agenda was not marriage per se, but that marriage is unavoidably linked with sex. No one ever thought to link the presence of opposite-sex families in the school readers and math problems to the message that men and women could have sex with one another, teaching six-year-olds about heterosexual sex. Heterosexual marriages have the prime advantage of being around for so long that no one really thinks about what they mean.

But from its creation as a category—people who have sex with others of the same gender—in the mid-nineteenth century, "homosexuality" has always been about sex. All Schubert Flint had to do was light up the "sex" in same-sex marriage to put the issue on the table.

On October 8, ProtectMarriage went up on TV with an ad, "Princes." In "Princes," which aired first briefly on Spanish-language TV, a young Hispanic girl comes home and tells her mother, "Guess what I learned in school today. I learned how a prince married a prince, and I can marry a princess!" Studies of polling after the fact reveal that the support for same-sex marriage dropped a point every other day for two weeks following the ad. As a technical matter, at the time of Prop 8 California law allowed families to opt out of "health" (read, sex) lessons, but no matter. The polling showed parents of small children going over to support Prop 8 in droves.

That the No forces would have been caught unprepared for a save-the-children pitch reflects a mind-boggling level of historical illiteracy. The whole Anita Bryant–led campaign to roll back the civil rights initiatives three decades before had been called "Save Our Children"; one centerpiece of the campaign for Colorado's Amendment 2 was a cartoon about gay workers at a day-care center.

When the polling started rolling in, the California gay organizations resisting Prop 8 ran to an actual gay political consultant, Los Angeles's Chad Griffin, to film a response to "Princes." Griffin, then thirty-one, the coolest guy in the class, had come to California after a stint as the youngest person in the Clinton White House to open a consulting firm. He never believed the polls that showed that the gay no on Proposition 8 position was polling so far ahead of the anti–gay marriage initiative. Now with the gay side polling at 38 or 39 percent, he knew that the only possible escape was "to crush them, utterly crush their message." He and his partner in the ad business, Doug Armour, brought in the only person in California with the credibility to do that—the superintendent of Public Education, Jack O'Connell. Griffin and Armour tried to take the sex out. They made an ad with O'Connell saying that gay marriage had nothing to do with public schools. This is technically true, but cowardly, and Griffin knew it would make the gay community uncomfortable. The right answer is, as Griffin admits, that "maybe we should teach these things." But at the time, he said, "We were trying to get a no vote and to me it doesn't matter how you do it." The no side got to 48 percent. And that's where it stayed until Election Day, November 4, 2008. It was never going to be easy, Griffin reflects. "I've never seen a perfect campaign," Griffin charitably says. "With a perfect campaign we might have gotten 51 percent."

Or they might never have gotten to 51 percent. As the great movement thinkers since Harry Hay have known, you can't take the sex out of homosexual, and certainly not in the context of marriage. The first right in the Constitution of the post-Stonewall Gay Activists Alliance was "the right to our own feelings," including the right to feel attracted to the beauty of members of their own sex and "the right to express our feelings in action through making love." In that regard, gay men and lesbian women are different. When they try to make themselves into carbon copies of the nongay population, they usually fail.

They had fierce adversaries. The Catholic archbishop of San Francisco had spent eleven years as bishop of Salt Lake City; when he reached out to the Mormon Church to help pass Prop 8, all the relationships were already in place. Mormons, Schubert says, gave the campaign a staggering 40 percent of the millions they raised in the last months of the campaign and provided a huge number of foot soldiers. Polling reveals that it was a last Sunday effort by the churches that raised the support needed to pass Prop 8.

Even in California, marriage is the hardest battle. People the gay community thought it could count on abandoned them in droves. Parents of young children voted against them. Majorities of Hispanic and African American populations, with their heavy churchgoing component, voted against them. Cleve Jones remembers union leaders coming to him time after time during the weeks before the November 4 election date and warning him. We are turning out voters for Obama, they told Jones, and our voters are going to vote yes on forbidding same-sex marriage.

Where Were You on November 4?

Chad Griffin was in a suite at the posh St. Francis Hotel in San Francisco, with his friend Mayor Gavin Newsom and *Milk* movie producer Bruce Cohen, when the election returns came in. Griffin had always thought Prop 8 was a losing proposition for the gay community, but he still felt "profoundly conflicted." While the country had elected its first African American president, California, a state that had always symbolized the best of the American dream to Chad, had wrenchingly let its people down.

Lesbian community-college teacher Robin McGehee was standing in a little meeting room at the Holiday Inn in downtown Fresno with LGBT people watching the Prop 8 results. The Democratic party was in a large ballroom at the same Holiday Inn. She could hear the cheers for Obama: "I was sitting in a room the size of a hotel room and I could hear them celebrating, and I thought, 'We're separated.' It wasn't that the Democratic group was in there sharing our pain. My hands were in the air saying he's won and I was sucker punched at the same time."

Milk screenwriter Dustin Lance Black was not surprised. When the heroic biopic of slain gay leader Harvey Milk, *Milk*, had its preopening premiere at the Castro Theatre in San Francisco on October 28, 2008, everybody in the project wore their "No on 8" buttons on the red carpet. But Lance Black had been in his home state of Virginia working for Obama earlier that month. Returning home, he played his answering machine and heard a robo-call with Obama's voice on it. The antigay forces were leaving messages playing candidate Obama's statement that he was opposed to same-sex marriage.

Matt Foreman, the program director for gay and lesbian rights at the Haas, Jr. Fund, and Evan Wolfson's first funder, saw the early returns and turned off the TV. He could not understand what the fuss was about. Prop

8 was like the twentieth or thirtieth defense of marriage amendment. The marriage plan never involved fighting in California so soon. Have a little patience, he thought. Those California gays, always thinking everything has to go their way.

What Was to Be Done?

Griffin had a power lunch.

McGehee planned a big rally not in West Hollywood but in the outback.

Black wrote himself an Academy Award acceptance speech making a plea for marriage.

Chad Griffin and his business partner Kristina Schake were commiserating over lunch with Rob Reiner and his wife, Michele, at the legendary Polo Lounge at the Beverly Hills Hotel. Griffin had met the liberal actor and producer in 1995, when his West Wing bosses assigned the nineteen-year-old aide the job of minding Reiner, who was touring the White House in preparation for making the film *The American President*. Reiner, the big, straight Jewish movie producer, and Griffin, the slender, gay Arkansas Baptist, became instant friends. Reiner says even their handwriting is identical. When, years later, Griffin was contemplating opening his own consulting firm, Reiner was one of his first clients. Reiner had long been involved in liberal politics in California, devoting years away from his lucrative filmmaking business to the cause of early-childhood education, and he used Griffin's consulting firm to work on the ballot measures to get money for kids.

By the time Griffin and Reiner had lunch, lots of people had been talking about taking the marriage battle to federal court. The federal avenue would settle the question nationwide. And, unlike the decision from the California courts, if the Supreme Court interpreted the US Constitution to forbid laws against same-sex marriage, it would be almost impossible to reverse the decision. Even at the high-water mark of the conservative revival in 2004, President Bush's call for a federal marriage amendment had gone absolutely nowhere. Reiner, for his part, felt burned by the ballot process and was looking for a more efficient avenue to political outcomes. Nothing beats a victory in the Supreme Court for getting the most bang for your movement bucks. As the Reiners lingered over lunch, a friend, Kate Molene, whose sister had once been married to the legendary conservative lawyer Ted Olson, came by. Later that day she called Michele and said, "You know, if you wanted to try a federal action, Ted Olson would be with you on this."

Reiner and Michele looked at each other. If that's true, if that's really true, this is a political home run. Olson, who had represented candidate George W. Bush successfully in the Supreme Court case that decided the 2000 election, was an icon of conservative America. Did he really mean it? A few weeks after the power lunch, Olson visited the legendarily liberal Reiners in Los Angeles and persuaded them of his sincerity. Same-sex marriage was fundamentally conservative behavior and his libertarian commitments dictated leaving people's sex lives up to them. He thought there were five justices who would vote their way. Olson suggested that they get a liberal to balance his presence so it wouldn't look like a stunt. He proposed liberal lion David Boies, who had been his opponent in the presidential election case *Bush v. Gore*, as cocounsel, and the home run began to look to Reiner like nothing short of a grand slam.

Americans for Equal Rights: The Top-down Strategy

Another organization? Various institutions in the gay movement had been fighting for same-sex marriage since a local organizer filed a suit for Ninia Baehr in Hawaii in 1991. Starting with a prescient initial grant from the Haas, Jr. Fund, the father of the same-sex marriage movement, Evan Wolfson, had been running the Freedom to Marry initiative entirely on that one issue for more than five years. Up in Boston, Mary Bonauto's Gay and Lesbian Advocates and Defenders were about to score their second victory, getting a promarriage ruling from the state supreme court in Connecticut. Lambda Legal had taken a stab at the heartland, bringing a winning suit in the state courts of Iowa. Wolfson funder Matt Foreman didn't think long-term marriage advocates actually needed Ted Olson and David Boies to tell them what to do. One state at a time, the conventional gay movement was moving the ball forward over difficult terrain. When Boies and Olson filed the federal suit in spring 2009, the traditional groups claimed they were taken completely by surprise. The gay legal establishment had a long record of treating the federal option with kid gloves. Wolfson pretty well sums up their position when he says, "The choice is do we keep winning which is what we're doing or do we trigger a premature, problematic, difficult, burdensome, and potentially troublesome result."

Boies and Olson filed an unremarkable complaint to strike down Prop 8, pitting two couples, Kris Perry and Sandy Stier, and Jeff Zarillo and Paul Katami, against Governor Arnold Schwarzenegger and the other officials charged with enforcing California law. Like the lawsuits the establishment gay legal teams had been filing under the equal protection language of the state constitutions in Massachusetts and elsewhere, *Perry v. Schwarzenegger* told the story of their plaintiffs wanting to make a life together, invoking, instead of the state charters, the protections of equality and due process from the federal Constitution. It didn't take Olson and Boies to figure out that they had to make their case look as much as possible like Larry Tribe's successful argument in *Romer v. Evans.* The voters of California, the complaint says, just decided to cut gay and lesbian people off from all the rights and status that come along with marriage, to create a group uniquely disfavored in the law. The Supreme Court had forbidden the states to separate interracial couples forty years before in *Loving v. Virginia. Turner v. Safley*, a constitutional decision made in 1987, protected marriage rights, even for prisoners with life sentences. Once again, the voters, in referendum, had relegated gays and lesbians to a status lower than felons. Like

Colorado's Amendment 2, the repeal of California's right to same-sex marriage can be explained only by a bare desire to hurt a historically disfavored group. It wasn't a big theoretical stretch from *Romer* to *Perry*. The only question was whether the Supreme Court was ready.

Forget legal theory; when Boies and Olson stepped up to the podium at a press conference to announce their representation of the cause of same-sex marriage on May 27, 2009, the scene looked like nothing so much as their separate press conferences that surrounded the 2000 election contest *Bush v. Gore*. CNN was there and Fox News, the *Los Angeles Times*, and the *New York Times*. Like the memorable backdrops created for the warring sides in *Bush v. Gore*, Griffin had surrounded his champions with red, white, and blue.

But instead of representing the irreconcilable halves of an evenly divided nation, this time Olson and Boies together symbolized a unified nation, red and blue, liberal and conservative, Democratic and Republican, all agreed on the bedrock American principle of equal rights. It was the Christmas truce in the culture wars. Boies and Olson did a good imitation of Alphonse and Gaston, each deferring to the other, and admiring journalists uncovered stories of the two adversaries' previously unreported joint bicycle trips and long, wine-soaked dinners in the years following their legendary confrontation.

Why does it matter that Boies and Olson took the case? At about the same time as the *Perry* filing, a private lawyer in California had brought a federal suit, *Smelt v. United States*, with much the same theory, challenging the constitutionality of the Defense of Marriage Act. Three months before *Perry*, Mary Bonauto, who had represented the successful plaintiffs in Massachusetts, filed a constitutional suit in Massachusetts to stop the United States from enforcing the part of the Defense of Marriage Act that withholds all federal benefits from married same-sex couples. If Massachusetts says you're married, Bonauto asserted, the federal government has no business substituting its judgment for the state.

Bonauto's DOMA case, *Gill v. Office of Personnel Management*, could have been decided on somewhat narrower grounds than the head-on confrontation in *Perry*, just holding that the federal government must defer to the states about what constitutes a valid marriage. However, *Gill* also raised the broader issue—that treating same-sex marriages differently is unconstitutional, period. The *Gill* complaint is just as skillfully drawn as Boies and Olson's was. It was inherently just as newsworthy as *Perry*. Bonauto was in many ways a more appropriate symbol for same-sex marriage than the straight white men in California. She is married to a same-sex partner; the two are raising two children; she won the first victory in *Goodridge*. But when Bonauto filed *Gill*, there was no bunting, no CNN. Boies and Olson were rock stars. When they came on board, the movement changed.

In January 2010, the media gathered once again in San Francisco, this time to watch the first day of the trial in the case billed as the gay *Brown v. Board of Education*. The courtroom was filled to overflowing—media, showbiz celebs like Rob Reiner, and famous activists like Cleve Jones. The first witness to testify was Kris Perry, lesbian mother of four, who had been trying for years, as marriage went in and out under California law, to marry her longtime partner, Sandra Stier. Questioned by Olson, Kris told the story of how she tried to just be a mom in the stands at her sons' ball games. Every day she faced the question of whether to come out, sometimes to perfect strangers like the clerk holding a charge card form with a box to check: marital status. The effort that this very private woman made to tell her story publicly, while her adorable young sons sat in the courtroom, left not a dry eye in the house. When she stepped down, the godfather of the conservative legal establishment, Ted Olson, wrapped his arms around her. For twelve days of trial, in the courtroom and live blogged, the media and the community witnessed the gay and lesbian couples and the two most famous lawyers in America, every day, all day, including at lunch. At the rally after the judge ruled in their favor a few months later, plaintiff Paul Katami hugged Ted Olson back. The picture was all over the Internet.

Ya gotta have friends in high places. As a matter of pure constitutional logic, once the US Supreme Court categorized marriage as a fundamental civil right in *Loving* and all the cases that followed, the state should have

David Boies and Ted Olson hugging their clients, 2011.
Paul Katami (far left), Jeffrey Zarillo (second from right), Ted Olson (second from left), and David Boies, (right). (AP Photo/Eric Risberg)

to show some convincing reason beyond pure distaste to limit membership in the club. The idea that stories with opposite-sex marriages are chaste, while tales of same-sex marriages will turn the children into little satyrs, so effective in the TV ads, should not survive the rational fact-finding process of the legal system. But even the courts are not immune to social politics. In the real world, before the courts will act, there is almost always some shift in social legitimacy. Nowhere is this more the case than those areas like marriage that feel distant from the purely political world. Civil rights litigation often speeds up the process of social legitimation, because it forces people to take sides in public, but it is almost never the first step.

When Boies and Olson filed their suit, the gay movement had been hammering on the marriage establishment with claims of formal equality brought by their own movement lawyers since 1991, with limited success. The sexual-privacy cases they relied on only reinforced the idea of sexual relationships as outside the structure of civil society; they were about the right to be left alone, not the right to be approved. Although the Supreme Court clearly categorized marriage as fundamental in the race-marriage case, *Loving*, the law in that case was intrusive; it made it *criminal* for a white person and another "to cohabit as man and wife" in Virginia, especially pursuant to an interracial marriage from a more permissive state. *Loving* also smelled to high heaven of Hitler-era eugenics, with all the talk of mongrel races and pure blood.

The revolution's demand for gay marriage, however, went far beyond the tolerance-based arguments in *Loving*. The gay revolution affirmatively demands that the states bless gays' unions—to admit them to the state-run social club called "marriage." In the fight over Prop 8, Schubert Flint cannily figured this out, adopting as their goal separating *respect* for gay and lesbian rights from *approval* of their application to join the club. On Election Day, millions of citizens of the state of California had voted their RSVPs, regretfully declining to attend same-sex weddings.

Perry started the process of gathering sponsors for gay candidates for the marriage club almost immediately after the suit was filed. Attorney General Jerry Brown, and, later, Governor Arnold Schwarzenegger, weighed in, refusing to defend Prop 8. They thought it was unconstitutional, too. The extremely antigay Pugno Protect Marriage coalition had to move to intervene, a costly move. Politically, instead of a neutral, high government official defending the well-established voting process that just happened to turn up an antigay result, the new defendant, the offspring of State Senator Pete Knight's long-standing antigay campaign, graphically symbolized the record of antigay prejudice that fueled Prop 8.

Moreover, a shrewd public official might have tried to pull off a defense of Prop 8 as distasteful, but within the broad constitutional tolerance for democratic self-governance, a position for which there is a lot of support regardless of the content of the decision. ProtectMarriage.com, however, actually tried to show that gay marriage would hurt society. The ProtectMarriage lawyer even tried the "Princes" move ("would you want school children to learn about gay marriages?") in cross-examining legendary gay historian George Chauncey. Chauncey, however, had learned his history lessons. "Why not?" he asked. "Shouldn't children be allowed to read books in which interracial couples marry and live happily ever after?" After legendary cross-examiner David Boies had his way with the defense's so-called "expert" witnesses to the gay marriage threat during pretrial proceedings, most of them refused to come to court. The one witness brave enough to face Boies in the courtroom was rewarded by having his testimony dismantled by Boies's cross-examination and then failing to qualify as an expert anyway. During the two years of litigation, ProtectMarriage spent almost as much time keeping the trial from being broadcast to the public as they did defending Prop 8. Even ProtectMarriage must have realized that watching them replay their political campaign in the reason-driven precincts of the courtroom would not help their cause.

On the gay side, what with all the hugging and the toasting and the handsome men in their business suits, the rally after the judge ruled for the plaintiffs looked for all the world like a wedding reception. Speaking everywhere and being on the news every time something happened in the case, Boies and Olson put their social capital in the bank for marriage equality. Probably no one else in the country could have done more. On August 8,

2011, the American Bar Association awarded Boies and Olson their highest honor, a medal won in previous years by lawyers like justices Oliver Wendell Holmes and Thurgood Marshall.

The Fierce Advocate

Unlike the happy postpartisan Boies-Olson twins, six months into his first term the newly elected Democratic president of the United States, Barack Obama, found himself in the same illiberal camp as the usually liberal California electorate. His Justice Department filed a brief defending the Defense of Marriage Act (DOMA) in the first of many challenges to come, *Smelt v. United States*. Someone sent the brief to blogger John Aravosis. The government had made arguments, common in the litigation over same-sex marriage, that gays and lesbians have no special constitutional rights, that DOMA was rational, which is all that's required if gays aren't a protected class. If all you're looking for is a rational basis for a law, the United States argued, the government has ample power to restrict marriage, as it does in cases, for example, of incest or underage children. The brief seemed, to an official at the ex-gay group Exodus International, to be pleasingly "repeating social conservative arguments." Gay marriage = Incest! Pedophilia!!

The Democratic administration may be excused for not realizing the price it was going to pay for the brief in *Smelt*. After all, scores of Democrats in Congress had voted for DOMA in the first place, with no apparent electoral or other cost to them. The state and local Democratic parties had done nothing to stave off the anti–gay marriage amendment tsunami in 2004.

And they had reason to want to stay away from the issue. In the fifteen years since Bill Clinton took office in 1993, the deep structure of the American electoral map had changed very little. Any national candidate would need to peel off some of the consistently Republican states in order to win the White House. The core Republican-base states map almost perfectly onto the strongholds of the religious right, and gay marriage raised the Sinful horseman of the gay apocalypse like no other issue had since the AIDS epidemic.

Doubtless mindful of the electoral reality it faced, the Obama campaign had repeatedly insulted or ignored the gay movement. Early in the 2008 primary season, the Obama campaign had put together a gospel tour, targeted at the African American voters of South Carolina. For their headliner, the Obama campaign chose Donny McClurkin, who all the locals knew was the poster boy for being cured of gayness through finding God. Activists would never know whether the Obama campaign had just gratuitously insulted them because it did not care about the gay constituency or because the campaign was too ignorant of gay issues to know who they had hired. Exactly as the activists feared, the campaign gave McClurkin the stage, and he told the audience that God had delivered him from homosexuality. After the McClurkin episode blew up at them, the Obama campaign suddenly acceded to repeated requests from gay magazine the *Advocate* for an interview with the candidate, and their political reporter Kerry Eleveld got fifteen minutes to listen to Obama recite his record on support for LGBT issues while a state senator. It was the first time a presidential candidate had ever given an interview to an official gay publication.

A month after the campaign ended, Obama's team picked California evangelical minister Rick Warren to give the invocation at the game-changing president's inauguration. Warren's positions on poverty and AIDS had given him some distance from the hard-right profile of the ordinary evangelical, but he had e-mailed his thirty thousand followers just before the election, urging them to pass Prop 8 and "preserve the Biblical definition of marriage." Gay activists were incensed at the inclusion of an antigay preacher to open the presidential inauguration. Again, Obama turned to the media to emphasize the good heart that underlay his offensive actions. At a press conference shortly after the Warren explosion, Obama described himself as "a fierce advocate for gay and lesbian Americans." The establishment gay organization Human Rights Campaign invited the president to address their big dinner. It looked like nothing had changed since the A-gays failed to buy their way in to the Democratic Party in 1993. An electoral minority, concentrated in states already safe for the liberal-leaning party, their options looked pretty bleak.

But by the time the Justice Department compared same-sex marriage to incest in federal court, the movement had changed. The gay blogosphere, now five years old, was made for this. John Aravosis's version of the *Smelt* brief went viral faster than the Spanish flu and instantly crossed into the mainstream media, which also now included a number of out gay journalists and opinion writers. No one needed to remind Aravosis or the fourth estate that Gay Was Good. Presidential press secretary Robert Gibbs found himself defending the brief under heavy fire from ABC's Jake Tapper, and the *Washington Post*'s Jonathan Capehart wrote a column about how donors were bailing out on an upcoming Obama fund-raiser. As Rick Jacobs, head of the liberal and progay California Courage Campaign, astutely observed, gay people were already furious about the loss on Prop 8. Now some of that anger was turning on the president. The Obama administration hurried up its new executive order extending partnership benefits to the same-sex couples employed by the federal government, in a transparent effort to calm the waters.

Clinton's old gay adviser Richard Socarides, who would become one of the "fierce advocate"'s fiercest critics, dates his radicalization to the day he heard about the Rick Warren invocation. Because Socarides was a lawyer and an insider during the Clinton years, he was also relentless on the Justice Department's persistent claim that when it came to DOMA, it had no choice but to defend the federal law. Socarides knew that almost every modern president had refused to defend some law on grounds that it's unconstitutional. Socarides went public on MSNBC and in the *Wall Street Journal*, reaming the president in the indignant tones of someone who knows he's being lied to.

When an old Nixon appointee, Judge Joseph Tauro, struck down DOMA as unconstitutional in the broadest terms in Mary Bonauto's case, *Gill*, in 2010, the stakes for the Obama administration rose sharply. The Justice Department had been defending DOMA in the proliferating challenges. Would it now appeal a federal ruling of unconstitutionality, arguing that it must defend a law because it's constitutional in order to argue that the law is constitutional?

Get Equal: The Bottom-up Strategy

Democratic National Committee critic and partner of former DNC employee Donald Hitchcock, Paul Yandura, was loving this. When Fresno rally organizer Robin McGehee turned up in Washington in 2009, Yandura was ready for some insurgency. Like Yandura, McGehee had had a Cinderella rise. During the Prop 8 battle, lesbian mother McGehee had been an increasingly visible voice of the gay and lesbian community in her little California town. After Prop 8 passed, the priest at her son's private Catholic school asked her to step down as president of the PTA. As McGehee was organizing a rally in the Central Valley, where she felt the California gay establishment had done little to support the local activists, she also had to find a new school for little Sebastian. The cost to her family enriched the fuel of her indignation as little else could have done. When she heard Cleve Jones speak at a conference right after Prop 8, she asked him if he would come to her little rally. An unheard-of five thousand people showed up.

Jones figured he had found a natural. When David Mixner put out a call on his blog in May 2009 for a national march—the first in decades—on Washington, Jones asked McGehee if she would help organize it. "Be the mom," he said. "So I can be just Uncle Cleve." When McGehee needed some money to pay for scholarships to come to the march, someone put her in touch with Yandura, who had long had the ear of the gay heir to the Progressive Insurance fortune, Jonathan Lewis. Lewis, "the only lone wolf," as McGehee says, in gay philanthropy, started funding the insurgency.

Around a quarter of a million people showed up at the march. Not by chance, the insurgents arrived at the National Mall on October 11, 2009, the day after Barack Obama's appearance at the Human Rights Campaign (HRC) dinner. The local production of *Hair* closed its doors and sent the cast to sing for the new rebels: "Let the Sunshine In." A few months later, Jonathan Lewis pledged to pay for a meeting of all the new factions at the legendary Highlander civil rights center in Tennessee. They would learn to do direct action and civil disobedience all over again. The Highlander meeting gave birth to a new group, GetEqual, led by McGehee and another California youngster, Kip Williams, and dedicated to direct action for LGBT rights.

But even as the new insurgents marched in October 2009, ten months into Barack Obama's presidency, the administration was still defending DOMA. Despite a clear and unequivocal commitment to repeal don't ask/don't tell in the Democratic platform and during the campaign, the Democrats had let the Defense Authorization Act go through Congress in May without a murmur about DADT. Less than a month after the March for Equality, that November, the people of the state of Maine did exactly what California did and passed a referendum reversing the law authorizing same-sex marriage, which the Maine legislature had just passed the year before. This time, the loss came after a campaign that presented the real faces of same-sex couples, as the critics of the California campaign had suggested. No help. Schubert Flint put up the schoolchildren and the thing went down like déjà vu all over again.

It was a watershed moment in the movement. All the pieces were in place. Activists in the blogosphere and beyond were clear on the fact of their difference. A critical number of movement players were unambivalent about their moral rectitude. They were disabused of the reliability of their so-called progressive allies. They were acting up. But nothing changed. The old folks from ACT UP and the insurgent youngsters were singing songs from *Hair* and the establishment gays from HRC were dining with the president. All social movements come to an end eventually and all end short of their goals. Was this the end?

12

Victory: The Civil Rights March of Our Generation

On March 20, 2009, infantry lieutenant Dan Choi, fresh from his tour of duty in the Iraq War, appeared on MSNBC's *Rachel Maddow Show.*

"I'm gay," he announced. And I'm not lying anymore.

Not more than a week later, New York's young, newly appointed senator, Kirsten Gillibrand, heard from one of her girlfriends from her law practice days.

"I want you to meet one of my clients. Dan Choi."

The Soldier and the Girl (Senator)

West Point graduate, Iraq War veteran, trained Arabic linguist, Dan Choi was a movement dream. Trying, again, to move the least liberal institutions in Western society, marriage and the military, the movement task was to claim the goods of sacrifice and heroism for the historically denigrated gay population. Who better suited to do the job for the movement than a tall, handsome young soldier?

"I want nothing but to serve my country and even die for my country," Choi told the senator. "I believe in its values. Everything about the military is about honor," he said, "except if you're gay."

"What a horrible way to live your life," thought Gillibrand, a young wife and mother herself. "I cannot imagine being in any job without being able to tell my coworkers and my colleagues about my husband or my children or what I do on the weekend or the other things that are most important to me."

A couple of months after Choi's appearance, California's online progressive organization, the Courage Campaign, scooped up the articulate Lieutenant Choi and organized a demonstration at an Obama fund-raiser in Los Angeles. The Courage Campaign, which sprang from founder Rick Jacobs's experience with the new-media Howard Dean campaign in 2004, gathered a hundred thousand signatures online asking Obama not to discharge Choi. At that first demonstration, Choi debuted *his* signature move—he stepped beyond the protesters who had been obediently observing the police no-protest zone and stood saluting the commander in chief as the cameras snapped. When safely inside the event, President Obama worked the friendly crowd, musing aloud about what the protesters could possibly be demanding, but the next morning Choi was all over the news.

Gillibrand's office launched an online-story project. The senator from the memoir generation understood how to present the movement's romantic, moralistic issue: "Dan Choi's story had an overwhelming impact on me, inspiring me and infuriating me," she explains. "We had about a dozen stories from people who were the victims of DADT and thousands more signed petitions to repeal it." (Gillibrand also realized that she could pitch repeal as a straight story of military readiness. Losing all those good soldiers could not be good for the country's defense.)

When she started, Gillibrand assumed that one of the ninety-nine senators senior to her was already actively working on the issue. After all, there had been bills to repeal don't ask/don't tell hanging around Congress for years. Turns out, Senator Ted Kennedy, who had been point man on repealing DADT, was dying, and Gillibrand knew that in the time he had left, he would not be diverted from his role in health-care reform. So this newest senator wrote a bill designed to be complementary to existing bills, in this case to have an eighteen-month moratorium on discharges.

Gillibrand was not surprised that she was leading an eminently winnable fight. "Gay rights is a generational issue," she believes. "It is the civil rights march of *our* generation. We have lived very different lives than our older colleagues; we have friends who are gay throughout our entire educational life. We have friends of my generation who are now raising children, making a very different profile of gay families today." And the personal is still the political. "I also had a number of friends in my law firm," Gillibrand says. "Gay friends who I spent my vacations with when I lived in New York. They were my family away from home so their lives and their loved ones are very important to me."

The path for the new civil rights march had been well laid. Maybe the supposedly liberal California electorate and the supposedly liberal politicos at the White House wouldn't help them, but the tide was turning anyway. In the early nineties, the incendiary controversy around marriage and the military had cost the gay revolution dearly. While the "morality politics" defeats outside the liberal state were piling up, however, the civil rights victories of the 1990s and early 2000s moved gays and lesbians into the sphere of normal citizenship in the liberal state. By 2009, the polls were overwhelmingly in favor of allowing gays to serve.

And so, as Gillibrand met with more and more senators, she realized there was more support than people thought. This included Carl Levin, powerful chairman of the Senate Armed Services Committee, which would eventually have to hear the matter. "I'm with you," Levin said. "Just keep me posted." She even got encouraging words from her gal pals across the aisle, senators Susan Collins and Olympia Snowe. She submitted her legislation. Thanks in part to Rachel Maddow and Lieutenant Dan Choi, the media were actually paying some attention to the issue, and a reporter cornered Majority Leader Harry Reid.

The Nevada senator, who had met Dan Choi at a Human Rights Campaign (HRC) black-tie dinner in Las Vegas, didn't think the army should kick out an Arabic linguist, or anyone else the country needed, for that matter. He said he supported full repeal and wrote a letter to President Obama asking him to help. In January 2010, Obama put the repeal of DADT in his State of the Union address.

Gillibrand asked Levin, chairman of the Senate Armed Services Committee, to hold a hearing on DADT, and, to her delight, he agreed. The February hearing was the first such meeting in sixteen years. Aubrey Sarvis, the deceptively mild-mannered former army sharpshooter and telecommunications lobbyist who had been running the Servicemembers Legal Defense Network (SLDN) for four or five years at that point, says the hearing was the turning point. When the chairman of the Senate Armed Services Committee calls, the Pentagon listens. Secretary of Defense Robert Gates and Chairman of the Joint Chiefs Admiral Mike Mullen had to appear and they had to take a position on DADT. The days of quizzical or genial rhetoric from the commander in chief were numbered.

The hearing was the tip, but SLDN was the iceberg. In its decade and a half of compelling the military to recognize the personhood of its members, gay or not, SLDN had won the respect of the military establishment. Leaders like Michelle Benecke had even been invited to lecture at the military training colleges. In 2009, SLDN had arranged a meeting between Admiral Mullen and straight movement allies Admiral Jamie Barnett and General John Adams. Sarvis, well aware of the role of romantic stories in the fight for acceptance in a premodern institution, sent an SLDN board member, retired Navy captain Joan Darrah.

Like so many of the pivotal people in the battles, Darrah, a naval intelligence officer, had a great story. In her third decade of closeted service, she went to a meeting at the Pentagon. Minutes after she left the building on 9/11, the third terrorist airplane slammed into the room where she had been meeting, killing seven of her colleagues. Having concealed her relationship, Darrah realized that had she died there, her long-term partner would have found out about her death on CNN. A few months later she retired. "Joan led the discussion at the meeting with Admiral Mullen, and talked a lot about integrity," Sarvis reports. At the committee hearing a year later, Mullen told Congress, "For me personally it comes down to integrity—theirs as individuals and ours as an institution." "When Admiral Mullen said, 'This policy undermines the integrity and effectiveness of the service,'" Senator Gillibrand thought, "Omigod, we're going to repeal don't ask/don't tell."

But no. First, the White House told the junior senator it wanted Connecticut independent senator Joe Lieberman, a moderate and a senior person on the Armed Services Committee, to be the leader on this. So, Gillibrand recalls, she just asked Senator Lieberman almost daily for about two months to cosponsor the bill with her. "Having Senator Lieberman really made a difference," she graciously concedes. Maybe. But the bill just sat there. The military asked for ten months to do a study before the administration would get behind a repeal bill. That would put the repeal squarely at the end of the crowded congressional session in December 2010. The establishment gay organizations, including SLDN with reluctance, agreed to all the military demands in order to get a bill passed even conditioned on the outcome of the study. Still the Senate stalled.

Since the crucial last senators would not sign on until the Pentagon was satisfied, the military held all the cards. Sarvis got wind of Pentagon lobbyists telling senators not to move on the bill. There were rumors that the president leaned on Gates to speed things up, and that he threatened to quit. Led by the indefatigable Speaker Nancy Pelosi and the House Majority Leader Steny Hoyer, the House of Representatives actually did include provisions repealing DADT as part of the 2010 National Defense Authorization Act (NDAA). Pelosi, it is reported, said no one had asked *her* to make a deal with the Pentagon. Activists remained hopeful that when the NDAA reached the Senate the repeal would pass with it.

But then the polling data that showed a Republican takeover of the House of Representatives in November 2010 began to roll in, and the Republicans decided they wouldn't join with the Democrats to pass anything, not even, for the first time, the National Defense Authorization Act. Dan Choi announced he was going on a hunger strike, but no one paid him any mind. It was summer 2010. A conservative political train was coming, and the beautiful young senator and the courageous young soldier were tied to the tracks.

Activist Judges

Just when it seemed that all might be lost, the movement's federal-litigation initiative suddenly bore fruit. In 2004, inspired by the Supreme Court's decision protecting homosexual sodomy, an organization of gay conservatives, Log Cabin Republicans, had sued to challenge the constitutionality of DADT. In July 2010, Judge Virginia Phillips, a bespectacled Jane Austen–loving widow and Democratic appointee to the federal bench in California, struck down the law as unconstitutional and issued a nationwide injunction against its enforcement. Coincidentally, eighty-year-old Nixon appointee Joseph Tauro, of the US District Court for the District of Massachusetts, struck down the Defense of Marriage Act in *Gill v. OPM.* And California federal trial judge Vaughn Walker, the seventysomething, long-closeted homosexual protégé of the first George Bush, handed Boies and Olson the predictable constitutional victory on Prop 8.

The decision-laden summer of 2010 dealt a serious blow to the conservative strategy of excluding gay and lesbian citizens from the sacred precincts of love and war. As the decisions protecting gays' political rights in *Romer* and privacy in *Lawrence* reflected, the courts are important guardians of the liberal bargain. For reasons nowhere set forth in the document, however, the courts have long had a hands-off policy toward enforcing the constitutional principles of the liberal state to marriage or the military. When deciding challenges to military decisions, the courts extend a level of deference toward the military to control its own affairs unequaled in the rest of the constitutional scheme. On matters of the heart, it took thirteen full years after the Supreme Court struck down segregated schools for the court to forbid racial segregation of marriage. Even after they belatedly defined marriage as a fundamental right, the federal courts for years refused to become involved in domestic-relations cases otherwise within their jurisdiction; the policy was simply called the "domestic-relations exception." No authority required. Feminists speculate that the domestic-relations exception survives because federal judges do not consider women, otherwise citizens, to be citizens within marriage. With the courts forgoing their role as constitutional cops, the government-regulated realms of marriage and the military survived as relics of an unfree, unequal illiberal past long after the courts had played a role in imposing basic liberal values in the rest of the state.

But as the summer of 2010 revealed, it could not last. Citizenship in the liberal state confers a powerful dose of dignity on the people included. They are not animals, to be attacked or killed for sport: their lives are valuable. They are not crazies: they are entitled to rational pursuit of their self-interest in the democratic process. And they are not felons: their human intimacy is of constitutional status. Marriage and the military are different, but they are not completely disconnected from the rest of society, and ultimately they are answerable to the principles of the Constitution. The court did finally strike down the remaining laws against interracial marriage. The more gay and lesbian Americans took on the aspects of normal citizenship in the liberal state, the more incoherent their exclusion from even these remote precincts of modernity seemed.

So far had the gay revolution come that the lawyer for Log Cabin Republicans, a straight white Republican partner in the huge corporate law firm White and Case, had no qualms at all about leading the challenge to DADT. Dan Woods denies that he's in a category with heroes of social change like Thurgood Marshall. He says he finds his advocacy perfectly consistent with his conservative principle that every man should be treated strictly on his own merit. Anyway, the plaintiffs were Republicans: the gay political group, *Log Cabin Republicans.*

In the perfect logic of the constitutional system, Woods could have rested his case on the thirty or more years of studies all concluding that openly gay participants would not harm the military. But Woods had digested the lesson from the failed past efforts to extend the constitutional norms into areas of love and war. Like Senator Gillibrand in Congress and the activists from SLDN, Woods believed he needed the romance of their gallantry.

Luckily, among the many victims of DADT eager to tell their stories to the federal judge, Woods had the gallant Major Michael Almy to put on the stand. Major Almy, whose father and two uncles were career military, joined up in 1993 with a valuable skill in information technology. A decade later, when Almy finished his third deployment to Iraq, he left his government computer behind. The next person to use it decided to open his private e-mail file. (As an information specialist, Almy knew no one was ever supposed to read his e-mail.) There, amid hundreds of e-mails to his mother, were a handful of e-mails reflecting a same-sex relationship. Major Almy, festooned with awards and medals and trailing the unstinting praise of superiors and inferiors, was discharged from the service. His next major public appearance was as the first example in Judge Phillips's sweeping opinion striking down DADT.

The government got a reprieve in the military arena when the United States Court of Appeals for the Ninth Circuit stayed Judge Phillips's injunction by a two-to-one vote of the three-judge panel and the Supreme Court affirmed the stay. The stay only applied, however, until the appeals court ruled on the government's appeal of the underlying ruling that DADT is unconstitutional. Since the Obama administration was firmly on record as opposing DADT, the administration held a trump card—it could stop defending the law and Judge Phillips's order would become final.

The possibility that some court might actually just order the military to stop DADT on a dime sent a chill down the back of the Defense Department. As the lame-duck Congress reconvened after the Republicans won a majority of the House in November 2010, Secretary Gates, who had resisted the provisional bill the previous spring, and Admiral Mullen held a press conference, fretting publicly about the dangers in a court-ordered repeal. In early December they leaked the favorable report and then released it publicly before the lame-duck Congress could go home, taking with them the last chance for a legislative repeal.

Military Victory

Aubrey Sarvis puts it baldly, "I don't care what anyone says, no one had a secret plan to have two votes in the lame-duck session after the Democrats have lost control of the House."

In the years since the 2008 election, the gay revolution has often seemed more like a silent movie serial than a well-planned political campaign. This is actually not surprising. As Senator Gillibrand found out when she took up repealing DADT, a critical portion of elite decision makers were on the gay side. But the racial and feminist movements have deep roots in American history, high visibility in a racially diverse world, and a substantial presence in the electorate. The people involved in the gay revolution, a tiny minority of voters and with comparatively small resources, struggle constantly to make a majority of legislators, however sympathetic, consider them a priority. This tension produces one cliff-hanger after another. Sarvis thinks, for example, that there were people around the president who would have been okay with DADT going over into the next Congress, which was tantamount to complete failure.

In repealing DADT, then, the movement benefited, as it often had, from a relatively small handful of committed allies. As the clock of the lame-duck session ticked toward recess, the core DADT-repeal activists, Gillibrand, Collins, and Lieberman, along with the scion of the legendary progressive Udall clan, Colorado senator Mark Udall, were meeting every day. At one point they even threatened to hold the Senate over Christmas.

After several near misses, on December 9, Joe Lieberman and Republican Susan Collins introduced the repeal as a stand-alone bill, stripped from the larger NDAA. The change in format meant that the House would have to pass another bill. All day, every day of the weekend of December 10,

House Majority Leader Steny Hoyer worked the phones of the senators, to be sure that there really were enough votes to break a filibuster and repeal DADT. Despite the sky-high approval numbers in the polls, gay rights were toxic for so long it seems that he worried about his surviving House Democrats taking what was seen as a politically risky vote for nothing. But, on Wednesday, December 15, former Army captain and Bronze Star–winner Democratic representative Patrick Murphy introduced and the House passed the bill repealing don't ask/don't tell. Early on the cold Saturday morning of December 18, Orthodox Jewish senator Joe Lieberman, whose religion forbids riding on the Sabbath, left his house in Georgetown to walk to the Capitol to vote. Reflecting the support that had long been there, the bill passed the Senate by sixty-five votes, five more than needed to break a filibuster.

It feels like a victory, but it pays to remember that it's hardly D-day. This is what passes for a civil rights victory in the "civil rights march of this generation"—undoing the discriminatory law the government inflicted on itself in its orgy of revulsion in 1993. And even then the repeal probably would not have happened but for the lucky break that the parties couldn't agree on some other issue, opening up enough time to pass the first federal gay equality measure in the history of the Republic.

And a Thousand Fathers

As the votes reflected, Congress, looking at a 67 percent approval rate for gay service, did not expect a negative response to repealing DADT. But everyone was surprised at the intensity of the praise. Newspaper editorials called it the only good thing to come out of the lame-duck session. Lawmakers returned to their districts to find their progressive allies showering them with kudos for their record-breaking action.

In the seventeen years since Sam Nunn led his camera crew into the shower room of the submarine, America had changed. Heck, even Sam

Nunn had changed his mind about gays in the military, coming out for it (after he was against it in 1993).

And the military had changed. The youngsters who make up most of the armed services had, like Kirsten Gillibrand, grown up with openly gay people all around them. In the army a person can become a major while still in his or her thirties and even occasionally a full-bird colonel, one rank below brigadier general. By 2010, even the officer corps, which so totally commanded the loyalty of then Chief of Staff Colin Powell in 1993, was of a different generation. The officers were running an institution that had come to resemble the liberal state. Members of an all-volunteer force fighting two wars in 2010, they had experienced firsthand the difficulty of meeting their recruitment goals, competing with the market economy for the best and the brightest. They cringed every time they saw a great candidate turn away because they did not want to run the gauntlet of DADT.

Ironically, as the military became more modern, the gay revolution looked more traditional. Their second assault on the military citadel was not motivated primarily by a desire for a springboard to equality in civil society. Since 1993, the gay revolution had made great strides in the liberal state. Most of the gay and lesbian linguists and nurses and information technologists discharged from the military for violating DADT were perfectly capable of living openly and earning a living in the civilian society to which they were consigned. Serving openly in the military was their primary end, not the means to a more familiar civil rights goal. In this, the gay campaign for military service was a piece of the morally ambitious gay movement agenda. Not satisfied with rights alone, the end gays sought was honor, the honor of serving their country's military. Congressional liberals lobbied their colleagues with conservative arguments that gay soldiers were good for national security. The moral self-confidence that has characterized the successful parts of the gay revolution from the beginning won the day. World War II veteran and movement founder Franklin Kameny, tossed out of the Army Mapping Service as a security risk half a century before, said it: Gay Is Good.

In the quest for honor, it was the soldiers who made the last push. Whether it was Dan Choi, who chained himself to the White House fence that spring, or less well-known representatives like Michael Almy or Joan Darrah, someone coming forward with a desire to serve was the most powerful motivator for the change. Choi stood in a line of people stretching all the way back to that moment in 1993 when veterans Michelle Benecke and Dixon Osburn pulled up chairs to borrowed desks and turned on their castoff computers to tell the stories of the gay men and lesbian women who only wanted to serve their country.

Ironically, the Pentagon actually triggered what it most feared, a court order to repeal. The repeal law allowed the Pentagon an open-ended amount of time to prepare their troops and certify to the president that DADT could be lifted. Seven months after Congress voted, the military still had not given the president the requisite green light. On July 6, 2011, the Ninth Circuit Court of Appeals, which was sitting on the appeal in the Log Cabin Republicans case, finally lost patience with the military and ordered it to stop enforcing DADT. The government was reduced to agreeing not to discharge anyone while it crept toward certification in order to stop the court from forcing it to immediately accept gay enlistees. The administration's failure to close the deal even after repeal passed did not surprise one well-placed Senate staffer who had been watching the whole shebang. "The White House staff had to be dragged kicking and screaming the whole way toward repeal," he says.

DOMA Is a Legal Orphan

A week or two after the Senate vote, HRC president Joe Solmonese went to a liberal fund-raiser in Los Angeles for Ohio Democratic senator Sherrod Brown. What were the straight progressive funders talking about? The senator's role in repealing don't ask/don't tell. Best thing he'd ever done, they said.

New activists up against the fence, 2010
(photograph by Talk About Equality, courtesy of GetEQUAL)

The progressives' pleasure in what Congress had done put real pressure on Democratic president Barack Obama. The government was still defending the Defense of Marriage Act, and the time for appealing Judge Joseph Tauro's ruling was approaching fast. Then in February, legal cupid Mary Bonauto filed the same lawsuit she had tried in Massachusetts, this time in the federal court in Connecticut. The funders were high-fiving and the blogosphere was waiting for Obama's next move. Obama, who kept saying things like he was "evolving" in his position on gay marriage, would clearly have preferred to remain above the fray and just let ProtectMarriage.com and the rest suggest that marriage was a constitution-free zone. Polling in favor of same-sex marriage had not yet crossed the 50 percent mark and there was little electoral will in Congress to repeal DOMA.

But litigation, whether ultimately successful or not, plays a crucial role in a social movement. The minute the gay activists started forcing the government to articulate why gays and lesbians should be excluded from marriage in the secular and reason-driven precincts of the courthouse, the Defense of Marriage Act became a hot potato. It's one thing to be silent in face of bigotry and another thing to express bigoted positions yourself. There was no neutral ground. The Obama administration had to figure out a way to drop it. And dropping it was a political act.

Gay activist and Obama critic Richard Socarides was watching with great interest. A few months before, he'd gotten a call to a meeting from some midlevel lawyers at the White House Office of Legal Counsel. He'd been such a big mouth about how Bill Clinton hadn't defended a law he thought was unconstitutional, maybe he could help the current White House. WWCD? they wanted to know: What Would Clinton Do? Clinton, Socarides said, would have asked what the best outcome was—politically or policy-wise—and then whether it was legal.

On February 23, 2011, Attorney General Eric Holder sent a letter to Congress: the Justice Department will not be defending your law anymore. The administration tried its best to make the decision look like a neutral application of legal principles rather than a Clintonesque pursuit of the best political option the law allowed. It settled on the difference between Connecticut, where the new case was filed, and all the other cases. The federal court of appeals in the jurisdiction including Connecticut had not yet issued an opinion about how to treat discrimination based on sexual orientation. Believing that antigay discrimination was suspect, and absent binding precedent to the contrary from the court of appeals in Connecticut, Justice would have to ask the Connecticut federal courts to scrutinize the act closely. Justice did not believe the law could survive heightened scrutiny. The United States would stay in the case, the letter said, but the Justice Department was going to tell the court the law was unconstitutional. Congress would have to defend its own legislation.

Even the people—Socarides, blogger John Aravosis—who had been screaming the loudest for the administration to stop defending DOMA, were flabbergasted. Could it be that the president was a fierce advocate after all? On the right, Bush Justice Department alum and conservative legal blogger Edward Whelan wrote, "The Obama administration has been sabotaging DOMA litigation from the outset. Today's action at least has the modest virtue of bringing that sabotage out into the open." In the end, it looked like the political potato of defending DOMA had finally gotten too hot, even for cool hand Barack.

Although the movement had gotten no traction at all in getting the administration to work for repeal of DOMA, by forcing it to drop the defense of marriage in court, gay activists extracted a big deposit to the movement's social capital. Whelan, who had been a Supreme Court clerk and official in the very political Office of Legal Counsel in the Bush administration, recognized exactly what was at stake in what may look like a somewhat technical matter: "The optics matter an awful lot politically and I think to the court, too." It's one thing to have the orderly, institutionally legitimate defenders (the "Justice" Department) of the presumptively legitimate law of Congress blessing the law when it's challenged, and another to have defense of the law relegated to the arms of private hired guns.

Then, in a brilliant stroke, the movement took the fight to the next level—the legal profession. The Obama administration had waited until the election of a Republican Congress to decide to bail on the DOMA cases, and, not surprisingly, the House Republicans voted to have Congress take the case over from the Department of Justice. New speaker John Boehner went off to hire them a lawyer.

On March 23, Joe Solmonese, the president of Human Rights Campaign, sent a letter to the law firms that made the *American Lawyer* magazine's biggest and richest list, the AmLaw 200. The House Republicans would be looking for a lawyer, he heard. "On behalf of the Human Rights Campaign (HRC)," he wrote, "I . . . urge your firm, if it is even considering taking that case, not to do so." Don't volunteer to be the next institution comparing same-sex marriage to bestiality. Reflecting the transformation of the legal culture, law firms had become among the best places in America for gay and lesbian employees, Solmonese pointed out. "The legal sector has the largest number of top-scoring companies in HRC's Corporate Equality Index," an annual measure of how equitably large private businesses in the United States treat their lesbian, gay, bisexual, and transgender employees, consumers, and investors. Don't screw it up.

On April 18, Bush administration solicitor general Paul Clement, now a partner at behemoth firm King & Spalding, agreed to represent the House. Within hours, the firm, which had scored 95 percent on the HRC Index, heard from HRC: "The firm of King & Spalding has brought a shameful stain on its reputation in arguing for discrimination against loving, married couples." The next day, HRC announced that it would take ads in mainstream and legal publications and send informational letters to the firm's clients, organizations to which they had made charitable contributions, and the nation's top law schools informing them of K&S's decision to promote discrimination. E-mail and Twitter would start among HRC's more than one million members and supporters. The blogosphere lit up.

On April 25, just as GetEqual was gathering its demonstrators outside King & Spalding's Washington offices (SHAME ON YOU KING & SPALDING), King & Spalding announced it was withdrawing from its defense of

DOMA and Paul Clement would be leaving the firm. Clement would go to Bancroft PLLC, a firm of eight mostly Bush-administration alums, and take his client with him. GetEqual demonstrators were marking up their placards with felt tip pens, SHAME ON YOU, ER, BANCROFT.

It was not clear at first whether Solmonese's bold stroke had paid off. Quick as you could say, "To Kill a Mockingbird," the political establishment, which had largely been silent on the matter, turned Paul Clement, the defender of the punitive and discriminatory Defense of Marriage Act, into Atticus Finch. Editorial writers compared Congress's desire to defend DOMA in a civil suit to the right of a criminal defendant, presumed innocent, to counsel. The *New York Times* said that Thurgood Marshall, the legal architect of desegregation, was no different from his opponent John W. Davis, who defended the segregationist school boards. The Obama administration, obviously sensing an opportunity to demonstrate fealty to the rule of law after the transparently strategic decision to bail on DOMA, piled on. Attorney General Eric Holder lauded "great lawyer" Paul Clement for "doing what lawyers do when we're at our best," a sentiment reiterated by President Obama's press secretary, and, astonishingly, by newly appointed Supreme Court justice Elena Kagan, in a marked departure from the discretion that normally governs the justices' public pronouncements.

The legal arguments about why he shouldn't ask law firms to turn down the DOMA case made no sense to Solmonese. "Even in the midst of the storm," he says, "none of these process people was willing to argue that it was lawyering 'at its best' to defend racial segregation or that a firm should defend a statute forbidding women to practice law." The way Solmonese saw it, the controversy had nothing to do with legal ethics. Everyone knows a law firm can turn cases away. They do it every day. For a half century, the gay movement had been asserting that mistreating and discriminating against them was not only illegal, it was immoral. Solmonese had just tested the limits of that core principle. The establishment wasn't sure exactly whether gays had come far enough.

But sometimes just acting like you're rich makes you rich. Like the new military, law firms needed to compete in the market economy for employees and for clients. Indignant King & Spalding lawyers leaked to the press that the superstar partner had neglected to take the obligatory step of submitting the contract to the firm's business-review committee, which first learned of the controversial commitment from the media and when K&S's furious gay and gay-sympathetic employees poured into their offices. Word was, signature-firm client Coca-Cola was not happy. Regardless of what the *Times* thought, it turns out, very few law students dream of being the man who *defended* segregation.

Solmonese ran into a prominent Washington lawyer at a cocktail party: "I hope," the advocate told him, "you appreciate that from this day forward, the top two hundred law firms in America will never again go near anything that even remotely smells antigay."

Rainbow Empire State

Still it looked like the classes versus the masses: life-tenured federal judges for same-sex marriage, the people of the state of California and the voters spooking the Obama political machine against. Marriage equality lost in heavily Democratic state legislatures in Maryland and Rhode Island. Then, popular New York governor Andrew Cuomo announced in May 2011 that he was going to lead the charge in the Empire State, something he had promised in his campaign. It's hard to imagine that Cuomo was unaware of the hosannas that greeted the repeal of don't ask/don't tell. But same-sex marriage had just gone down to defeat in New York two years before and the state senate was again controlled by Republicans; it seemed like a long shot. Three months later, he signed the bill into law. The lights on the Empire State Building blazed red, yellow, green, blue, a rainbow of celebration.

Victory in New York involved every strength the movement possessed. By fiat of nature, everyone has a gay friend or relative. Cuomo's girlfriend Sandra Lee's brother was an out gay man. By all accounts, Cuomo ran a pitch-perfect operation. He pulled all the fractious gay organizations into one coalition, New Yorkers United for Marriage. The libertarian New York mayor, Michael Bloomberg, and the Republicans from Wall Street had all come to see gay and lesbian people as citizens and, as citizens, entitled to access to marriage, just as if it were a garden-variety institution of the liberal state. Gently coaxed by the governor, they put their clout and money behind the effort. Unlike the failed effort in the Democratic-controlled legislature in 2009, Cuomo controlled his own party, delivering every Democrat except the intransigently homophobic Reverend Ruben Diaz of the Bronx.

The legal profession helped. As Republican marriage supporter Mark Grisanti said on the night of the vote, "I am not here only as a Catholic. I am here with a background as an attorney through which I look at things and I apply reason." Bill Smith, from the ubiquitous Gill Action, which, in 2010, had brought down three of the four vulnerable state senators who had voted against marriage equality in 2009, was just occasionally seen hanging out with the governor while the action went on. But even a glimpse of Gill's Smith was probably a bracing experience for a vulnerable legislator. Four Republicans joined the Democrats to pass the bill.

Of course, New York is not Kansas, but the New York vote may be the turning point for this last, hardest-fought issue. It is still the media capital of the country. In one act, the New York legislature doubled the number of people eligible for same-sex marriages in America and pulled ahead of California for one of the first times since the gay revolution began. The vote revealed a dent in the previously unbroken Republican opposition to marriage. Polling consistently shows the members of the public have crossed the 50 percent mark in supporting the unions. The positive numbers in New York at the time of the vote were trending much higher.

And in a society ultimately committed to self-government, the masses matter. It completely violates the concept of the independent life-tenured judicial branch, but as Mr. Dooley said, the Supreme Court does sort of follow the election returns. When Justice Kennedy puts on his robes some morning in the 2012–2013 Supreme Court term, or whenever *Gill* or *Perry* or whatever case makes the inevitable appearance before that evenly divided court, he won't be thinking he's about to address an issue that could pass only in Massachusetts.

The Third Weekend in July

The New York law set the date for weddings to begin four weeks from passage: Sunday, July 24. Late that Friday, the media black hole for unpopular announcements, President Obama announced that the Defense Department had finally okayed the lifting of don't ask/don't tell. Open gay military service would begin in September.

Later that same night, Lieutenant Dan Choi lifted his saber over DADT-victim former drill sergeant Jeanette Coleman, and her bride-to-be, Kawane Harris, as they shared a kiss at their prenuptial celebration in his new apartment in New York. On Sunday, he was their bridesmaid.

Epilogue

"Do you really think you ought to call it *Victory*?" Richard Socarides asked. I had called him to ask about the Justice Department's dropping of DOMA and mentioned this book was almost done.

"Why in the world not?" I asked. "This is an amazing story."

"But there's so much that has not been done," he replied. "People will think you're saying it's over and everyone should go home."

Of course there is a lot left to be done. While things are improving on the coasts and in the upper Midwest, twenty-eight states have little or no affirmative law on any aspect of gay victory. In these states, there is no recognition of gay couples of any sort, no antidiscrimination laws or acknowledgment of bullying of gay kids in the schools. Nineteen of the antigay states have super DOMAs, forbidding recognition not only of marriage but also of civil unions or any consensual relationship, including any claim to the couples' children. Almost a half century after Bella Abzug dropped the first gay antidiscrimination bill in the hopper in 1973, Congress still has not passed a national employment antidiscrimination law. And for the transgendered people, often not covered by even the existing gay and lesbian antidiscrimination and hate-crimes laws, the situation is even worse. In so many states, it's as if the gay revolution has taught the society little or nothing.

And it is a fact of modern American life that whichever progressive movement is on the rise is the first to suffer from a conservative resurgence. Nixon's southern strategy crippled the racial civil rights movement; the 1978 eruption of the religious right ended any possibility of passing the feminists' Equal Rights Amendment. The state-based gay legal initiative largely hit a wall when the election of 2010 turned over many promising state legislatures or governorships to the Republicans. The legendary GayTM may make great headlines, but only 3.4 percent of all gay and lesbian adults contribute more than thirty-five dollars to any identifiably gay cause. The ten largest antigay organizations—Focus on the Family and the like—have twice the $500 million in revenues of all the gay organizations put together.

So celebrating the Victory of the gay revolution does not mean an imaginary gay commander in chief should land on an aircraft carrier in a flight suit with a "Mission Accomplished" sign behind him.

To celebrate gay Victory is to walk up the broken, weed-choked path to the tiny house in Northwest DC, where eighty-six-year-old Frank Kameny (1925–2011) lived for forty years. In 2009, the district named 5020 Cathedral Avenue a DC historic landmark. "For thirteen fiery years," the *Washington Post* said, reporting the designation, the modest house was "the epicenter of the gay-rights movement in the nation's capital." A year or two before Kameny decided he'd fight back in 1957, another federal civil servant, whose name we will never know, put a gun to his head at the corner of Twenty-first and Virginia and blew his brains out. Peter Szluk, the self-described "hatchet man" of the McCarthy-era State Department, had just called the victim in to tell him he'd been outed and was no longer eligible for employment in the United States government. When they called Kameny, he pushed back, and now his house is a landmark.

To celebrate gay Victory is to march among a hundred thousand celebrants in the 2011 Pride Parade down the streets of New York City, streets once so dangerous for gay men that Martin Boyce and his pals used to peer around corners to see who was there before they would venture on. Until he or one of his cross-dressing friends picked up a copper penny at the Stonewall Inn one hot June night in 1969 and threw it at the coppers, the people who were supposed to keep them safe. We die, they said at last, reaching for the bricks at a nearby construction site. We do something. "Every Queen in that riot changed."

To celebrate gay Victory is to know that you will never party with Larry Kramer. As thousands of ecstatic New York couples were donning impeccably tasteful and imaginative wedding garb and marrying everywhere from Niagara Falls to the steps of city hall in 2011, he submitted a statement to the *New York Times* complaining about the gay couples' inability to get tax relief. Yet he is the father of perhaps the biggest victory of all. Screaming and yelling and playwrighting and polemicizing, he, not single-handedly, but irreplaceably, lit the fire under the gay community first in New York and then nationwide. ACT UP didn't stop the dying: the numbers kept climbing to a horrendous high of almost fifty thousand in 1996, the year before the effective drugs came online. But they did something. One year before ACT UP, the Supreme Court of the United States ruled that gays' claim to be citizens under the Constitution was "facetious." In 1987, ACT UP shut down Wall Street, in 1988 the FDA, then the NIH, and then the church. If gays were going to die, the United States was going to do something. In 2010, the United States government spent over $3 billion on AIDS. In 2011, the United States Centers for Disease Control and Prevention announced that new drugs, taken immediately, can stop the disease from ever getting started and end the danger that an infected person will have sex and infect another.

To celebrate gay Victory is to attend the 2010 revival of playwright Tony Kushner's Tony Award–winning play, *Angels in America*. "The world only spins forward," his prophetic character Prior Walter told the audience at the end of the second installment in 1993. "We will be citizens." That year, the gay community in Colorado sued the state to overthrow its new constitutional amendment barring gays from politics. Three years later, in 1996, the Supreme Court presented the gay legal movement with its first supreme Victory. "It is not," Justice Kennedy concluded, "within our constitutional tradition to enact laws of this sort."

To celebrate gay Victory is to attend the marriage of Phyllis Lyon and Del Martin, the first couple to be married by San Francisco mayor Gavin Newsom in 2004, when he defied the California law limiting marriages to persons of opposite sexes. Del and Phyllis were certainly not thinking about marriage when they hung curtains across their living room window high above San Francisco Bay in 1955. The handful of lesbian women who made up the discussion group Daughters of Bilitis were afraid Del and Phyllis's neighbors would see them dancing. Almost fifty years later to the day, Del and Phyllis stood on the steps of San Francisco City Hall. Straight movement ally Newsom had heard President George W. Bush advocate for social death for the relationships of people like Phyllis and Del, proposing to amend the United States Constitution to forbid any state to recognize their union. They die? Newsom was going to do something.

And to celebrate gay Victory is to raise a glass of champagne at the wedding of navy lieutenant Gary Ross to his partner of eleven years. After decades of lying, as he defended his country as a surface-warfare officer, Ross flew to Vermont so he could marry in public one minute after DADT was repealed at midnight on September 21.

No matter how the saying goes, the arc of history more wiggles than bends toward justice. The Victory was not only the funding of AIDS research or the legalization of same-sex marriage in California or the *Will and Grace* television show or the Supreme Court ruling that the sodomy laws were unconstitutional. But all these events together, plus many more, have served to slowly bend the arc of history toward justice.

The Victory is in the doing. In doing the work, gay activists ennoble themselves and, by proxy, other people in their community. When the story of *Victory* opened, people whose sexual orientation was toward people of the same gender were considered sinful, criminal, crazy, and treasonous. In 2010, Gallup, which has been asking a question about the moral approval of homosexuality for years, saw the moral approval line cross 50 percent. So far had this movement come as a symbol of social justice that, when beleaguered President Barack Obama needed to highlight his values in anticipation of the 2012 election, he ordered his administration to use foreign aid to promote gay rights abroad, and his secretary of state, Hillary Rodham Clinton, delivered a blazing speech in defense of gay rights as human rights at the big UN meeting in Geneva.

Tim Gill, the Colorado mogul, made a bazillion dollars developing QuarkXPress, the computer program for desktop publishing. Since the Amendment 2 fight in Colorado in 1992, he has devoted his time and resources to the gay revolution. Just recently, a Gill beneficiary, the Movement Advancement Project, produced some fascinating data about the movement. Gill money brought down three of the four vulnerable state senators who opposed marriage equality in New York in 2009. Two years later, Gill hit-man Bill Smith was spotted behind the scenes when the crucial Republican New York state senators suddenly found it in their interest to support marriage equality. Gill is doubtless proud of the work he did to amass his fortune, but can there be any doubt that he's prouder of the movement work that followed?

No one said it better than Niccolò Machiavelli: "It ought to be remembered that there is nothing more difficult to take in hand, more perilous to conduct, or more uncertain in its success, than to take the lead in the introduction of a new order of things." As this most marginalized group of Americans fought for full inclusion in the social order, they didn't only change their world; they changed everyone's world. Because they were different, the makers of the gay revolution could not take the easy path of showing they were acceptable citizens under an old order. They had to change the meaning of the core concepts of citizenship—morality, sanity, loyalty—itself.

Although it's always hard to say exactly when a new order comes in, from the long view of history, gay men and lesbian women made a new world. And we are all living in it.

On the Shoulders of Giants

There was a time when working on gay history was a sure path off the tenure track. Blessedly, that time is past. Many of the witnesses to the story in the early chapters of this book are dead, often untimely so. Hopefully, that time is also past. Meanwhile, there are George Chauncey, Brett Beeman, Elizabeth Kennedy and Madeline Davis, Allan Bérubé, Larry Gross, Craig Rimmerman, Kenneth Wald, Clyde Wilcox, Lillian Faderman, Stuart Timmons, John D'Emilio, Martin Duberman, Andrew Sullivan, David Johnson, David Allyn, David Carter, Ronald Bayer, Randy Shilts, Jennifer Brier, Deborah Gould, John-Manuel Andriote, Stephen Branford, Gary Mucciaroni, Lisa Keen, Suzanne Goldberg, Steven Epstein, Ellen Ann Anderson, Nathaniel Frank, Stephen Bransford, Pat Cain, Paisley Currah, Richard Juang and Shannon Price Minter, Neil Miller, Adam Nagourney and Dudley Clendinen, and dozens more, who thoroughly researched and lovingly preserved the past, so that we latecomers could see. Details of the debt are in the endnotes. A special bow to Sarah Schulman and Jim Hubbard for the ACT UP Oral History Project, an accessible record of incomparable value to anyone who wants to learn about that crucial time in gay history.

Acknowledgments

Heterosexual people usually take their opportunity to marry for granted. One of the many positive externalities of the gay movement is to make us aware of how meaningful that opportunity is. I should not have needed reminding. Since 1989, I have had the privilege of being married to David Forkosh. Neither this book nor most of the other elements of my good life would have been possible without the consistent love and support he has so generously bestowed upon me during our life together.

Victory has the proverbial multiple ancestors. The incomparable editor Gail Winston figured out that it should be and what it should be in the course of a lunch. Then she encouraged, supported, read, edited, and listened to endless narcissistic blather from the author for the ensuing two years. This tale of the brilliant gay revolution would never have come into being without her courage, judgment, skill, and generosity of spirit. Not only the (narcissistic) author but everyone involved in the movement and who will learn from its victory is in her debt.

The other parent, literary agent David Kuhn, took on a complete stranger and shepherded her through a thousand iterations. Lunch with Gail Winston was just one of his endlessly resourceful and creative ideas about how to get from notion to publication. His commitment to this project was unswerving and his tough-minded judgment dead on at all the crucial junctures. The term "agent" does not do him justice; he is a full partner in his clients' enterprises.

In many ways I owe my brilliant career to the gentle ministrations of my private editor and guru Sarah Blustain, who was, once again, responsible for clarity of thought and expression.

Thanks are also due to the team at HarperCollins, especially Gail's smart and interesting assistant, Maya Ziv, and the omniscient copy editor, Stephen Wagley.

I'm not Dante, but Virgils abound. Cleve Jones, Robby Browne, Sue Hyde, Richard Socarides, Rick Jacobs, Rex Wockner, Michael Rogers, and John Aravosis deserve special thanks for passing me along to everyone they thought might help. Almost without exception, they all did.

No one did more for this enterprise than the writer and historian Eric Marcus and journalist Karen Ocamb. Eric's *Making Gay History: The Half-Century Fight for Lesbian and Gay Equal Rights* was a significant source in almost every chapter of this book. His friendship and support, however, were beyond any measure of significance. Karen's blog, LGBTPOV, guided me brilliantly through the thickets of the California wing, and her good offices of introduction were just the visible manifestation of her generous spirit. When I met Eric, at the 2009 NGLJA panel on the fortieth anniversary of Stonewall, I was a complete stranger to him. When I met Karen, outside the courthouse door on the first day of trial in *Perry v. Schwarzenegger*, in January 2010, I was a complete stranger to her. How lucky for me to start this story of the gay revolution, dependent, after all, on the kindness of strangers.

Chronology

THE GAY REVOLUTION	AMERICAN HISTORY
	1890–1914 Mass migration to cities
1897 First homosexual rights group forms in Germany	
1903 Raid on gay bathhouse	
	1920 Prohibition established by Eighteenth Amendment
1927 Authorities close Mae West's *The Drag*	
	1933 Prohibition repealed by Twenty-first Amendment
1934 New York State law demands "orderly" bars	
1941 Psychiatrists screen draft inductees for homosexuality	1941–1945 US involvement in World War II
1943–1945 Military's general discharge of homosexual soldiers	
	1948–1954 McCarthy period
1950 State Department announces homosexual discharges First American gay rights organization: Mattachine Society	
1953 Mattachine Society divided by Red Scare	
	1954 *Brown v. Board of Education*
1955 Daughters of Bilitis founded	
	1957 Free speech protected by Supreme Court
1958 Mattachine's *ONE* magazine protected by Supreme Court's ruling in *Roth*	

1960 Mattachine DC founded	1960 First civil rights sit-in
	1963 *Feminine Mystique* published
1964 California gay groups founded	1964 Civil Rights Act passed
1965 Radicals take over Mattachine New York	1965 *Griswold v. Connecticut*: Constitution protects birth control for married couples Antiwar movement ramps up
	1967 *Loving v. Virginia*: Constitution protects interracial marriage
	1968 Riots at the Democratic National Convention in Chicago
1969 Stonewall Gay Liberation Front founded	
1970 Radicalesbians founded	
1973 American Psychiatric Association rules homosexuality not a psychiatric illness	1973 *Roe v. Wade*: Constitution protects abortion
1975 US Civil Service drops gay and lesbian hiring ban	
	1976 Jimmy Carter elected president, only Democratic president between 1968 and 1992
1977 Anita Bryant founds Save Our Children and overturns Dade County ordinance	
1979 Harvey Milk killed; thousands march in San Francisco	1979 Jerry Falwell forms Moral Majority
1980 Human Rights Campaign Fund founded	1980 Ronald Reagan elected president; Margaret Heckler named Health and Human Services secretary CNN founded as cable news network

CHRONOLOGY

1981 CDC's Weekly *Mortality and Morbidity Report* finds Kaposi's sarcoma and *Pneumocystis carinii* pneumonia among homosexual men First meeting of Gay Men's Health Crisis	
	1986 National Science Foundation Network (NSFNET) provides access to supercomputer sites; commercial Internet service providers emerge in late '80s
1987 Kramer speech sparks ACT UP	
1992 Bob Hattoy speaks at Democratic National Convention, then goes to work for Clinton	**1992** Bill Clinton elected president
1993 Don't Ask/Don't Tell (DADT) passed *Angels in America* wins the Pulitzer Prize	
1996 Congress passes Defense of Marriage Act (DOMA) Supreme Court rules gays can't be fenced out of politics in *Romer*	**1996** Highly effective antiretroviral treatment for AIDS released
1997 AIDS deaths drop significantly Ellen DeGeneres comes out on *Ellen*	
1998 Matthew Shepard killed	
1978–1999 Hate crimes bills passed in many states	
	2000 Andrew Sullivan starts blog, the Daily Dish
	2001 9/11 attacks
2003 Massachusetts Supreme Judicial Court rules that the state may not deny same-sex marriage Supreme Court rules criminalizing sodomy unconstitutional in *Lawrence*	
2008 Proposition 8 passes, repeals same-sex marriage in California	**2008** Barack Obama elected president
2010 DADT repealed	

Notes

Introduction

xi **Robert M. "Robby" Browne, 2007 Corcoran Real Estate:** Robby Browne, interview by the author, April 2010.

xii **compelling American society to acknowledge them:** "President Obama Signs Byrd Shepard Hate Crimes Bill into Law," http://www.baywindows.com/index.php?ch=news&sc=glbt&sc2=news&sc3=&id=98285; the website of the Human Rights Campaign keeps a rolling list of all state laws, http://www.hrc.org/laws_and_elections/state_law_listing.asp; history of support for ENDA since 1974, http://www.hrc.org/issues/workplace/5635.htm.

xii **In July 2010, a federal judge:** *Lesbian/Gay Law Notes*, at New York Law School, maintains running coverage of the rapidly expanding and evolving legal campaign, http://www.nyls.edu/centers/harlan_scholar_centers/justice_action_center/publications/lesbiangay_law_notes.

xiii **gay media are now pooh-poohing:** "John Rich Says Chely Wright Misunderstood When He Asked Her If She Was Gay," Celebitchy, May 6, 2010, http://www.celebitchy.com/category/coming_out/.

xiii **a *New York Times* editorial called same-sex marriage:** "A Basic Civil Right," *New York Times,* June 11, 2010, viewed online at www.nytimes

.com/2010/06/11/opinion/11fri1.html. Gallup poll on same-sex marriage, viewed online at http://www.gallup.com/poll/147662/first-time-majority-americans-favor-legal-gay-marriage.aspx.

xiii **were considered sinful by the church:** Dudley Clendinen and Adam Nagourney, *Out for Good*, 12; Johnson, passim.

xiii **what we philosophers call a "liberal (small *L*) state":** For a perfectly serviceable summary of the liberal tradition, see Gerald Gaus and Shane D. Courtland, "Liberalism," *The Stanford Encyclopedia of Philosophy* (Spring 2011 edition).

xiv **"oppositional consciousness":** Jane Mansbridge and Aldon D. Morris, *Oppositional Consciousness*; Mancur Olson, *The Logic of Collective Action*.

xv **New social-movement theorists:** Carol McClurg Mueller, "Building Social Movement Theory," in Aldon D. Morris and Carol McClurg Mueller, *Frontiers in Social Movement Theory*, 3–25.

xv **Classical or new, each of the movements:** Inter alia, the three volumes of Taylor Branch's *America in the King Years*; Richard Kluger, *Simple Justice*; Ruth Rosen, *The World Split Open*; Gail Collins, *When Everything Changed*, 104–5; Gerald N. Rosenberg, *The Hollow Hope*.

xvi **liberalism pretends to be morally neutral:** Inter alia, Michael J. Sandel, *Liberalism and the Limits of Justice*.

xvi **"Is Good":** Franklin Kameny, interview by author, September 30, 2009.

xvi **"It was more than just being gay":** Arthur Evans, interview by author, January 13, 2010.

Chapter 1

Like everyone writing about anything to do with the movement after the publication of *Gay New York* in 1996, I am immeasurably indebted to the seminal work of historian George Chauncey on the period 1890–1940. The picture of the "gay male community" pieced together from his painstaking archival work held up remarkably well when applied to the later period, for which there are still living witnesses.

1 **When twenty-year-old "Jeb Alexander":** *Jeb and Dash*, edited by Ina Russell, 31. Jeb is a pseudonym. Jeb's diaries, published just as Chauncey was finishing *Gay New York*, provide an ongoing original source for this chapter. All references to Jeb and his circle come from the diaries, except where otherwise noted. Since Jeb's niece, Ina Russell, who published the diaries, chose to call him by his first "name," I will follow suit.

1 **The word "homosexual":** Jim Miller, *"Democracy Is in the Streets,"* Introduction, xi–xvii; George Chauncey, *Gay New York*, 12.

2 **flooded into American cities:** Chauncey, *Gay New York*, 11–12.

2 **chain of migration to American cities:** Ibid., 271–2.

2 **whole neighborhoods:** Ibid., chapter 6.

3 **women would have to wait decades:** Elizabeth Lapovsky Kennedy and Madeline D. Davis, "I Could Hardly Wait to Get Back to That Bar," in Brett Beemyn, ed., *Creating a Place for Ourselves*, 28–29.

3 **divided into subcultures:** Chauncey, *Gay New York*, 182–3.

4 **a secret language:** Ibid., 286–8.

5 **Prohibition had transformed the urban restaurant scene:** Ibid., 164–7.

5 **The making of the gay male world:** Thomas Hobbes, *On the Citizen (De Cive)*, chapter 8.

6 **semipublic institutions of gay culture**: Chauncey, *Gay New York*, chapters 8 (on the baths) and 9 (on the balls).

7 **so crowded with men having sex**: Chad C. Heap, *Slumming*, 271.

7 **However comforting camp culture was**: Chauncey, *Gay New York*, 296.

8 **he left his diaries**: Ina Russell, interview by the author, September 2009.

8 ***from other gay men* whom he happened to meet:** Chauncey, *Gay New York*, 276.

9 **openly advertised drag entertainment:** Ibid., chapter 11.

10 **New York when the state liquor authority:** Ibid., chapter 12.

11 **"Arden" was initiated into lesbian life**: Elizabeth Lapovsky Kennedy and Madeline D. Davis, *Boots of Leather, Slippers of Gold*, 34–36.

11 **keeping the gay patrons to the most exquisite standards:** Chauncey, *Gay New York*, 350–51.

11 **diarist Donald Vining:** Like *Jeb and Dash*, Donald Vining's diary, *A Gay Diary, 1933–1946*, is another original source of the material from the early years. Vining's deflowering appears in Chauncey, *Gay New York*, 152.

12 **The only bar that fought back:** Chauncey, *Gay New York*, 338.

12 **they had found a place:** Esther Newton, *Cherry Grove, Fire Island*, 35.

13 **San Francisco's North Beach became a center of integration:** Nan Boyd, "'Homos Invade S.F.!'" in Beemyn, *Creating a Place for Ourselves*, 79–84.

14 **World War II changed the lives of everyone:** Allan Bérubé, *Coming Out Under Fire*. Bérubé is the George Chauncey of "gay men and women in World War II."

15 **Robert Fleischer:** Ibid., 8.

15 **Richard von Krafft-Ebing:** Ronald Bayer, *Homosexuality and American Psychiatry*, 19–20.

16 **Magnus Hirschfeld:** Ibid., 21.

16 **treatments like electric shock:** J. Bancroft and I. Marks, "Electric Aversion Therapy."

16 **a scientific analysis of homosexual case studies:** Henry L. Minton, *Departing from Deviance.*

17 **psychiatrists, Drs. Henry Sullivan and Winfred Overholser:** Bérubé, *Coming Out Under Fire*, 9–11.

18 **Vining did the obvious thing:** Vining, *A Gay Diary, 1933–1946*, 278, 300.

19 **civilians poached military uniforms:** Bérubé, *Coming Out Under Fire*, 107–8.

19 **Marty Klausner, who was caught in the closet door:** Ibid., 102.

19 **the army had replaced:** Ibid., 139–41.

20 **it was the doctors' diagnosis:** Ibid., 133, 140.

20 **a "blue" discharge as mentally unfit:** Ibid., 228.

20 **"Why they don't just round us all up and kill us":** Ibid., 232.

20 **aided by the nascent racial civil rights movement:** Ibid., 238–49.

21 **They were explicitly excluded:** Ibid., 243.

21 **Jewish family didn't look scary to Fleischer:** Ibid., 250.

21 **how many gay veterans:** David K. Johnson, *The Lavender Scare*, 163–4.

22 **The New York Veterans Benevolent Association:** Bérubé, *Coming Out Under Fire*, 249.

23 **Macdonald had warned Duncan not to sign his name:** Ibid., 250–1; Ekbert Faas, *Young Robert Duncan*, 147–60.

25 **when she discovered his boyhood journals:** *Perry v. Brown*, trial day 6, http://www.johnirelandonline.com/Trial/day6.html.

26 **the community of African Americans:** Mark Newman, *The Civil Rights Movement*, 8–26.

26 **split the racial civil rights movement:** Eugene Robinson, *Disintegration: The Splintering of Black America*, 51–60.

26 **The women of the feminist movement:** Ruth Rosen, *The World Split Open*, 335–6; Linda R. Hirshman, *Get to Work*, passim.

27 **gay-rights organization was born:** Stuart Timmons, *The Trouble with Harry Hay*, 144.

Chapter 2

29 **Stalin didn't much like homosexuals:** Stuart Timmons, *The Trouble with Harry Hay*, 96.

29 **a traitor to his class:** Ibid., chapters 1–4 for Harry's early years.

31 **There were crowds:** Ina Russell, ed., *Jeb and Dash*, 51–162.

31 **aristocrats called it madness**: Auguste Comte, *Course of Positive Philosophy* (1830–1842); for a translation of Comte's work, see *The Positive Philosophy of Auguste Comte*, translated by Harriet Martineau; see also Robert A. Nisbet, "The French Revolution and the Rise of Sociology in France."

32 **There was nothing political to discuss, Geer said:** Timmons, *The Trouble with Harry Hay*, 69.

32 **Technically, Geer was right:** Grant Farred, "Endgame Identity?"is a good example of the long dialogue.

32 **Stalin was moved to address the subject:** In 1913, Stalin wrote a description; Joseph Stalin, "Marxism and the National Question," 303–14, in Stalin, *Works*, vol. 2, 417, n. 130.

33 **Hay believed:** Timmons, *The Trouble with Harry Hay*, 136.

33 **they gained a foothold:** Mark Newman, *The Civil Rights Movement*, 21.

33 **the ideas that he would use:** Timmons, *The Trouble with Harry Hay*, 132.

34 **fabulous head shot:** Ibid., cover.

34 **not reconcile his two worlds:** Ibid., 97–101.

35 **learning and teaching every aspect of Marxist thought:** Ibid., 101–22.

35 **"Music, the Barometer of the Class Struggle":** Harry Hay, *Radically Gay*, 122–6.

35 **what he had to say:** David K. Johnson, *Lavender Scare*, 169–70.

35 **Red and lavender, the scares began:** Ibid., 15–39.

36 **"we had to get started":** Timmons, *The Trouble with Harry Hay*, 132.

36 **what else might be possible:** Ibid., 132–5.

36 **Bachelors for Wallace:** Hay, *Radically Gay*, 60–77.

37 **could not find one person to join him:** Timmons, *The Trouble with Harry Hay*, 136–8.

37 **Hay, always thinking:** http://www.outhistory.org/wiki/Harry_Hay:_Founding_the_Mattachine_Society,_1948–1953.

38 **a few male cross-dressers:** Paisley Currah, Richard M. Juang, and Shannon Price Minter, eds., *Transgender Rights*, 171.

38 **"beyond the melting pot":** Nathan Glazer and Daniel P. Moynihan, *Beyond the Melting Pot.*

38 **Rudi Gernreich:** Timmons, *The Trouble with Harry Hay*, 139–42.

40 **the gay movement in America was officially launched:** Ibid., 143–4.

40 **Dale Jennings:** Ibid., 144.

40 **Mattachines:** Ibid., 150.

41 **organized in cells:** Ibid.

42 **as many as 150 people:** Ibid., 154–6.

42 **"We're going to make an issue of this thing":** Ibid., 164–5.

43 **a major civil rights initiative:** Ibid., 165–6.

43 **"Victory!":** Ibid., 167–71.

44 **The first issue of *ONE* magazine:** January 1953, http://www.onearchives.org/collections.

44 **they sent a questionnaire:** Timmons, *The Trouble with Harry Hay*, 174.

44 **a column about their "strange new pressure group":** John D'Emilio, *Sexual Politics, Sexual Communities*, 76–77.

45 **HUAC was particularly feared in California:** Richard A. Schwartz, "How the Film and Television Blacklists Worked," http://comptalk.fiu.edu/blacklist.htm.

45 **HUAC was holding hearings:** D'Emilio, *Sexual Politics, Sexual Communities*, 76.

46 **the fuss over Welles:** Johnson, *Lavender Scare*, 65–7.

46 **"I was fired for *disloyalty*":** Ibid., 67.

46 **behaviors were immoral and their feelings were crazy:** Ibid., 112–8.

47 **after 1950 the homosexual security threat was a legislative fact:** Ibid., 101–16.

47 **Executive Order 10450:** Ibid., 103.

47 **Historian David Johnson estimates:** Ibid., 166–9.

48 **"boom—right on the corner of Twenty-first and Virginia":** Ibid., 158.

48 **called a meeting:** Timmons, *The Trouble with Harry Hay*, 176–7.

48 **terms of argument for the gay revolution:** D'Emilio, *Sexual Politics, Sexual Communities*, 78–79.

49 **content of their character:** Ibid., 79.

49 **their greatest contribution:** Ibid., 81.

49 **disappearance into the heterosexual society:** Currah, Juang, and Minter, eds., *Transgender Rights*, 177.

50 **McCarthy who won (again):** Timmons, *The Trouble with Harry Hay*, 177–9.

50 **"highest possible public respect":** D'Emilio, *Sexual Politics, Sexual Communities*, 81.

50 **The last thing they wanted:** Letter from Kinsey, ibid., 84.

50 **a tiny group of San Francisco lesbians:** Phyllis Lyon, interview by the author, March 23, 2011.

51 **the Mattachine Society couldn't have chosen a worse time to cave in:** "Have You No Sense of Decency," http://www.senate.gov/artandhistory/history/minute/Have_you_no_sense_of_decency.htm.

52 **"You want to do something?":** Lyon, interview by the author.

52 **Allen Ginsberg was reciting his poem:** D'Emilio, *Sexual Politics, Sexual Communities*, 177.

53 **a young gay man named Cleve Jones:** Cleve Jones, interview by the author, February 1, 2010.

53 **prosecute the bookstore owner:** D'Emilio, *Sexual Politics, Sexual Communities*, 177–81.

53 ***Roth v. United States*:** 354 U.S. 476 (1957).

53 **a local judge acquitted Ferlinghetti:** *California v. Ferlinghetti* (1957), http://mason.gmu.edu/~kthomps4/363-s02/horn-howl.htm.

53 **"*ONE* Is Not Grateful":** ONE archive.

54 ***ONE* sued the postmaster in Los Angeles, Otto K. Oleson:** *One, Inc. v. Oleson*, 241 F.2d 772 (1957), rev'd., 355 U.S. 371 (1958).

56 ***ONE* did on the issue that followed:** *ONE* archive.

56 **Frank Kameny was, he says, innocently taking a piss:** *Kameny v. Brucker*, petition for a writ of certiorari, no. 676, U.S. Supreme Court (1960), Kameny Papers, Library of Congress.

57 **they picked on Kameny:** Franklin Kameny, interview by the author, September 30, 2009; Eric Marcus, *Making Gay History*, 81.

57 **As a boy:** Kameny, interview by the author, July 23, 2010.

58 **that homosexuals were no more deserving of persecution:** Kameny, interview by the author, September 30, 2009.

58 **subversive, and so not eligible for an equal share in the liberal state:** http://www.glbtq.com/social-sciences/aclu_lgbt_aids_project.html.

58 **Kameny wrote:** *Kameny v. Brucker.*

58 **no no no no no no no no, never:** Kameny, interview by the author, July 23, 2010.

59 **commenced doing everything:** Kameny, interviews by the author, September 30, 2009, and July 23, 2010.

59 **formed a confederation:** D'Emilio, *Sexual Politics, Sexual Communities*, 161.

59 **Kameny helped found a DC chapter of the ACLU:** Kameny, interview by the author, September 30, 2009.

Chapter 3

61 **the Michigan sky erupted in light:** Jim Miller, *"Democracy Is in the Streets,"* 123.

61 **"It was the Sixties that did it":** Franklin Kameny, interview by the author, September 30, 2009.

62 **Jim Fouratt:** Martin B. Duberman, *Stonewall*, 59–60; Jim Fouratt, interview by the author, October 24, 2009.

62 **Being who you were:** Todd Gitlin, *The Sixties: Years of Hope, Days of Rage*, 19–21.

62 **the new generation was a crowd:** Gitlin, *The Sixties*, 16–21; Todd Gitlin, interview by the author, December 9, 2009.

63 **terminally boring and the terrifyingly terminal:** Gitlin, *The Sixties*, 23; Allen Young, interview by the author, September 1, 2010.

63 **Burning books:** Young, interview.

63 **Gitlin, whose family story:** Gitlin, interview.

64 **checking her bedroom for Nazis:** Gitlin, *The Sixties*, 25.

64 **explosive reports:** Hannah Arendt, *Eichmann in Jerusalem*.

64 **Carol Ruth Silver:** Carol Ruth Silver, interview by the author, December 2009.

64 **Martha Shelley:** Martha Shelley, interview by the author, November 28, 2009.

65 **Dick Leitsch came to New York:** Dick Leitsch, interview by the author, October 26, 2009.

65 **HUAC visit to San Francisco:** Gitlin, *The Sixties*, 82–83.

66 **They sat down at the lunch counter:** Ibid., 81–82.

66 **James Pepper, sixteen-year-old homosexual scion:** James Pepper, interview by the author, August 21, 2010.

66 **a little band of homosexuals sat down at a bar:** D'Emilio, *Sexual Politics, Sexual Communities*, 207–8.

67 **Kameny watched the various movement marches:** Kameny, interview by the author, September 30, 2009.

67 **Rustin was its John the Baptist:** D'Emilio, *Lost Prophet*, 326–58.

68 **led ten homosexuals to their places in front of the White House:** Ibid., 165.

68 **Carl Wittman had had it up to here:** "Wittman, Carl," in http://www.williamapercy.com/wiki/images/Wittman.pdf, citing "Us and the New Left," *Fag Rag* 22/23 (Fall 1978), 1, 22.

68 **the eruption of women from the Left:** Gitlin, *The Sixties*, 362–77.

69 **psychiatrists had advanced the idea:** Ronald Bayer, *Homosexuality and American Psychiatry*, 15–40.

70 **Randy Wicker really did not like most women:** Randy Wicker, interview by the author, November 2, 2009.

70 **Dick Leitsch thinks:** Leitsch, interview.

70 **he has never read "Sex and Caste":** Jim Fouratt, interview by the author, August 17, 2010.

70 **"A Gay Manifesto":** http://library.gayhomeland.org/0006/EN/A_Gay_Manifesto.htm.

71 **it certainly aroused lesbian women:** http://www.amazon.com/Encyclopedia-Gender-Society-Jodi-OBrien/dp/1412909163#reader_1412909163.

71 **Daughters of Bilitis and their newsletter, *The Ladder*:** Marcia M. Gallo, *Different Daughters*, 159–62.

71 **describes Randy Wicker:** "Randolfe Wicker," in http://www.williamapercy.com/wiki/images/Randolfe_wicker.pdf.

71 **Wicker was an everything activist:** D'Emilio, *Sexual Politics, Sexual Communities*, 158–9.

72 **Wicker made the connection:** Wicker, interview.

72 **regime of criminal laws governing people's sexual practices:** Kathleen London, "The History of Birth Control," http://www.yale.edu/ynhti/curriculum/units/1982/6/82.06.03.x.html; Lawrence A. Friedman, *A History of American Law,* 444–9.

72 **from the illiberal institution of the church:** James A. Brundage, *Law, Sex and Christian Society in Medieval Europe*, 245–8.

72 **The roots of the injunctions:** Mark D. Jordan, *The Invention of Sodomy in Christian Theology*, 30–31.

72 **Catholic theologian Thomas Aquinas said:** Brent Pickett, "Homosexuality," *The Stanford Encyclopedia of Philosophy* (Spring 2011 edition), http://plato.stanford.edu/archives/spr2011/entries/homosexuality/; Michael Carden, *Sodomy: A History of a Christian Biblical Myth*, 183–5.

72 **with the writings of the ancient pagan Greek philosophers:** Ralph McIn-

erny and John O'Callaghan, "Saint Thomas Aquinas," *The Stanford Encyclopedia of Philosophy* (Winter 2010 edition), http://plato.stanford.edu/archives/win2010/entries/aquinas/.

72 **Aristotle believed:** Graham White, "Medieval Theories of Causation," *The Stanford Encyclopedia of Philosophy* (Fall 2009 edition), http://plato.stanford.edu/archives/fall2009/entries/causation-medieval/.

73 **Presto, sins against nature:** George E. Haggerty, *Gay Histories and Cultures: An Encyclopedia*, 225; "The Law in England, 1290–1885," http://www.fordham.edu/halsall/pwh/englaw.asp.

73 **obviously has some connection to survival (or is harmless):** A. Camperio Ciani, P. Cermelli, and G. Zanzotto, "Sexually Antagonistic Selection in Human Male Homosexuality," *PLoS ONE* 3, no. 6 (2008), e2282.doi:10.1371/journal.pone.0002282.

73 **"the Sex Freedom League":** Wicker, interview; David Allyn, *Make Love, Not War*, 44–47.

73 **flying semen:** Ibid., 46.

74 **"filthy-speech" protest movement:** Ibid., 48.

74 ***Fanny Hill*:** *Memoirs v. Massachusetts*, 383 U.S. 413 (1966).

75 **Alfred Kinsey reported:** Alfred Kinsey and the Institute for Sex Research, *Sexual Behavior in the Human Female* (1953).

75 **a biologist:** Allyn, *Make Love, Not War*, 33.

75 **a nudie-magazine publisher:** Ibid., 26–27.

75 **middle-aged copywriter:** Ibid., 19–21.

76 **the Playboy Foundation:** Marilyn Haft, interview by the author, November 4, 2009.

77 **Connecticut, for example, had a century-old law:** Allyn, *Make Love, Not War*, 37.

77 **the legal campaign for consequence-free sex:** John W. Johnson, Griswold v. Connecticut*: Birth Control and the Constitutional Right of Privacy.*

78 **people sure don't want the state:** Linda Greenhouse, "The Law: Echo of '87 Bork Uproar Rings Softly in Abortion Debate," *New York Times*, April 28, 1989, http://www.nytimes.com/1989/04/28/us/the-law-echo-of-87-bork-uproar-rings-softly-in-abortion-debate.html.

80 **New York gay radicals were different in kind:** Leitsch, interview; Wicker, interview; Fouratt, interview; D'Emilio, *Sexual Politics, Sexual Communities*, 158–60.

82 **Kameny to give one of their monthly lectures:** D'Emilio, *Sexual Politics, Sexual Communities*, 163.

82 **four years of activism:** Ibid., 164–75.

82 **For the first time the DC circuit court reversed:** Ibid., 154–5; Kameny, interview, September 30, 2009.

83 ***Norton v. Macy*:** 417 F.2d 1161 (D.C. Cir. 1969).

83 **getting the police out of the bathrooms and the bars:** Leitsch, interview.

85 **Leitsch and his same-sex bar liberators continued to push the envelope:** Ibid.

86 **Jim Fouratt remembers:** Fouratt, interview.

86 **movement stalwart Carl Wittman, had a harder time:** Liz Highleyman, "Past Out," http://www.sgn.org/sgnnews34_18/page30.cfm; Todd Gitlin, interview by the author, September 8, 2010.

87 **Wittman's sexual commitment:** David Mungello, interview by the author, September 7, 2010.

87 **a "refugee camp" for "homosexuals" from "Amerika":** Wittman, "Gay Manifesto," http://library.gayhomeland.org/0006/EN/A_Gay_Manifesto.htm; D'Emilio, *Sexual Politics, Sexual Communities*, 186–95.

87 **Presto, a "newspaper":** Lillian Faderman and Stuart Timmons, *Gay L.A.*, 159.

89 **called the 1964 New Year's ball:** D'Emilio, *Sexual Politics, Sexual Communities*, 195.

90 **Wittman's "Gay Manifesto":** There are copies of Wittman's Gay Manifesto on the Internet, as noted above, and it is collected in any number of anthologies, including Karla Jay and Allen Young, *Out of the Closets*, 330–42.

91 **the flaws that would ultimately take them down:** Mark Newman, *The Civil Rights Movement*, 125–8; Ruth Rosen, *The World Split Open*, 82–86.

92 **Allen Young, the big-deal journalist:** Young, interview.

Chapter 4

95 **schedule a meeting:** David Carter, *Stonewall*, 210, 216.

96 **one of the first histories:** Martin B. Duberman, *Stonewall.*

96 **scathing criticism:** Jim Fouratt, interview by the author, October 24, 2009; Randy Wicker, interview by the author, November 2, 2009.

96 **what a dump:** Carter, *Stonewall*, 66–88.

97 **a bunch of runaway street kids:** Ibid., 57–66.

98 **From the moment the police entered the bar:** The basic factual description of the events of June 28 is from Carter, *Stonewall*; the Pine quotation is on page 147.

99 **a very different movement:** Todd Gitlin, *The Sixties: Years of Hope, Days of Rage*, 242–60.

100 **"'OK boys, you've become men'":** Ibid., 252.

100 **Stonewall was its child:** Fouratt, interview; Carter, *Stonewall*, 134, 148; "Stonewall Rebellion Discussion," http://www.housing.wisc.edu/diversity/lgbtclass/stonewall.php.

101 **Every queen in that riot changed:** Martin Boyce, "40 Years Across the Table, Stonewall Vets Talk with LGBT Youth," http://www.youtube.com/watch?v=DAdNqF0137g.

102 **a ruling from the New York Court of Appeals:** Alice Echols, *Hot Stuff: Disco and the Remaking of American Culture*, 44.

102 **the homosexual state of nature:** Boyce, "40 Years."

103 **The next night:** Carter, *Stonewall*, 182–94.

104 **he wrote a manifesto:** Ibid., 195–6.

104 **burn down the nearby offices of the *Village Voice*:** Ibid., 201–5.

105 **"Some of my best friends are gay":** Lucian Truscott IV, interview by the author, September 16, 2010.

105 **The last thing Mattachine president Dick Leitsch wanted:** Dick Leitsch, interview by the author, October 26, 2009; Carter, *Stonewall*, 210.

106 **not any lesbian:** Martha Shelley, interview by the author, November 28, 2009.

107 **John O'Brien had reserved a meeting room at Alternate U:** Carter, *Stonewall*, 217–8.

108 **Hoose's story:** Jerry Hoose, interview by the author, October 6, 2010.

108 **GLF stalwart Steven Dansky:** Steven Dansky, interview by the author, October 8, 2010.

109 **both used the word "chills":** Hoose, interview; Dansky, interview.

110 **five hundred dollars to the Black Panthers:** Carter, *Stonewall*, 232, http://tobymarotta.com/contents.htm; John O'Brien, interview by the author, October 10, 2010.

111 **newfound identity:** Carter, *Stonewall*, 232.

112 **"Artemis March" (née March Hoffman) went to meetings every night:** Artemis March, interview by the author, August 23, 2010.

112 **The gay men's movement was too hot:** D'Emilio, *Sexual Politics, Sexual Communities*, 236–7; Dudley Clendinen and Adam Nagourney, *Out for Good*, 88–95.

113 **The new organization, the Radicalesbians:** Ellen Shumsky, "The Radical Lesbian Story: An Evolution of Consciousness," in Tommi Avicolli Mecca, *Smash the Church, Smash the State!*, 190–95.

114 **no way Arthur Evans was going to make any of those mistakes:** Arthur Evans, interview by the author, January 13, 2010.

115 **Evans and Bell and the other two critical renegades:** Clendinen and Nagourney, *Out for Good*, 46–51.

116 **"You can't get much more American than that":** Evans, interview.

116 **the constitution and bylaws of their new organization:** http://www.outhistory.org/wiki/images/6/66/Preamble.jpg.

118 **They bought an abandoned firehouse:** Clendinen and Nagourney, *Out for Good*, 76.

118 **"existence precedes essence":** Evans, interview.

119 **the Snake Pit:** Clendinen and Nagourney, *Out for Good*, 51–56.

119 **the indefatigable Marty Robinson:** Evans, interview; Tommy Langan-Schmidt, interview by the author, October 13, 2010.

120 **the GAA determined to bring lawless disorder to the officials:** Evans, interview.

121 **right on the museum steps:** Clendinen and Nagourney, *Out for Good*, 52.

122 **When the racial movement moved north:** Mark Newman, *The Civil Rights Movement*, 115–6.

122 **they were met with mockery and derision:** Norman Mailer, "The Prisoner of Sex," *Harper's*, March 1971; Joan Didion, "The Women's Movement,"

New York Times, July 30, 1972, http://www.nytimes.com/1972/07/30/books/didion-movement.html.

124 **Rodwell, as always, was undeterred:** Martin Duberman, *Stonewall*, 226–7, 270–80.

125 **a parade about Stonewall:** The details about the planning of the parade are largely from Elizabeth A. Armstrong and Suzanna M. Crage, "Movements and Memory: The Making of the Stonewall Myth."

126 **Just showing up is a political statement:** Toby Marotta, *The Politics of Homosexuality*, 167.

126 **both Los Angeles and Chicago:** Ellen Ann Andersen, *Out of the Closets and into the Courts*, 741.

127 **As the months before the march passed, Rodwell had:** Duberman, *Stonewall*, 276–80; Michael Lavery, interview by the author, November 11, 2010.

Chapter 5

129 **"I march in that parade every year now":** Richard Socarides, interviews by the author, May 27, 2010, June 7, 2010, and June 9, 2010.

130 **"Marched in 1970 Parade":** Observation by the author, June 28, 2010.

131 **Frank Kameny had had his eye on:** Franklin Kameny, interview by the author, September 30, 2009.

131 **Feminism battled Freud:** Ruth Rosen, *The World Split Open*, 17–18, 149–50.

131 **a band of activists disrupted the San Francisco meeting:** Ronald Bayer, *Homosexuality and American Psychiatry*, 102–3. This first action was in alliance with feminist activists.

131 **homosexuals speak for themselves:** Ibid., passim.

133 **the scene in the Regency Room:** "Zapping the Shrinks," http://www.rainbowhistory.org/apazap.htm.

133 **"never needed a microphone to be heard":** Kameny, interview, September 30, 2009.

134 **Evelyn Hooker:** Eric Marcus, *Making Gay History*, 3–5, 33–35, 59. I am indebted to Eric Marcus for introducing me to the critical role played by this early nongay ally.

134 **He speculated about whether homosexuality:** Bayer, *Homosexuality and American Psychiatry*, 21–28.

135 **homosexuality was listed:** Ibid., 39.

135 **studying its homosexual patients for signs of "cure":** Ibid., 28–38.

135 **Robert Spitzer would later admit:** Robert Spitzer, interview by the author, December 10, 2009.

135 **every weapon in the psychiatric arsenal:** J. Bancroft and I. Marks, "Electric Aversion Therapy of Sexual Deviations."

135 **a veritable psychiatric gauntlet:** Paisley Currah, Richard M. Juang, and Shannon Price Minter, eds., *Transgender Rights*, 276–9; Allan Horwitz, *Creating Mental Illness*, 15.

136 **some scientifically defensible diagnoses and provable treatments:** Herb Kutchins and Stuart A. Kirk, *Making Us Crazy*.

136 **Szasz and the other "antipsychiatrists":** Bayer, *Homosexuality and American Psychiatry*, 54–60.

136 **gay militants started disrupting:** Ibid., 92.

137 **going to a psychiatrist was considered collaboration:** Ibid., 96.

137 **divisions within the profession:** Alfred Freedman, interview by the author, November 17, 2009.

137 **Robert Spitzer:** Spitzer, interview.

138 **Gold took Spitzer with him:** Bayer, *Homosexuality and American Psychiatry*, 124–6.

139 **"Victory for Homosexuals":** "Doctors Rule Homosexuality Not Abnormal," *New York Times*.

139 **on December 15, 1999:** Freedman, interview.

140 **it was the gay challenge that started him down the road of rethinking:** Spitzer, interview.

140 ***DSM III* and Spitzer:** Alix Spiegel, "The Dictionary of Disorder: How One Man Revolutionized Psychiatry," *The New Yorker*, January 3, 2005, http://www.newyorker.com/archive/2005/01/03/050103fa_fact.

141 **Perry decided to die:** Troy Perry, interview by the author, April 16, 2010. Unless otherwise indicated, the MCC story is derived from this interview.

142 **called Perry:** Dennis Altman, *The Homosexualization of America*, 27.

143 **beat him to death:** Elizabeth A. Armstrong and Suzanna M. Crage, "Movements and Memory," 735.

144 **During the AIDS epidemic:** Troy Perry, interview by the author, April 27, 2010.

147 **Michael Lavery was in that temple of reason:** Michael Lavery, interview by the author, November 11, 2010.

148 **NAACP Legal Defense Fund:** Mark Newman, *The Civil Rights Movement*, 5.

148 **The ACLU had played a major role:** "Tribute: The Legacy of Ruth Bader Ginsburg and the WRP Staff," http://www.aclu.org/womens-rights/tribute-legacy-ruth-bader-ginsburg-and-wrp-staff.

148 **New York judges didn't think "homosexual":** Ellen Ann Andersen, *Out of the Closets and into the Courts*, 1–2.

148 **the church-inflected world of benevolence and charity:** Gareth H. Jones, *History of the Law of Charity*, 3–4.

149 **Lambda was a sorry bunch:** Andersen, *Out of the Closets*, 28–31.

149 **Haft was determined to make a name for herself:** Marilyn Haft, interview by the author, November 4, 2009.

151 **the civil service lifted the prohibition on employment of gay people:** George B. Lewis, "Lifting the Ban on Gays in the Civil Service."

151 **California led the way:** Lillian Faderman and Stuart Timmons, *Gay L.A.*, 180.

152 **struck down the New York sodomy laws:** *People v. Onofre*, 415 N.E. 2d 936 (NY 1980); Patricia A. Cain, *Rainbow Rights*, 169.

153 **was the improbable game changer:** Dudley Clendinen and Adam Nagourney, *Out for Good*, 154–7.

153 **Mrs. Feinstein sought out the assistance of the new gay organization:** Carol Ruth Silver, interview by the author, December 2009.

154 **Jim Foster, head of the SIR political committee, knew:** Gary Miller, interview by the author, April 11, 2009.

154 **Foster was one of the many socially privileged guys:** Clendinen and Nagourney, *Out for Good*, 161–2.

155 **California Democratic Council:** California Democratic Council, "About Us," http://www.cdc-ca.org/page.php?27.

155 **the Alice B. Toklas Democratic Club held its first meeting:** Clendinen and Nagourney, *Out for Good*, 161–3; Miller, interview.

155 **the New York clubs were organized:** Mark Townsend, "Democratic Party in Manhattan," http://gomyd.com/2010/03/17/democratic-party-in-manhattan/.

156 **They really didn't think they needed a parade:** Miller, interview; Silver, interview.

156 **Foster mobilized:** Clendinen and Nagourney, *Out for Good*, 132–6.

157 **Voeller and a handful of other bourgeois professionals abandoned:** Ibid., 188–95; Marcus, *Making Gay History*, 187–8.

157 **found them unpalatable allies:** Currah, Juang, and Minter, eds., *Transgender Rights*, 142.

157 **the most conventional movement script:** Clendinen and Nagourney, *Out for Good*, 193–5.

158 **The Task Force was not clearly destined for survival:** Ibid., 196–8.

158 **alliance between gay men and lesbian women:** Ibid., 261–3.

159 **I rolled over in bed:** Eric Marcus, interview by the author, November 16, 2011. Costanza presented the meeting to Marcus as just a part of her normal duties as public liaison. When Marcus interviewed O'Leary for *Making Gay History* she swore him to secrecy about how she proposed the meeting since Costanza was still not publicly out.

159 **Homosexuals at the White House:** Clendinen and Nagourney, *Out for Good*, 287–9.

160 **the Gay Rights National Lobby was launched:** Ibid., 258–60.

161 **a gay political action committee (PAC):** Ibid., 432–40; Vic Basile, interview by the author, June 3, 2010.

161 **the rise of Harvey Milk:** Randy Shilts, *The Mayor of Castro Street*, passim; Shilts did much of the original research on the Milk story; Silver, interview; Cleve Jones, interview by the author, February 1, 2010.

162 **fell out of fashion in social movement theory:** James Jasper, *Passion and Purpose: Action Theory of Social Movements*, chapter 1, "After the Big Paradigms: Social Movement Theory Today," http://www.hks.harvard.edu/cchrp/hrsm/pdf/JamesJasper_SM_Theory.pdf.

164 **a shift in the story:** Probably the most revealing sentence in Randy Shilts's entire Milk hagiography is the quotation of Milk's favorite saying: "You're never given power. You have to take it." Shilts, *The Mayor of Castro Street*, 193.

164 **the Alice folks were too timid:** Ibid., 73–75.

165 **President Jimmy Carter's Internal Revenue Service:** Milton Cerny, "Tax Exempt Organizations: It's Been a Memorable Twenty Years," McGuire-Woods blog, http://www.mcguirewoods.com/news-resources/publications/taxation/tax-exempt%20organizations.pdf; Robert P. Dugan Jr., *Winning the New Civil War*, 127–9.

165 **Anita Bryant, who started an organization:** Clendinen and Nagourney, *Out for Good,* 291–330; Marcus, *Making Gay History*, 213–5.

165 **The successful fight against the Briggs initiative:** Clendinen and Nagourney, *Out for Good*, 365–9, 377–90; Shilts, *The Mayor of Castro Street*, 238–50.

166 **Milk's death:** Ibid., 267–9, 324–39.

166 **They turned their political wrath:** Ibid., 340–1.

166 **Milk became an icon:** Ibid., passim; Rob Epstein, *The Times of Harvey Milk* (documentary, 1984); Dustin Lance Black, *Milk* (screenplay).

Chapter 6

169 **When Steve Endean arrived in Washington:** Dudley Clendinen and Adam Nagourney, *Out for Good*, 396–8.

169 **Williams was mostly in the bag:** Ibid., 440.

169 **Chicago's Howard Brown Clinic:** "Howard Brown Health Center," http://www.howardbrown.org/hb_aboutus.asp?id=153.

169 **was praying he would not get caught:** Taylor Branch, "Closets of Power," *Harper's*, October 1982.

169 **activist Cleve Jones:** Cleve Jones, interview by the author, February 1, 2010.

170 **Human Rights Campaign (HRC) had:** Human Rights Campaign, 1996 Report, http://www.novelguide.com/a/discover/sigs_0001_0001_0/sigs_0001_0001_0_00077.html.

170 **The president of the United States spoke:** "Remarks by President Clinton

at Human Rights Campaign Dinner," http://www.critpath.org/pflag-talk/ClintonHRC.html.

170 **(GMHC) was spending $30 million:** Donald Suggs, "True Colors," http://www.poz.com/articles/242_1737.shtml.

170 **But Roscoe Browne's mother had to pay:** Robby Browne, interview by the author, November 6, 2010; Barbara Campbell, interview by the author, November 23, 2010; Jennifer Warren and Richard C. Paddock, "Randy Shilts, Chronicler of AIDS Epidemic, Dies," *Los Angeles Times*, February 18, 1994; Cleve Jones, interview.

171 **"We die/they do nothing":** "ACT UP Action at the FDA and HHS Rally," DIVA TV documentary 01299 (1988), New York Public Library, http://www.actupny.org/nypl/divatv.html.

172 **the boat dock on the river Styx:** Alvin Friedman-Kien, interview by the author, February 12, 2009.

173 **At almost exactly the same moment:** Randy Shilts, *And the Band Played On*, 55–56.

173 **On June 5, 1981:** Ibid., 68.

173 **the world's emergency squad:** Ibid., 4.

174 **he knew immediately that a crisis was at hand:** Don Francis, interview by the author, January 13, 2010.

174 **the last issue the conservative Reagan administration:** Charles Perrow and Mauro F. Guillén, *AIDS Disaster*, 50–54.

174 **Mayor Ed Koch had little time:** Edward I. Koch, interview by the author, December 18, 2009.

174 **his job did not include:** Shilts, *And the Band Played On*, 310.

174 **National Institutes of Health (NIH), also did as little as it could:** Ibid., 93–95; Francis, interview; "Summary of the Workshop on Kaposi's Sarcoma," http://history.nih.gov/NIHInOwnWords/assets/media/pdf/unpublished/unpublished_05.pdf.

175 **"they were not interested in a disease that affects gay men":** Friedman-Kien, interview.

175 **the august Dr. Gallo:** John Crewdson, *Science Fictions*, 39; Shilts, *And the Band Played On*, 151, 173, 201.

175 **Tim Westmoreland was on a routine visit to the CDC:** Tim Westmoreland, interview by the author, December 17, 2010.

175 **Waxman did what he could:** Shilts, *And the Band Played On*, 143–4.

175 **And so it went:** Westmoreland, interview; Jennifer Brier, *Infectious Ideas*, 82–83.

176 **Fifteen hundred people died from AIDS in 1983:** AIDS deaths cited are from CDC MMWR, "Update: Trends in AIDS Incidence, Deaths, and Prevalence—United States, 1996," http://www.cdc.gov/mmwr/preview/mmwrhtml/00046531.htm#00001188.gif; there is always slippage and recalculation in mortality reports, but the numbers are clearly roughly accurate.

176 **Great, Friedman-Kien thought:** The story about Friedman-Kien at Kramer's apartment is endemic to the AIDS literature. This particular version comes from the author's interview with Friedman-Kien.

177 **only thing they were angry about was being told:** Shilts, *And the Band Played On*, 91; Brier, *Infectious Ideas,* 32–40.

177 **Cleve Jones was reported to be:** Jones, interview.

177 **"NO WAY," they caroled merrily:** Michael VerMeulen, "The Gay Plague," *New York*, May 31, 1982.

177 **When Roscoe Browne told his brother:** Robby Browne, interview by the author, November 6, 2010.

178 **what would the gay revolution have achieved:** Brier, *Infectious Ideas*, 29, 32.

178 **who was on their side:** Ibid., 80–81; Perrow and Guillén, *AIDS Disaster*, 8.

178 **professional morality of medicine completely obscured all other considerations:** Anthony Fauci, interview by the author, November 22, 2010; Friedman-Kien, interview; Francis, interview.

179 **educating interest groups in how to lobby him:** Westmoreland, interview.

179 **"Most of us still didn't have a clue":** Steve Endean, *Bringing Lesbian and Gay Rights into the Mainstream*, 128–9.

179 **Lambda did find its docket:** Abby Rubenfeld, interview by the author, March 31, 2011.

180 **first recognized the magnitude of the peril:** Deborah B. Gould, *Moving Politics*, 92–93; Clendinen and Nagourney, *Out for Good*, 476–7.

180 **make a bedrock change:** John-Manuel Andriote, *Victory Deferred*, 223.

182 **He wrote furious hortative essays:** "1,112 and Counting" is reproduced from the *New York Native*, many places, inter alia, http://queerrhetoric.com/2010/03/14/1112-and-counting/.

182 **the founders of GMHC threw him out:** Shilts, *And the Band Played On*, 275.

182 **essentially started all its programs:** Ibid., 150.

182 **By 1985, GMHC had volunteers:** Perrow and Guillén, *AIDS Disaster*, 107–12; "Joan Tisch: Face to Face with a Living Legend," http://www.gmhc.org/news-and-events/press-releases/joan-tisch-face-to-face-with-a-living-legend.

183 **money manager Jim Pepper out:** James Pepper, interview by the author, August 21, 2010.

184 **a "heroic narrative of early AIDS activism":** Gould, *Moving Politics*, 142.

184 **Dr. Francis joined the flood of men:** Francis, interview; Marc Conant, interview by the author, January 10, 2010.

185 **only San Francisco had the public-private collaboration:** Andriote, *Victory Deferred*, 138.

Chapter 7

187 **learned that their life expectancy:** The oral histories of ACT UP at the New York Public Library and the San Francisco Main Library, http://www.actuporalhistory.org/about/index.html, include many stories that implicitly reveal the link between the discovery of infected status while there was still time for extended activism. Published stories include, for example, "Lone PWA Survivor Remembers," http://www.xtra.ca/public/Vancouver/Lone_PWA_survivor_remembers–9915.aspx.

188 **Supreme Court decision radicalized the gay movement:** The most extended analysis and treatment of the *Bowers* effect is Deborah B. Gould, *Moving Politics.* Although I disagree with her that there was a paucity of political opportunities in 1986, see, infra, at pp. 188–93; clearly, the

emotive power of the government's insult greatly fueled the eruption of militant activism.

188 **Thirty-nine-year-old Victor Bender:** Patricia Morrisroe, "AIDS: One Man's Story," *New York*, August 19, 1985.

189 **FODs (Friends of Dan):** Vic Basile, interview by the author, June 3, 2010; Barbara Campbell, interview by the author, November 23, 2010; David Mixner, *Stranger Among Friends*, 233–4.

189 **Larry Kramer's article of the same name:** Gould, *Moving Politics*, 93–100.

191 **talk of possible treatments increased exponentially:** Steven Epstein, *Impure Science*, 187–94.

191 **In 1984, someone leaked to congressional staffer Tim Westmoreland:** Tim Westmoreland, interview by the author, December 17, 2010.

192 **money for research began resembling a meaningful response:** Randy Shilts, *And the Band Played On*, 492–3; Craig A. Rimmerman, Kenneth D. Wald, and Clyde, Wilcox, eds., *The Politics of Gay Rights*, 232.

192 **sent its lobbyists to Lowell Weicker:** Basile, interview.

192 **elites were divided:** Anthony Fauci, interview by the author, November 22, 2010; Jennifer Brier, *Infectious Ideas*, 89.

192 **Old activists stirred to life:** Dudley Clendinen and Adam Nagourney, *Out for Good*, 543; Gould, *Moving Politics*, 129–30; Avram Finkelstein, interview by the author, January 7, 2011.

193 **the Nazi analogy:** Gould, *Moving Politics*, 128, 168–9; Finkelstein, interview.

193 **Supreme Court justice Lewis Powell's gay law clerk:** Joyce Murdoch and Deb Price, *Courting Justice.*

193 ***Bowers v. Hardwick*:** 478 U.S. 186 (1986).

194 ***Bowers* was an ugly surprise:** Patricia A. Cain, *Rainbow Rights*, 172–9.

194 **The Supreme Court decision triggered street protests:** Gould, *Moving Politics*, 175–6; Cain, *Rainbow Rights*, 179–81.

195 **Lavender Hill Mob traveled to Atlanta:** Gould, *Moving Politics*, 129; Clendinen and Nagourney, *Out for Good*, 543.

195 **Larry Kramer had agreed:** Gould, *Moving Politics*, 131; Clendinen and Nagourney, *Out for Good*, 547.

195 **Kramer told the crowd:** Larry Kramer, *Reports from the Holocaust*, 127–36.

195 **booked the room for a meeting every week:** "Historical Story of Kramer's 1987 Speech," via LGBT Center website, http://www.actupny.org/20th-year-anniversary/index.html.

196 **he decided he'd go to the follow-up meeting:** Michael Nesline, interview March 24, 2002, by Sarah Schulman, ACT UP Oral History Project, A Program of Mix—The New York Lesbian & Gay Experimental Film Festival.

196 **"gay white men realized they did not have the privilege they thought they had":** Ann Northrop, interview by the author, November 17, 2010.

196 **White men have contacts:** Northrop, interview; Larry Kramer, interview by the author, November 13, 2009.

197 **attracts the cameras:** Benjamin Shepard and Ronald Hayduk, *From ACT UP to the WTO*, 89.

197 **On March 24, 1987:** http://www.actupny.org/documents/1stFlyer.html; http://www.actupny.org/divatv/synopsis75.html.

197 **ACT UP demonstrators handed out an information sheet:** http://www.actupny.org/documents/1stFlyer.html.

197 **the normally well-behaved HRC demonstrated:** Gould, *Moving Politics*, 153; Basile, interview.

198 **Every radical movement, gay or not, that came after:** Shepard and Hayduk, *From ACT UP to the WTO*, 1–9.

198 **"ACT UP was the single most important thing the gay population ever achieved":** Kramer, interview.

198 **put together some contemporary teaching materials:** Shepard and Hayduk, *From ACT UP to the WTO*, x–xii.

198 **How did they do it:** Jim Eigo, ACT UP Oral History Project, March 5, 2004; "Mainstream Strategy for AIDS Group," *New York Times*, July 22, 1988, http://www.nytimes.com/1988/07/22/nyregion/mainstream-strategy-for-aids.

199 **"I ran the show just like I used to produce the news":** Northrop, interview.

200 **ACT UP artists:** Marlene McCarty, interview by the author, November 19, 2010.

200 **"It was my life":** Greg Bordowitz, interview, ACT UP Oral History Project, December 17, 2002.

201 **Seize control of the FDA:** http://www.actupny.org/divatv/synopsis75.html; Michelangelo Signorile, ACT UP Oral History Project, September 20, 2003.

201 **the Food and Drug Administration had it coming:** Daniel Henninger, "Drug Lag," in *The Concise Encyclopedia of Economics*; for a less ideological analysis, see Henry I. Miller, *To America's Health: A Proposal to Reform the Food and Drug Administration,* and Adil E. Shamoo, *Principles of Research Data Audit.*

204 **speeding up the process:** Brier, *Infectious Ideas*, 166; Fauci, interview.

205 **The St. Patrick's action:** Northrop, interview; Michael Petrelis, ACT UP Oral History Project, April 21, 2003.

206 **But the price was high:** Petrelis, interview; John-Manuel Andriote, *Victory Deferred*, 247–8; Gould, *Moving Politics*, 285–6.

207 **Dr. Anthony Fauci looked out:** Fauci, interview; "HIV Frontlines: An Interview with Anthony Fauci, M.D.," The Body, http://www.thebody.com/content/art47390.html?mtrk=8858344; "The Age of AIDS: Interviews: Larry Kramer," *Frontline* (PBS), http://www.pbs.org/wgbh/pages/frontline/aids/interviews/kramer.html.

208 **he must have seemed like a god:** Epstein, *Impure Science*, 286–7.

208 **ACT UP was always a provisional alliance:** Andriote, *Victory Deferred*, 250–3; Gould, *Moving Politics*, 303–20; Epstein, *Impure Science*, 287–94.

209 **conventional movement trap:** Andriote, *Victory Deferred*, 250–3; Gould, *Moving Politics*, 328–94; Epstein, *Impure Science*, 287–94.

209 **"save the whales":** Gould, *Moving Politics*, 354.

209 **the split between the men and the women:** Brier, *Infectious Ideas*, 179–82; Sarah Schulman, interview by the author, November 19, 2010; Marion Banzhaf, ACT UP Oral History Project, April 18, 2007.

210 **the sessions were, to put it mildly, contentious:** Epstein, *Impure Science*, 292.

210 **be suspended:** Gould, *Moving Politics*, 366. Gould notes the confusion in the debates, citing the oral history interviews with the various factions.

210 **Treatment Action Group:** Brier, *Infectious Ideas*, 183–4; Kramer, interview; Northrop, interview.

211 **Cleve Jones had figured this out:** Cleve Jones, interview by the author, February 1, 2010.

212 **the NAMES Project took the quilt:** The Names Project, "History of the Quilt," http://www.aidsquilt.org/history.htm.

212 **One of them was for Roscoe Browne:** Robby Browne, interview by the author, November 6, 2010.

214 **well over a billion dollars a year on AIDS research:** Andriote, *Victory Deferred*, 256.

215 **Cleve Jones got out of his deathbed:** Jones, interview.

Chapter 8

217 **gorgeous day in Hollywood, California:** Details of the evening from the video on file with author.

217 **What a way it had been:** David B. Mixner, *Stranger Among Friends*; David B. Mixner, interview by the author, May 21, 2010.

218 **start the first gay political action committee:** Dudley Clendinen and Adam Nagourney, *Out for Good*, 356–7.

218 **In a stunning debut:** Mixner, *Stranger Among Friends*, 132–3.

218 **Human Rights Campaign Fund:** Clendinen and Nagourney, *Out for Good*, 433.

218 **Senator Edward Kennedy was the keynote speaker:** Ibid., 472.

219 **competition within the Democratic Party:** Mixner, *Stranger Among Friends*, 196–200.

219 **The flood of money:** Ibid., 201; Guide to the Human Rights Campaign Records, 1975–2005, Collection number 7712, Division of Rare and Manuscript Collections, Cornell University Library, http://rmc.library.cornell.edu/EAD/htmldocs/RMM07712.html; "The Victory Fund: A Brief History," http://www.victoryfund.org/our_story/history.

219 **lawyers' organization had an income:** Ellen Ann Andersen, *Out of the Closets and into the Courts*, 45–46.

220 **"We can't do this":** Clendinen and Nagourney, *Out for Good*, 529; Mixner, *Stranger Among Friends*, 152.

221 **a call from his old friend Bill Clinton:** Mixner, *Stranger Among Friends*, 204; Mixner, interview.

221 **Lesbian activists found out:** Sue Hyde, interview by the author, February 15, 2011.

221 **Some soldiers started asking:** Nathaniel Frank, *Unfriendly Fire*, 17–18.

221 **racial civil rights movement:** Ronald R. Krebs, *Fighting for Rights*, 171–5.

221 **Massachusetts senator Paul Tsongas:** Mixner, *Stranger Among Friends*, 204–7.

222 **When Bill and Hillary Clinton came:** Ibid., 210–2.

224 **When Mixner went:** Ibid., 161.

224 **connected to the gay community:** Mixner, interview.

224 **regulations governing gays in the military would be changed:** Mixner, *Stranger Among Friends*, 4–5.

225 **gay organizations had a field day:** Frank, *Unfriendly Fire*, 77–78.

225 **Task Force got involved:** Hyde, interview.

225 **found his voice:** Joseph Steffan, interview by the author, February 22, 2011; Frank, *Unfriendly Fire*, 19–22.

226 **Congressman Barney Frank explained:** David Morton Rayside, *On the Fringe*, 237.

227 **the three antigay crusaders:** Frank, *Unfriendly Fire*, 28.

228 **"your reasoning would have kept you from the mess hall a few decades ago":** Karen DeYoung, *Soldier*, 230.

229 **"change the meaning of who they are":** Frank, *Unfriendly Fire*, 275–6, quoting Gerald Garvey and John DiIulio in *The New Republic*, April 1993.

229 **roadmap to the social change:** Frank, *Unfriendly Fire*, 78–79.

230 **chained himself to the White House fence:** Mixner, *Stranger Among Friends*, 338.

230 **a harder target: marriage:** Evan Wolfson, interviews by the author, May 10, 2010, and May 12, 2010.

232 **goes back to antiquity:** Vernon L. Provencal, "The Family in Aristotle," vernon .provencal@acadiau.ca, http://www.mun.ca/animus/2001vol6/provencal6.htm.

233 **renewed agitation for marriage equality:** Jonathan Rauch, *Gay Marriage*, 4; Paula Ettelbrick, "Since When Is Marriage a Path to Liberation?"

233 **sue the state:** Evan Wolfson, *Why Marriage Matters*, 29–32.

233 **the Hawaii Supreme Court reversed:** *Baehr v. Lewin*, 74 Haw. 530, 852 P.2d 44 (1993), reconsideration and clarification granted in part, 74 Haw. 645, 852 P.2d 74 (1993).

234 **"full faith and credit":** U.S. Constitution, Article IV.

234 **the 1996 presidential primary season:** Frank Rich, "Journal: Bashing to Victory," *New York Times,* February 14, 1996.

234 **to draft a law:** http://ontheissues.org/News_Gay_Rights.htm; http://www.lectlaw.com/files/leg23.htm.

235 **chaired by . . . Henry Hyde:** *Hearing before the Subcommittee on the Constitution of the Committee on the Judiciary*, H.R., 108th Cong., Second Session, March 30, 2004, Serial No. 70; *Defense of Marriage Act (DOMA)*, H.R. Report 104–664 (1996).

236 **Socarides says he argued as hard as he could:** Richard Socarides, interviews by the author, May 27, June 7, and June 9, 2010.

236 **federal study of the impact:** Letter from Dayna Shal to Senator Bill Frist, http://www.gao.gov/new.items/d04353r.pdf.

236 **he had a plan:** Wolfson, interviews.

236 **big winds at his back:** George Chauncey, *Why Marriage?* At nn. 12–14; note 10; Evan Wolfson, "Fighting to Win and Keep the Freedom to Marry," 259.

237 **"the ick factor":** Evan Thomas, "The War over Gay Marriage," *Newsweek*, July 7, 2003.

238 **people with otherwise conventional desires:** Jonathan Rauch, "Families Forged by Illness," *New York Times*, June 4, 2006.

238 **marriage was a realm of insecurity and inequality:** Nancy F. Cott, *Public Vows: A History of Marriage and the Nation*.

239 **the state had long deferred to the church:** Ibid., 5–6.

239 **converted to Catholicism :** Tim Drake, "From the Ark to the Barque: Hadley Arkes Speaks About His Reception into the Catholic Church," *National*

Catholic Register Daily News, August 24, 2010, http://www.ncregister.com/daily-news/from-the-ark-to-the-barque/1%20of#ixzz1WcLBT5HG.

240 **doing something extra:** Ronald R. Krebs, *Fighting for Rights*, 4.

Chapter 9

243 ***Romer v. Evans***: 517 U.S. 620 (1996).

244 **political efforts at the local level:** Craig A. Rimmerman, Kenneth D. Wald, and Clyde Wilcox, eds., *The Politics of Gay Rights*, 269–87.

245 **a perfect example of the process:** Jerry Gerash, "Beth Chayim Chadashim Drash," October 12, 2001, http://www.denvergayrevolt.com/origins_of_center.html.

245 **passed an ordinance:** Lisa Keen and Suzanne B. Goldberg, *Strangers to the Law*, 5–6.

246 **But there were the queens:** http://www.impcourt.org/icis/who/founder.html.

247 **Once there was community, politics followed:** Pat Steadman, interview by the author, March 14, 2011; Tea Schook, interview by the author, March 21, 2011; Ina Russell, interview by the author, September, 2009; Phil Nash, interview by the author, April 4, 2011.

247 **In 1990, Denver policewoman Angela Romero:** Keen and Goldberg, *Strangers to the Law*, 27.

248 **Colorado for Family Values:** Ibid., 3–4, 7–9; Ellen Ann Andersen, *Out of the Closets and into the Courts*, 153.

248 **Colorado for Family Values proposed:** *Romer v. Evans*.

249 **had never succeeded in enacting measures to make life radically worse:** Rimmerman, Wald, and Wilcox, eds., *The Politics of Gay Rights*, 164–5.

249 **Pat Steadman was anything but a stranger to the law:** Steadman, interview.

249 **the coach announced:** Jean Hardisty, "Constructing Homophobia."

250 **eight-page broadside:** On file with author.

250 **having a very bad feeling:** Schook, interview; Mary Celeste, interview by the author, May 3, 2011.

251 **she had promised to represent them:** Steadman, interview; Jean Dubofsky, interview by the author, March 18, 2011.

251 **the legal profession's role in the gay revolution:** Dale Carpenter, "How the Law Accepted Gays," *New York Times*, April 28, 2011.

253 **The lawyers and the lawsuits came in perfect sync:** Matt Coles, interview by the author, March 29, 2011.

253 ***Romer* was it:** The strategy is set forth in Keen and Goldberg, in Dubofsky, interview, and in Coles, interview.

255 **a Supreme Court precedent:** *Department of Agriculture v. Moreno*, 413 U.S. 528 (1973).

256 **the Colorado Supreme Court agreed:** *Evans v. Romer*, 854 P.2d 11270 (Colo. 1993).

257 **The Colorado Supreme Court:** *Evans v. Romer*, 882 P.2d 1335 (Colo. 1994).

258 **Larry Tribe wrote a brief:** Reagan Wm. Simpson and Mary R. Vasaly, *How to Be a Good Friend to the Court*, 67–79.

258 **representatives of a whole range of thinking:** Philip B. Kurland, "The Supreme Court, 1963 Term: Foreword," 143; John Hart Ely, "The Wages of Crying Wolf: A Comment on *Roe v. Wade*," 920.

260 **On October 10, 1995:** *Romer v. Evans* Oral Argument, http://www.oyez.org/cases/1990–1999/1995/1995_94_1039/argument; Dubofsky, interview.

260 **something like *Dred Scott*:** Laurence Tribe, interview by the author, April 7, 2011.

262 **there was literally "no presence" from the LGBT community:** Lisa Turner, interview by the author, April 19, 2011.

264 **Task Force started a federation:** http://www.thetaskforce.org/press/releases/pr117_071897; transgender, http://www.transgenderlaw.org/aboutTLPI.htm; for the Sylvia Rivera Law Project, see Paisley Currah, Richard M. Juang, and Shannon Price Minter, eds., *Transgender Rights*, 226.

264 **a scared freshman:** Tim Gill, e-mail interview by the author, June 29, 2011.

265 **Gill and his allies:** Joshua Green, "They Won't Know What Hit Them," *The Atlantic*, March 2007.

266 **arrested him and another man:** *Lawrence v. Texas*, 539 U.S. 558 (2003); Douglas Martin, "Tyron Garner, 39, Plaintiff in Pivotal Sodomy Case, Dies,"

New York Times, September 14, 2006, http://www.nytimes.com/2006/09/14/obituaries/14garner.html. A recent book heavily contests the facts as recited in the opinion. Dale Carpenter, *Flagrant Conduct* (New York, W. W. Norton, 2012).

266 **not spoiling for a federal fight:** Andersen, *Out of the Closets*, 101–11; Rubenfeld, interview.

267 **One of the people waiting was Larry Tribe:** Tribe, interview.

269 **Matthew Shepard's short life was ebbing:** John Aravosis, Matthew Shepard Online Resources Archive, http://www.wiredstrategies.com/shepard2.html; Loffreda, *Losing Matt Shepard*; "New Details Emerge in Matthew Shepard Murder," http://abcnews.go.com/2020/story?id=277685&page=2; Judy Shepard, *The Meaning of Matthew.*

270 **John Aravosis was sitting at his computer:** John Aravosis, interview by the author, June 2, 2010.

271 **Kevin Berrill thought he'd heard everything:** Kevin Berrill, interview by the author, May 5, 2011.

272 **he went to the ADL:** The ADL Hate Crimes website is at http://www.adl.org/combating_hate/.

275 **efforts in the states:** Donald P. Haider-Markel, "Lesbian and Gay Politics in the States," in Rimmerman, Wald, and Wilcox, eds., 204–6; Task Force Timeline, http://www.thetaskforce.org/issues/hate_crimes_main_page/timeline; Task Force history, http://www.thetaskforce.org/issues/hate_crimes_main_page/overview; Donald P. Haider-Markel, "The Politics of Social Regulatory Policy: State and Federal Hate Crime Policy and Implementation Effort."

275 **The 1995 murder of anatomically female Brandon Teena:** Currah, Juang, and Minter, eds., *Transgender Rights*, 183.

276 **it would not pass:** Jared Miller, "Opponents Say Existing Statutes Sufficient; State Avoids Hate Crime Legislation," *Star-Tribune* (Casper, Wyoming) Capital Bureau, October 11, 2008, http://trib.com/news/state-and-regional/article_d636eb76–665b–5593-b186-f69a96d32a37.html.

276 **seemed to be working perfectly:** Dave Cullen, "Quiet Bombshell in Matthew Shepard Trial," http://www.salon.com/news/feature/1999/11/01/

gay_panic; Loffreda, *Losing Matt Shepard*, 138–9; Matthew Shepard Online Resources, http://www.wiredstrategies.com/mrshep.htm.

279 **It was the foundation's biggest donor:** International Court System website, http://www.impcourt.org/icis/info/News/MSF–021510.html.

279 **Matthew Shepard and James Byrd, Jr., Hate Crimes Prevention Act:** "Obama Signs Hate Crimes Bill into Law," http://articles.cnn.com/2009-10-28/politics/hate.crimes_1_crimes-gay-rights-human-rights-campaign?_s=PM:POLITICS.

279 **the usual opponents:** *Glenn, Yuille, Ouellette, and Combs v. Holder*, United States Court of Appeals for the Sixth Circuit 10–2273 (6th Cir. 2010); James B. Jacobs and Kimberly Potter, *Hate Crimes: Criminal Law and Identity Politics*; Andrew Sullivan, "What's So Bad about Hate," *New York Times Magazine*, September 26, 1999.

279 **attacked forty-nine-year-old gay Jack Price:** "Man Beaten in Apparent Anti-Gay Attack," Associated Press, October 12, 2009, http://www.nypost.com/p/news/local/queens/item_wqxpVGb5BEcLhuHFmCMJYJ#ixzz1WpcYa82s.

280 **the play saved more gay lives:** Greg Reiner, interview by the author, fall 2010.

280 **It was time, Kaufman felt:** The Laramie Project DVD: Moises Kaufman Interview, http://www.movieweb.com/dvd/DVz7kBzBo9EZDz/moises-kaufman-interview.

281 **"I'm never getting out of here":** Greg Pierotti, "Laramie Sequel Gives Voice to Shepard's Killer: Greg Pierotti Interviewed Convicted Killer Aaron McKinney for 10 Hours," Associated Press, http://today.msnbc.msn.com/id/33074488/ns/today-entertainment/t/laramie-sequel-gives-voice-shepards-killer/#.TmI9UmpXGgA.

Chapter 10

283 **the April 30, 1997, episode of the sitcom *Ellen*:** http://www.youtube.com/watch?v=bhuiJINpRww.

285 **They would be the Servicemembers Legal Defense Network:** Michelle Be-

necke, interview by the author, April 14, 2011; Nathaniel Frank, *Unfriendly Fire*, 179, 182, 190.

287 **the press started taking the goings-on seriously:** Jennifer Egan, "Uniforms in the Closet: The Shadow Life of a Gay Marine," *New York Times Magazine*, June 28, 1998; "Advocacy Group Says Military Rooting Out Gays," February 26, 1997, http://articles.cnn.com/1997–02–26/us/9702_26_gays.military_1_michelle-benecke-homosexuals-servicemembers-legal-defense-network?_s=PM:US; "Don't Ask, Don't Tell, Don't Pursue," a Digital Library Project of the Robert Crown Law Library at Stanford Law School, http://dont.stanford.edu/commentary/index.htm.

288 **issued a guideline:** "Memorandum for Secretaries of the Military Departments, Chairman of the Joint Chiefs of Staff, Inspector General of the Department of Defense," March 24, 1997, http://dont.stanford.edu/regulations/memo3.htm.

288 **Not soon enough for Private (FC) Barry Winchell:** Frank, *Unfriendly Fire*, 193–7; Benecke, interview.

289 **a bill to repeal DADT:** Rick Klein, "Meehan Targeting 'Don't Ask, Don't Tell,'" *Boston Globe*, November 18, 2006, http://www.boston.com/news/nation/washington/articles/2006/11/18/meehan_targeting_dont_ask_dont_tell.

289 **order the state to marry same-sex couples:** *Goodridge v. Dept. of Public Health*, 798 N.E.2d 941 (Mass. 2003).

290 **tried to take control of events:** Scott L. Cummings and Douglas NeJaime, "Lawyering for Marriage Equality," 1235; Kate Spencer, "Same Sex Couples and the Right to Marry—European Perspectives," 155, http://www.srcf.ucam.org/cslr/index.php?option=com_journal&task=article&mode=pdf&format=raw&id=93; Kees Waaldijk, "Others May Follow: The Introduction of Marriage, Quasi-Marriage, and Semi-Marriage for Same-Sex Couples in European Countries," 569, http://www.nesl.edu/userfiles/file/lawreview/vol38/3/11-Waaldijk-PDF.pdf.

290 **Massachusetts Supreme Judicial Court chief justice Margaret:** Emily Bazelon, "A Bold Stroke," http://www.legalaffairs.org/issues/May-June–2004/feature_bazelon_mayjune.

294 **the second year it failed:** Frank Phillips, "Legislators Vote to Defeat Same-Sex Marriage Ban," *Boston Globe* City and Region Desk, June 14, 2007, http://www.boston.com/news/globe/city_region/breaking_news/2007/06/legislators_vot_1.html.

294 **part of their wedding vows:** http://www.elegala.com/.

295 **must enact a constitutional amendment:** George W. Bush, 2004 State of the Union Address, http://www.americanrhetoric.com/speeches/stateoftheunion2004.htm.

295 **Michael Rogers got pissed:** Michael Rogers, interview by the author, June 3, 2010; Jose Antonio Vargas, "Gay Rights Site Runs 'Outing' Ad Aimed at the Hill," *Washington Post*, July 9, 2004.

295 **John Aravosis, had the same reaction:** John Aravosis, interview by the author, June 2, 2010.

296 **tech-savvy gay guys:** Andy Towle, interview by the author, April 16, 2011; Bil Browning, interview by the author, April 9, 2011.

297 **Rex Wockner had been the secret information system:** Rex Wockner, interview by the author, April 17, 2011, and numerous times thereafter.

297 **the OutGiving conference:** http://www.outgiving.org/about/.

297 **eQualityGiving:** Juan and Ken Ahonen-Jover, interview by the author, July 10, 2011.

298 **He dispatched his adviser:** Lisa Turner, interview by the author, April 19, 2011.

298 **was furious:** Paul Yandura, interview by the author, June 3, 2010.

Chapter 11

301 **Newsom was going to order his clerk to start issuing marriage licenses:** Daniel R. Pinello, *America's Struggle for Same-Sex Marriage*, 73–80; Therese Stewart, interview by the author, May 3, 2011; Kate Kendell, interview by the author, April 13, 2011.

302 **the agreement to wait:** Scott L. Cummings and Douglas NeJaime, "Lawyering for Marriage Equality," 1269–71.

303 **the anti–gay-marriage forces:** Ibid., 1293–4; ProtectMarriage.com, http://www.facebook.com/pages/ProtectMarriagecom/211390365541709.

303 **Schubert Flint Public Affairs:** Frank Schubert and Jeff Flint, "Case Studies: Passing Prop 8," February 1, 2009, http://www.campaignsandelections.com/case-studies/176127/passing-prop–8.thtml.

304 **the schoolkids campaign sent the ball clear out of the park:** David Fleischer, "What Defeat in California Can Teach Us about Winning Future Ballot Measures on Same-Sex Marriage," LGBT Mentoring Project, August 3, 2010, https://7382575426631341557-a-lgbtmentoring-org-s-sites.googlegroups.com/a/lgbtmentoring.org/prop–8-report/TheProp8Report.pdf?attachauth=ANoY7coq7hzcTJeGlEjkz-lqlkdlqrGNcQ–5CEG3x7Y0SgVXnvR1ltuDJoaneQcIGQArBXCBtc–8j4jJ0NMxVGthqZqkwLpJBu9lfXvgmHTNqiXkcNBsK3wu5Fv3-Oxz2NPIRx-cTB7eriPZGQcdRzlOUC4kP7ZGq_wAuNBV2GYMO18RhFdPXLncmfoKc6WZ7aBc1fFn-j1qOeiVVz–69KrZoDbZJ1xltA%3D%3D&attredirects=0.

305 **the option got less attractive:** NELLCO Legal Scholarship Repository, Columbia Public Law and Legal Theory Working Papers, Columbia Law School, March 11, 2010; Olatúnde C. Johnson, "The Story of *Bob Jones University v. United States.*"

306 **ran to an actual gay political consultant, Los Angeles's Chad Griffin:** Chad Griffin, interview by the author, April 13, 2010, and April 19, 2011.

308 **Chad Griffin was in a suite at the posh St. Francis Hotel:** Griffin, interview, April 19, 2011.

308 **Lesbian community-college teacher Robin McGehee was:** Robin McGehee, interview by the author, March 4, 2011.

308 ***Milk* screenwriter Dustin Lance Black was not surprised:** Lance Black, interview by the author, April 12, 2010.

308 **Evan Wolfson's first funder, saw:** Matt Foreman, interview by the author, April 18, 2011.

309 **became instant friends:** Rob Reiner, interview by the author, April 14, 2010.

311 **claimed they were taken completely by surprise:** Chuleenan Svetvilas, "Challenging Prop. 8: The Hidden Story: How Hollywood Activists Seized Control of the Fight for Gay Marriage," http://www.callawyer.com/story.cfm?eid=906575&evid=1.

312 **admiring journalists uncovered stories:** Ross Todd, "Marriage Brokers: Behind the Scenes of the Odd Couple's Groundbreaking Litigation," http://www.gibsondunn.com/news/Documents/GibsonDunnMarriageBrokers-AmLaw-3-11.pdf.

312 ***Smelt v. United States*:** C.D.Cal. Case No. 8:2009-cv-00286.

312 ***Gill v. Office of Personnel Management*:** 699 F.Supp.2d 374 (2010).

313 **The picture was all over the Internet:** http://www.daylife.com/photo/00NC0Dlb7cgEx?__site=daylife&q=Jeffr.

316 **refusing to defend Prop 8:** Lambda Legal Newsroom, July 27, 2011, *Perry v. Brown* (formerly known as *Perry v. Schwarzenegger*), http://www.lambdalegal.org/in-court/cases/perry-v-schwarzenegger.html.

316 **Pugno Protect Marriage coalition had to move to intervene:** http://oldsite.alliancedefensefund.org/userdocs/SchwarzeneggerMTI.pdf.

316 **"Why not?" he asked:** Americans for Equal Rights Trial Transcript, http://www.afer.org/wp-content/uploads/2010/01/Perry-Vol-3-1-13-10.pdf.

316 **David Boies had his way with the defense's so-called "expert" witnesses:** Stewart, interview.

316 **The one witness brave enough to face Boies in the courtroom:** http://www.afer.org/wp-content/uploads/2010/01/Perry-Vol-12-1-27-10.pdf.

316 **keeping the trial from being broadcast to the public:** *Hollingsworth v. Perry*, http://www.scotusblog.com/wp-content/uploads/2010/01/Stay-TV-on-Prop-8-trial-1-9-10.pdf.

317 **the American Bar Association awarded Boies and Olson:** Rachel M. Zahorsky, "Sometime-Foes Boies and Olson Honored with ABA Medal for Successful Joint Efforts," http://www.abajournal.com/news/article/sometime_foes_boies_and_olson_honored_with_aba_medal_for_joint_efforts.

317 **Someone sent the brief to blogger John Aravosis:** John Aravosis, "Obama Defends DOMA in Federal Court. Says Banning Gay Marriage Is Good for the Federal Budget. Invokes Incest and Marrying Children," America Blog, June 12, 2009, http://www.americablog.com/2009/06/obama-justice-department-defends-doma.html.

318 **God had delivered him from homosexuality:** "Obama Supporter: 'God Delivered Me from Homosexuality,'" Politicalticker blog, October 29, 2007, http://politicalticker.blogs.cnn.com/2007/10/29/obama-supporter-god-delivered-me-from-homosexuality/.

318 **given an interview to an official gay publication:** Kerry Eleveld, interview by the author, April 15, 2011.

318 **evangelical minister Rick Warren to give the invocation:** Amy Sullivan, "Inaugural Pastor: The Two Faces of Rick Warren," *Time*, January 18, 2009, http://www.time.com/time/nation/article/0,8599,1872453,00.html#ixzz1X0JKG.

319 **instantly crossed into the mainstream media:** Kristina Wong, "Today's Qs for O's WH—6/17/2009," June 17, 2009, http://abcnews.go.com/blogs/politics/2009/06/todays-qs-for-os-wh-6172009/; Jonathan Capehart, "For Obama, a Hit and a Miss on Gay Rights," *Washington Post*, June 21, 2009, http://www.washingtonpost.com/wp-dyn/content/article/2009/06/19/AR2009061902746.html.

319 **dates his radicalization:** Richard Socarides, interviews by the author, May 27, June 2, 7, and 9, 2010.

319 **Judge Joseph Tauro, struck down DOMA:** http://www.glad.org/current/news-detail/federal-court-strikes-down-doma-section–3/.

320 **McGehee had had a Cinderella rise:** McGehee, interview.

320 **Jones figured he had found a natural:** Ibid.

320 **showed up at the march:** "Photo Flash: HAIR at the National Equality March in Washington, D.C.," *Broadway World*, October 13, 2009, http://broadwayworld.com/article/Photo_Flash_HAIR_at_the_National_Equality_March_in_Washington_DC_20091013#ixzz1X0YsDWBs.

321 **without a murmur about DADT:** Aubrey Sarvis, interview by the author, May 9, 2011.

321 **déjà vu all over again:** Devin Dwyer, "Maine Votes 'No' on Gay Marriage," ABC News, November 4, 2009, http://abcnews.go.com/Politics/maine-voters-weigh-gay-marriage-referendum/story?id=8978779.

Chapter 12

323 **"I'm gay," he announced:** http://www.youtube.com/watch?v=YiWSPdRGvC0.

323 **newly appointed senator, Kirsten Gillibrand:** Kirsten Gillibrand, interview by the author, May 10, 2011.

324 **organized a demonstration:** "Rally for LGBT Equality with President Obama," http://www.couragecampaign.org/page/event/detail/wrv7.

324 **The Courage Campaign:** Rick Jacobs, interview by the author, April 15, 2010.

324 **Choi debuted *his* signature move:** http://www.youtube.com/watch?v=Bczbe2RjxMQ.

324 **what the protesters could possibly be demanding:** "Obama Makes Demonstration a Punchline," http://unitethefight.blogspot.com/2009/05/obama-demonstration-demanding-end-to.html.

325 **the polls were overwhelmingly in favor of allowing gays to serve:** "In U.S., Broad, Steady Support for Openly Gay Service Members," Gallup, May 10, 2010, http://www.gallup.com/poll/127904/Broad-Steady-Support-Openly-Gay-Service-Members.aspx.

326 **wrote a letter to President Obama:** http://big.assets.huffingtonpost.com/Reid2Prez.pdf.

326 **says the hearing was the turning point:** Aubrey Sarvis, interview by the author, May 9, 2011.

327 **but no one paid him any mind:** Ambreen Ali, "Why Hunger Strikes Fail: It's an Extreme Tactic, Yet It's Also One That Rarely Works," Congress.org, June 7, 2010, http://origin-www.congress.org/news/2010/06/07/why_hunger_strikes_fail.

328 **the movement's federal-litigation initiative suddenly bore fruit:** *Log Cabin Republicans v. Gates*, http://graphics8.nytimes.com/packages/pdf/13military/031111036345.pdf; *Gill v. OPM*, 699 F.Supp.2d 374 (D.Mass., 2010); *Perry v. Schwarzenegger*, http://documents.nytimes.com/us-district-court-decision-perry-v-schwarzenegger.

328 **unequaled in the rest of the constitutional scheme:** Kelly E. Henriksen, "Note & Comment: Gays, The Military, and Judicial Deference: When the

Courts Must Reclaim Equal Protection as Their Area of Expertise," 1273; *Goldman v. Weinberger*, 475 U.S. 503.

329 **to be citizens within marriage:** Emily J. Sack, "The Domestic Relations Exception, Domestic Violence, and Equal Access to Federal Courts."

329 **the lawyer for Log Cabin Republicans:** Dan Woods, interview by the author, May 20, 2011.

330 **Secretary Gates:** Rachel Slajda, "Gates to Congress: Repeal DADT Now," TPMMuckraker, November 30, 2010, http://tpmmuckraker.talkingpointsmemo.com/2010/11/dadt_report_allowing_gays_poses_little_risk_to_mil.php.

331 **repeal as a stand-alone bill:** Carl Hulse, "Senate Repeals Ban against Openly Gay Military Personnel," *New York Times*, December 19, 2010, http://www.nytimes.com/2010/12/19/us/politics/19cong.html.

332 **House Majority Leader Steny Hoyer worked the phones:** Russell Berman, "Gay-Rights Advocates Say Dem Leader Hoyer Saved 'Don't Ask' Repeal," *The Hill*, December 21, 2010, http://thehill.com/homenews/campaign/134763-gay-rights-advocates-say-hoyer-saved-dont-ask-repeal.

333 **And the military had changed:** Sarvis, interview.

334 **who chained himself to the White House fence that spring:** Brian Montopoli, "Dan Choi, Other Gay Rights Protesters Arrested after Chaining Selves to White House Fence," CBS News, April 20, 2010, http://www.cbsnews.com/8301–503544_162–20002942–503544.html.

334 **finally lost patience with the military:** John Schwartz, "Court Rules against Ban on Gays in the Military," *New York Times*, July 7, 2011, http://www.nytimes.com/2011/07/07/us/politics/07gays.html?_r=1&ref=dontaskdonttell.

334 **well-placed Senate staffer:** Anonymous, interview by the author, June 26, 2011.

334 **Solmonese went to a liberal fund-raiser:** Joe Solmonese, interview by the author, May 2, 2011.

336 **legal cupid Mary Bonauto filed the same lawsuit:** http://www.justice.gov/opa/pr/2011/February/11-ag–223.html.

336 **Richard Socarides was watching:** Richard Socarides, interview by the author, June 2, 2011.

337 **"sabotage out into the open":** Ed Whelan, "Obama's Dive on DOMA," *National Review*, February 23, 2011, http://www.nationalreview.com/bench-memos/260523/obama-s-dive-doma-ed-whelan.

337 **recognized exactly what was at stake:** Edward Whelan, interview by the author, June 2, 2011.

338 **sent a letter to the law firms:** http://www.hrcbackstory.org/wp-content/uploads/2011/03/AmLaw–200-Letter-RE-DOMA-Defense.pdf.

338 **Paul Clement, now a partner at behemoth firm King & Spalding:** Ryan J. Reilly, "Boehner Picks Bush Solicitor General Paul Clement to Defend DOMA," TPMMuckraker, April 18, 2011, http://tpmdc.talkingpoints memo.com/2011/04/boehner-picks-bush-solicitor-general-paul-clement-to-defend-doma.php.

338 **heard from HRC:** http://www.hrc.org/15539.htm.

338 **The blogosphere lit up:** Roman, "DOMA-Defending Law Firm Employees Targeted by Online Campaign," All-Lawyers Info, April 23, 2011, http://blog.all-lawyers.info/doma-defending-law-firm-employees-targeted-by-online-campaign.

338 **withdrawing from its defense of DOMA:** John Aravosis, post on Gay .Americablog, "GetEQUAL Protests Bancroft PLLC over Defense of Bigoted DOMA Law," April 25, 2011, http://gay.americablog.com/2011/04/getequal-protests-bancroft-pllc-over.html.

339 **into Atticus Finch:** Editorial, "The Duty of Counsel," *New York Times*, April 28, 2011, http://www.nytimes.com/2011/04/28/opinion/28thu4 .html?_r=3&partner=rssnyt&emc=rss; Josh Gerstein, "Eric Holder Rejects Attacks on Paul Clement over DOMA Defense," Politico, April 26, 2011, http://www.politico.com/blogs/joshgerstein/0411/Eric_Holder_rejects_attacks_on_Paul_Clement_over_DOMA_defense.html; Robert Barnes, "Kagan Defends Former Bush Official Who Is Representing House in Same-Sex Marriage Case," *Washington Post*, April 29, 2011, http://www .washingtonpost.com/politics/kagan-defends-former-bush-official-who-is-representing-house-in-same-sex-marriage-case/2011/04/29/AFoDR0GF_story.html.

340 **Victory in New York:** Michael Barbaro, "Behind N.Y. Gay Marriage, an Unlikely Mix of Forces," *New York Times*, June 26, 2011, http://www.nytimes.com/2011/06/26/nyregion/the-road-to-gay-marriage-in-new-york.html?pagewanted=all; Evan Wolfson, interview by the author, May 6, 2011.

342 **they shared a kiss:** Clarknt67, "Live from NY! Jeanette Is Marrying Kawane Today," Milk Men and Women, Daily Kos, July 24, 2011, http://www.dailykos.com/story/2011/07/24/998035/-Live-From-NY!-Jeanette-Is-Marrying-Kawane-Today.

Epilogue

343 **there is a lot left to be done:** Right after I spoke to Socarides, one of the million institutions Colorado's Tim Gill sponsors, Movement Advancement Project, issued a "Momentum Report," an analysis of LGBT equality in the US, which sums it up nicely. The report to Gill's annual Outgiving Conference was much more blunt than the written report released later. Here's the presentation: http://www.youtube.com/watch?v=YIP0JO3XQNE. And here's the link to the Equality Maps: http://www.lgbtmap.org/equality-maps.

345 **high of almost fifty thousand in 1996:** http://www.kff.org/hivaids/upload/The-HIV-AIDS-Epidemic-in-the-U-S-Fact-Sheet.pdf.

Bibliography

Interviews

Interviews are by the author unless otherwise indicated.

Achtenberg, Roberta, January 11, 2010.

Ahonen-Jover, Juan, July 10, 2011.

Ahonen-Jover, Ken, July 10, 2011.

Anonymous, June 26, 2011.

Aravosis, John, June 2, 2010.

Banzhaf, Marion, ACT UP Oral History, April 18, 2007.

Basile, Vic, June 3, 2010.

Bellamy, Carol, December 18, 2009.

Benecke, Michelle, April 14, 2011.

Berrill, Kevin, May 5, 2011.

Black, Dustin Lance, April 12, 2010.

Bordowitz, Greg, ACT UP Oral History Project, December 17, 2002.

Boutrous, Theodore, May 2, 2011.

Browne, Robby, April and November 6, 2010.

Browning, Bil, April 9, 2011.

Buchanan, Wade, March 31, 2011.

Campbell, Barbara, November 23, 2010.

Carey, Rea, June 3, 2010.

Carter, David, September 23, 2010.

Cathcart, Kevin, November 12, 2009.

Celeste, Mary, May 3, 2011.

Choi, Dan, June 26, 2010.

Cohen, Bruce, April 16, 2010.

Coles, Matt, March 29, 2011.

Conant, Marc, January 10, 2010.

Dansky, Steven, October 8, 2010.

Dubofsky, Jean, March 18, 2011.

Eigo, Jim, ACT UP Oral History Project, March 5, 2004.

Eleveld, Kerry, April 15, 2011.

Evans, Arthur, January 13, 2010.

Fauci, Anthony, November 22, 2010.

Finkelstein, Avram, January 7, 2011.

Foreman, Matt, April 18, 2011.

Fouratt, Jim, October 24, 2009; August 17, 2010.

Francis, Don, January 13, 2010.

Freedman, Alfred, November 17, 2009.

Friedman-Kien, Alvin, February 12, 2009.

Garvy, Helen, September 10, 2010.

Gill, Tim, e-mail interview, June 29, 2011.

Gillibrand, Kirsten, May 10, 2011.

Gitlin, Todd, December 9, 2009; September 8, 2010.

Gold, Mitchell, March 17, 2011.

Griffin, Chad, April 13 and April 19, 2011.

Haft, Marilyn, November 4, 2009.

Hoose, Jerry, October 6, 2010.

Hyde, Sue, February 15, 2011.

Jacobs, Rick, April 15, 2010.

Jones, Cleve, February 1, 2010.

Kameny, Franklin, September 30, 2009; July 23, 2010.

Kaufman, Moises, The Laramie Project DVD, MovieWeb, undated.

Kelley, Bill, July 24, 2011.

Kendell, Kate, April 13, 2011.

Kilhefner, Don, April 13, 2010.

Koch, Edward I., December 18, 2009.

Kors, Geoffrey, April 27, 2011.

Kramer, Larry, November 13, 2009.

Kushner, Tony, October 2, 2010.

Lanigan-Schmidt, Tommy, October 13, 2010.

Lavery, Michael, November 2010.

Leitsch, Dick, October 26, 2009.

Lyon, Phyllis, March 23, 2011.

Marans, Jon, October 24, 2009.

March, Artemis (née March Hoffman), August 23, 2010.

Marcus, Eric, July 29, 2009; November 16, 2011.

Martin, Keith, October 2, 2010.

McCarty, Marlene, November 19, 2010.

McGehee, Robin, March 4, 2011.

Miller, Gary, April 11, 2009.

Mixner, David B., May 21, 2010.

Mungello, David, September 7, 2010.

Nash, Phil, April 4, 2011.

Nesline, Michael, interview by Sarah Schulman, ACT UP Oral History Project, March 24, 2002.

Northrop, Ann, November 17, 2010.

O'Brien, John, October 10, 2010.

Ocamb, Karen, April 25, 2011.

Pepper, James, August, 21, 2010.

Perry, Troy, April 16 and April 27, 2010.

Petrelis, Michael, ACT UP Oral History Project, April 21, 2003.

Pomerantz, Leslie Fay, February 2, 2011.

Reiner, Greg, fall 2010.

Reiner, Rob, April 14, 2010.

Rogers, Michael, June 3, 2010.

Rubenfeld, Abby, March 31, 2011.

Russell, Glenda, April 16, 2011.

Russell, Ina, September 2009.

Sarvis, Aubrey, May 9, 2011.

Schook, Tea, March 21, 2011.

Schulman, Sarah, November 19, 2010.

Shelley, Martha, November 28, 2009.

Signorile, Michelangelo, ACT UP Oral History Project, September 20, 2003.

Silver, Carol Ruth, December 2009.

Socarides, Richard, May 27, June 2, June 7, and June 9, 2010.

Solmonese, Joe, May 2, 2011.

Solomon, Marc, April 15, 2010.

Spitzer, Robert, December 10, 2009.

Steadman, Pat, March 14, 2011.

Steffan, Joseph, February 22, 2011.

Stewart, Therese, May 3, 2011.

Towle, Andy, April 16, 2011.

Tribe, Laurence, April 7, 2011.

Truscott, Lucian, IV, September 16, 2010.

Turner, Lisa, April 19, 2011.

Van Sant, Gus, April 16, 2010.

Westmoreland, Tim, December 17, 2010.

Whelan, Edward, June 2, 2011.

Wicker, Randy, November 2, 2009.

Wockner, Rex, April 17, 2011, and numerous times thereafter.

Wolfson, Evan, May 6, May 10, and May 12, 2010.

Woods, Dan, May 20, 2011.

Yandura, Paul, June 3, 2010.

Yee, Sylvia, March 24, 2011.

Young, Allen, September 1, 2010.

Books and Journal Articles

Allyn, David. *Make Love, Not War: The Sexual Revolution: An Unfettered History.* Boston and New York: Little, Brown, 2001.

Altman, Dennis. *The Homosexualitzation of America: The Americanization of the Homosexual.* New York: St. Martin's Press, 1982.

Andersen, Ellen Ann. *Out of the Closets and into the Courts: Legal Opportunity Structure and Gay Rights Litigation.* Ann Arbor: University of Michigan Press, 2006.

Andriote, John-Manuel. *Victory Deferred: How AIDS Changed Gay Life in America.* Chicago and London: University of Chicago Press, 1999.

Arendt, Hannah. *Eichmann in Jerusalem: A Report on the Banality of Evil.* New York: Viking Press, 1963.

Armstrong, Elizabeth A., and Suzanna M. Crage. "Movements and Memory: The Making of the Stonewall Myth." *American Sociological Review* 71 (2006): 724–51.

Ayers, Ian, and Jennifer Gerarda Brown. *Straightforward: How to Mobilize Heterosexual Support for Gay Rights.* Princeton, N.J., and Oxford: Princeton University Press, 2005.

Baim, Tracy, ed. *Obama and the Gays: A Political Marriage.* Chicago: Prairie Avenue Productions, 2010.

Bancroft, J., and I. Marks. "Electric Aversion Therapy of Sexual Deviations." *Proceedings of the Royal Society of Medicine* 61 (1968): 796–9.

Bayer, Ronald. *Homosexuality and American Psychiatry: The Politics of Diagnosis.* Princeton, N.J.: Princeton University Press, 1981.

Beemyn, Brett, ed. *Creating a Place for Ourselves: Lesbian, Gay, and Bisexual Community Histories.* New York: Routledge, 1997.

Bérubé, Allan. *Coming Out Under Fire: The History of Gay Men and Women in World War II,* 20th anniversary ed. Chapel Hill: University of North Carolina Press, 2010. The first edition was published in 1990.

Boyd, Nan Alamilla. "'Homos Invade S.F.!': San Francisco's History as a Wide-Open Town." In *Creating a Place for Ourselves: Lesbian, Gay, and Bisexual Community Histories,* edited by Brett Beemyn, 73–84. New York: Routledge, 1997.

Branch, Taylor. *At Canaan's Edge: America in the King Years, 1965–68.* New York: Simon and Schuster, 2006.

———. *Parting the Waters: America in the King Years, 1954–63.* New York: Simon and Schuster, 1988.

———. *Pillar of Fire: America in the King Years, 1963–65.* New York: Simon and Schuster, 1998.

Bransford, Stephen. *Gay Politics vs. Colorado and America: The Inside Story of Amendment 2.* Cascade, Colo.: Sardis Press, 1994.

Brier, Jennifer. *Infectious Ideas: U.S. Political Responses to the AIDS Crisis.* Chapel Hill: University of North Carolina Press, 2009.

Bronski, Michael. *A Queer History of the United States.* Boston: Beacon Press, 2011.

Brundage, James A. *Law, Sex, and Christian Society in Medieval Europe.* Chicago and London: University of Chicago Press, 1987.

Cain, Patricia A. *Rainbow Rights: The Role of Lawyers and Courts in the Lesbian and Gay Civil Rights Movement.* Boulder, Colo.: Westview Press/Perseus Books Group, 2000.

Canaday, Margot. *The Straight State: Sexuality and Citizenship in Twentieth-Century America.* Princeton, N.J., and Oxford: Princeton University Press, 2009.

Carden, Michael. *Sodomy: A History of a Christian Biblical Myth.* London and Oakville, Conn.: Equinox, 2004.

Carpenter, Edward. *The Intermediate Sex.* Fairford, Gloucester, U.K.: Echo Library, 2007. Originally published in 1912.

Carter, David. *Stonewall: The Riots That Sparked the Gay Revolution.* New York: St. Martin's Griffin, 2004.

Chauncey, George. *Gay New York: Gender, Urban Culture, and the Making of the Gay Male World, 1890–1940.* New York: BasicBooks, 1994.

———. *Why Marriage? The History Shaping Today's Debate over Gay Equality.* New York: Basic Books, 2004.

Clendinen, Dudley, and Adam Nagourney. *Out for Good: The Struggle to Build a Gay Rights Movement in America.* New York: Simon and Schuster, 1999.

Cohen, Peter F. *Love and Anger: Essays on AIDS, Activism, and Politics.* New York: Haworth Press, 1998.

Collins, Gail. *When Everything Changed: The Amazing Journey of American Women, from 1960 to the Present.* New York: Little, Brown, 2009.

Comte, Auguste. *The Positive Philosophy of Auguste Comte.* Translated by Harriet Martineau. Bristol, England: Thoemmes, 2001. Reprint of the 1853 edition.

Cott, Nancy F. *Public Vows: A History of Marriage and the Nation.* Cambridge, MA: Harvard University Press, 2000.

Crewdson, John. *Science Fictions: A Scientific Mystery, a Massive Cover-up, and the Dark Legacy of Robert Gallo.* Boston, New York, and London: Little, Brown, 2002.

Crimp, Douglas. *Melancholia and Moralism: Essays on AIDS and Queer Politics.* Cambridge, Mass., and London: MIT Press, 2002.

Cummings, Scott L., and Douglas NeJaime. "Lawyering for Marriage Equality." *UCLA Law Review* 57 (June 2010): 1235.

Currah, Paisley, Richard M. Juang, and Shannon Price Minter, eds. *Transgender Rights.* Minneapolis and London: University of Minnesota Press, 2006.

D'Emilio, John. *Sexual Politics, Sexual Communities: The Making of a Homosexual Minority in the United States, 1940–1970.* Chicago and London: University of Chicago Press, 1983.

———. *Lost Prophet: The Life and Times of Bayard Rustin.* New York: Free Press, 2003.

DeYoung, Karen. *Soldier: The Life of Colin Powell.* New York: Alfred A. Knopf, 2006.

Duberman, Martin B. *About Time: Exploring the Gay Past.* New York: Meridian Books, 1991.

———. *Stonewall.* New York: Plume Books, 1993.

———. *Waiting to Land: A (Mostly) Political Memoir, 1985–2008.* New York and London: New Press, 2009.

Dugan, Robert P., Jr. *Winning the New Civil War.* New York: Multnomah Books, 1991.

Echols, Alice. *Hot Stuff: Disco and the Remaking of American Culture,* New York: W. W. Norton, 2010.

Ely, John Hart. "The Wages of Crying Wolf." *Yale Law Journal* 82, no. 5 (April 1973): 920–49.

Endean, Steve. *Bringing Lesbian and Gay Rights into the Mainstream: Twenty Years of Progress.* New York: Harrington Park Press, 2006.

Engel, Stephen M. *The Unfinished Revolution: Social Movement Theory and the Gay and Lesbian Movement.* Cambridge, U.K.: Cambridge University Press, 2001.

Epstein, Steven. *Impure Science: AIDS, Activism, and the Politics of Knowledge.* Berkeley, Los Angeles, and London: University of California Press, 1996.

Ettelbrick, Paula. "Since When Is Marriage a Path to Liberation?" Chapter Four in *Same-Sex Marriage Pro and Con,* edited by Andrew Sullivan. New York: Vintage Books, 1997.

Evans, Arthur. *Critique of Patriarchical Reason.* San Francisco: White Crane Press, 1997.

Faas, Ekbert. *Young Robert Duncan: Portrait of the Poet as a Homosexual in Society.* Santa Barbara, Calif.: Black Sparrow Press, 1983.

Faderman, Lillian, and Stuart Timmons. *Gay L.A.: A History of Sexual Outlaws, Power Politics, and Lipstick Lesbians.* Berkeley, Los Angeles, and London: University of California Press, 2006.

Farred, Grant. "Endgame Identity? Mapping the New Left Roots of Identity Politics." *New Literary History* 31, no. 4 (2000): 627–48.

Fisher, James. *Understanding Tony Kushner.* Columbia: University of South Carolina Press, 2008.

Frank, Nathaniel. *Unfriendly Fire: How the Gay Ban Undermines the Military and Weakens America.* New York: St. Martin's Griffin, Thomas Dunne Books, 2009.

Friedman, Lawrence M. *A History of American Law,* 3rd ed. New York: Simon and Schuster, 2005.

Gallo, Marcia M. *Different Daughters: A History of the Daughters of Bilitis and the Rise of the Lesbian Rights Movement.* New York: Carroll and Graf, 2006.

Gerstmann, Evan. *Same-Sex Marriage and the Constitution*, 2nd ed. Cambridge, U.K.: Cambridge University Press, 2005.

Gitlin, Todd. *The Sixties: Years of Hope, Days of Rage.* New York: Bantam, 1987.

Glazer, Nathan, and Daniel P. Moynihan. *Beyond the Melting Pot*, 2nd ed. Cambridge, Mass.: MIT Press, 1970.

Gould, Deborah B. *Moving Politics: Emotion and ACT UP's Fight Against AIDS.* Chicago and London: University of Chicago Press, 2009.

Gross, Larry. *Up from Invisibility: Lesbians, Gay Men, and the Media in America.* New York: Columbia University Press, 2001.

Gross, Larry, and James D. Woods, eds. *The Columbia Reader on Lesbians and Gay Men in Media, Society, and Politics.* New York: Columbia University Press, 1999.

Haider-Markel, Donald P. "Lesbian and Gay Politics in the States: Interest Groups, Electoral Politics, and Public Policy." In *The Politics of Gay Rights*, edited by Craig A. Rimmerman, Kenneth D. Wald, and Clyde Wilcox. Chicago: University of Chicago Press, 2000.

———. "The Politics of Social Regulatory Policy: State and Federal Hate Crime Policy and Implementation Effort." *Political Research Quarterly* 51, no. 1 (March 1998): 69–88.

Haggerty, George E. *Gay Histories and Cultures: An Encyclopedia.* New York: Garland, 2000.

Hay, Harry. *Radically Gay: Gay Liberation in the Words of Its Founder.* Edited by Will Roscoe. Boston: Beacon Press, 2001.

Heap, Chad C. *Slumming: Sexual and Racial Encounters in American Nightlife, 1885–1940.* Chicago and London: University of Chicago Press, 2009.

Henriksen, Kelly E. "Note & Comment: Gays, the Military, and Judicial Deference: When the Courts Must Reclaim Equal Protection as Their Area of Expertise." *Administrative Law Journal* 9 (Winter 1996): 1273.

Hirshman, Linda R. *Get to Work: A Manifesto for Women of the World.* New York: Viking, 2006.

Hobbes, Thomas. *On the Citizen.* Edited and translated by Richard Tuck and Michael Silverthorne. Cambridge, UK, and New York: Cambridge University Press, 1998. Translation of *De Cive.*

Hodges, Ben, ed. *Forbidden Acts: Pioneering Gay and Lesbian Plays of the Twentieth Century.* New York: Applause Theatre and Cinema Books, 2003.

Jacobs, James B., and Kimberly Potter. *Hate Crimes: Criminal Law and Identity Politics.* New York: Oxford University Press, 1998.

Jay, Karla, and Allen Young. *Out of the Closets: Voices of Gay Liberation.* New York and London: New York University Press, 1992.

Jones, Gareth H. *History of the Law of Charity, 1532–1827.* London: Cambridge University Press, 1969.

Johnson, David K. *The Lavender Scare: The Cold War Persecution of Gays and Lesbians in the Federal Government.* Chicago and London: University of Chicago Press, 2004.

Johnson, John W. Griswold v. Connecticut: *Birth Control and the Constitutional Right of Privacy.* Lawrence: University of Kansas Press, 2005.

Johnson, Olatunde C. "The Story of *Bob Jones University v. United States:* Race, Religion, and Congress' Extraordinary Acquiescence." In *Statutory Interpretation Stories,* edited by William Eskridge and Elizabeth Garrett. New York: Foundation Press, 2010. *Columbia Public Law Research Paper No. 10–229.*

Jordan, Mark D. *The Invention of Sodomy in Christian Theology.* Chicago and London: University of Chicago Press, 1997.

Keen, Lisa, and Suzanne B. Goldberg. *Strangers to the Law: Gay People on Trial.* Ann Arbor: University of Michigan Press, 1998.

Kennedy, Elizabeth Lapovsky, and Madeline D. Davis. *Boots of Leather, Slippers of Gold: The History of a Lesbian Community.* New York: Penguin Books, 1993.

———. "I Could Hardly Wait to Get Back to That Bar; Lesbian Bar Culture in Buffalo in the 1930s and 1940s." In *Creating a Place for Ourselves: Lesbian, Gay, and Bisexual Community Histories,* edited by Brett Beemyn, 29–66. New York: Routledge, 1997.

Kinsey, Alfred C., and the Institute for Sex Research. *Sexual Behavior in the Human Female.* Philadelphia: W. B. Saunders, 1953.

Kinsey, Alfred C., et al. *Sexual Behavior in the Human Male.* Philadelphia: W. B. Saunders; Bloomington: Indiana University Press, 1948.

Kluger, Richard. *Simple Justice: The History of* Brown v. Board of Education *and Black America's Struggle for Equality.* New York: Alfred A. Knopf, 1975.

Kramer, Larry. *Faggots.* New York: Grove Press, 2000.

———. *Reports from the Holocaust: The Story of an AIDS Activist.* New York: St. Martin's Press, 1994.

Krebs, Ronald R. *Fighting for Rights: Military Service and the Politics of Citizenship.* Ithaca, N.Y., and London: Cornell University Press, 2006.

Kurland, Philip B. "The Supreme Court, 1963 Term: Foreword: Equal in Origin and Equal in Title to the Legislative and Executive Branches of the Government." *Harvard Law Review* 78 (November 1964): 143–76.

Kutchins, Herb, and Stuart A. Kirk. *Making Us Crazy: DSM: The Psychiatric Bible and the Creation of Mental Disorders.* New York: Free Press, 1997.

Lewis, George B. "Lifting the Ban on Gays in the Civil Service." *Public Administration Review* 57, no. 5 (September–October 1997): 387–95.

Loffreda, Beth. *Losing Matt Shepard: Life and Politics in the Aftermath of Anti-Gay Murder.* New York: Columbia University Press, 2000.

Mansbridge, Jane, and Aldon D. Morris. *Oppositional Consciousness: The Subjective Roots of Social Protest.* Chicago and London: University of Chicago Press, 2001.

Marcus, Eric. *Making Gay History: The Half-Century Fight for Lesbian and Gay Equal Rights.* New York: Perennial, 2002.

Marotta, Toby. *The Politics of Homosexuality.* Boston: Houghton Mifflin, 1981.

Mecca, Tommi Avicolli, ed. *Smash the Church, Smash the State! The Early Years of Gay Liberation.* San Francisco: City Lights Books, 2009.

Miller, Henry I. *To America's Health: A Proposal to Reform the Food and Drug Administration.* Stanford, Calif.: Hoover Institution Press, 2000.

Miller, Jim. *"Democracy Is in the Streets": From Port Huron to the Siege of Chicago.* New York: Simon and Schuster, 1987.

Miller, Neil. *Out of the Past: Gay and Lesbian History from 1869 to the Present*, revised and updated. New York: Alyson Books, 2006.

Minton, Henry L. *Departing from Deviance: A History of Homosexual Rights and Emancipatory Science in America.* Chicago and London: University of Chicago Press, 2002.

Mixner, David. *Stranger Among Friends.* New York: Bantam Books, 1996.

Mohr, Richard D. *The Long Arc of Justice: Lesbian and Gay Marriage, Equality, and Rights.* New York: Columbia University Press, 1994.

Morris, Aldon D., and Carol McClurg Mueller. *Frontiers in Social Movement Theory.* New Haven, Conn., and London: Yale University Press, 1992.

Mucciaroni, Gary. *Same Sex, Different Politics: Success and Failure in the Struggles over Gay Rights.* Chicago and London: University of Chicago Press, 2008.

Mueller, Carol McClurg. "Building Social Movement Theory." In *Frontiers in Social Movement Theory,* edited by Aldon D. Morris and Carol McClurg Mueller, 3–25. New Haven, Conn., and London: Yale University Press, 1992.

Murdoch, Joyce, and Deb Price. *Courting Justice: Gay Men and Lesbians v. the Supreme Court.* New York: Basic Books, 2002.

Murray, Stephen O. *American Gay.* Chicago and London: University of Chicago Press, 1996.

Newman, Mark. *The Civil Rights Movement.* Westport, Conn., and London: Praeger, 2004.

Newton, Esther. *Cherry Grove, Fire Island: Sixty Years in America's First Gay and Lesbian Town.* Boston: Beacon Press, 1993.

Nicolas, Peter, and Mike Strong. *The Geography of Love: Same-Sex Marriage and Relationship Recognition in America (The Story in Maps).* University of Washington School of Law Research Paper No. 2011–15.

Nimmons, David. *The Soul Beneath the Skin: The Unseen Hearts and Habits of Gay Men.* New York: St. Martin's Press, 2002.

Nisbet, Robert A. "The French Revolution and the Rise of Sociology in France." *American Journal of Sociology* 49, no. 2 (September 1943).

Olson, Mancur, Jr. *The Logic of Collective Action: Public Goods and the Theory of Groups.* Cambridge, Mass.: Harvard University Press, 1965.

Perrow, Charles, and Mauro F. Guillén. *The AIDS Disaster: The Failure of Organizations in New York and the Nation.* New Haven, Conn., and London: Yale University Press, 1990.

Pinello, Daniel R. *America's Struggle for Same-Sex Marriage.* Cambridge, U.K.: Cambridge University Press, 2006.

Rauch, Jonathan. *Gay Marriage: Why It Is Good for Gays, Good for Straights, and Good for America.* New York: Times Books/Henry Holt, 2004.

Rayside, David Morton. *On the Fringe: Gays and Lesbians in Politics.* Ithaca, N.Y.: Cornell University Press, 1998.

Rimmerman, Craig A., Kenneth D. Wald, and Clyde Wilcox, eds. *The Politics of Gay Rights.* Chicago and London: University of Chicago Press, 2000.

Robinson, Eugene. *Disintegration: The Splintering of Black America.* New York: Doubleday, 2010.

Rosen, Ruth. *The World Split Open: How the Modern Women's Movement Changed America.* New York: Viking, 2000.

Rosenberg, Gerald N. *The Hollow Hope: Can Courts Bring About Social Change?* 2nd ed. Chicago and London: University of Chicago Press, 2008.

Russell, Ina, ed. *Jeb and Dash: A Diary of Gay Life, 1918–1945.* Boston and London: Faber and Faber, 1994.

Sack, Emily J. "The Domestic Relations Exception, Domestic Violence, and Equal Access to Federal Courts." *Washington University Law Review* 84, no. 6 (2006): 1441–1512.

Sandel, Michael J. *Liberalism and the Limits of Justice*, 2nd ed. Cambridge, U.K., and New York: Cambridge University Press, 1998.

Schiavi, Michael. *Celluloid Activist: The Life and Times of Vito Russo*. Madison: University of Wisconsin Press, 2011.

Schulman, Sarah. *My American History: Lesbian and Gay Life During the Reagan/Bush Years*. New York: Routledge, 1994.

Shamoo, Adil E. *Principles of Research Data Audit*. New York: Routledge, 1989.

Shepard, Benjamin, and Ronald Hayduk. *From ACT UP to the WTO: Urban Protest and Community Building in the Era of Globalization*. London and New York: Verso, 2002.

Shepard, Judy. *The Meaning of Matthew: My Son's Murder in Laramie, and a World Transformed*. New York: Hudson Street Press, 2009.

Shilts, Randy. *And the Band Played On: Politics, People, and the AIDS Epidemic*. New York: St. Martin's Griffin, 1987.

———. *The Mayor of Castro Street: The Life and Times of Harvey Milk*. New York: St. Martin's Press, 1982.

Shumsky, Ellen. "The Radical Lesbian Story: An Evolution of Consciousness." In *Smash the Church, Smash the State!* edited by Tommi Avicolli Mecca. Pages 190–95.

Simpson, Reagan Wm., and Mary R. Vasaly. *The Amicus Brief: How to Be a Good Friend to the Court*, 2nd ed. Chicago: Tort Trial & Insurance Practice Section, American Bar Association, 1998.

Spencer, Kate. "Same Sex Couples and the Right to Marry—European Perspectives." *Cambridge Students Law Review* 6 (2010): 155.

Stalin, Joseph. "Marxism and the National Question." In Stalin, *Works*, vol. 2, 303–14. Moscow: Foreign Languages Publishing House, 1953.

Sullivan, Andrew. *Virtually Normal: An Argument About Homosexuality*. New York: Knopf, 1995.

Svetvilas, Chuleenan. "Challenging Prop. 8: The Hidden Story: How Hollywood Activists Seized Control of the Fight for Gay Marriage." *California Lawyer*, January 2010.

Tarrow, Sidney. *Power in Movement: Social Movements and Contentious Politics*, 2nd ed. Cambridge, U.K.: Cambridge University Press, 1998.

Thompson, Mark, ed. *Long Road to Freedom:* The Advocate *History of the Gay and Lesbian Movement*. New York: St. Martin's Press, 1994.

Timmons, Stuart. *The Trouble with Harry Hay: Founder of the Modern Gay Movement.* Boston: Alyson, 1990.

Tobin, Kay, and Randy Wicker. *The Gay Crusaders.* New York: Paperback Library, 1972.

Todd, Ross. "Marriage Brokers: Behind the Scenes of the Odd Couple's Groundbreaking Litigation." *The American Lawyer,* March 2011.

Vaid, Urvashi. *Virtual Reality: The Mainstreaming of Gay and Lesbian Liberation.* New York: Doubleday Anchor Books, 1995.

Vining, Donald. *A Gay Diary, 1933–1946.* New York: Hard Candy Books, 1979.

Waaldijk, Kees. "Others May Follow: The Introduction of Marriage, Quasi-Marriage, and Semi-Marriage for Same-Sex Couples in European Countries." *New England Law Review* 38, no. 3 (2003): 569.

Wescott, Glenway. *Continual Lessons: The Journals of Glenway Wescott, 1937–1955.* Edited by Robert Phelps with Jerry Rosco. New York: Farrar, Strauss and Giroux, 1990.

White, C. Todd. *Pre-gay L.A.: A Social History of the Movement for Homosexual Rights.* Urbana and Chicago: University of Illinois Press, 2009.

Wilson, James Q. *The Amateur Democrat: Club Politics in Three Cities.* Chicago and London: University of Chicago Press, 1966.

Wolfson, Evan. "Fighting to Win and Keep the Freedom to Marry: The Legal, Political, and Cultural Challenges Ahead." *National Journal of Sexual Orientation Law* 1 (1995): 259–301.

———. *Why Marriage Matters: America, Equality, and Gay People's Right to Marry.* New York: Simon and Schuster, 2004.

Newspaper Articles, Magazine Articles, Documentaries, and Media Reports

Barbaro, Michael. "Behind N.Y. Gay Marriage, an Unlikely Mix of Forces." *New York Times,* June 26, 2011.

Barnes, Robert. "Kagan Defends Former Bush Official Who Is Representing House in Same-Sex Marriage Case." *Washington Post,* April 29, 2011.

Branch, Taylor. "Closets of Power." *Harper's Magazine,* October, 1982.

Capehart, Jonathan. "For Obama, a Hit and a Miss on Gay Rights." *Washington Post,* June 21, 2009.

Carpenter, Dale. "How the Law Accepted Gays." *New York Times,* April 28, 2011.

Didion, Joan. "The Women's Movement." *New York Times*, July 30, 1972.

Drake, Tim. "From the Ark to the Barque: Hadley Arkes Speaks About His Reception into the Catholic Church." *National Catholic Register Daily News*, August 24, 2010.

Dwyer, Devin. "Maine Votes 'No' on Gay Marriage." ABC News, November 4, 2009.

"Editorial: A Basic Civil Right," *New York Times*, June 11, 2010.

"Editorial: The Duty of Counsel," *New York Times*, April 28, 2011.

Egan, Jennifer. "Uniforms in the Closet: The Shadow Life of a Gay Marine." *New York Times Magazine*, June 28, 1998.

Epstein, Rob. *The Times of Harvey Milk*. Documentary, 1984.

Garvey, Gerald, and John DiIulio. "Only Connect?" *The New Republic*, April 26, 1993.

Green, Joshua. "They Won't Know What Hit Them." *The Atlantic*, March 2007.

Greenhouse, Linda. "The Law: Echo of '87 Bork Uproar Rings Softly in Abortion Debate." *New York Times*, April 28, 1989.

Hulse, Carl. "Senate Repeals Ban against Openly Gay Military Personnel." *New York Times*, December 19, 2010.

Klein, Rick. "Meehan Targeting 'Don't Ask, Don't Tell.'" *Boston Globe*, November 18, 2006.

Kramer, Larry. "1,112 and Counting." *New York Native*, March 14–27, 1983.

Mailer, Norman. "The Prisoner of Sex." *Harper's*, March 1971.

Martin, Douglas. "Tyron Garner, 39, Plaintiff in Pivotal Sodomy Case, Dies." *New York Times*, September 14, 2006.

Miller, Jared. "Opponents Say Existing Statutes Sufficient; State Avoids Hate Crime Legislation." *Star-Tribune* (Casper, Wyoming) Capital Bureau, October 11, 2008.

Montopoli, Brian. "Dan Choi, Other Gay Rights Protesters Arrested After Chaining Selves to White House Fence." CBS News, April 20, 2010.

Morgan, Thomas. "Mainstream Strategy for AIDS Group." *New York Times*, July 22, 1988.

Morrisroe, Patricia. "AIDS: One Man's Story." *New York*, August 19, 1985.

Phillips, Frank. "Legislators Vote to Defeat Same-Sex Marriage Ban." *Boston Globe* City and Region Desk, June 14, 2007.

Rauch, Jonathan. "Families Forged by Illness." *New York Times*, June 4, 2006.

Rich, Frank. "Journal: Bashing to Victory." *New York Times*, February 14, 1996.

Schwartz, John. "Court Rules Against Ban on Gays in the Military." *New York Times*, July 7, 2011.

Spiegel, Alix. "The Dictionary of Disorder: How One Man Revolutionized Psychiatry." *The New Yorker*, January 3, 2005.

Sullivan, Amy. "Inaugural Pastor: The Two Faces of Rick Warren." *Time*, January 18, 2009.

Sullivan, Andrew. "What's So Bad about Hate." *New York Times Magazine*, September 26, 1999.

Thomas, Evan. "The War over Gay Marriage." *Newsweek*, July 7, 2003.

Vargas, Jose Antonio. "Gay Rights Site Runs 'Outing' Ad Aimed at the Hill." *Washington Post*, July 9, 2004.

VerMeulen, Michael. "The Gay Plague," *New York*, May 31, 1982.

Warren, Jennifer, and Richard C. Paddock. "Randy Shilts, Chronicler of AIDS Epidemic, Dies." *Los Angeles Times*, February 18, 1994.

Whelan, Ed. "Obama's Dive on DOMA." *National Review*, February 23, 2011.

Wong, Kristina. "Today's Qs for O's WH." ABC News, June 17, 2009.

Zahorsky, Rachel M. "Sometime-Foes Boies and Olson Honored with ABA Medal for Successful Joint Efforts." *ABA Journal*, August 8, 2011.

Online Articles and Blog Posts

"Advocacy Group Says Military Rooting Out Gays." CNN. Posted February 26, 1997. http://articles.cnn.com/1997–02–26/us/9702_26_gays.military_1_michelle-benecke-homosexuals-servicemembers-legal-defense-network?_s=PM:US.

Ali, Ambreen. "Why Hunger Strikes Fail: It's an Extreme Tactic, Yet It's Also One That Rarely Works." Congress.org, June 7, 2010, http://origin-www.congress.org/news/2010/06/07/why_hunger_strikes_fail.

Aravosis, John. "GetEQUAL Protests Bancroft PLLC over Defense of Bigoted DOMA Law." Gay.Americablog. Posted April 25, 2011. http://gay.americablog.com/2011/04/getequal-protests-bancroft-pllc-over.html.

———. "Obama Defends DOMA in Federal Court. Says Banning Gay Marriage Is Good for the Federal Budget. Invokes Incest and Marrying Children." America blog. Posted June 12, 2009. http://www.americablog.com/2009/06/obama-justice-department-defends-doma.html.

Bazelon, Emily. "A Bold Stroke." LegalAffairs. Posted May/June 2004. http://www.legalaffairs.org/issues/May-June-2004/feature_bazelon_mayjune.

Berman, Russell. "Gay-Rights Advocates Say Dem Leader Hoyer Saved 'Don't Ask' Repeal." The Hill, December 21, 2010, http://thehill.com/homenews/campaign/134763-gay-rights-advocates-say-hoyer-saved-dont-ask-repeal.

Boyce, Martin. "40 Years Across the Table, Stonewall Vets Talk with LGBT Youth." YouTube video. Posted June 13, 2009. http://www.youtube.com/watch?v=DAdNqF0l37g.

Camperio, A., Ciani P. Cermelli, and G. Zanzotto. "Sexually Antagonistic Selection in Human Male Homosexuality." *PLoS ONE* 3, no. 6 (2008): e2282.

Cerny, Milton. "Tax Exempt Organizations: It's Been a Memorable Twenty Years." *Tax Notes,* November 12, 1992. McGuireWoods blog. http://www.mcguirewoods.com/news-resources/publications/taxation/tax-exempt%20organizations.pdf.

Clarknt67. "Live from NY! Jeanette Is Marrying Kawane Today." Milk Men and Women, Daily Kos. Posted July 24, 2011. http://www.dailykos.com/story/2011/07/24/998035/-Live-From-NY!-Jeanette-Is-Marrying-Kawane-Today.

Clinton, Bill. "Remarks by President Clinton at Human Rights Campaign Dinner." PFLAG Talk and TGS PFLAG Virtual Library. Posted November 8, 1997. http://www.critpath.org/pflag-talk/ClintonHRC.html.

Cullen, Dave. "Quiet Bombshell in Matthew Shepard Trial." *Salon*. Posted November 1, 1999. http://www.salon.com/news/feature/1999/11/01/gay_panic.

Ellen puppy episode. YouTube video. Posted April 30, 1997. http://www.youtube.com/watch?v=bhuiJINpRww.

Gaus, Gerald, and Shane D. Courtland. "Liberalism." The Stanford Encyclopedia of Philosophy (Spring 2011 edition), edited by Edward N. Zalta. http://plato.stanford.edu/archives/spr2011/entries/liberalism/.

Gerash, Jerry. "Beth Chayim Chadashim Drash." Denver Gay Revolt. Posted October 12, 2001. http://www.denvergayrevolt.com/origins_of_center.html.

Gerstein, Josh. "Eric Holder Rejects Attacks on Paul Clement over DOMA Defense." Politico, April 26, 2011, http://www.politico.com/blogs/joshgerstein/0411/Eric_Holder_rejects_attacks_on_Paul_Clement_over_DOMA_defense.html.

Hardisty, Jean. "Constructing Homophobia: Colorado's Right-Wing Attack on Homosexuals." *Public Eye* (March 1993), http://www.publiceye.org/magazine/v07n1/conshomo.html.

"Have You No Sense of Decency." http://www.senate.gov/artandhistory/history/minute/Have_you_no_sense_of_decency.htm.

Henninger, Daniel. "Drug Lag." In *The Concise Encyclopedia of Economics.* http://www.econlib.org/library/CEE.html.

Highleyman, Liz. "Past Out: Who Was Carl Wittman." Seattle Gay News. Posted May 5, 2006. http://www.sgn.org/sgnnews34_18/page30.cfm.

Human Rights Campaign. Report, 1996. http://www.novelguide.com/a/discover/sigs_0001_0001_0/sigs_0001_0001_0_00077.html.

"In U.S., Broad, Steady Support for Openly Gay Service Members," Gallup Poll, May 10, 2010. http://www.gallup.com/poll/127904/Broad-Steady-Support-Openly-Gay-Service-Members.aspx.

Jasper, James. *Passion and Purpose: Action Theory of Social Movements.* Chapter 1, "After the Big Paradigms: Social Movement Theory Today." http://www.hks.harvard.edu/cchrp/hrsm/pdf/JamesJasper_SM_Theory.pdf.

"John Rich Says Chely Wright Misunderstood When He Asked Her If She Was Gay." Celebitchy. Posted May 6, 2010. http://www.celebitchy.com/category/coming_out/.

"KABC on LGBT Rights Protest Greeting President Obama." YouTube video. Posted May 28, 2009. http://www.youtube.com/watch?v=Bczbe2RjxMQ.

London, Kathleen. "The History of Birth Control." Yale–New Haven Teachers Institute. http://www.yale.edu/ynhti/curriculum/units/1982/6/82.06.03.x.html.

Maddow, Rachel. "Right to Serve w/Lt. Dan Choi of Knights Out." YouTube video. Posted March 31, 2009. http://www.youtube.com/watch?v=YiWSPdRGvC0.

"Man Beaten in Apparent Anti-Gay Attack." Associated Press; *New York Post*. Posted October 12, 2009. http://www.nypost.com/p/news/local/queens/item_wqxpVGb5BEcLhuHFmCMJYJ#ixzz1WpcYa82s.

McInerny, Ralph, and John O'Callaghan. "Saint Thomas Aquinas." The Stanford Encyclopedia of Philosophy (Winter 2010 edition), edited by Edward N. Zalta. http://plato.stanford.edu/archives/win2010/entries/aquinas/.

"New Details Emerge in Matthew Shepard Murder." ABC News *20/20*. Posted November 26, 2004. http://abcnews.go.com/2020/story?id=277685&page=2.

"Obama Makes Demonstration a Punchline." Unite the Fight blog. Posted May 28, 2009. http://unitethefight.blogspot.com/2009/05/obama-demonstration-demanding-end-to.html.

"Obama Signs Hate Crimes Bill into Law." CNN Politics. Posted October 28, 2009. http://articles.cnn.com/2009-10-28/politics/hate.crimes_1_crimes-gay-rights-human-rights-campaign?_s=PM:POLITICS.

"Obama Supporter: 'God Delivered Me from Homosexuality.'" CNN Politicalticker blog. Posted October 29, 2007. http://politicalticker.blogs.cnn.com/2007/10/29/obama-supporter-god-delivered-me-from-homosexuality/.

"Photo Flash: HAIR at the National Equality March in Washington, D.C." Broadway World. Posted October 13, 2009. http://broadwayworld.com/article/Photo_Flash_HAIR_at_the_National_Equality_March_in_Washington_DC_20091013#ixzz1X0YsDWBs.

Pickett, Brent. "Homosexuality." The Stanford Encyclopedia of Philosophy (Spring 2011 edition), edited by Edward N. Zalta. http://plato.stanford.edu/archives/spr2011/entries/homosexuality/.

Pierotti, Greg. "Laramie Sequel Gives Voice to Shepard's Killer: Greg Pierotti Interviewed Convicted Killer Aaron McKinney for 10 Hours." Associated Press; MSNBC.com. Posted September 29, 1999. http://today.msnbc.msn.com/id/33074488/ns/today-entertainment/t/laramie-sequel-gives-voice-shepards-killer/#.TmI9UmpXGgA.

"President Obama Signs Byrd Shepard Hate Crimes Bill into Law." Bay Windows. Posted October 28, 2009. http://www.baywindows.com/index.php?ch=news&sc=glbt&sc2=news&sc3=&id=98285.

Proposition 8 Trial Re-enactment. MarriageTrial.com. Posted January 11–27, 2010, and June 16, 2010. http://www.johnirelandonline.com/Trial.

Provencal, Vernon L. "The Family in Aristotle." http://www.mun.ca/animus/2001vol6/provencal6.htm.

Reilly, Ryan J. "Boehner Picks Bush Solicitor General Paul Clement to Defend DOMA." TPMMuckraker, April 18, 2011, http://tpmdc.talkingpointsmemo.com/2011/04/boehner-picks-bush-solicitor-general-paul-clement-to-defend-doma.php.

Roman. "DOMA-Defending Law Firm Employees Targeted by Online Campaign." All-Lawyers Info. Posted April 23, 2011. http://blog.all-lawyers.info/doma-defending-law-firm-employees-targeted-by-online-campaign.

Schubert, Frank, and Jeff Flint. "Case Studies: Passing Prop 8." Campaigns and Elections.

Posted February 1, 2009, http://www.campaignsandelections.com/case-studies/176127/passing-prop-8.thtml.

Schwartz, Richard A. "How the Film and Television Blacklists Worked." http://comptalk.fiu.edu/blacklist.htm.

Shal, Dayna. Letter to Senator Bill Frist. January 23, 2004. http://www.gao.gov/new.items/d04353r.pdf.

Slajda, Rachel. "Gates to Congress: Repeal DADT Now." TPMMuckraker, November 30, 2010, http://tpmmuckraker.talkingpointsmemo.com/2010/11/dadt_report_allowing_gays_poses_little_risk_to_mil.php.

Suggs, Donald. "True Colors." POZ. Posted July 1997. http://www.poz.com/articles/242_1737.shtml.

Townsend, Mark. "Democratic Party in Manhattan." Manhattan Young Democrats blog. Posted March 17, 2010. http://gomyd.com/2010/03/17/democratic-party-in-manhattan/.

White, Graham. "Medieval Theories of Causation." The Stanford Encyclopedia of Philosophy (Fall 2009 edition), edited by Edward N. Zalta. http://plato.stanford.edu/archives/fall2009/entries/causation-medieval/.

Wolfson, Evan. "The Law of Interstate Marriage Recognition: A Summary of Legal Issues." Wider Church and Justice and Witness Ministries, United Church of Christ, 1996. http://www.ucc.org/assets/pdfs/emr23.pdf.

Wong, Kristina. "Today's Qs for O's WH—6/17/2009." ABC News blog. Posted June 17, 2009. http://abcnews.go.com/blogs/politics/2009/06/todays-qs-for-os-wh–6172009/.

Websites

Note: These are the websites used in assembling the historical materials for the book, not the sites for current blogging and politics. For a review of the gay revolution online, see chapter 11.

ACT UP Oral History Project: http://www.actuporalhistory.org/about/index.html. The ACT UP Oral History Project is a collection of interviews with surviving members of the AIDS Coalition to Unleash Power, New York. The project is coordinated by Jim Hubbard and Sarah Schulman, with camera work by James Wentzy (in New York) and (on the West Coast) S. Leo Chiang and Tracy Wares.

BIBLIOGRAPHY

AIDS Quilt: http://www.aidsquilt.org/history.htm. All about the quilt, its history and travels.

Anti-Defamation League Hate Crimes: http://www.adl.org/combating_hate/.

Bay Windows: http://www.baywindows.com/. The website of the New England gay newspaper, *Bay Windows*; general coverage.

"Don't Ask, Don't Tell, Don't Pursue": http://dont.stanford.edu/commentary/index.htm. Digital Library Project of the Robert Crown Law Library at Stanford Law School.

Gay Homeland Foundation: http://library.gayhomeland.org. The Gay Homeland Foundation collects important political works and recommendations for books, articles, and other media.

GLBTQ: http://www.glbtq.com/. The largest website devoted to gay, lesbian, bisexual, transgender, and queer education and culture and houses the largest, most comprehensive encyclopedia of GLBTQ culture in the world. Helpful essays on almost every subject.

Human Rights Campaign Archives: http://rmc.library.cornell.edu/EAD/htmldocs/RMM07712.html. The Human Rights Campaign Archives back to 1975 are at Cornell. This is a guide to the collection.

Internet History Sourcebooks Project: http://www.fordham.edu/Halsall/index.asp/.

LGBT Movement Advancement Project: http://www.lgbtmap.org/equality-maps. The link to the Equality Maps of the LGBT Movement Advancement Project.

LGBTQ Civil Rights Movement: http://www.housing.wisc.edu/diversity/lgbtclass/index.php. Website of a course at the University of Wisconsin–Madison, "The LGBTQ Civil Rights Movement 1960–1990: Exploring History and Current Consequences."

Matthew Shepard Online Resources: http://www.wiredstrategies.com/shepardx.html. John Aravosis's archives, including material about Matthew Shepard.

New York Law School: http://www.nyls.edu/centers/harlan_scholar_centers/justice_action_center/publications/lesbiangay_law_notes. *Lesbian/Gay Law Notes*, at New York Law School, maintains running coverage of the rapidly expanding and evolving legal campaign.

New York Public Library: http://legacy.www.nypl.org/research/chss/spe/rbk/faids/igic.html. The online guide to the extensive, well-catalogued collection of materials at the New York Public Library Gay and Lesbian Collections and AIDS/HIV Collections.

OutHistory.org: http://www.outhistory.org/. OutHistory.org is produced by the Center for

Lesbian and Gay Studies (CLAGS), located at the City University of New York Graduate Center. The site is directed by Jonathan Ned Katz. A collaborative history site with a wide range of historical essays.

Perry v. Brown: http://marriagetrial.com/. A complete reenactment of the Boies/Olson challenge to Prop 8, *Perry v. Schwarzenegger*, now *Perry v. Brown*. A pdf of the *Perry v. Schwarzenegger* transcript is at the Americans for Equal Rights website, http://www.afer.org/wp-content/uploads/2010/01/Perry-Vol-3-1-13-10.pdf.

Queer Rhetoric Project: http://queerrhetoric.com/mission/. The Queer Rhetoric Project is a free online archive of political texts, speeches, and activism relating to gay, lesbian, bisexual, and transgender rights.

Rainbow History Project: http://www.rainbowhistory.org/index.html: Archive of the history, arts, and culture relevant to sexually diverse communities in metropolitan Washington, DC.

Stanford Encyclopedia of Philosophy: http://plato.stanford.edu/about.html. The Stanford Encyclopedia of Philosophy (SEP) is an invitation-only, online encyclopedia. All entries and substantive updates are refereed by members of a distinguished editorial board before they are made public. Scholarly yet readable essays on a wide range of topics in philosophy.

The Body: http://www.thebody.com/index.html?ic=3001. Online site for all things AIDS.

University of Southern California: http://www.onearchives.org/collections. Gay and Lesbian archives at the University of Southern California in Los Angeles, collection with a special emphasis on Los Angeles, and a collection of all the back issues of *ONE* magazine.

Various organizations have websites. Most of them include useful reports and surveys. They include:

Alliance Defense Fund: http://oldsite.alliancedefensefund.org.

American Civil Liberties Union: http://www.aclu.org.

American Rhetoric Online Speech Bank: http://www.americanrhetoric.com.

California Democratic Council: http://www.cdc-ca.org.

Centers for Disease Control: http://www.cdc.gov.

Courage Campaign: http://www.couragecampaign.org. The Courage Campaign focuses heavily on California politics and includes a big element of online activism, "Take Action" buttons on each subject.

EleGALA.com: http://www.elegala.com. A wedding-planning website.

Gallup Poll: http://www.gallup.com.

Gay and Lesbian Advocates and Defenders: http://www.glad.org. Gay and Lesbian Advocates and Defenders includes a very useful feature with the full text of important decisions.

Gay Men's Health Crisis: http://www.gmhc.org.

Howard Brown Health Center, Chicago: http://www.howardbrown.org.

Human Rights Campaign: http://www.hrc.org/index.htm. The Human Rights Campaign website includes a very useful state by state law feature.

Human Rights Campaign: http://www.hrc.org/issues/workplace/5635.htm. The Human Rights Campaign website includes the history of support for the Employment Non-Discrimination Act (ENDA) since 1974.

International Court System: http://www.impcourt.org. Information and links about the International Court System.

Kaiser Family Foundation: http://www.kff.org.

Lambda Legal: http://www.lambdalegal.org.

'Lectric Law Library: http://www.lectlaw.com/files/leg23.htm.

LGBT Mentoring Project: http://lgbtmentoring.org.

National Center for Lesbian Rights: http://www.nclrights.org/site/PageServer.

National Gay and Lesbian Task Force: http://www.thetaskforce.org. The National Gay and Lesbian Task Force website includes useful pdf's of their reports.

National Institutes of Health: http://www.nih.gov.

On the Issues: http://ontheissues.org/News_Gay_Rights.htm. Blog that focuses on politicians' positions on gay rights.

OutGiving: http://www.outgiving.org/about.

PBS: www.pbs.org.

ProtectMarriage.com: http://www.ProtectMarriage.com.

Toby Marotta Community-Roots Archive: http://tobymarotta.com/contents.htm.

Transgender Law and Policy Institute: http://www.transgenderlaw.org. Along with its sister organization, http://transgenderlawcenter.org/cms/, provides a range of resources about transgender law and policy, including recent decisions and legislation state by state.

United States Department of Justice: http://www.justice.gov.

United States Senate: http://www.senate.gov.

Wider Church and Justice and Witness Ministries of the United Church of Christ: http://www.ucc.org.

Victory Fund: http://www.victoryfund.org/home. The website of the Victory Fund includes useful information about its history.

William H. Percy: http://www.williamapercy.com.

Legal Cases and Government Reports

Baehr v. Lewin, 74 Haw. 530, 852 P.2d 44 (1993); reconsideration and clarification granted in part, 74 Haw. 645, 852 P.2d 74 (1993).

Bowers v. Hardwick, 478 U.S. 186 (1986).

California v. Ferlinghetti (1957).

Department of Agriculture v. Moreno, 413 U.S. 528 (1973).

Evans v. Romer, 854 P.2d 11270 (Colo. 1993).

Evans v. Romer, 882 P.2d 1335 (Colo. 1994).

Gill v. Office of Personnel Management, 699 F.Supp.2d 374 (D.Mass. 2010).

Glenn, Yuille, Ouellette, and Combs v. Holder, 10–2273 (6th Cir. 2010).

Goldman v. Weinberger, 475 U.S. 503.

Goodridge v. Dept. of Public Health, 798 N.E.2d 941 (Mass. 2003).

Griswold v. Connecticut, 381 U.S. 479 (1965).

Hollingsworth v. Perry, 130 S.Ct. 705 (2010).

Kameny v. Brucker, petition for a writ of certiorari, no. 676, U.S. Supreme Court (1960). Kameny Papers, Library of Congress.

Lawrence v. Texas, 539 U.S. 558.

Log Cabin Republicans v. Gates, 10–56634 (9th Cir. 2010).

Memoirs v. Massachusetts, 383 U.S. 413 (1966).

Norton v. Macy, 417 F.2d 1161 (D.C. Cir. 1969).

One, Inc. v. Oleson, 241 F.2d 772 (1957), rev'd., 355 U.S. 371 (1958).

People v. Onofre, 415 N.E. 2d 936 (NY 1980).

Perry v. Brown (formerly known as *Perry v. Schwarzenegger*), 10–16696 (9th Cir. 2011).

Romer v. Evans, 517 U.S. 620 (1996).

Roth v. United States, 354 U.S. 476 (1957).

Smelt v. United States, C.D.Cal. Case No. 8:2009-cv-00286.

Defense of Marriage Act (DOMA), H.R. Report 104–664 (1996).

Hearing before the Subcommittee on the Constitution of the Committee on the Judiciary, H.R., 108th Cong., Second Session, March 30, 2004, Serial No. 70.

"Memorandum for Secretaries of the Military Departments, Chairman of the Joint Chiefs of Staff, Inspector General of the Department of Defense," March 24, 1997, http://dont.stanford.edu/regulations/memo3.htm.

Index

Page numbers in italics refer to photographs.

INDEX

About the Author

Linda Hirshman, a lawyer and pundit, is the author of *Get to Work: A Manifesto for Women of the World* and many other books. She received her JD from the University of Chicago Law School and her PhD in philosophy from the University of Illinois at Chicago, and she taught philosophy and women's studies at Brandeis University. In recent years, she has appeared on network and cable television shows, including *60 Minutes* and *The Colbert Report*. She has also written for the *New York Times*, the *Washington Post*, *Slate*, *Newsweek*, the *Daily Beast*, and *Salon*.